The
Writer's World

Essays

THIRD EDITION

Lynne Gaetz

Lionel Groulx College

Suneeti Phadke

St. Jerome College

PEARSON

Boston   Columbus   Indianapolis   New York   San Francisco   Upper Saddle River

Amsterdam   Cape Town   Dubai   London   Madrid   Milan   Munich   Paris   Montreal   Toronto

Delhi   Mexico City   Sao Paulo   Sydney   Hong Kong   Seoul   Singapore   Taipei   Tokyo

Executive Editor: Matthew Wright
Editorial Assistant: Laura Marenghi
Senior Development Editor: Marion Castellucci
Development Editor: Erica Nikolaidis
Senior Supplements Editor: Donna Campion
Executive Digital Producer: Stefanie Snajder
Content Specialist: Erin Jenkins
Digital Editor: Sara Gordus
Director of Marketing: Roxanne McCarley
Project Manager: Denise Phillip Grant

Project Coordination, Text Design, and Electronic
    Page Makeup: Laserwords Private Limited
Cover Designer/Manager: Wendy Ann Fredericks
Cover Photos: © Shutterstock
Text Permissions: Aptara
Photo Researcher: Integra
Senior Manufacturing Buyer: Dennis Para
Printer/Binder: R.R. Donnelley/Crawfordsville
Cover Printer: Lehigh-Phoenix Color/Hagerstown

Credits and acknowledgments borrowed from other sources and reproduced, with permission, in this textbook appear on the appropriate page within text and on pages 618–619.

Library of Congress Cataloging-in-Publication Data
Gaetz, Lynne, 1960–
  The writer's world : essays / Lynne Gaetz, Lionel Groulx College, Suneeti Phadke, St. Jerome College. — Third Edition.
    pages cm
  ISBN-13: 978-0-321-89904-0 (Student Edition : alk. paper)
  ISBN-10: 0-321-89904-0 (Student Edition : alk. paper)   1. English language—Rhetoric—Problems, exercises, etc.
2. Report writing—Problems, exercises, etc.   I. Phadke, Suneeti, 1961– II. Title.
  PE1413.G34 2014
  808.4—dc23
                                                                                                    2013048660

2 3 4 5 6 7 8 9 10—DOC—17 16 15 14

Student Edition ISBN-13:   978-0-321-89904-0
Student Edition ISBN-10:   0-321-89904-0

A la Carte Edition ISBN-13:   978-0-321-89911-8
A la Carte Edition ISBN-10:   0-321-89911-3

Contents

Part III More College and Workplace Writing   238

Part IV Editing Handbook   304

Readings Listed by Rhetorical Mode

Preface

Thank you for making the second edition of *The Writer's World: Essays* a resounding success. We are delighted that the book has been able to help so many students across the country. This new edition, too, can help your students produce writing that is technically correct and richly detailed, whether your classes are filled with students who have varying skill levels, whether students are native or nonnative speakers of English, or whether they learn better through the use of visuals.

When we started the first edition, we set out to develop practical and pedagogically sound approaches to these challenges, and we are pleased to hear that the book is helping students succeed in their writing courses. We began with the idea that this project should be a collaboration with other developmental writing teachers. So we met with more than forty-five instructors from around the country, asking for their opinions and insights regarding (1) the challenges posed by the course, (2) the needs of today's ever-changing student population, and (3) the ideas and features we were proposing in order to provide them and you with a more effective teaching and learning tool. Pearson also commissioned dozens of detailed manuscript reviews from instructors, asking them to analyze and evaluate each draft of the manuscript. These reviewers identified numerous ways in which we could refine and enhance our key features. Their invaluable feedback was incorporated throughout *The Writer's World*. The text you are seeing is truly the product of a successful partnership between the authors, publisher, and more than one hundred developmental writing instructors.

What's New in the Third Edition?
Deeper MyWritingLab Integration

New to this edition, resources and assessment designed specifically for *The Writer's World* are in the MyWritingLab/eText book-specific module along with all the diagnostic, practice, and assessment resources of MyWritingLab. Students can use MyWritingLab to access media resources, practice, and assessment for each chapter of *The Writer's World*. When they see MyWritingLab™ in the text, students have the option of completing the practice online in the MyWritingLab/eText book-specific module. Practice assessments will flow to your instructor Gradebook in MyWritingLab, reducing grading time and allowing you to focus attention on those students who may need extra help and practice.

- All Writer's Room exercises can be completed in MyWritingLab, giving students access to a wide range of customizable instruction, practice, and assessment.
- Students can now answer additional reading comprehension questions for readings in Chapter 40 in MyWritingLab, offering extra practice and assessment and helping students strengthen their grasp of the readings.
- All "At Work" paragraphs (see page 79 for an example) appear in MyWritingLab with additional commentary and annotations, helping students to see how the paragraphs are constructed.

A New Look

A new clean and modern design streamlines instruction and increases usability, allowing students to more effectively find and retain the information covered.

New Grammar Themes and Practices

Most of the grammar practices in Part IV: The Editing Handbook are new, providing updated grammar instruction through the lens of topical and culturally relevant content. In addition, two new grammar themes have been added to engage student interest: Section 3: Travel and Survival and Section 4: Inventions and Discoveries.

Updated College and Workplace Writing Section

Part III: More College and Workplace Writing has been extensively revised. Chapter 16, "Summarizing," now focuses specifically on summary writing. Chapter 17, "The Research Essay," features integrated information on paraphrasing, summarizing, and quotations. We've also provided new citation information about online dictionaries and e-books.

New Readings

In Chapter 40, five new readings relate to the grammar themes. Thought-provoking essays from Josh Freed, Yannick LeJacq, Robert Rodriguez, and John D. Carl discuss the isolating effects of technology, bullying, the competitive world of marketing new inventions, and how cults become religions. Finally, new to the third edition is the inclusion of a short story, "The Veldt," written by celebrated science fiction author Ray Bradbury. Students can write response essays (reports) about that short story.

Updated Film Writing Prompts

The film writing prompts in Chapters 6–14 have been updated to include newer and more recent movies, as well as a range of independent and mainstream selections, such as *Zero Dark Thirty*, *Les Miserables*, and *Lincoln*.

Expanded "At Work" Paragraphs

Chapters 6–14 feature examples of the nine writing modes applied to real-world contexts. In the third edition, these "At Work" paragraphs have been expanded and annotated to highlight the individual elements of each paragraph (thesis statement, supporting ideas, and concluding statement).

New and More Images

This edition presents new dynamic and vibrant images—photos of graffiti and diverse countries and cities—that will engage students and prompt critical thinking.

How *The Writer's World* Meets Students' Diverse Needs

We created *The Writer's World* to meet your students' diverse needs. To accomplish this, we asked both the instructors in our focus groups and the reviewers at every stage not only to critique our ideas but also to offer their suggestions and recommendations for features that would enhance the learning process of their students. The result has been the integration of many elements that are not found in other textbooks, including our **visual program, coverage of nonnative speaker material, and strategies for addressing the varying skill levels students bring to the course**.

The Visual Program

A stimulating, full-color book with more than 160 photos, *The Writer's World* recognizes that today's world is a visual one, and it encourages students to become better communicators by responding to images. Chapter-opening visuals in Parts I, II, and III help students to think about the chapter's key concept in a new way.

The visuals in Part II provide students with another set of opportunities to write in response to images, with Media Writing activities that encourage them to respond using particular paragraph and essay patterns.

Throughout *The Writer's World*, words and images work together to encourage students to explore, develop, and revise their writing.

Seamless Coverage for Nonnative Speakers

Instructors in our focus groups noted the growing number of nonnative/ESL speakers enrolling in writing courses. Although some of these students have special needs related to the writing process, many of you still have a large portion of native speakers in your courses whose more traditional needs must also be satisfied. In order to meet the challenge of this rapidly changing dynamic, we have carefully implemented and integrated content throughout to assist these students.

The Writer's World does not have separate ESL boxes, ESL chapters, or tacked-on ESL appendices. Instead, information that traditionally poses a challenge to nonnative speakers is woven seamlessly throughout the book. In our extensive experience teaching writing to both native and nonnative speakers of English, we have learned that both groups learn best when they are not distracted by ESL labels. With the seamless approach, nonnative speakers do not feel self-conscious and segregated, and native speakers do not tune out detailed explanations that may also benefit them. Many of these traditional problem areas receive more coverage than you would find in other textbooks, arming the instructor with the material to effectively meet the needs of nonnative speakers. Moreover, the *Annotated Instructor's Edition* provides more than seventy-five ESL Teaching Tips designed specifically to help instructors better meet the needs of their nonnative-speaking students.

Issue-Focused Thematic Grammar

In surveys, many of you indicated that one of the primary challenges in teaching your course is finding materials that are engaging to students in a contemporary context. This is especially true in grammar instruction. **Students come to the course with varying skill levels**, and many students are simply not interested in grammar. To address this challenge, we have introduced **issue-focused thematic grammar** into *The Writer's World*.

Each chapter centers on a theme that is carried out in examples and activities. These themes include topics related to conflict, urban development, travel and survival, inventions and discoveries, our natural world, and human development. The thematic approach enables students to broaden their awareness of subjects important to American life, such as understanding advertising and consumerism. The thematic approach makes reading about grammar more engaging. And the more engaging grammar is, the more likely students are to retain key concepts—raising their skill level in these important building blocks of writing.

We also think that it is important to teach grammar in the context of the writing process. Students should not think that grammar is an isolated exercise. Therefore, each grammar chapter includes a warm-up writing activity.

What Tools Can Help Students Get the Most from *The Writer's World*?

Overwhelmingly, focus group participants and reviewers asked that both a larger number and a greater diversity of exercises and activities be incorporated into *The Writer's World*. In response, we have developed and tested the following learning aids in *The Writer's World*. We are confident they will help your students become better writers.

Hints

In each chapter, **Hint** boxes highlight important writing and grammar points. Hints are useful for all students, but many will be particularly helpful for nonnative speakers. For example, in Chapter 14, one Hint encourages students to state an argument directly and a second Hint explains how research can strengthen an essay. In Chapter 22, a Hint discusses word order in embedded questions. Hints include brief discussions and examples so that students will see both concept and application.

Vocabulary Boosts

Throughout Part II of *The Writer's World*, Vocabulary Boost boxes give students tips to improve their use of language and to revise and edit their word choices. For example, a Vocabulary Boost in Chapter 6 asks students to replace repeated words with synonyms, and the one in Chapter 8 explains how to use vivid language. These lessons give students concrete strategies and specific advice for improving their diction.

The Writer's Desk

Parts I, II, and III include **The Writer's Desk** exercises, which help students get used to practicing all stages and steps of the writing process. As the chapter progresses, students warm up with a prewriting activity and then use specific methods for developing, organizing (using paragraph and essay plans), drafting, and finally, revising and editing to create a final draft.

The Writer's Room

The Writer's Room contains writing activities that correspond to general, college, and workplace topics. Some prompts are brief to allow students to freely form ideas while others are expanded to give students more direction.

There is something for every student writer in this end-of-chapter feature. Students who respond well to visual cues will appreciate the media writing prompts in The Writer's Room in Part II: Essay Patterns. To help students see how grammar is not isolated from the writing process, there are also The Writer's Room activities at the ends of sections 1–6 in Part IV: The Editing Handbook.

The Writer's World eText

Accessed through the MyWritingLab/eText course (www.mywritinglab.com), students now have the eText for *The Writer's World* at their fingertips while completing the various exercises and activities within MyWritingLab and in the new book-specific module. Students can highlight important material and add notes to any section for further reflection and/or study throughout the semester.

How We Organized *The Writer's World*

The Writer's World: Essays is separated into five parts for ease of use, convenience, and ultimate flexibility.

Part I: The Writing Process
Part I teaches students (1) how to formulate ideas (Exploring); (2) how to expand, organize, and present those ideas in a piece of writing (Developing); and (3) how to polish writing so that they convey their message as clearly as possible (Revising and Editing). The result is that writing a paragraph or an essay becomes far less daunting because students have specific steps to follow.

Part II: Essay Patterns
Part II gives students a solid overview of the patterns of development. Using the same easy-to-understand process (Exploring, Developing, and Revising and Editing), each chapter in this section explains how to convey ideas using one or more writing patterns. As they work through the practices and write their own essays, students begin to see how using a writing pattern can help them fulfill their purpose for writing.

Part III: More College and Workplace Writing
Part III covers topics ranging from the letter and résumé to the research essay. This section also explains how to respond to films and literary works and how to prepare for essay exams.

Part IV: The Editing Handbook
Part IV is a thematic grammar handbook. In each chapter, the examples correspond to a theme, such as conflict, inventions and discoveries, and human development. As students work through the chapters, they hone their grammar and editing skills while gaining knowledge about a variety of topics. In addition to helping build interest in the grammar practices, the thematic material provides a spark that ignites new ideas that students can apply to their writing.

Part V: Reading Strategies and Selections
Part V offers tips, readings, and follow-up questions. Students learn how to write by observing and dissecting what they read. The readings relate to the themes found in Part IV: The Editing Handbook, providing more fodder for generating writing ideas.

Pearson Writing Resources for Instructors and Students

Book-Specific Ancillary Material

Annotated Instructor's Edition for *The Writer's World: Essays, 3/e* ISBN 0-321-89909-1 The AIE offers in-text answers, marginal annotations for teaching each chapter, links to the *Instructor's Resource Manual* (IRM), and MyWritingLab teaching tips. It is a valuable resource for experienced and first-time instructors alike.

Instructor's Resource Manual for *The Writer's World: Essays, 3/e* ISBN 0-321-89905-9 The material in the IRM is designed to save instructors time and provide them with effective options for teaching their writing classes. It offers suggestions for setting up their course; provides lots of extra practice for students who need it; offers quizzes and grammar tests, including unit tests; furnishes grading rubrics for each rhetorical mode; and supplies answers in case instructors want to print them out and have students grade their own work. This valuable resource is exceptionally useful for adjuncts who might need advice in setting up their initial classes or who might be teaching a variety of writing classes with too many students and not enough time.

PowerPoint Presentation for *The Writer's World: Essays, 3/e* ISBN 0-321-89908-3 PowerPoint presentations to accompany each chapter consist of classroom-ready lecture outline slides, lecture tips and classroom activities, and review questions. Available for download from the Instructor Resource Center.

Answer Key for *The Writer's World: Essays, 3/e* ISBN 0-321-89913-X The Answer Key contains the solutions to the exercises in the student edition of the text. Available for download from the Instructor Resource Center.

MyWritingLab MyWritingLab™

MyWritingLab is where practice, application, and demonstration meet to improve writing!

MyWritingLab, a complete online learning program, provides additional resources and better practice exercises for developing writers. MyWritingLab accelerates learning through layered assessment and a personalized learning path utilizing the Knewton Adaptive Learning Platform™, which customizes standardized educational content to piece together the perfect personalized bundle of content for each student. With over eight thousand exercises and immediate feedback to answers, the integrated learning aids of MyWritingLab reinforce learning throughout the semester.

What makes the practice, application, and demonstration in MyWritingLab more effective?

Diagnostic Testing: MyWritingLab's diagnostic Path Builder test comprehensively assesses students' skills in grammar. Students are provided with an individualized learning path based on the diagnostic's results, identifying the areas where they most need help.

Progressive Learning: The heart of MyWritingLab is the progressive learning that takes place as students complete the Overview, Animations, Recall, Apply, and Write exercises along with the Post-test within each topic. Students move from preparation (Overview,

Animation) to literal comprehension (Recall) to critical understanding (Apply) to the ability to demonstrate a skill in their own writing (Write) to total mastery (Post-test). This progression of critical thinking enables students to truly master the skills and concepts they need to become successful writers.

Online Gradebook: All student work in MyWritingLab is captured in the online Gradebook. Instructors can see what and how many topics their students have mastered. They can also view students' individual scores on all assignments throughout MyWritingLab, as well as overviews by student and class performance by module. Students can monitor their progress in new Completed Work pages, which show them their totals, scores, time on task, and the date and time of their work by module.

eText: The eText for *The Writer's World* is accessed through MyWritingLab. Students now have the eText at their fingertips while completing the various exercises and activities within MyWritingLab and in the new book-specific module. The MyWritingLab logo is used throughout the book to indicate exercises or writing activities that can be completed in the new book-specific module and submitted through MyWritingLab (results flow directly to the Gradebook where appropriate).

Additional Resources

Pearson is pleased to offer a variety of support materials to help make writing instruction easier for teachers and to help students excel in their coursework. Many of our student supplements are available for free or at a greatly reduced price when packaged with *The Writer's World: Essays, 3/e*. Visit www.pearsonhighereducation.com, contact your local Pearson sales representative, or review a detailed listing of the full supplements package in the *Instructor's Resource Manual* for more information.

Acknowledgments

Many people have helped us produce *The Writer's World*. First and foremost, we would like to thank our students for inspiring us and providing us with extraordinary feedback. Their words and insights pervade this book.

We also benefited greatly from the insightful comments and suggestions from more than one hundred instructors across the nation, all of whom are listed in the opening pages of the *Annotated Instructor's Edition*. Our colleagues' feedback was invaluable and helped shape *The Writer's World* series content, focus, and organization.

Reviewers

The following reviewers provided insight and assistance in the latest revision of *The Writer's World* series:

Justin Bonnett, Saint Paul College; Cheryl Borman, Hillsborough Community College, Ybor City Campus; Adam Carlberg, Tallahessee Community College; Judith L. Carter, Amarillo College; Zoe Ann Cerny, Horry-Georgetown Technical College; Cathy J. Clements, State Fair Community College; Cynthia Dawes, Edgecombe Community College; Mary F. Di Stefano Diaz, Broward College; Stephanie Fischer, Southern Connecticut State University; Paul Gallagher, Red Rocks Community College; Kim Allen Gleed, Harrisburg Area Community College; Karen Hindhede, Central Arizona College; Schahara Hudelson,

South Plains College; Dianna W. Hydem, Jefferson State Community College; Stacy Janicki, Ridgewater College; Patrice Johnson, Dallas County Community College District; Jennifer Johnston, Hillsborough Community College; Julie Keenan, Harrisburg Area Community College; Patricia A. Lacey, Harper College; Nicole Lacroix, Red Rock Community College; Ruth K. MacDonald, Lincoln College of New England; Joy McClain, Ivy Technical Community College, Evansville; Ellen Olmstead, Montgomery College; Deborah Peterson, Blinn College; Rebecca Portis, Montgomery College; Sharon Race, South Plains College; Stephanie Sabourin, Montgomery College; Sharisse Turner, Tallahassee Community College; Jody Wheeler, Saint Paul College; Julie Yankanich, Camden County College

Lynne Gaetz in the Dominican Republic

We are indebted to the team of dedicated professionals at Pearson who have helped make this project a reality. They have boosted our spirits and have believed in us every step of the way. Special thanks to Erica Nikolaidis for her magnificent job in polishing this book and to Matthew Wright for trusting our instincts and enthusiastically propelling us forward. We owe a deep debt of gratitude to Yolanda de Rooy, whose encouraging words helped ignite this project. Michelle Gardner's attention to detail in the production process kept us motivated and on task and made *The Writer's World* a much better resource for both instructors and students.

Finally, we would like to dedicate this book to our families who supported us and who patiently put up with our long hours on the computer. Manu and Murray continually encouraged us, as did Diego, Rebeka, Kiran, and Meghana.

A Note to Students

Your knowledge, ideas, and opinions are important. The ability to clearly communicate those ideas is invaluable in your personal, academic, and professional life. When your writing is error-free, readers will focus on your message, and you will be able to persuade, inform, entertain, or inspire them. *The Writer's World* includes strategies that will help you improve your written communication. Quite simply, when you become a better writer, you become a better communicator. It is our greatest wish for *The Writer's World* to make you excited about writing, communicating, and learning. Enjoy!

Suneeti Phadke in the Caribbean

Lynne Gaetz and Suneeti Phadke
writingrewards@pearson.com

Call for Student Writing!

Do you want to be published in *The Writer's World*? Send your paragraphs and essays to us along with your complete contact information. If your work is selected to appear in the next edition of *The Writer's World*, you will receive credit for your work and a copy of the book!

Lynne Gaetz and Suneeti Phadke
writingrewards@pearson.com

Part I

The Writing Process

The writing process is a series of steps that most writers follow to advance from thinking about a topic to preparing the final draft.

Before you begin the next chapters, review the steps in the writing process.

CHAPTER 1	CHAPTERS 2,3,4	CHAPTER 5
▶ **EXPLORING**	▶ **DEVELOPING**	▶ **REVISING AND EDITING**
• Think about your topic.	• Express your main idea.	• Revise for unity.
• Think about your audience.	• Develop your supporting ideas.	• Revise for adequate support.
• Think about your purpose.	• Make a plan or an outline.	• Revise for style.
• Try exploring strategies.	• Write your first draft.	• Edit for technical errors.

MODEL PARAGRAPH

[handwritten: A paragraph is a series of sentences. They are about a Can be part of longer work such as a essay for report]

A paragraph is a series of sentences that are about one central idea. Paragraphs can stand alone, or they can be part of a longer work such as an essay or report. The topic sentence expresses the main idea, and body sentences develop that idea. Most paragraphs end with a concluding sentence that brings the paragraph to a satisfactory close.

Many people protest that their vote doesn't matter, but each vote can make a difference. For instance, in Vermont's 1997 election, representative Sydney Nixon lost by one vote. In the 1974 senate election in New Hampshire, there was a two-vote difference between Louis Wyman and John A. Durkin. Also, large enough groups of like-minded people can change policies and laws, so voting can lead to concrete results. Everyone should remember that each and every vote counts!

> The **topic sentence** expresses the main point of the paragraph.

> The **supporting ideas** contain details and examples.

> The **concluding sentence** brings the paragraph to a satisfactory close.

MODEL ESSAY

An essay contains several paragraphs that revolve around one central idea. The introductory paragraph includes a thesis statement that expresses the main idea of the essay. Body paragraphs support the thesis statement. The essay closes with a concluding paragraph that sums up the main ideas.

Roma Ahi
Dan Rowen
English 102
12 Nov. 2013

The Importance of Voting

Most people get involved in politics for the right reasons. For instance, those who knew Canadian politician Jack Layton said that he simply wanted to make a difference. Each person in the country can also make a difference. Every time there is an election, there is an action that everyone should take. Everyone should vote for three reasons.

> The **introduction** generates interest in the topic. The **thesis statement** expresses the essay's topic and controlling idea.

First, it is easy to vote. During each election, students and workers are given enough hours to present themselves to polling stations. There are a lot of volunteers who ensure that the voting process is smooth. Those with limited mobility can get a ride to the polling station, usually by a team from the party that they are supporting. College student Luc Robitaille says, "It only took twenty minutes of my time to vote."

Furthermore, many people protest that their vote doesn't matter, but each vote can make a difference. For instance, in Vermont's 1997 election, representative Sydney Nixon lost by one vote. In the 1974 senate election in New Hampshire, there was a two-vote difference between Louis Wyman and John A. Durkin. Also, large enough groups of like-minded people can change policies and laws, so voting can lead to concrete results. Everyone should remember that each and every vote counts.

Finally, Americans should value their right to vote, remembering that people in other nations suffer horribly just because they want democracy. In many nations, pro-democracy supporters are sent to prison. Myanmar politician Aung San Suu Kyi spent almost fifteen years under house arrest because she wanted free and open elections. In 2011, Iranian officials arrested and jailed the leader of the reform movement, Mir-Hossein Mousavi. Also, during the past few years, protesters in Egypt, Tunisia, and Libya have been killed during their fight to have free and open elections. When people live in a nation that has a thriving democracy, it is their duty to support it.

Unfortunately, many people are cynical about politics. But each vote is important, and the right to vote is a historical right that everyone should respect. As critic and editor George Jean Nathan said, "Bad officials are elected by good citizens who do not vote."

Each **body paragraph** begins with a **topic sentence** that supports the thesis and contains details and examples.

The **concluding paragraph** briefly restates the main points and ends with a suggestion, prediction, or quotation.

Exploring 1

Before planting seeds or shrubs, a gardener might look for ideas in magazines, on the Internet, or in nurseries. Similarly, a writer uses various prewriting strategies to explore topics for writing.

LEARNING OBJECTIVES

LO 1 Follow the key steps in exploring. **(p. 5)**

LO 2 Define topic. **(p. 6)**

LO 3 Define audience. **(p. 6)**

LO 4 Define purpose. **(p. 7)**

LO 5 Use exploring strategies. **(p. 10)**

LO 6 Keep a journal and writing portfolio. **(p. 13)**

Key Steps in Exploring

LO 1 Follow the key steps in exploring.

Essay-length prose is the backbone of written communication in and out of college. Throughout your life, you will use principles of essay writing in various written communications, including research papers, e-mails, reports, formal letters, newsletters, and Web pages. Essays help you explore ideas and share those thoughts with others. By reading through this text and completing the many helpful writing practices in it, you will significantly improve your chances of getting more out of your courses and jobs. Enjoy the journey!

Perhaps you recently received a writing assignment and have been staring at the blank page, thinking, "I don't know what to write." Well, it is not necessary to write a good essay immediately. There are certain things that you can do to help you focus on your topic.

5

Understand Your Assignment

As soon as you are given an assignment, make sure that you understand your task. Answer the following questions about the assignment.

+ How many words or pages does the assignment require?
+ What is the due date for the assignment?
+ Are there any special qualities my writing should include? For example, should my writing be double-spaced? Should I include a list of works cited?

After you have thought about your assignment, consider the following four key steps in the exploring stage of the writing process.

> ▶ **EXPLORING**

STEP 1   **Think about your topic.** Determine what you will write about.

STEP 2   **Think about your audience.** Consider your intended readers and what interests them.

STEP 3   **Think about your purpose.** Ask yourself what your goal is.

STEP 4   **Try exploring strategies.** Experiment with different ways to generate ideas.

LO2 Define topic.

Topic

Your **topic**, or **subject**, is what you are writing about. When an instructor gives you a writing topic, narrow the topic and find an angle that interests you. When you think about your topic, ask yourself the following questions.

+ What special knowledge do I have about the topic?
+ What subtopics are most relevant to me?
+ What aspect of the topic do I care deeply about?

LO3 Define audience.

Audience

Your **audience** is your intended reader. In your personal, academic, and professional life, you will often write for a specific audience. You can keep your readers interested by adapting your tone and vocabulary to suit them.

Tone shows your general attitude or feeling toward a topic. You might write in a tone that is humorous, sarcastic, or serious. For example, imagine that you are preparing an invitation to an event. To determine the design and phrasing, you need to know important information about your recipients. What are their ages and lifestyles? Are they mainly male or female? Would they prefer printed invitations, e-mails, or text messages? Questions like these help you connect with your audience.

Knowing your reader is especially important when you are preparing academic or workplace documents. When you consider your audience, ask yourself the following questions.

◆ Who will read my essay? Will my instructor be my only reader, or will others also read it?
◆ What does my audience already know about the topic?
◆ What information will my readers expect?
◆ Should I use formal or informal language?
◆ How should I adjust my vocabulary and tone to appeal to my readers?

HINT ◀ Instructor as the Audience

Your instructor represents a general audience. Such an audience of educated readers will expect you to use correct grammar and to reveal what you have learned or understood about the topic. Do not leave out information because you assume that your instructor is an expert in the field. Your ideas should be presented in a clear and organized manner.

Purpose

LO 4 Define purpose.

Your **purpose** is your reason for writing. Sometimes you may have more than one purpose. When you consider your purpose, ask yourself the following questions.

◆ Is my goal to **entertain**? Do I want to tell a personal story or anecdote?
◆ Is my goal to **persuade**? Do I want to convince readers that my point of view is the correct one?
◆ Is my goal to **inform**? Do I want to explain something or present information?

HINT ◀ General and Specific Purpose

Your **general purpose** is to entertain, inform, or persuade. Your **specific purpose** is your more precise reason for writing. For example, imagine that you are writing about music. You can have the following general and specific purposes.

> **General purpose:** to inform
> **Specific purpose:** to explain how to become a better musician

PRACTICE 1

As you read the following messages, consider the differences in both the tone and the vocabulary the writer uses. Then answer the questions that follow.

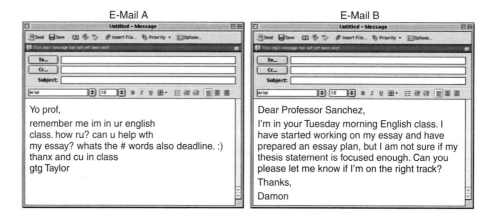

E-Mail A

Yo prof,
remember me im in ur english
class. how ru? can u help wth
my essay? whats the # words also deadline. :)
thanx and cu in class
gtg Taylor

E-Mail B

Dear Professor Sanchez,
I'm in your Tuesday morning English class. I
have started working on my essay and have
prepared an essay plan, but I am not sure if my
thesis statement is focused enough. Can you
please let me know if I'm on the right track?
Thanks,
Damon

1. Why is the language inappropriate in the first instant message?

_____

_____

2. What judgments, based on the messages, might the instructor make about the two students?

_____

_____

PRACTICE 2

The following selections are all about food; however, each excerpt has a different purpose, has been written for a different audience, and has been taken from a different source. Read each selection carefully. Then underline any language clues (words or phrases) that help you identify the selection's source, audience, and purpose. Finally, answer the questions that follow each selection.

EXAMPLE:

slang ➤
slang ➤
slang, informal tone ➤

    I just made my very first dessert. It looks <u>awesome</u>. I hope it tastes alright. I almost <u>freaked out</u> when I realized I forgot to turn the oven on. My instructor is <u>super</u>, and he's got a <u>great sense of humor</u> with me and the other students. Next, I am going to try to make a more complicated dessert.

What is the most likely source of this paragraph?

a. Web site article   b. (personal journal)   c. textbook   d. memoir

What is its primary purpose? _to inform_

Who is the audience? _friend or family member_

1.   I never mastered the art of the thump. Whether the melon is ripe or not, the thump sounds the same to me. Each one I cut, however, seems to be at its pinnacle—toothy crispness, audacious sweetness. . . . Sitting on the stone wall, sun on my face, big slice of watermelon—I'm seven again, totally engrossed in shooting seeds between my fingers and spooning out circles from the dripping quarter moon of fruit.

What is the most likely source of this paragraph?

(a.) Web site article   b. personal journal   c. textbook   (d.) memoir

What is its primary purpose? _to entertain_

Who is the audience? _People_

2.   Eat regularly. Eating is one of life's great pleasures, and it is important to take time to stop, relax, and enjoy mealtimes and snacks. By scheduling eating times, people do not miss meals. People may not get adequate nutrients if they miss a meal, and they might not be able to compensate for a lack of nutrients by eating a subsequent meal. So eating meals regularly is especially important for school-age children, adolescents, and older adults.

What is the most likely source of this paragraph?

a. Web site article   b. personal journal   c. textbook   d. memoir

What is its primary purpose? _____

Who is the audience? _____

3.   About 5,000 years ago, another revolution in technology was taking place in the Middle East, one that would end up changing the entire world. This was the discovery of agriculture, large-scale cultivation using plows harnessed to animals or more powerful energy sources. So important was the invention of the animal-drawn plow, along with other breakthroughs of the period—including irrigation, the wheel, writing, numbers, and the use

of various metals—that this moment in history is often called "the dawn of civilization."

What is the most likely source of this paragraph?

a. Web site article   b. personal journal   c. textbook   d. memoir

What is its purpose? _____

Who is the audience? _____

_____

LO 5 Use exploring strategies.

Exploring Strategies

After you determine your topic, audience, and purpose, try some **exploring strategies**—also known as **prewriting strategies**—to help get your ideas flowing. Four common strategies are *freewriting*, *brainstorming*, *questioning*, and *clustering*. It is not necessary to do all of the strategies explained in this chapter. Find the strategy that works best for you.

You can do both general and focused prewriting. If you have writer's block and do not know what to write about, use **general prewriting** to come up with possible writing topics. Then, after you have chosen a topic, use **focused prewriting** to find an aspect of the topic that is interesting and that could be developed in your essay.

HINT ◄ **When to Use Exploring Strategies**

You can use the exploring strategies at any stage of the writing process:
- To find a topic
- To narrow a broad topic
- To generate ideas about your topic
- To generate supporting details

Narrow Your Topic

An essay has one main idea. If your topic is too broad, you might find it difficult to write a focused essay about the subject. For example, imagine that you are given the topic "music." If you don't narrow the topic, it will be difficult to have a clear and focused point. To narrow the topic, think about more specific topics, such as *the best types of music, the value of music education,* or *censorship of lyrics.* Find one aspect of the topic that you know a lot about and that you personally find interesting. If you have a lot to say and you think the topic is compelling, chances are that your reader will also like your topic.

Review the following examples of general and narrowed topics.

Topic	Narrowed Topic
jobs	preparing for a job interview
music	protest songs from the past and present

To help narrow and develop your topic, you can use the following exploring strategies: freewriting, brainstorming, questioning, and clustering.

Freewriting

Freewriting gives writers the freedom to write without stopping for a set period of time. The goal of this exercise is to record the first thoughts that come to mind. If you run out of ideas, don't stop writing. Simply fill in the pause with phrases like "blah blah blah" or "What else can I write?" As you write, do not be concerned with word choice, grammar, or spelling. If you use a computer, let your ideas flow and do not worry about typing mistakes. You could try typing without looking at the screen.

Alicia's Freewriting

College student Alicia Parera thought about mistakes college students make. During her freewriting, she wrote down everything that came to mind.

> What mistakes do students make? I procrastinate too much. I just avoid working until the last minute and then I cram. It's not healthy. What else? Not asking for help. I feel shy to tell the teacher if I don't understand something. Also immaturity. Students goof off. Colin keeps skipping classes and acts like he's in high school. Can't think of other ideas. What about Amanda and that family crisis? She dropped classes after the course-dropping deadline. Finances are also hard. I work so many hours I sometimes can't keep up with schoolwork . . . It's hard.

Brainstorming

Brainstorming is like freewriting, except that you create a list of ideas and you can take the time to stop and think when you create your list. As you think about the topic, write down words or phrases that come to mind. Do not worry about grammar or spelling; the point is to generate ideas.

Alicia's Brainstorming

Topic: Mistakes that college students make

—party too much
—not doing homework
—feeling too shy to speak with instructors when they have problems
—getting too stressed

—choosing the wrong career path
—don't know what they want to do
—feeling intimidated in class

Questioning

Another way to generate ideas about a topic is to ask yourself a series of questions and write responses to them. The questions can help you define and narrow your topic. One common way to do this is to ask yourself *who, what, when, where, why,* and *how* questions.

Alicia's Questioning

What kinds of mistakes do college students make?
—not doing homework, missing classes, partying too much

Who makes the most mistakes?
—first-year students because they aren't always prepared for college life

Why do some students miss classes?
—feel as if there are no consequences, don't feel interested in their program

When do most students drop out?
—administrators say that November is the most common month that students drop out

How should colleges encourage students who are at risk of dropping out?
—give more financial aid, offer career counseling

Where can students get help?
—guidance counselors, instructors, friends, family, professionals doing students' dream jobs

Why is this topic important?
—new students can learn about pitfalls to avoid, administrators can develop strategies for helping students

Clustering

Clustering is like drawing a word map; ideas are arranged in a visual image. To begin, write your topic in the middle of the page and draw a box or a circle around it. That idea will lead to another, so write the second idea and draw a line connecting it to your topic. Keep writing, circling, and connecting ideas until you have groups, or "clusters," of them on your page.

Alicia's Clustering

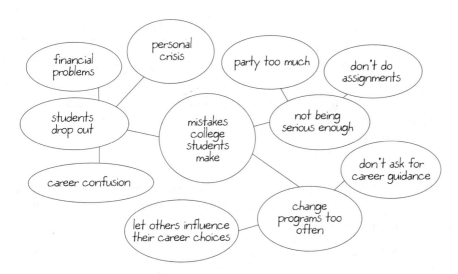

Explore the next three topics. Use a different exploring strategy for each topic. You can choose to do freewriting, brainstorming, questioning, or clustering.

health   overconsumption   volunteer work

Journal and Portfolio Writing

Keeping a Journal

LO 6 Keep a journal and writing portfolio.

You may write for work or school, but you can also practice writing for pleasure. One way to practice your writing is to keep a journal. A **journal** can be a book, computer file, or even a blog where you record your thoughts, opinions, ideas, and impressions. Journal writing gives you a chance to practice your writing without worrying about the audience and what they might think about it. It also gives you a source of material when you want to write about a topic of your choice.

In your journal, you can write about any topic that appeals to you. Here are some possible topics for journal writing.

- Your reflections and feelings about your personal life, your career goals, your college courses, your past and future decisions, and your work
- Your reactions to controversies in your family, neighborhood, college, city, or country, or in the world
- Your reflections on the opinions and philosophies of others, including those of your friends or of people whom you read about in your courses

Keeping a Portfolio

A **writing portfolio** is a place (a binder or an electronic file folder) where you keep samples of all of your writing. The purpose of keeping a portfolio is to have a record of your writing progress. In your portfolio, keep all the drafts of your writing assignments. When you work on new assignments, review your previous work in your portfolio. Identify your main problems, and try not to repeat the same errors.

MyWritingLab™

Complete these writing assignments at mywritinglab.com

MyWritingLab™   **THE WRITER'S ROOM**

Writing Activity 1: Topics

Choose one of the following topics, or choose your own topic. Then generate ideas about the topic. You may want to try the suggested exploring strategy.

General Topics

1. Try freewriting about people who have helped you succeed.
2. Brainstorm a list of thoughts about different types of fear.
3. Create a cluster diagram about problems with technology.
4. Ask and answer questions about voting.

College and Work-Related Topics

5. Try freewriting about a mistake you made at work or at college. Include any emotions or details that come to mind.
6. Brainstorm a list of ideas about noisy work environments.
7. Ask and answer questions about bosses.
8. Create a cluster diagram about different types of students.

Writing Activity 2: Photo Writing

Use questioning to generate ideas about the following image. Ask and answer *who*, *what*, *when*, *where*, *why*, and *how* questions.

Checklist: Exploring

When you explore a topic, ask yourself these questions.

☐ What is my **topic**? Consider what you will write about.

☐ Who is my **audience**? Think about your intended reader.

☐ What is my **purpose**? Determine your reason for writing.

☐ Which exploring strategy will I use? You could try one strategy or a combination of strategies.

Freewriting is writing without stopping for a limited period of time.

Brainstorming is making a list.

Questioning is asking and answering a series of questions.

Clustering is drawing a word map.

2 Developing the Main Idea

LEARNING OBJECTIVES

LO 1 Follow key steps in developing the main idea. **(p. 16)**

LO 2 Write a thesis statement. **(p. 17)**

LO 3 Develop the supporting ideas. **(p. 23)**

Faced with so many plant and flower varieties, a gardener narrows down which ones are most appropriate for his or her garden. Similarly, a writer considers many ideas before choosing a main idea for an essay.

LO 1 Follow key steps in developing the main idea.

Key Steps in Developing the Main Idea

In Chapter 1, you learned how to consider your reading audience and your purposes for writing. You also practiced using exploring strategies to formulate ideas. In this chapter, you will focus on developing a main idea that can be expanded into a complete essay. There are two key steps in this process.

▶ DEVELOPING THE MAIN IDEA

STEP 1 **Write a thesis statement.** Write a statement that expresses the main idea of the piece of writing.

STEP 2 **Develop your supporting ideas.** Find facts, examples, or anecdotes that best support your main idea.

Writing a Thesis Statement

LO2 Write a thesis statement.

Your **thesis** is the main idea that you want to express. A clear thesis statement presents the topic of the essay, and it includes a **controlling idea** that expresses the writer's opinion, attitude, or feeling about the topic. The controlling idea can appear at the beginning or end of the thesis statement.

      topic   controlling idea

Volunteer work should be compulsory for all high school students.

         controlling idea   topic

Extra credit should be given to **high school students who do volunteer work**.

PRACTICE 1

Circle the topic and underline the controlling idea in each thesis statement.

EXAMPLE: You can overcome shyness by practicing the next three steps.

1. Our government should stop spending money on space exploration.

2. There are many reasons for the high rate of youth unemployment.

3. The new museum in our town has an interesting design.

4. There are three types of overindulgent parents.

5. A superstorm is not just a rare weather event; it is a warning to humans about the effects of severe climate change.

6. At my high school prom, I embarrassed myself.

Writing an Effective Thesis Statement

When you develop your thesis statement, ask yourself the following questions to help you avoid thesis statement errors.

1. **Is my thesis a complete statement?**
    Make sure that your thesis does not express an incomplete idea or more than one idea. A thesis statement should reveal one complete thought.

Incomplete	Allergies: so annoying. (This is not a complete statement.)
More than one idea	There are many types of allergens, and allergies affect people in different ways. (This statement contains two distinct ideas. Each idea could become an essay.)
Thesis statement	Doctors suggest several steps people can take to relieve symptoms related to pet allergies.

2. **Does my thesis statement have a controlling idea?**
   Rather than announcing the topic, your thesis statement should make a point about the topic. It should have a controlling idea that expresses your attitude or feeling about the topic. Avoid phrases such as *My topic is* or *I will write about.*

Announces	I will write about computers.
	(This sentence says nothing relevant about the topic. The reader does not know what the point of the essay is.)
Thesis statement	When Microsoft develops a new operating system, there are political, financial, and environmental consequences.

3. **Can I support my thesis statement in an essay?**
   Your thesis statement should express an idea that you can support in an essay. If it is too narrow, you will find yourself with nothing to say. If it is too broad, you will have an endless composition.

Too broad	There are many childless couples in our world.
	(This topic needs a more specific and narrow focus.)
Too narrow	The average age of first-time mothers is approximately twenty-six years old.
	(It would be difficult to write an entire essay about this fact.)
Thesis statement	Many couples are choosing to remain childless for several reasons.

4. **Does my thesis statement make a valid and interesting point?**
   Your thesis statement should make a valid point. It should not be a vaguely worded statement or an obvious and uninteresting comment.

Vague	Censorship is a big problem.
	(For whom is it a big problem?)
Obvious	The Internet is important.
	(So what? Everyone knows this.)
Invalid	The Internet controls our lives.
	(This statement is difficult to believe or prove.)
Thesis statement	The Internet has become a powerful presence in our personal, social, and working lives.

PRACTICE 2

Examine each statement.

- Write **TS** if it is an effective thesis statement.
- Write **I** if it is an incomplete idea.

- Write **M** if it contains more than one complete idea.
- Write **A** if it is an announcement.

EXAMPLE: This essay is about spousal abuse. _____A_____

1. The high price of gas. _____

2. My college has a great sports stadium, but it needs to give more help to female athletes. _____

3. Nursing is extremely demanding. _____

4. My subject is the torture of war prisoners. _____

5. There are many excellent commercials on television, but some are too violent. _____

6. The loss of a job can actually have positive effects on a person's life. _____

PRACTICE 3

Examine each statement.

- Write **TS** if it is a complete thesis statement.
- Write **V** if it is too vague.
- Write **O** if it is too obvious.

EXAMPLE: Americans are more nationalistic. _____V_____

1. New York has a large population. _____

2. We had a major problem. _____

3. Some adult children have legitimate reasons for moving back into their parents' homes. _____

4. The roads are very crowded during holiday periods. _____

5. There are several ways to do this. _____

6. Children in our culture are changing. _____

PRACTICE 4

Examine each pair of sentences.

- Write **B** if the sentence is too broad.
- Write **TS** if the sentence is an effective thesis statement.

EXAMPLE: _____B_____ Plants can help people.

_____TS_____ Learning to care for plants gave me unexpected pleasure.

1. _____ Music is important around the world.

   _____ Some simple steps can help you successfully promote your music.

2. _____ My neighborhood is being transformed by youth gangs.

   _____ Violence is a big problem everywhere.

3. _____ My life has been filled with mistakes.

   _____ My jealousy, insecurity, and anger ruined my first marriage.

4. _____ The car accident transformed my life.

   _____ Everybody's life has dramatic moments.

PRACTICE 5

Examine each pair of sentences.

* Write **N** if the sentence is too narrow.
* Write **TS** if the sentence is an effective thesis statement.

EXAMPLE: ____N____ I grow coriander in my garden.

   ____TS____ Learning to care for plants gave me unexpected pleasure.

1. _____ Our roads are very icy.

   _____ Driving in the winter requires particular skills.

2. _____ Carjacking rates have increased by 20 percent in our city.

   _____ You can avoid being a carjacking victim by taking the next steps.

3. _____ I hurt myself in various ways during my three days on the beach.

   _____ There are many sharp pieces of shell on the local beach.

4. _____ Identical twins who are raised together have distinct personalities.

   _____ My twin sisters have similar birthmarks on their necks.

Revising Your Thesis Statement

A thesis statement is like the foundation that holds up a house. If the thesis statement is weak, it is difficult to construct a solid and compelling essay. Most writers must revise their thesis statements to make them strong, interesting, and supportable.

When you plan your thesis, ask yourself if you can support it with at least three ideas. If not, you have to modify your thesis statement. To enliven a dead-end statement, ensure that your thesis can answer the *why*, *what*, or *how* questions. Sometimes, just by adding a few words, you can turn a dead-end statement into a supportable thesis.

Weak thesis   Many students drop out of college.

(How could you develop this into an essay? It is a dead-end statement.)

Better thesis   Students drop out of college **for several reasons**.

(You could support this thesis with at least three ideas. This thesis statement answers the question "Why?")

HINT ◀ **Writing a Guided Thesis Statement**

Give enough details to make your thesis statement interesting. Your instructor may want you to guide the reader through your main points. To do this, mention your main and supporting ideas in your thesis statement. In other words, your thesis statement provides a map for the readers to follow.

Weak   My first job taught me many things.

Better   My first job taught me about the importance of responsibility, organization, and teamwork.

PRACTICE 6

The next thesis statements are weak. First, identify the problem with the statement (write *vague, obvious, incomplete, announces*, and so on) and ask yourself questions to determine how you might be able to revise it. Then revise each statement to make it more forceful and focused.

EXAMPLE: Teenagers don't do enough exercise.

Comments: Invalid. Is this statement really true?

Revision: Teenagers should be encouraged to do regular exercise.

1. The speed limit in school zones is 20 mph.

   Comments: _____

   Revision: _____

   _____

2. Americans feel afraid.

   Comments: _____

   Revision: _____

   _____

3. My topic is about homework.

   Comments: _____

   Revision: _____

   _____

4. Obesity in America is a health issue.

Comments: _____

Revision: _____

_____

5. Major league sports.

Comments: _____

Revision: _____

_____

Overview: Writing a Thesis Statement

To create a forceful thesis statement, you should follow the next steps.

Step 1

Find your topic. You can use exploring strategies to get ideas.

General topic: Traditions

Brainstorming:

- Commercialization of holidays
- My family traditions
- Important ceremonies
- Why do we celebrate?
- Benefits of traditions
- Initiation ceremonies

Step 2

Narrow your topic. Decide what point you want to make.

Narrowed topic: Initiation ceremonies

Point I want to make: Initiation ceremonies can help people make the transition from childhood to adulthood.

Step 3

Develop a thesis statement that you can support with specific evidence. You may need to revise your statement several times.

Initial thesis statement: Initiation ceremonies serve a valuable function.

Revised thesis statement: Meaningful initiation ceremonies benefit individuals, families, and communities.

THE WRITER'S DESK   **Write Thesis Statements**

Write a thesis statement for each of the next topics. If you explored these topics in Chapter 1, you can use those ideas to help you write your thesis statement. If you have not explored these topics yet, then spend a few minutes exploring them. Brainstorm some ideas for each topic to help you define and narrow it. Then develop a thesis statement that makes a point and is not too broad or too narrow.

health   overconsumption   volunteer work

EXAMPLE: Topic: Mistakes students make

Narrowed topic: *Reasons students drop out*

Thesis statement: *Students may drop out of college because they are unprepared, have financial problems, or experience an emotional crisis.*

1. _____

   _____

2. _____

   _____

3. _____

   _____

Developing the Supporting Ideas

LO3 Develop the supporting ideas.

The next step in essay writing is to plan your supporting ideas. Support is not simply a restatement of the thesis. The body paragraphs must develop and prove the validity of the thesis statement.

Each body paragraph has a **topic sentence** that expresses the main idea of the paragraph. Like a thesis statement, a topic sentence must have a controlling idea. Details and examples support the topic sentence. In the following illustration, you can see how the ideas flow in an essay. Topic sentences support the thesis statement, and details bolster the topic sentences. Every idea in the essay is unified and helps to strengthen the essay's thesis.

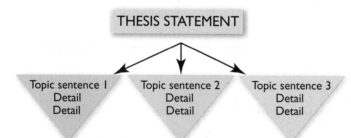

PRACTICE 7

Write a thesis statement for each group of supporting ideas. Make sure that your thesis statement is clear, makes a point, and is not too broad or too narrow.

EXAMPLE: Thesis: _When you buy a car, make an informed decision._

   a. Ask family members what type of car they would prefer.
   b. Research on the Internet or in car guides to find information about specific models that interest you.
   c. Keeping your budget in mind, compare new and used cars.

1. Thesis: _____

   _____

   a. First, keeping teens off the street at night will ensure that they do not become victims of crime.
   b. Next, requiring adolescents to remain at home will prevent them from committing delinquent acts.
   c. Finally, parents won't need to worry about the whereabouts of their children after dark.

2. Thesis: _____

   _____

   a. When boys are in all-male classrooms, teachers can modify their activities to keep the boys' attention.
   b. All-female classrooms permit the female students to focus on the material and show their intelligence.
   c. Unlike co-education classrooms, same-gender classrooms are easier for teachers to control.

3. Thesis: _____

   _____

   a. First, internalize and believe in your sales pitch.
   b. Speak softly, and do not scare the customer with a commanding voice or aggressive mannerisms.
   c. Finally, involve the customer in your sales presentation.

PRACTICE 8

Read the full essay in this practice and then do the following.

1. First, determine the topic of each body paragraph. Then write a topic sentence for each body paragraph. Your topic sentence should have a controlling idea and express the main point of the paragraph.

2. Next, ask yourself what this essay is about. Finally, compose a thesis statement that sums up the main point of the essay. You might look in the concluding paragraph to get some ideas.

   (Introduction) Paparazzi are photographers who take pictures of celebrities. For a shocking photograph of a well-known person, a tabloid photographer can earn more than $100,000. Thus, such photographers hunt for unusual and possibly embarrassing images of well-known people.

   Thesis statement: _____

   _____

(Body 1) Topic Sentence: _____

_____

When people read gossip magazines, or even watch TV channels like *VH1*, they always see paparazzi surrounding the stars. They also see celebrities jumping into cars and trying to get away from the photographers. This type of behavior can cause serious accidents. The most famous case was the death of Princess Diana. Trying to escape from paparazzi, she died in a car crash in 1997. Other celebrities have been injured while trying to escape photographers.

(Body 2) Topic Sentence: _____

_____

Some paparazzi stalk celebrities and take photos from trees, rooftops, helicopters, or boats. For instance, Jennifer Hudson, a former *American Idol* contestant, lived through a great personal tragedy. Her mother, brother, and nephew were murdered. Photographers and reporters were seen hounding Hudson with questions and taking photographs of her during this misfortune.

(Body 3) Topic Sentence: _____

_____

Magazine covers regularly display photographs of celebrities' spouses and children. The family members may not want or appreciate the attention. For example, the children of Brad Pitt and Angelina Jolie are exposed to scrutiny, criticized for their clothing choices, and occasionally ridiculed. Several years ago, Pierce Brosnan's wife was mocked for gaining weight.

(Conclusion) Paparazzi hurt people rather than help them. It is almost sickening to think of what a photographer is willing to do to get a story. The public should stop buying gossip magazines so photographers will not be able to earn a living by committing gross invasions of privacy.

Generating Supporting Ideas

When you plan your supporting ideas, make certain that they develop and provide evidence for the central point that you are making in the thesis statement. To generate ideas for body paragraphs, you could use the exploring strategies (brainstorming, freewriting, questioning, or clustering) that you learned in Chapter 1.

Review the process that student Alicia Parera went through. First, she created a list to support her thesis statement. Then she reread her supporting ideas and removed ideas that she did not want to develop in her essay. She also grouped together related ideas.

Initial Ideas

Draft Thesis Statement: Students drop out of college for many reasons.

Supporting ideas:

—can't adapt to college life

—feel confused about career goals ⟩——— **A**

—don't have study skills

—can't afford tuition

—part-time job takes time away from schoolwork ⟩——— **B**

—financial problems

—lose a family member

—undergo an emotional crisis such as a breakup ⟩—— **C**

—~~want to start their own business~~

After critically examining her supporting ideas, Alicia chose three that could become body paragraphs. She evaluated each set of linked ideas and summarized the connections between ideas in the set. These sentence summaries then became her topic sentences.

Revised Thesis and Supporting Points

Thesis Statement: Students may drop out of college because they are unprepared, have financial problems, or experience an emotional crisis.

    Topic Sentence: Many students are unable to adapt to college life.

    Topic Sentence: Some students face overwhelming financial burdens.

    Topic Sentence: Furthermore, students may undergo an emotional crisis.

HINT ◄ Look Critically at Your Supporting Ideas

After you have made a list of supporting ideas, look at it carefully and ask yourself the next questions.

- **Which ideas could I develop into complete paragraphs?** Look for connections between supporting ideas. Group together ideas that have a common thread. Then create a topic sentence for each group of related ideas. In Alicia's example, three of her ideas became topic sentences.

- **Does each idea support my thesis?** Choose ideas that directly support the thesis statement, and drop any ideas that might go off topic. In Alicia's example, the last idea, "Want to start their own business," does not support her thesis, so she crossed it out.

PRACTICE 9

Brainstorm three supporting ideas for the next thesis statements. Find ideas that do not overlap, and ensure that your ideas support the thesis. (You can brainstorm a list of ideas on a separate sheet of paper, and then add the three best ideas here.)

EXAMPLE: Sex education classes should be mandatory in middle schools.

—students will receive the correct information about their bodies

—students will be able to make more informed decisions about becoming sexually active

—students will be more comfortable with their own sexuality as they grow into adults

1. Insomnia can be caused by many factors.

2. College internships are a valuable tool for graduating students.

3. Americans can avoid being victims of identity theft by taking a few simple precautions.

THE WRITER'S DESK   Generate Supporting Ideas

Brainstorm supporting ideas for two or three of your thesis statements from the previous Writer's Desk on pages 22–23. Look critically at your lists of supporting ideas. Ask yourself which supporting ideas you could expand into body paragraphs, and then drop any unrelated ideas.

MyWritingLab™

Complete these writing assignments at mywritinglab.com

MyWritingLab™   THE WRITER'S ROOM   Topics to Develop

Writing Activity 1

Choose one of the Writer's Room topics from Chapter 1 and write a thesis statement. Using an exploring strategy, develop supporting ideas for your thesis.

Writing Activity 2

Narrow one of the following topics. Then develop a thesis statement and some supporting ideas.

General Topics

1. social networking
2. saving money
3. delaying childbirth
4. traditions

College and Work-Related Topics

5. pressures students face
6. salary for college athletes
7. compulsory attendance for college students
8. benefits of extracurricular activities

Checklist: Thesis Statement and Topic Sentences

When you write a thesis statement and topic sentences, ask yourself these questions.

☐ Is my thesis a complete sentence?

☐ Does it contain a narrowed topic and a controlling idea?

☐ Is my main point clear and interesting?

☐ Can the thesis be supported with several body paragraphs? (Verify that the topic is not too narrow, or you will hit a dead end with it. Also check that the topic is not too broad. Your essay requires a clear focus.)

☐ Can I think of details, examples, and other ideas to support the thesis?

☐ Is my thesis forceful and direct, and not too vague or obvious?

☐ Does my thesis make a valid point?

☐ Do I have good supporting ideas?

☐ Does each topic sentence have a controlling idea and support the thesis statement?

3 Developing the Essay Plan

LEARNING OBJECTIVES

LO 1 Follow key steps in developing the essay plan. **(p. 30)**

LO 2 Organize supporting ideas. **(p. 31)**

LO 3 Develop an essay plan. **(p. 35)**

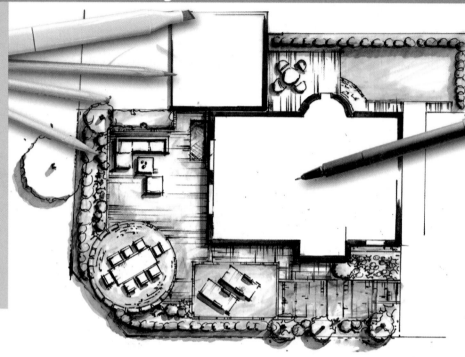

Like gardens, essays require careful planning. Some ideas thrive while others do not. Writers develop essay plans to help them decide which ideas support the main idea most effectively and where to place those ideas so that readers can understand them.

LO 1 Follow key steps in developing the essay plan.

Key Steps in Developing the Essay Plan

In the previous chapters, you learned how to use exploring strategies to formulate ideas and narrow topics. You also learned to develop main ideas for essays. In this chapter, you will focus on the third stage of the essay writing process: developing the essay plan. There are two key steps in this process.

▶ **DEVELOPING THE ESSAY PLAN**

STEP 1 **Organize your supporting ideas.** Choose an appropriate method of organization.

STEP 2 **Write an essay plan.** Place your main and supporting ideas in an essay plan.

Organizing Supporting Ideas

LO 2 Organize supporting ideas.

Once you have a list of main ideas that will make up the body paragraphs in an essay, you need to organize those ideas in a logical manner using time, space, or emphatic order.

Time Order

To organize an essay using **time order (chronological order)**, arrange the details according to the sequence in which they occurred. Time order can be effective for narrating a story, explaining how to do something, or describing an event.

When you write essays using time order, you can include the following transitional expressions to help your readers understand when certain events happened. (There is a more extensive list of transitions on page 63 in Chapter 5.)

after that	first	later	next
eventually	in the beginning	meanwhile	suddenly
finally	last	months after	then

PRACTICE 1

The writer uses time order to organize supporting ideas for the following thesis statement.

THESIS STATEMENT: My one and only ferry ride was a disaster.

1. To begin with, the only available seat was in a horrible location near the back of the boat.

2. Next, the rain began, and the passengers on deck rushed inside.

3. After that, the ferry began to rock, and some passengers became ill.

One paragraph from the essay also uses time order. Underline any words or phrases that help show time order.

> Next, the rain began, and the passengers on deck started to move inside. Suddenly, a sprinkle became a downpour. I was in the middle of the crowd, and water was running in rivulets down my face and down the back of my neck. Then, those behind me got impatient and began to shove. The doorway was narrow, and many people were

jostling for position. I was pushed to the right and left. Meanwhile, I was soaked, tired, and cranky. The crowd squeezed me more and more. Finally, I was pushed through the door; I stumbled and tried not to fall. The inner cabin was so crowded that I had to stand in the aisle holding on to the back of one of the seats.

Space Order

Organizing ideas using **space order** helps the reader to visualize what you are describing in a specific space. For example, you can describe someone or something from top to bottom or bottom to top, from left to right or right to left, or from far to near or near to far.

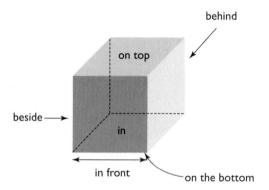

Help readers find their way through your essay by using the following transitional expressions.

above	beneath	nearby	on top
behind	closer in	on the bottom	toward
below	farther out	on the left	under

PRACTICE 2

The writer uses space order to organize supporting ideas for the following thesis statement.

THESIS STATEMENT: Spending very little money, local students helped turn a tiny old house into a vibrant youth center.

1. Working outdoors, two students cleared the yard.

2. Focusing on the exterior surfaces of the building, a second team of students painted and made minor repairs.

3. Inside the house, some students turned the living room into a recreation and meeting place.

One paragraph from the essay also uses space order. Underline any words or phrases that indicate space order.

> Working outdoors, two students cleared the yard. At the front edge of the property, there were paper bags, fast-food wrappers, and broken bottles. Wearing gloves, the students picked up the mess and put the items in the garbage. In the center of the yard, some of the grass was dying, so the students planted new grass seeds. Leading up to the front of the house was a stone walkway. The students repaired the paving stones. Under the front windows were two empty flower boxes. The boxes were gray with peeling paint. One student sanded the boxes, and the other repainted them. When they finished their work, the yard looked inviting.

Emphatic Order

To organize the supporting details of an essay using **emphatic order**, arrange them in a logical sequence. For example, you can arrange details from the least to the most important, from general to specific, from the least appealing to the most appealing, and so on.

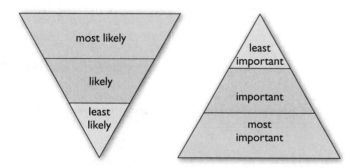

Here are some transitional expressions that help readers understand which ideas you want to emphasize the most or the least in the body paragraphs of an essay.

above all	first	moreover	principally
clearly	in particular	most importantly	the least important
especially	last	of course	the most important

HINT ◀ Using Emphatic Order

When you organize details using emphatic order, use your own values and opinions to determine what is the most or the least important, upsetting, remarkable, and so on. Another writer may organize the same ideas in a different way.

PRACTICE 3

The writer uses emphatic order to organize supporting ideas for the following thesis statement.

THESIS STATEMENT: Chronic stress creates immense costs for American society.

1. First, American businesses lose millions of dollars because of employee stress.

2. In addition, psychological stress can take a toll on interpersonal relationships.

3. Above all, untreated stress may shorten the lives of many Americans.

One paragraph from the essay also uses emphatic order. Underline any words or phrases that help show emphatic order.

> American businesses lose millions of dollars because of employee stress. First, work-related stress often causes employees to miss work. Employers must deal with lost productivity and replacement costs of absent employees. Next, highly stressed workers may develop grievances against the company. As a means of forcing the employers to recognize a legitimate injustice, employees may sue employers. Most importantly, overly stressed employees might not be able to perform at their peak. Stress can negatively influence a person's intellectual and emotional ability. An employee might not be able to react creatively and logically in a crisis because stress diminishes a person's ability to think through a problem. Clearly, businesses must look at ways to reduce employee stress.

HINT ◀ Combining Time, Space, and Emphatic Order

You will probably use more than one type of organizational method in an essay. For example, in a time order essay about a journey, one paragraph might be devoted to a particular place that you visited, and in that paragraph, you might use space order to describe the scene.

PRACTICE 4

Read each list of supporting ideas, and number the items in a logical order. Then write *time*, *space*, or *emphatic* to indicate the organization method.

EXAMPLE: Thesis Statement: Painting a picture can be a rewarding experience.

   _1_ Choose a location that you find particularly peaceful.

   _3_ Add colors to your sketch that best represent the mood you are feeling.

   _2_ Settle in and make a preliminary sketch of the place.

Order: ___*time*___

1. Thesis Statement: As I sat in my back garden, I pinpointed the locations of various loud sounds.

    ____ Two cardinals were fluttering above their nest in the tree top and squawking desperately.

    ____ Pierce, my sister's cocker spaniel, sat at the foot of a spindly tree, barking angrily at the cat.

    ____ A cat, perched precariously on the branch, was hissing at the birds.

    Order: _____

2. Thesis Statement: Julius faced a series of problems as he rushed to his job interview.

    ____ On his way to the interview a half an hour later, he was stuck in a traffic jam.

    ____ Right after breakfast, Julius tried to start his car and panicked when it made funny noises.

    ____ After advancing only a half a block in twenty minutes, he decided to park the car and walk to his interview.

    Order: _____

3. Thesis Statement: Top college athletes should get paid to play on sports teams.

    ____ Coaches and colleges receive millions of dollars in revenues when college sports teams win.

    ____ Top athletes raise a school's profile and help attract more students to the college.

    ____ Many college athletes don't receive enough scholarship money to cover the costs of going to college.

    Order: _____

Developing an Essay Plan

LO 3 Develop an essay plan.

A contractor would never build a house without making a drawing or plan of it first. In the same way, an essay plan can help you organize your ideas before you write the first draft. Planning your essay actually saves you time because you have already figured out your supporting ideas and how to organize them so your readers can easily follow them. To create an essay plan, follow the next steps.

* Looking at the list of ideas that you created while prewriting, identify the ones that most effectively support your thesis statement.

- Next, write topic sentences that express these main supporting ideas.
- Finally, add details under each topic sentence.

A formal essay plan uses Roman numerals and letters of the alphabet to identify main and supporting ideas. A formal plan also contains complete sentences. The basic structure is shown below.

Thesis Statement: _____

     I. _____

        A. _____

        B. _____

    II. _____

        A. _____

        B. _____

Concluding Idea: _____

In the planning stage, you do not have to develop your introduction and conclusion. It is sufficient to simply write your thesis statement and an idea for your conclusion. Later, when you write your essay, you can develop the introduction and conclusion.

Alicia's Essay Plan

Alicia Parera wrote topic sentences and supporting examples and organized her ideas into a plan. Notice that she begins with her thesis statement, and she indents her supporting ideas. Also notice that she uses emphatic order.

Thesis Statement: Students may drop out of college because they have financial problems, experience an emotional crisis, or are unprepared for college life.

    I.   Some students face overwhelming financial burdens.

        A. They may have a part-time job to pay for such things as tuition and rent.

        B. Moreover, a part-time job leaves little time for studying and homework.

        C. Also, transportation may be expensive and beyond a student's means.

    II. Furthermore, some students are faced with life-changing events and must leave college to cope.

        A. A pregnancy and childbirth consume energy and attention.

        B. Also, a serious illness or death in the family can cause a student to miss classes, and it becomes too difficult to catch up.

        C. Of course, a broken relationship can cause a student to feel emotionally fragile and unable to concentrate.

III.   Finally, they may be unprepared for college life.

        A. They might have poor study skills.

        B. Furthermore, some students cannot respect schedules.

        C. The increased freedom in college causes some students to skip too many classes.

        D. Additionally, many students feel confused about career goals and decide to leave college.

PRACTICE 5

Read the following essay plan. Brainstorm and develop three supporting ideas for each topic sentence.

THESIS STATEMENT: Each generation has produced influential musical icons.

Topic Sentence: In the 1960s, some amazing singers and bands influenced their generation.

_____

_____

_____

_____

Topic Sentence: During the 1980s, certain musical stars made lasting impressions.

_____

_____

_____

_____

Topic Sentence: From 2000 to 2010, a wide variety of music styles became popular.

_____

_____

_____

_____

PRACTICE 6

Read the following essay plan. Brainstorm and develop three supporting ideas for each topic. Include specific anecdotes.

THESIS STATEMENT: I learned valuable life lessons in primary and secondary school.

    Topic Sentence: Through various activities, I learned to get along with others.

_____

_____

_____

_____

    Topic Sentence: I learned about the importance of knowledge.

_____

_____

_____

_____

    Topic Sentence: Finally, I learned self-discipline.

_____

_____

_____

_____

THE WRITER'S DESK Write an Essay Plan

Brainstorm ideas for an essay on a separate piece of paper. You can choose ideas that you developed in Chapter 2. Then do the following.

1. Highlight at least three ideas from your list that you think are the most compelling and most clearly illustrate the point you are making in your thesis statement. These three ideas will make up your body paragraphs.

2. Group together any related ideas with the three supporting ideas.

3. Organize your ideas for the body paragraphs using time, space, or emphatic order.

4. Create a complete essay plan.

MyWritingLab™ **THE WRITER'S ROOM** Topics to Develop

MyWritingLab™
Complete these
writing assignments at
mywritinglab.com

Writing Activity 1

Choose one of the Writer's Room topics from Chapter 2, and create an essay plan. Using an exploring strategy, develop supporting ideas for your thesis.

Writing Activity 2

Create a list of supporting ideas for one of the next thesis statements. Then develop an essay plan.

General Topics

1. Single people should (or should not) have the right to adopt children.

2. The three talents I would most like to have are . . .

3. Driver education classes should (or should not) be compulsory.

4. There are good reasons to live near (or move away from) family members.

College and Work-Related Topics

5. New employees make three types of common mistakes.

6. An elected official should have the following characteristics.

7. College tuition should be free for three reasons.

8. (Choose a story, novel, or film) has important lessons for all of us.

Checklist: Essay Plan

When you develop an essay plan, ask yourself these questions.

☐ Does my thesis statement express the main idea of the essay?

☐ In my plan, does each body paragraph contain a topic sentence?

☐ Does each topic sentence support the thesis statement?

☐ In each body paragraph, do the sentences support the topic sentence?

☐ Are my ideas well organized?

4 Developing the First Draft

LEARNING OBJECTIVES

LO 1 Follow key steps in developing the first draft. **(p. 40)**

LO 2 Write an introduction. **(p. 41)**

LO 3 Write complete body paragraphs. **(p. 46)**

LO 4 Write a conclusion. **(p. 49)**

LO 5 Choose an essay title. **(p. 51)**

LO 6 Write the first draft. **(p. 54)**

By preparing the soil and planting seeds and shrubs, a gardener creates a landscape's basic foundation. In the same way, a writer plans the main idea, develops the plan, and then prepares the first draft of a writing assignment.

LO 1 Follow key steps in developing the first draft.

Key Steps in Developing the First Draft

In previous chapters, you learned how to develop a thesis statement, support it with ideas, and create an essay plan. To develop a first draft, follow the next five steps.

▶ DEVELOPING THE FIRST DRAFT

STEP 1 **Write an introduction.** Try to attract the reader's attention in the first paragraph of your essay.

STEP 2 **Write complete body paragraphs.** Expand each supporting idea with specific details.

STEP 3 **Write a conclusion.** Bring your essay to a satisfactory close.

STEP 4 **Title your essay.** Sum up your essay topic in a few words.

STEP 5 **Write the first draft.** Tie the introduction, body paragraphs, and conclusion into a cohesive essay.

Writing an Introduction

L02 Write an introduction.

The **introductory paragraph** establishes the subject of your essay and contains the thesis statement. A strong introduction will capture the reader's attention and make him or her want to read on. Introductions may have a lead-in, and they can be developed in several different ways.

The Lead-In

The point of writing an essay is to have people read it. Your essay should entertain, inform, or persuade readers. So, you can try to grab your readers' attention in the first sentence. There are three common lead-ins:

- ◆ a quotation
- ◆ a surprising or provocative statement
- ◆ a question

Introduction Styles

You can develop the introduction in several ways. Experiment with any of the following introduction styles.

- ◆ **Give general or historical background information** that gradually leads to your thesis. For example, in an essay about gender stereotypes in movies, you might begin by discussing some classic films.
- ◆ **Tell an interesting anecdote** or a story that leads to your thesis statement. For example, you might begin your essay about film violence by describing how aggressive your younger brother and his friends became after they watched the movie *The Dark Knight Rises*.
- ◆ **Describe something in vivid detail**, and then state your thesis. For example, you might begin your essay about the beauty myth by describing a cosmetic surgery procedure.

- **Define a term**, and then state your thesis. For example, in an essay about ways to avoid marital conflicts, you can begin by defining a happy marriage.
- **Present a contrasting position**, which is an idea that is the opposite of the one you will later develop, and then offer your thesis. Your readers will not expect you to present one side and then to argue for the other side. For example, in an essay about abortion, you might begin by presenting the arguments of those who would not agree with your particular point of view on the debate.
- **Pose several questions**, and end with a thesis statement. The purpose may be to engage your readers by inviting them to think about the topic. You might also ask questions that you will answer in your essay. For instance, in an essay about lotteries, you might ask, *Have you ever bought a lottery ticket? Why do so many people play lotteries?*

The next example presents the structure of a typical introduction.

Lead-in ➤

Historical background information ➤

Thesis statement ➤

> **Have good manners disappeared?** In past centuries, a gentleman would spread his cloak over a muddy road so that his lady wouldn't dirty her feet. Twenty years ago, an elderly man or woman would never have to stand in a bus because other passengers would offer up their seats. Times have certainly changed. Today, many people lack consideration for others. **Parents and schools should teach children basic good manners**.

PRACTICE 1

Read the following introductions. Underline each thesis statement, and determine what introduction style the writer used.

1.   The year 1929 was not the best time to be a movie mogul. By the end of the year, 8,700 theatres had been wired for sound, at great expense. Many silent stars made the transition to sound; some didn't. But the new stars, the ones who were created by talkies, would never have been so successful in silent films as they were in sound. Dialogue made actors real, and the kind of dialogue that audiences fell in love with was tough, slangy, and above all, colloquial. For the first time, the life depicted on the screen was as feisty as American movie audiences had always been. Sound made the movies democratic.

    —adapted from *Flashback* by Louis Giannetti and Scott Eyman

    a. Underline the thesis statement.

    b. What is the introduction style? Indicate the best answer.

    _____ historical background   _____ anecdote

    _____ definition   _____ contrasting position

2.   Adolescent males are dangerous. They join gangs, and they are responsible for most of the crime in our society. They drive too fast, causing accidents on our highways. They all experiment with drugs, and they annoy others with their loud music. But is such a portrayal of our nation's young men really fair? In fact, most stereotypes about adolescent males are incorrect and misleading.

—Abeer Hamad, student

    a. Underline the thesis statement.

    b. What type of lead-in did the writer use?

       _____ quotation   _____ question   _____ surprising statement

    c. What is the introduction style? Indicate the best answer.

       _____ historical background   _____ anecdote

       _____ definition   _____ contrasting position

3.   Where did you buy that blouse? I heard the question every time I wore it. It was a truly lovely designer model that had been marked down to $40. It was pale blue with swirling tiny flower buds running down each front panel. The little buttons were topped with imitation pearls. Unfortunately, the middle button kept coming undone. People at a certain angle to my left could peek in and view the lace eyelets on my brassiere. When I wore the blouse, my head kept bobbing down, looking to see if I was exposing myself. Over the years, I have had several humorous and embarrassing wardrobe and makeup malfunctions.

—Catalina Ortega, student

    a. Underline the thesis statement.

    b. What type of lead-in was used?

       _____ quotation   _____ question   _____ surprising statement

    c. What is the introduction style? Indicate the best answer.

       _____ general background   _____ contrasting position

       _____ definition   _____ description

4.   The term *cool jazz* refers to modern jazz that tends to be softer and easier than the bebop of Charlie Parker and Dizzy Gillespie. Cool jazz avoids roughness and brassiness. The term *cool jazz* has been applied to the music of saxophonist Lester Young and some of the musicians whom he and Count Basie influenced. Though musicians inspired by Basie and Young were found in almost all regions of America, many of them were based in California during the 1950s. The West Coast became one center of innovation in cool jazz.

—Mark C. Gridley, *Concise Guide to Jazz*

    a. Underline the thesis statement.

    b. What is the introduction style? Indicate the best answer.

       _____ general background   _____ anecdote

       _____ definition   _____ contrasting position

5.   "All the men were frightened," Julius Matthews said. On June 6, 1944, he, along with other young men, landed on the French beach. German bullets were flying all around him. He ran as fast as he could towards the cliffs, but his heavy boots sank into the sand, slowing him down. He saw men around him fall to the ground as bullets penetrated their bodies. On that day, many of the best-laid military plans went awry.

                           —Niles Logan, journalist

    a. Underline the thesis statement.

    b. What type of lead-in was used?

       _____ quotation   _____ question   _____ surprising statement

    c. What is the introduction style? Indicate the best answer.

       _____ general background   _____ anecdote

       _____ definition   _____ questions

6.   Why do some hip-hop artists embed jewels and gold in their teeth? Are the grills meant to impress others, or do the grills fit some deep need on the part of the artists to show that they matter? Is the hip-hop artist who shows off his "bling" any different from the accountant who buys a BMW to show that she has succeeded, or the corporate executive who marries a beautiful trophy wife? Showing off one's wealth is not new. In fact, throughout history, people have found extravagant ways to flaunt their wealth.

                           —Jamal Evans, student

    a. Underline the thesis statement.

    b. What type of lead-in was used?

       _____ quotation   _____ question   _____ surprising statement

    c. What is the introduction style? Indicate the best answer.

       _____ general background   _____ anecdote

       _____ definition   _____ questions

PRACTICE 2

Write interesting lead-ins (opening sentences) for the next topics. Use the type of lead-in that is indicated in parentheses.

EXAMPLE: College tuition (question)

　　　　　How much student debt do you have?
_____

1. Minimum wage (a quotation)

   _____

   _____

2. Drug use in sports (a provocative statement)

   _____

   _____

3. Celebrity culture (a question)

   _____

   _____

PRACTICE 3

Choose *one* of the next thesis statements. Then write three introductions using three different introduction styles. Use the same thesis statement in each introduction.

1. Physical education courses should be compulsory for college students.

2. American films and television shows do not reflect the cultural diversity of the nation.

3. Censorship is sometimes necessary for the welfare of society.

You can choose any three of the following introduction styles:

- general or historical background
- anecdote
- description
- definition
- contrasting position
- series of questions

THE WRITER'S DESK **Write Two Introductions**

In Chapter 3, you prepared an essay plan. Now, on a separate piece of paper, write two different styles of introductions for your essay. Use the same thesis statement in both introductions. Later, you can choose the best introduction for your essay.

LO3 Write complete body paragraphs.

Writing Complete Body Paragraphs

In your essay plan, you developed supporting ideas for your topic. When you prepare the first draft, you must flesh out those ideas. As you write each body paragraph, make sure that it is complete. Do not offer vague generalizations, and do not simply repeat your ideas. Provide evidence for each topic sentence by inserting specific details. You might include examples, facts, statistics, anecdotes, or quotations.

Examples are people, places, things, or events that illustrate your point. To support the view that some local spots are eyesores, the writer could give the following examples.

> The bowling alley on Kennedy Street needs to be renovated.
>
> The children's park in our neighborhood looks shabby.
>
> The Allen Drive mini-mall has tacky signs and cracked store windows.

Facts are objective details that can be verified by others. **Statistics** are facts that are expressed in numbers. (Make sure that your statistics are from reliable sources.) To support the view that transportation costs are too high for students, you could give the following facts and statistics as evidence.

> A one-way bus ticket now costs $3.50 for students.
>
> The monthly subway pass just increased to $260 for students.
>
> In a college survey of four hundred students, 70 percent expressed concern about the recent rate increases in public transportation.

Anecdotes are true experiences that you or someone else went through. An anecdote tells the story of what happened. **Quotations** are somebody's exact words, and they are set off in quotation marks. To support the view that lack of sleep can have dangerous consequences, you could include the following anecdote and quotation as evidence.

> When Allen Turner finished his night shift, he got into his car and headed home. On Forest Drive, he started to nod off. Luckily, a truck driver in another lane noticed that Turner's car was weaving, and the trucker honked. Turner said, "My eyes snapped open, and I saw a wall growing larger in front of me. I slammed on my brakes just before smashing into it."

Essay with Sample Body Paragraphs

Read the next body paragraphs. Notice how they are fleshed out with specific evidence.

Thesis Statement: For personal and financial reasons, a growing number of adult children are choosing to live with their parents.

Body Paragraphs

The cost of education and housing is very high, so it is more economical to live at home. First, rents have increased dramatically since the 1990s. In *The Daily Journal*, Anna Reinhold states that rents tripled in   ◄ fact
the past ten years. During the same period, student wages have not risen as much as the rents. In fact, the minimum wage is only $7.25 an hour. Also, college fees are increasing each year. Tuition and fees at four-year   ◄ fact
public colleges rose $399, or 4.8 percent this year, to an average of $8,655,   ◄ statistic
according to the College Board's annual "Trends in College Pricing" report.

Many young people want to build a nest egg before moving out of the family home. If they remain at home, they can save income from part-time jobs. "I've saved $14,000 by staying in my parents' place," says   ◄ quotation
Kyle Nehme, a twenty-four-year-old student at the University of Texas. Such students do not need to worry about student loans. According to financial analyst Raul Gomez, "Students who stay in the family home reap   ◄ quotation
significant financial benefits."

Students who remain in their parents' home have a much more relaxed and comfortable lifestyle. Often, the parents do the shopping and housework. For example, Liz Allen, a twenty-six-year-old marketing student,   ◄ anecdote
moved back in with her parents last May. She discovered how much more convenient it was when someone else did the vacuuming, laundry, and cooking. Moreover, such students feel more secure and safe in the cocoon of their parents' home. In a *Daily Journal* survey of ninety adults who live at home, 64 percent cited "comfort" as their major reason.   ◄ statistic

---

HINT ◄ Using Research to Support Your Point

Your instructor might ask you to back up your ideas with research. You can investigate several resources, including books, magazines, and the Internet, for relevant quotations, statistics, and factual evidence. For more information about doing research, see Chapter 17, "The Research Essay."

PRACTICE 4

Make the next body paragraphs more complete by adding specific examples. You can include the following:

* examples
* anecdotes from your own life or from the lives of others

 ♦ quotations (for this exercise, you can make up punchy quotations)
 ♦ facts, statistics, or descriptions of events that you have read about or seen

Do not add general statements. Check that the details you add are very specific.

THESIS STATEMENT: Prospective pet owners should become informed before buying an animal.

Body Paragraph 1 First, when families choose a dog, they should consider the inconvenience and possible dangers. Some breeds of dogs can become extremely aggressive. _____

_____

_____

_____

_____ Moreover, dog owners must accept that dogs require a lot of time and attention. _____

_____

_____

_____ Furthermore, it is very expensive to own a dog. _____

_____

_____

Body Paragraph 2 Some new pet owners decide to buy exotic pets. However, such pets come with very specific problems and require particular environments.

_____

_____

_____

Also, some exotic pets seem interesting when they are young, but they can become distinctly annoying or dangerous when they reach maturity. _____

_____

_____

_____

HINT ◄ Making Detailed Essay Plans

You can shorten the time you spend developing the first draft if you make a very detailed essay plan. In addition to your main ideas, your plan can include details for each supporting idea. Notice the detailed evidence in the following excerpt from an essay plan.

Thesis Statement: For personal and financial reasons, a growing number of adult children are choosing to live with their parents.

I. **Topic Sentence:** The cost of education and housing is very high.
   A. Rents have increased dramatically in the past ten years.
     Evidence: *The Daily Journal* states that rents have tripled in the past ten years.   ◄ fact
   B. Student wages have not risen as much as the rents.
     Evidence: The minimum wage is only $7.25 an hour.   ◄ fact
   C. Tuition fees are very high.
     Evidence: Tuition and fees at four-year public colleges rose $399, or 4.8 percent this year, to an average of $8,655, according to the College Board's annual "Trends in College Pricing" report.   ◄ statistic

THE WRITER'S DESK Make Complete Body Paragraphs

In Chapter 3, you prepared an essay plan. Now write complete body paragraphs for your essay. Make certain that each body paragraph contains specific details.

Writing a Conclusion

LO 4 Write a conclusion.

The **concluding paragraph** gives you one last chance to impress the reader and to make your point clear. A good conclusion makes the essay seem complete. One common and effective way to conclude a composition is to summarize the main ideas. The essay then comes full circle, and you remind the reader of your strongest points.

To make your conclusion more interesting and original, you could also close with a prediction, a suggestion, a quotation, or a call to action.

HINT ◄ Linking the Conclusion to the Introduction

One effective way to conclude an essay is to continue an idea that was introduced in the introduction.

• If you began an anecdote in the introduction, you can finish it in the conclusion.

• If you posed some questions in the introduction, you can answer them in the conclusion.

• If you highlighted a problem in the introduction, you might suggest a solution in the conclusion.

Look at the concluding paragraph to an essay about etiquette in our technological age.

Do not hide behind technology as your excuse for displaying rude or annoying behavior. Avoid posting insulting comments on social networking sites. If someone is writing an e-mail, do not read over his or her shoulder. Also, never text or fumble with your phone while driving.

The last sentence in the essay could be one of the following.

Prediction	If you follow the basic rules of etiquette, you will ensure that your friends and colleagues maintain their respect for you.
Suggestion	The next time you go out with friends, turn off your smartphone.
Quotation	As the French author Colette once said, "It is wise to apply the oils of refined politeness to the mechanism of friendship."
Call to Action	To help the next generation learn good manners, offer to teach a class to local high school students about etiquette in the technological age.

PRACTICE 5

Read the following conclusions and answer the questions.

A. Though creative cities will grow more attractive for empty-nest retirees and young graduates alike, we won't all be moving to New York. Many Americans will still prefer the space of the suburbs—including the parking spaces. "People want to balance the privacy of the suburbs with more public and social areas," says Dunham-Jones. But the result will be a U.S. that is more sustainable—environmentally and economically.

—Bryan Walsh, "Reclycling the Suburbs"

1. What method does the author use to end the conclusion? _____

B. Mr. Mishra arrived alone in New York in July, and was later joined by two of his sisters. He had been bracing for "serious cultural shock," he said, but his fears evaporated when he walked into the building. "The moment I'm about to enter my apartment, there were dozens of Bhutanese around me," he recalled. "Some looked like my mother, and some looked like my father. They said, 'You will be O.K.'"

—Kirk Semple, "Bhutanese Refugees Find a Toehold in the Bronx"

2. What method does the author use to end the conclusion? _____

C.   In this new millennium, let's put the concept of IQ to rest, once and for all. Stop giving IQ tests. Stop all the studies on IQ and birth order, IQ and nutrition, or IQ and Mozart. Let's find newer, more fluid, and more fair ways to debate and enable human potential. Let's use our heads for a change.

—Dorothy Nixon, "Let's Stop Being Stupid About IQ"

3. What method does the author use to end the conclusion? _____

HINT ◂ **Avoiding Conclusion Problems**

In your conclusion, do not contradict your main point, and do not introduce new or irrelevant information. Also, avoid ending your essay with a rhetorical question, which is a question that cannot be answered, such as "When will humans stop having wars?"

THE WRITER'S DESK **Write a Conclusion**

Write a conclusion for the essay you've been preparing in the previous Writer's Desk exercises.

Choosing an Essay Title

LO 5 Choose an essay title.

Think of a title *after* you have written your essay because you will have a more complete impression of your essay's main point. The most effective titles are brief, depict the topic and purpose of the essay, and attract the reader's attention.

GRAMMAR HINT ◂ **Capitalizing Titles**

Place your title at the top center of your page. Capitalize the first and last words of your title. Also capitalize the main words except for prepositions (*in, at, for, to,* etc.) and articles (*a, an, the*). Leave about an inch of space between the title and the introductory paragraph.

Descriptive Titles

Descriptive titles are the most common titles in academic essays. They depict the topic of the essay clearly and concisely. Sometimes, the writer takes key words from the thesis statement and uses them in the title. Here are two examples of descriptive titles.

Etiquette in the Technological Age

Avoiding Mistakes in the First Year of College

Titles Related to the Writing Pattern

You can also relate your title directly to the writing pattern of your essay. Here are examples of titles for different writing patterns.

Illustration:	Problems with Internet Dating
Narration:	My Worst Nightmare
Description:	The Anniversary Party
Process:	How to Handle a Workplace Bully
Definition:	The Meaning of Tolerance
Classification:	Three Types of Fathers
Comparison and Contrast:	Fads Versus Timeless Fashions
Cause and Effect:	The Reasons People Pollute
Argument:	Why Writing Matters

HINT ◂ Avoiding Title Pitfalls

When you write your title, watch out for problems.

- Do not view your title as a substitute for a thesis statement.
- Do not write a really long title because it can confuse readers.
- Do not put quotation marks around the title of your essay.

PRACTICE 6

Read the next introductions, and underline the thesis statements. Then write titles for each essay.

1.   Some people fear mistakes more than others fear snakes. Perfectionism refers to self-defeating thoughts and behaviors aimed at reaching excessively high, unrealistic goals. Unfortunately, nobody is perfect. In fact, there are many problems associated with the desire to be perfect.

   Title: _____

2.   Gang life, once associated with large urban centers in the United States, has become a common part of adolescent experience in towns and rural areas. Many of the gang members have no strong role models at home, and their gang affiliation makes them feel like part of a powerful group. To combat the problems associated with youth gangs, adults need to give adolescents more responsibilities.

   Title: _____

3.   "A person who is not initiated is still a child," says Malidoma Somé. Somé is from the Dagara tribe in West Africa, and he underwent a six-week initiation ceremony. Left alone in the bush with no food or clothing, he developed a profound appreciation of nature and of magic. When he returned to his

village, everyone welcomed him and other initiates with food and dancing. Somé had passed from childhood into adulthood and was expected to assume adult responsibilities. The ceremony helped Somé and the other initiates feel that they were valued participants in village life. Our culture should have formal initiation ceremonies for adolescents.

Title: _____

PRACTICE 7

Read the next body paragraphs of a short essay. First, underline the topic sentence in each body paragraph. Then, on a separate sheet of paper, develop a title, a compelling introduction with a thesis statement, and a conclusion.

ADD A TITLE

ADD AN INTRODUCTION

Body Paragraph 1

Celebrity psychologists offer superficial suggestions on quick-fix counseling shows. For example, Dr. Phil asks guests so-called probing questions and then offers simplistic solutions. Other shows such as *Intervention* or *Hoarders* give audiences a view into the private lives of vulnerable people. Addicts undergo rehabilitation treatments that are not always successful, and viewers do not see the complexity of an addiction. They believe that the celebrity psychologist has found a solution for the guests' complicated troubles.

Body Paragraph 2

Furthermore, celebrity doctors deliberately create controversy, confusion, and drama about medical treatments. For instance, Dr. Oz advertises upcoming segments of his show by using headlines such as "What Your Doctor Won't Tell You!" The theme of the show revolves around doctors debating alternative medicine that has not been scientifically tested or proven to be effective. Audiences may conclude that unproven alternative medicines are the key to improving their health. Other medical shows are theatrical. On *The Doctors*, the panelists resort to many visual images as well as jokes when discussing a medical topic. The important information gets lost in all the theatrics.

Body Paragraph 3

Most importantly, audiences must be very wary about accepting health information from celebrities. Generally, celebrities who offer opinions or advice on health are not health-care professionals. Tom Cruise has publicly stated that depression does not exist and that psychiatry is a pseudoscience. Suzanne Somers encourages people to use bioidentical hormone replacement therapy, an extremely controversial and unproven treatment. And Jenny McCarthy, who openly linked vaccines to autism in children, spread one of the worst cases of incorrect medical information. There is no medical evidence that vaccines cause autism in children.

ADD A CONCLUSION

LO 6 Write the first draft.

Writing the First Draft

After arranging the supporting ideas in a logical order, and after creating an introduction and conclusion, you are ready to write your first draft. The first draft includes your introduction, several body paragraphs, and your concluding paragraph.

THE WRITER'S DESK **Write the First Draft**

In the previous Writer's Desk exercises, you wrote an introduction, a conclusion, and an essay plan. Now write the first draft of your essay.

MyWritingLab™

Complete these writing assignments at mywritinglab.com

MyWritingLab™   **THE WRITER'S ROOM**   **Topics to Develop**

Writing Activity 1

Choose an essay plan that you developed for Chapter 3, and write the first draft of your essay.

Writing Activity 2

Write the first draft of an essay about one of the following thesis statements.

General Topics

1. The traditional role of males in this generation has (has not) changed significantly from previous generations.

2. Movies and television shows glorify crime and criminals.

3. Lying is appropriate in certain situations.

4. I would like to improve three of my traits.

College and Work-Related Topics

5. The following factors contribute to the academic success of college students.

6. Getting fired can be a liberating experience.

7. Learning from experience is more (less) effective than learning from books.

8. I would (would not) be a good salesperson for the following reasons.

Checklist: First Draft

When you develop the first draft, ask yourself these questions.

☐ Do I have a compelling introduction?

☐ Does my introduction lead into a clear thesis statement?

☐ Do my body paragraphs contain interesting and sufficient details?

☐ Do the body paragraphs support the idea presented in the thesis statement?

☐ Do I have an interesting title that sums up the essay topic?

☐ Does my conclusion bring my essay to a satisfactory close?

Revising and Editing

Revising and editing are similar to adding the finishing touches to a garden. A gardener adds new plants or transplants flowers and shrubs to enhance a garden. Similarly, a writer revises details and edits errors to improve an essay.

LO 1 Follow key steps in revising and editing.

Key Steps in Revising and Editing

The revising and editing stage is the final step in the writing process. When you **revise**, you modify your writing to make it stronger and more convincing. To revise, read your first draft critically and look for faulty logic, poor organization, and poor sentence style. Then reorganize and rewrite the draft, making any necessary changes. When you **edit**, you proofread your final draft for errors in grammar, spelling, punctuation, and mechanics.

There are five key steps to follow during the revising and editing stage.

▶ REVISING AND EDITING

STEP 1 **Revise for unity.** Make sure that all parts of your work relate to the main idea.

STEP 2 **Revise for adequate support.** Determine that your details effectively support the main idea.

STEP 3 **Revise for coherence.** Verify that your ideas flow smoothly and logically.

STEP 4 **Revise for style.** Make sure that your sentences are varied and interesting.

STEP 5 **Edit for technical errors.** Proofread your work, and correct errors in grammar, spelling, mechanics, and punctuation.

Revising for Unity

LO 2 Revise for unity.

Unity means that the ideas in an essay clearly support the focus of the essay. All information heads in the same direction, and there are no forks in the road. If an essay lacks unity, then some ideas drift away from the main idea a writer has expressed in the essay. To check for unity in an essay, consider the following:

*   Make sure that all topic sentences in the body paragraphs support the thesis statement of the essay.
*   Make sure that all sentences within a body paragraph support the topic sentence of that paragraph.

Every idea in an essay must move in the same direction just as this road goes straight ahead. There should be no forks in the road.

Essay Without Unity

The next essay plan looks at the reasons for deforestation. The third topic sentence veers away from the writer's central focus that deforestation has implications for the quality of life.

Do not take a detour from your main idea.

Thesis Statement: Deforestation in the Amazon has tremendous implications for people's quality of life.

Topic Sentence 1: First, logging, mining, and agriculture displace the indigenous population in the Amazon.

Topic Sentence 2: Also, scientists believe that deforestation in the Amazon will lead to a rapid increase in global climate change, which will affect people worldwide.

Topic Sentence 3: Many development experts are trying to find methods to have sustainable development in the Amazon.

◄ This topic sentence strays from the thesis of this essay.

PRACTICE 1

The following thesis statements have three supporting points that can be developed into body paragraphs. Circle the point that does not support the thesis statement.

1. North Americans have created a throw-away culture.
   a. First, waste from disposable containers and packaging has increased during the last one hundred years.
   b. Old appliances can be recycled.
   c. Consumers throw away about 40 percent of edible food.

2. Thesis Statement: International adoptions should be banned.
   a. Too many celebrities have adopted internationally.
   b. An internationally adopted child will often lose contact with his or her culture.
   c. By adopting from poor countries, wealthy Westerners contribute to the exploitation of mothers who cannot afford to keep their babies.

Paragraph Without Unity

Not only must your essay have unity, but each body paragraph must have unity. The details in the paragraph must support the paragraph's topic sentence. In the next paragraph, which is part of a larger work, the writer drifted away from his main idea. Some sentences do not relate to the topic sentence. If the highlighted sentences are removed, then the paragraph has unity.

The writer detours here. ➤

In her book *The Beauty Myth: How Images of Beauty Are Used against Women*, Naomi Wolf argues that women suffer psychologically because society indoctrinates them to value themselves based on their appearance. For example, the multibillion-dollar cosmetic and fashion industry markets its products by using very tall and thin supermodels. Most women cannot attain the physical standards of such an ideal and feel that they are failures if they cannot be thin and beautiful. Some companies depict regular and plus-sized women in their advertisements. For instance, Dove has used models of various sizes to sell some products. Even small children are affected. Many little girls idolize thin pop stars, and then become obsessed about their weight and physical appearance. Girls as young as nine years of age have been diagnosed with anorexia.

PRACTICE 2

Paragraphs A and B contain problems with unity. In each paragraph, underline the topic sentence and cross out any sentences that do not support the controlling idea.

Paragraph A

When Gita arrived in the United States, she suffered from culture shock. On the first day of classes, Gita noticed that some American students were eating or drinking as they walked in crowded places. Such behavior would be unthinkable in India. It is considered rude to eat in front of someone and not share food. Gita also noticed that American students were on familiar terms with their college instructors. Some students even called the instructors by their first names. Indian students would never call a professor by his or her first name. I was an exchange student in Seoul, South Korea. Korean students bow to their professors and elders. I also got into the habit of bowing each time I met my professors. Gita eventually adjusted to student life in the United States and today laughingly recounts her reactions to some of the cultural differences.

Paragraph B

The academic performance of students weakens if they are sleep deprived. Therefore, our college should implement a few rules to help students get enough sleep. First, the college should actively promote physical exercise for students. People who exercise regularly find it easier to fall asleep at night. Some people don't like to exercise, and they have physical problems that prevent them from exercising. Classes could also start one hour later to give students an extra hour to sleep. Or students could have an hour free in the afternoon. Some students would take advantage of this free period to take a nap. Finally, the college could offer seminars and sleep clinics to educate students about the consequences of too little sleep. If the college implements these small changes, students' grades may improve.

Like a bridge, main ideas should have adequate support.

Revising for Adequate Support

LO 3 Revise for adequate support.

A bridge is built using several well-placed stones. Like a bridge, an essay requires **adequate support** to help it stand on its own. When revising an essay for adequate support, consider the following:

◆ Make sure that your thesis statement is broad enough to be supported by several points. You may need to revise the thesis statement to meet the length requirements of the essay.

◆ When you write the body paragraphs of the essay, insert specific details and try to include vivid descriptions, anecdotes, examples, facts, or quotations.

Do not lead your reader in circles. Make a point and develop it.

Avoid Circular Reasoning

Circular reasoning means that a paragraph restates its main point in various ways but does not provide supporting details. Like a driver aimlessly going around and around a traffic circle, the main idea never seems to progress. Avoid using circular reasoning by directing your paragraph with a clear, concise topic sentence and by supporting the topic sentence with facts, examples, statistics, or anecdotes.

Paragraph with Circular Reasoning

The following paragraph contains circular reasoning. The main point is repeated over and over. The writer does not provide any evidence to support the topic sentence.

This writer leads the reader in circles. ➤

> Traveling is a necessary educational tool. Students can learn a lot by visiting other countries. Many schools offer educational trips to other places for their students. Students may benefit from such cultural introductions. Clearly, traveling offers students an important educational opportunity.

In the second version of this paragraph, the paragraph contains specific examples that help to illustrate the main point.

Revised Paragraph

Anecdotes and examples provide supporting evidence. ➤

> Traveling is a necessary educational tool. Students can learn a lot by visiting other places. Many schools and colleges offer educational trips. On such trips, students visit museums, art galleries, and historical sites. For example, the art department of our college sponsored a trip to Washington, D.C., and the students visited the Smithsonian. Other travel programs are work programs. Students may travel to another region or country to be involved in a community project. Students in the local high school, for instance, helped build a community center for children in a small town in Nicaragua. The students who participated in this project all said that they learned some very practical lessons, including organizational and construction skills. Clearly, traveling offers students an important educational opportunity.

PRACTICE 3

Read the following paragraphs, and write *OK* next to the ones that have adequate support. Underline the specific details in those paragraphs. Then, to the paragraphs that lack adequate support, add details such as descriptions, examples, quotations, or anecdotes. Use arrows to indicate where you should place specific details.

The next example is from an essay. In the first paragraph, the writer was repetitive and vague. After the writer added specific examples and vivid details, the paragraph was much more interesting.

Weak Support

To become a better dresser, follow the next steps. First, ask friends or family members what colors suit you. Also, don't be a slave to the latest fashion. Finally, spend money on a few good items rather than filling your closet with cheap outfits. My closet is half-full, but the clothing I have is of good quality.

Better Support with Details

To become a better dresser, follow the next steps. First, ask friends or family members what colors suit you. I love green, for instance, but when I wore an olive green shirt, a close friend said it brought out the green in my skin and made me look ill. Also, don't be a slave to the latest fashion. Although tank tops and low-rise jeans were popular for several years, I didn't have the right body type for that fashion because my belly spilled over the tops of my jeans. Instead, I wore longer shirts with my jeans, so I looked stylish but not ridiculous. Finally, spend money on a few good items rather than filling your closet with cheap outfits. My closet is half-full, but the clothing I have is of good quality.

1. **Many cyclists are inconsiderate.** Cyclists think that they don't have to obey traffic rules and that traffic signs are just for car drivers. Also, some cyclists are pretty crazy and do dangerous things and risk their lives or the lives of others. People have ended up in the hospital after a run-in with these two-wheeled rebels. Cyclists should take safety courses before they ride on public roads.

Write OK or add details

2. **During my first job interview, I managed to overcome my fright**. I sat in a small, brightly lit room in front of four interviewers. A stern woman stared at me intently and curtly asked me why I wanted the job. Perspiration dripped into my eyes as I stammered that I had seen an advertisement. She smirked and asked me to be more specific. Feeling that I didn't have a chance anyway, I relaxed and stopped worrying about the faces gazing at me. I spoke about my first experience in a hospital, and I described the nurses who took care of me and the respectful way the orderlies treated me. I expressed my heartfelt desire to work as an orderly, and I got the job.

Write OK or add details

LO 4 Revise for coherence.

Revising for Coherence

Make your writing as smooth as possible by using expressions that logically guide the reader from one idea to the next. When revising an essay for **coherence**, consider the following:

* Ensure that sentences within each body paragraph flow smoothly by using transitional expressions.
* Ensure the supporting ideas of an essay are connected to each other and to the thesis statement by using paragraph links.

Transitional Expressions

Just as stepping stones can help you cross from one side of the water to the other, **transitional expressions** can help readers cross from idea to idea in an essay.

Here are some common transitional expressions.

Function	Transitional Word or Expression		
Addition	again also besides finally first (second, third)	for one thing furthermore in addition in fact	last moreover next then
Comparison and contrast	as well equally even so however	in contrast instead likewise nevertheless	on the contrary on the other hand similarly
Concession of a point	certainly even so	indeed of course	no doubt to be sure
Effect or result	accordingly as a result consequently	hence otherwise then	therefore thus
Emphasis	above all clearly especially in fact	in particular indeed least of all most important	most of all of course particularly principally
Example	for example for instance in other words	in particular namely	specifically to illustrate
Reason or purpose	because for this purpose	for this reason the most important reason	
Space	above behind below beneath beside beyond closer in	farther out inside near nearby on one side/the other side on the bottom	on the left/right on top outside to the north/east/ south/west under
Summary or conclusion	generally in conclusion in other words in short	on the whole therefore thus	to conclude to summarize ultimately
Time	after that at that time at the moment currently earlier eventually first (second, etc.) gradually	immediately in the beginning in the future in the past later meanwhile months after now	one day presently so far subsequently suddenly then these days

Just as stepping stones link one shore to another, transitional expressions can link ideas in a paragraph and essay.

> ## HINT ◄ Use Transitional Expressions with Complete Sentences
>
> When you add a transitional expression to a sentence, make sure that your sentence is complete. Your sentence must have a subject and a verb, and it must express a complete thought.
>
> **Incomplete**   For example, violence on television.
>
> **Complete**   For example, violence on television <u>is very graphic</u>.

Adding Transitional Words Within a Paragraph

The next paragraph shows transitional words that link sentences within a paragraph.

> Have you ever started a workout program and after a few weeks stopped doing it? There are several steps that you can take to stay motivated. **First**, try activities that you like to do. For example, if you hate exercising on machines, you could try swimming. **Next**, schedule your exercise activities in advance. Choose a time and plan other activities around your workout times. **In addition**, participate in a variety of exercises. If you keep doing the same activity all the time, you will get bored and lose your motivation. **Finally**, promise yourself a little treat after you have completed your workout. A little self-indulgence is a good motivator, so reward yourself.

GRAMMAR LINK
For more practice using transitions in sentences, see Chapter 21, "Sentence Combining."

PRACTICE 4

Add appropriate transitional expressions to the following paragraph. Choose from the following list, and use each transitional word once. There may be more than one correct answer.

in addition	therefore	in fact	for instance
first	then	for example	moreover

Counterculture is a pattern of beliefs and actions that oppose the cultural norms of a society. _____ hippies are the best-known countercultural group in the recent past, and they are known for rebelling against authority. _____ they rejected the consumer-based capitalist society of their parents in favor of communal living arrangements. _____ the hippie generation valued peace and created a massive antiwar movement. _____ there were mass protests against the Vietnam War. _____ small religious groups belong to the countercultural current. These groups live with other like-minded people and turn away from widely accepted ideas on lifestyle. _____ the Amish reject modern technology. _____ militant groups and anarchist groups reject conventional laws. Some of these groups want to eliminate legal, political, and social institutions. There will always be countercultural movements in society.

PRACTICE 5

The next paragraph lacks transitional expressions. Add appropriate transitional expressions wherever you think they are necessary.

The United States has witnessed profound changes in sexual attitudes and practices. In the 1920s, millions of men and women migrated from farms to cities. Living apart from their families and meeting new people in the workplace, young people enjoyed considerable sexual freedom, one reason that decade became known as the "Roaring Twenties." In the 1940s and 1950s, a researcher, Alfred Kinsey, published the first study of sexuality in the United States, which raised eyebrows everywhere because it was published during a time when Americans were uneasy talking openly about sex. Kinsey's study encouraged a new openness toward sexuality. In the late 1960s, the revolution truly came of age. Youth culture dominated public life, and expressions like "sex, drugs, and rock-and-roll" summed up a new, freer attitude toward sex.

—John J. Macionis, *Sociology*, 14th edition

Making Links in Essays

To achieve coherence in an essay, try the following methods to move from one idea to the next.

1. **Repeat words or phrases from the thesis statement in the topic sentence of each body paragraph.** In this example, *giftedness* and *ambiguity* are repeated words.

Thesis Statement	Although many schools offer a program for <u>gifted</u> children, there continues to be <u>ambiguity</u> concerning the definition of <u>gifted</u>.
Body Paragraph 1	One <u>ambiguity</u> is choosing the criteria for assessing the <u>gifted</u>.
Body Paragraph 2	Another <u>ambiguity</u> pertains to defining the fields or areas in which a person is <u>gifted</u>.

2. **Refer to the main idea in the previous paragraph, and link it to your current topic sentence.** In the topic sentence for the second body paragraph, the writer reminds the reader of the first point (*insomnia*) and then introduces the next point.

Thesis Statement	Sleeping disorders cause severe disruption to many people's lives.
Body Paragraph 1	<u>Insomnia</u>, a common <u>sleep disorder</u>, severely limits the <u>sufferer's quality of life</u>.
Body Paragraph 2	The <u>opposite condition of insomnia</u>, narcolepsy also causes mayhem as the sufferer struggles to stay awake.

3. **Use a transitional word or phrase to lead the reader to your next idea.**

Body Paragraph 3	<u>Moreover</u>, when sufferers go untreated for their sleep disorders, they pose risks to the people around them.

LO 5 Revise for style.

Just as paint makes a fence more beautiful, revising for sentence style can make a piece of writing more appealing.

Revising for Style

When you revise for sentence **style**, you ensure that your essay has concise and appropriate language and sentence variety. You can ask yourself the following questions.

*   Have I used a variety of sentence patterns? (To practice using sentence variety, see Chapter 22.)

*   Are my sentences parallel in structure? (To practice revising for parallel structure, see Chapter 25.)

*   Have I used exact language? (To learn about slang, wordiness, and overused expressions, see Chapter 33.)

Alicia's Revision

In Chapter 3, you read Alicia's essay plan about college dropouts. After writing her first draft, she revised her essay. Look at her revisions for unity, support, coherence, and style.

Dropping Out of College   ◄ Add title.

   I live in a small coastal town on the Atlantic. The town attracts
tourists from all over the country. Because of its beautiful beach. My
college roommate, Farrad, works as a cook at the local pizza stand.
Last year, Farrad started working a few hours per week, but because
of his efficiency, his boss increased Farrad's hours. My roommate then
joined a growing group of people. He became a college dropout.

Students may drop out of college because they lack financial support,   ◄ Thesis
                                                                                   statement
experience an emotional crisis, or are unprepared for college life.

   First, some
   ~~Some~~ students drop out because they face overwhelming   ◄ Add transition.
financial burdens. Like Farrad, they may have a part-time job to

According to an Indiana government Web site, Investment Watch,
"Teenagers and young adults often find themselves in high debt with   ◄ Add detail.
little knowledge of basic savings and budgeting concepts. About
40 percent of Americans spend 110 percent of their income."

help pay for tuition and rent. If the job requires students to work for
many hours, they might not have time to study or to do homework.
The number of hours is overwhelming, and she may drop out of college.   ◄ Add detail.
Nadia, for exemple, works in the computer lab four nights a week.
Some students   ◄ Clarify pronoun.
~~They~~ also drop out because they live far from campus. Transportation
may be too expensive or inconvenient.

                                                        , and they
   Furthermore, some students undergo life-changing events. ~~They~~   ◄ Combine
                                                                               sentences.
In an interview with CNN, Dr. William Pepicello, president of the
University of Phoenix, stated that one reason that students drop   ◄ Add detail.
out is "life gets in the way."

must leave college. A college student may get married, or a female
student may become pregnant and taking care of a baby may
consume all of her time and energy. ~~There are public and private~~   ◄ Revise for unity.
                                       In addition, an   ◄ Add transition.
~~daycare centers. But parents must choose very carefully.~~ An illness in
the family may cause a student to miss too many classes. A student may
feel emotionaly fragile because of a broken relationship. The student
may not be able to cope with their feelings and wanted to leave college.

Find better word. ➤

adapt to

Moreover, some students may be unable to ~~get into~~ college life.

Some have poor study skills and fall behind in homework assignments.

Students may not be able to organize there time. Or a student might be

unused to freedom in college and skip too many classes. For instance,

In addition, not

Add transition. ➤ my lab partner has missed about six classes this semester. ~~Not~~ every

Add detail. ➤

According to the National Academic Advising Association (NACADA) Web site, 75 percent of first-year students do not have clear career goals.

student has career plans. Those who are unsure about their academic

futur may drop out rather than continue to study in a field they do not

For instance, my cousin realized she did not want to be an

Add detail. ➤ *engineer, so she left school until she could figure out what she really wanted to do.*

enjoy.

Even though students drop out of college for many good reasons,

For example,

Add transition. ➤ some decide to return to college life. Farrad hopes to finish his studies

Improve
conclusion. ➤

next year. *He knows he would have to find a better balance between work and school to succeed, but he is motivated to complete his education.*

HINT ◀ **Enhancing Your Essay**

When you revise, look at the strength of your supporting details. Ask yourself the following questions.

- Are my supporting details interesting, and will they grab my reader's attention? Should I use more vivid vocabulary?

- Is my concluding sentence appealing? Could I end the paragraph in a more interesting way?

LO 6 Edit for errors.

GRAMMAR LINK
To practice your editing skills, try the practices in Chapter 39.

Editing for Errors

When you **edit**, you reread your writing to make sure that it is free of errors. You focus on the language, and you look for mistakes in grammar, punctuation, mechanics, and spelling.

There is an editing guide on the inside back cover of this book. It contains some common error codes that your instructor may use. It also provides you with a list of errors to check for when you proofread your text.

Editing Tips

The following tips will help you to proofread your work more effectively.

* Put your text aside for a day or two before you do the editing. Sometimes, when you have been working closely with a text, you might not see the errors.

* Begin your proofreading at any stage of the writing process. For example, if you are not sure of the spelling of a word while writing the first draft, either you could highlight the word to remind yourself to verify it later, or you could immediately look up the word in the dictionary.

* Use the grammar and spelling checker that comes with your word processor. However, be vigilant when accepting the suggestions. Do not always choose the first suggestion for a correction. For example, a grammar checker cannot distinguish between when to use *which* and *that*. Make sure that suggestions are valid before you accept them.

* Keep a list of your common errors in a separate grammar log. When you finish a writing assignment, consult your error list and make sure that you have not repeated any of those errors. After you have received each corrected assignment from your instructor, you can add new errors to your list. For more information about a grammar and spelling log, see Appendix 6.

Alicia's Edited Essay

Alicia edited her essay about college dropouts. She corrected errors in spelling, punctuation, and grammar.

Dropping Out of College

I live in a small coastal town on the Atlantic. The town attracts

tourists from all over the country. ~~Because~~ *because* of its beautiful beach.

My college roommate, Farrad, works as a cook at the local pizza

stand. Last year, Farrad started working a few hours per week,

but because of his efficiency, his boss increased Farrad's hours.

My roommate then joined a growing group of people. He became a

college dropout. Students may drop out of college because they lack

financial support, experience an emotional crisis, or are unprepared

for college life.

First, some students drop out because they face overwhelming financial burdens. Like Farrad, they may have a part-time job to help pay for tuition and rent. According to an Indiana government Web site, *Investment Watch*, "Teenagers and young adults often find themselves in high debt with little knowledge of basic savings and budgeting concepts. About 40 percent of Americans spend 110 percent of their income." If the job requires students to work for many hours, they might not have time to study or to do homework. Nadia, for exemple *example*, works in the computer lab four nights a week. The number of hours is overwhelming, and she may drop out of college. Some students also drop out because they live far from campus. Transportation may be too expensive or inconvenient.

Furthermore, some students undergo life-changing events, and they must leave college. In an interview with CNN, Dr. William Pepicello, president of the University of Phoenix, stated that one reason that students drop out is "life gets in the way." A college student may get married, or a female student may become pregnant and taking care of a baby may consume all of her time and energy. In addition, an illness in the family may cause a student to miss too many classes. A student may also feel *emotionally* emotionaly fragile because of a broken relationship. The student may not be able to cope with their *his or her* feelings and *want* wanted to leave college.

Moreover, some students may be unable to adapt to college life. Some have poor study skills and fall behind in homework assignments. Also, students may not be able to organize there *their* time. Or a student might not be used to freedom in college and skip too many classes. For instance, my lab partner has missed about six classes this semester. In addition, not every student has career plans. According to the National Academic Advising Association

(NACADA) Web site, 75 percent of first-year students do not have

clear career goals. Those who are unsure about their academic

future

~~futur~~ may drop out rather than continue to study in a field they do

not enjoy. For instance, my cousin realized she did not want to be an

engineer, so she left school until she could figure out what she really

wanted to do.

    Even though students drop out of college for many good reasons,

some decide to return to college life. Farrad, for example, hopes to

will

finish his studies next year. He knows he ~~would~~ have to find a better

balance between work and school to succeed, but he is motivated to

complete his education.

THE WRITER'S DESK   **Revise and Edit Your Paragraph**

Choose an essay that you have written for Chapter 4, or choose one that you have written for another assignment. Carefully revise and edit the essay. You can refer to the Revising and Editing checklists on the inside back cover.

Peer Feedback

After you write an essay, it is useful to get peer feedback. Ask a friend, family member, or fellow student to read your work and give you comments and suggestions on its strengths and weaknesses.

HINT   **Offer Constructive Criticism**

When you peer-edit someone else's writing, try to make your comments useful. Phrase your comments in a positive way. Look at the examples.

Instead of saying . . .	You could say . . .
You repeat the same words.	Maybe you could find synonyms for some words.
Your paragraphs are too short.	You could add more details here.

You can use this peer feedback form to evaluate written work.

Peer Feedback Form

Written by _____ Feedback by _____

Date: _____

1. What is the main point of the written work? _____
   _____
   _____

2. Which details effectively support the thesis statement? _____
   _____
   _____

3. What, if anything, is unclear or unnecessary? _____
   _____
   _____
   _____

4. Give some suggestions about how the work could be improved. _____
   _____
   _____
   _____

5. What is the most interesting feature of this written work? _____
   _____
   _____
   _____

LO7 Write the final draft.

Writing the Final Draft

When you have finished making revisions on the first draft of your essay, write the final draft. Include all the changes that you have made during the revising and editing phases. Before you submit your final draft, proofread it one last time to make sure that you have caught any errors.

THE WRITER'S DESK Write Your Final Draft

You have developed, revised, and edited your essay. Now write the final draft.

HINT ◀ Spelling, Grammar, and Vocabulary Logs

- **Keep a Spelling and Grammar Log.** You probably repeat, over and over, the same types of grammar and spelling errors. You will find it very useful to record your repeated grammar mistakes in a Spelling and Grammar Log. You can refer to your list of spelling and grammar mistakes when you revise and edit your writing.

- **Keep a Vocabulary Log.** Expanding your vocabulary will be of enormous benefit to you as a writer. In a Vocabulary Log, you can make a list of unfamiliar words and their definitions.

See Appendix 6 for more information about spelling, grammar, and vocabulary logs.

MyWritingLab™   **THE WRITER'S ROOM**   **Essay Topics**

MyWritingLab™

Complete these writing assignments at mywritinglab.com

Writing Activity 1

Choose an essay that you have written for this course or for another course. Revise and edit that essay, and then write a final draft.

Writing Activity 2

Choose any of the following topics, or choose your own topic, and then write an essay. Remember to follow the writing process.

General Topics

1. taxing junk food
2. a problem in politics
3. unfair gender roles
4. privacy issues and social media sites

College and Work-Related Topics

5. something you learned in college
6. adjustments new college students have to make
7. unpleasant jobs
8. a longer school year

Checklist: Revising and Editing

When you revise and edit your essay, ask yourself the following questions.

☐ Does my essay have **unity**? Ensure that every paragraph relates to the main idea.

☐ Does my essay have **adequate support**? Verify that there are enough details and examples to support your main point.

☐ Is my essay **coherent**? Try to use transitional expressions to link ideas.

☐ Does my essay have good **style**? Check for varied sentence patterns and exact language.

☐ Does my essay have any errors? **Edit** for errors in grammar, punctuation, spelling, and mechanics.

☐ Is my **final draft** error-free?

Part II

Essay Patterns

What Is an Essay Pattern? A pattern or mode is a method used to express one of the three purposes: to inform, to persuade, or to entertain. Once you know your purpose, you will be able to choose which writing pattern to use.

Patterns may overlap, and you can combine writing patterns. You may use one predominant pattern, but you can also introduce other patterns in supporting material.

CHAPTER 6
▶ ILLUSTRATION

Illustrate or prove a point using specific examples.

CHAPTER 7
▶ NARRATION

Narrate or tell a story about a sequence of events that happened.

CHAPTER 8
▶ DESCRIPTION

Describe using vivid details and images that appeal to the reader's senses.

CHAPTER 9
▶ PROCESS

Inform the reader about how to do something, how something works, or how something happens.

CHAPTER 10
▶ DEFINITION

Explain what a term or concept means by providing relevant examples.

CHAPTER 11
▶ CLASSIFICATION

Classify or sort a topic to help readers understand different qualities about that topic.

CHAPTER 12

▶ COMPARISON AND CONTRAST

Present information about similarities (compare) or differences (contrast).

CHAPTER 13

▶ CAUSE AND EFFECT

Explain why an event happened (the cause) or what the consequences of the event were (the effects).

CHAPTER 14

▶ ARGUMENT*

Argue or take a position on an issue and offer reasons for your position.

*Argument is included as one of the nine patterns, but it is also a purpose in writing.

Just as fabric has a variety of textures and designs, writing also has different patterns and styles that depend on the writer's purpose.

Illustration

Health clubs advertise a variety of activities that customers can do to get in shape. In the same way, writers have a better chance of persuading readers when they illustrate their ideas using examples.

LEARNING OBJECTIVES

LO 1 Define illustration. (p. 78)

LO 2 Define the purpose of an illustration essay. (p. 79)

LO 3 Explore topics for an illustration essay. (p. 81)

LO 4 Write the thesis statement of an illustration essay. (p. 82)

LO 5 Generate the supporting details of an illustration essay. (p. 83)

LO 6 Develop an illustration essay plan. (p. 84)

LO 7 Write the first draft of an illustration essay. (p. 85)

LO 8 Revise and edit an illustration essay. (p. 86)

WRITERS' EXCHANGE

Work with a partner. You have three minutes to list as many words as you can that are examples of the following. For example, bungee jumping is a dangerous sport.

effective exercises   dangerous sports   comfort food

▶ **EXPLORING**

L01 Define
illustration.

What Is Illustration?

Illustration writing includes specific examples that help readers acquire a clearer, deeper understanding of an essay's subject. You illustrate or give examples each time you explain, analyze, narrate, or express an opinion. Examples might include something that you have experienced or observed, or they may include factual information, such as a statistic.

People use illustration every day. At home, a parent might list ways that a child's room is becoming messy. At college, classmates may share examples of how they have been given too much homework. At work, an employee could list examples of ways for the company to save money.

Visualizing Illustration

PRACTICE 1

Brainstorm supporting ideas for the following thesis statement. List examples on the lines provided.

THESIS STATEMENT: The average person's diet contains too much junk food.

Crisp and Salty

Oily

for example

for instance

The Illustration Essay

LO 2 Define the purpose of an illustration essay.

There are two effective ways to exemplify your main point and support your body paragraphs in an illustration essay.

1. Use a **series of examples**. When writing an essay about innovative commercials, you might list things that some directors do, such as using bizarre camera angles, introducing hilarious scenarios, adding amusing jingles, or creating catchy slogans.

2. Use an **extended example**, such as an anecdote or a description of an event. When writing about problems faced by first-year college students, you might tell a story about a specific student's chronic lateness.

ILLUSTRATION **AT WORK**

MyWritingLab™

Access the interactive "At Work" paragraphs in MyWritingLab

Employment recruiter Rene Delery has written a guide to help job seekers create satisfactory résumés.

Most job hunters know that a résumé should be grammatically correct, with relevant and truthful details. Yet even good résumés can sink because of silly mistakes. For example, an annoying problem is the use of a tiny font. The person reading the résumé should not have to squint. The best font size is 11 or 12. Also, job seekers sometimes try to be artsy and try to stand out, but their irregular headings and inconsistent spacing can clutter up an otherwise well-done résumé. Another mistake job hunters make, hoping the employer won't notice, is to leave out dates. Doing so gives the impression that the candidate has something to hide. Finally, it's important for a résumé to look professional, yet people often neglect to use a simple and clear e-mail address. Some silly e-mail handles that have crossed my desk are "wakeysmile" and "razorkitty." Such addresses make the job hunter appear childish. Anyone who is looking for employment should keep these tips in mind.

The **topic sentence** states the topic and controlling idea.

The **supporting sentences** provide details and examples.

The **concluding sentence** brings the paragraph to a satisfactory close.

A Student Essay

Read the student essay, and answer the questions that follow.

Priceless Euphoria

Lisa Monique

1   The Beatles recorded a song, satirically titled *Money*, in which they sing, "The best things in life are free." Undoubtedly, the best things in life *are* free. Although costs might be associated, these "things" are not purchased items. The best things are a common thread among all people regardless of gender,

race, religion, or nationality. In fact, the best things in life are not things but are precious segments in time involving and engaging us in experiences, emotions, and various states of being.

2   Nature provides us with many priceless treasures of breathtaking scenery. We might view a cascading waterfall, a brilliant sunset casting a serene, pink glow on the mountain jags and peaks, or the glistening beauty of a fresh, undisturbed snowfall. Each location we visit stimulates the senses. A day at the beach allows us to listen to crashing waves, watch a school of dolphins play, splash in the shallow water, or bury our feet in the gushy, wet sand. The desert is also a smorgasbord of sensations. Marvels include the mighty Saguaro cacti, the ethereal haze of the Palo Verde trees, and the grace and gentleness of a passing butterfly.

3   Emotional experiences, as well, are often the best "things" in life. Falling in love, viewing the birth of a child, having the first kiss, laughing and conversing with an old friend, and watching the klutzy steps of a puppy are some simple delights in life. Emotional experiences can occur with loved ones, but they can also be kindled in natural environments. A day at the beach is renewing and refreshing. Hiking in the desert helps us to feel wild, free, and reckless. The purity of a fresh snowfall makes us feel childlike and innocent.

4   Similarly, states of being bring great satisfaction, which is, yet again, a great thing. Good health after a prolonged illness or even after a short bout of the flu is a greatly appreciated state of being. Invaluable gratification is derived from meeting a deadline, winning a race, nurturing a garden, sculpting a creation, giving a gift, receiving a gift, dispensing good advice, accepting good advice, planning a successful event, helping someone in need, and achieving a well-earned goal.

5   Money does directly buy cars, jewelry, furs, vacations, large homes, designer clothing, or French perfume. Purchases are not the best "things" in life. It is true that crayons and paper are purchased, but coloring is free. Writing, dancing, laughing, loving, and learning are all beneficial activities with peripheral costs. The value is found in each experience. Consequently, "the best things in life are free" is not just a simple song lyric, but also a rather complex and admirable human philosophy.

PRACTICE 2

1. Who is the intended audience? _____

2. Highlight the essay's thesis statement.

3. Highlight the topic sentence in each body paragraph.

4. In body paragraphs 2, 3, and 4, what does the writer use?

   a. series of examples   b. extended examples

5. In paragraph 4, what does the writer mean by *states of being*? Using your own words, explain her point.

   _____

   _____

6. What organizational strategy does the writer use?

   a. time order   b. space order   (c.) emphatic order

7. Add one more example to each body paragraph.

   nature ____*rainbow*_____

   _____

   emotional experiences _____

   _____

   states of being ____*cooking, getting exercised.*_____

   _____

LO 3 Explore topics for an illustration essay.

Explore Topics

In the Writer's Desk Warm Up, you will try an exploring strategy to generate ideas about different topics.

THE WRITER'S DESK Warm Up

Read the following questions, and write the first ideas that come to your mind. Think of two to three ideas for each topic.

EXAMPLE: What can go wrong when you rent an apartment?

   —hard to find a landlord who will rent to a student

   —can't find a good apartment in a decent area on a student

   budget

   —roommate problems

1. What are some online addictions?

   _____

   _____

2. Think of some silly or unfounded fears that children have.

_____

_____

3. What are some status symbols in today's society?

_____

_____

▶ DEVELOPING

LO 4 Write the thesis statement of an illustration essay.

The Thesis Statement

The thesis statement of the illustration essay is a general statement that expresses both your topic and your controlling idea. To determine your controlling idea, think about what point you want to make. Remember to express an attitude or point of view about the topic.

topic   controlling idea

Newlyweds often have misconceptions about married life.

controlling idea   topic

I am unable to control **the mess in my work space**.

THE WRITER'S DESK   Write Thesis Statements

Write a thesis statement for each of the following topics. You can look for ideas in the Warm Up on the previous page. Each thesis statement should express your topic and controlling idea.

EXAMPLE: Topic: apartment rental problems

Thesis Statement: Students who want to rent an apartment may end up frustrated and disappointed.

1. Topic: online addictions

Thesis Statement: _____

_____

2. Topic: children's silly or unfounded fears

   Thesis Statement: _____

   _____

3. Topic: status symbols in our society

   Thesis Statement: _____

   _____

The Supporting Ideas

L05 Generate the supporting details of an illustration essay.

After you have developed an effective thesis statement, generate supporting ideas.

- Use prewriting strategies to generate a list of examples. Brainstorm a series of examples and extended examples that will best illustrate your main point.
- Choose the best ideas.
- Organize your ideas. Choose the best organizational method for this essay pattern.

THE WRITER'S DESK **Generate Supporting Ideas**

Choose one of your thesis statements from the previous Writer's Desk. List three or four examples that support the thesis statement.

EXAMPLE:

Thesis Statement: Students who want to rent an apartment may end up frustrated and disappointed.

Supports: —can't find an affordable place

—landlords might be hesitant to rent to them

—roommates may be immature

—not enough housing for students

—available housing is in dangerous neighborhoods

Thesis Statement: _____

_____

Supports: _____

_____

_____

_____

_____

LO 6 Develop an illustration essay plan.

The Essay Plan

When writing an outline for an illustration essay, make sure that your examples are valid and relate to the thesis statement. Also, include details that will help clarify your supporting examples and organize your ideas in a logical order.

Thesis Statement: Students who want to rent an apartment may end up frustrated and disappointed.

   I.   Landlords are often hesitant to rent to students.
         A.   Young people might be irresponsible.
         B.   They don't have credit ratings.

   II.   Students have money problems.
         A.   They have limited choices.
         B.   They cannot apply for nicer apartments because many are too expensive.
         C.   They must settle for dives and dumps.

   III. Sharing a place with another student can end badly.
         A.   The roommate might be very messy.
         B.   The roommate might be a party guy or girl.
         C.   There could be financial disputes over unpaid rent and bills.

   IV.   Some students choose to rent alone but have other problems.
         A.   They may feel lonely.
         B.   People living alone may feel unsafe.

THE WRITER'S DESK Write an Essay Plan

Refer to the information you generated in previous Writer's Desks, and prepare a detailed essay plan. Consider the order in which you list details.

The First Draft

LO 7 Write the first draft of an illustration essay.

After outlining your ideas in a plan, write the first draft using complete sentences. Also, include transitional words or expressions to help your ideas flow smoothly. Here are some transitional expressions that can help you introduce an example or show an additional example.

To introduce an example		To show an additional example	
for example	namely	also	in addition
for instance	specifically	first (second)	in another case
in other words	to illustrate	furthermore	moreover

THE WRITER'S DESK Write the First Draft

In the previous Writer's Desk, you developed an essay plan. Now write the first draft of your illustration essay. Remember to include details such as specific names, places, facts, or statistics to flesh out each body paragraph.

VOCABULARY BOOST

Here are some ways to vary sentences, which will help you avoid boring readers with repeated phrases.

1. Underline the opening word of every sentence in your first draft. Check to see if some words are repeated.

2. If you notice every sentence begins the same way, try introducing the sentence with an adverb, such as *usually*, *generally*, or *luckily*, or a prepositional phrase such as *With his help* or *Under the circumstances*. In the following example, *They* is repeated too many times.

Repeated first words

People make many mistakes with their finances. <u>They</u> want luxuries that they cannot afford. <u>They</u> buy items on credit. <u>They</u> do not consider the high interest rates that credit card companies charge.

Variety

People make many mistakes with their finances. Desiring luxuries that they cannot afford, consumers buy items on credit. Sadly, many do not consider the high interest rates that credit card companies charge.

▶ **REVISING AND EDITING**

LO 8 Revise and edit an illustration essay.

Revise and Edit an Illustration Essay

When you finish writing an illustration essay, review your work and revise it to make the examples as clear as possible to your readers. Make sure that the order of ideas is logical, and remove any irrelevant details. Before you work on your own essay, practice revising and editing a student essay.

A Student Essay

Read the essay, and then answer the questions that follow. As you read, correct any errors that you find and make comments in the margins.

FINDING AN APARTMENT

Shannon Nolan

1.   Renting an apartment for the first time is one of the defining rites of passage that marks the transition from adolescence to young adulthood. Many young people have a dream of what their first apartment will be like, whether it is the boho chic flat in a trendy neighborhood, the immaculate penthouse in the heart of downtown, or the ultimate party pad with a gang of best friends for roommates. Unfortunately, it is often harder to find that perfect apartment than it is to daydream about it. Students who want to rent an apartment may end up frustrated and disappointed.

2.   Finding an apartment—any apartment—can be hard enough. Landlords are often hesitant to rent to students for the very reasons students want an apartment. Young renters do not have credit ratings with banks, and they haven't proved that they're capable of handling responsability. They throw parties, make noise, and never stay in one place very long. Landlords usually require a reference from a former landlord and a security deposit, if not the co-signature of a parent or relative. However, landlords are far from the sainted beings their high standards might indicate. The ones who don't ask for references are usually equally lax about fixing blocked drains or leaking ceilings, and the ones who do demand references aren't necessarily any better.

3.   Money is another common issue for student renters. A student budget in most cases is fairly limited. Rent, bills, and tuition must be paid, on a part-time salary at best. Often after one weekend of apartment hunting, the dream of the perfect apartment goes up in smoke. The place advertised as a "spacious studio" turns out to be a sort of basement mausoleum with grime-covered slats for windows, more appropriate as the setting for a horror movie than a romantic year of independence. "One bedroom" means "walk-in closet." A trend emerges—if the price is right, everything else is wrong.

4. To reduce expenses, many people opt to share a place, but the joys of shared housekeeping can turn rapidly into a disaster. Students quickly wonder why did they want a roommate in the first place. A certain amount of messiness can be expected from first-time renters, but some people take this to an extreme. No one wants to end up rooming with the guy who starts a biology lab in the kitchen—studying the growth patterns of breakfast cereal mold (especially when he is a sociology major). Similarly, students who are serious about their studies do not want to live with a party guy or girl who is out all night, every night, and who seems to come home only for about five minutes at a time to puke in the sink.

5. Some students, unhappy with their experiences sharing a closet-sized bedroom in a dorm decide to rent a bachelor or studio apartment, prefering to pay a little more in exchange for peace of mind. Sandra, a second-year student, took this route and found that a whole new problem confronted her. "I couldn't believe how lonely I was the first few months," she said. "Even though I hated my roommate, I actually missed her. I spent so much time studying in coffee shops that I might as well have stayed in res." Besides loneliness, safety is another problem for those living alone. Many students, especially women, are worried about the risks of walking home alone.

6. The first year or so of independence can be a vulnerable time, and not just emotionally. Finding apartments is tough, and renting can be expensive. Sharing can be a solution—unless roommates become a nightmare. Then there is the dangers of being lonely and depressed or of having something bad happen with no one there to offer support. It might seem like the pitfalls of apartment renting outweigh the benefits. But the first step into true independence has its rewards as well, and after all, it's a step everyone must take.

PRACTICE 3

Revising

1. Highlight the thesis statement.

2. Highlight the topic sentence in paragraphs 2 and 4.

3. In paragraph 2, the writer veers off course. Cross out the sentences that do not support the topic sentence.

4. Paragraph 3 is missing a topic sentence. Which sentence best sums up the main point of paragraph 3?

   a. Many apartments are small and ugly.

   b. Landlords do not rent to students easily.

   c. Because students have limited budgets, they must settle for small, run-down apartments.

   d. Apartments are often not as nice as they are described in the advertisements.

5. Paragraph 5 is also missing a topic sentence. Which sentence best sums up the main point of paragraph 5?

   a. Furthermore, students who can afford to live alone might have problems.

   b. There are safety issues when renting an apartment.

   c. Sandra had her own studio apartment.

   d. Sometimes students who live alone feel lonely.

6. Which paragraph contains an extended example? ____

Editing

GRAMMAR LINK

See the following chapters for more information about these grammar topics:

Embedded Questions, Chapter 22

Commas, Chapter 35

Spelling, Chapter 34

Subject–Verb Agreement, Chapter 27

7. Paragraph 4 contains an embedded question error. (For information about embedded questions, see the Grammar Hint following this practice.) Underline and correct the error.

   Correction: _____

   _____

8. Paragraph 5 contains a comma error. Underline and correct the error.

   Correction: _____

9. This essay contains misspelled words in paragraphs 2 and 5. Underline and correct them.

   Corrections: _____   _____

10. Underline and correct a subject–verb agreement error in paragraph 6.

   Correction: _____

GRAMMAR HINT ◀ **Writing Embedded Questions**

When a question is part of a larger sentence, do not use the question word order. View the next examples.

   Error   I wondered how would I pay the rent.

   Correction   I wondered how <u>I would</u> pay the rent.

THE WRITER'S DESK   **Revise and Edit Your Essay**

Revise and edit the essay that you wrote for the previous Writer's Desk. You can refer to the revising and editing checklists at the end of this chapter and at the back of the book.

A Professional Essay

Al Kratina is a freelance writer and filmmaker who writes about films, music, and television. The next essay examines the way food is portrayed on television.

We're Watching What We Eat

Al Kratina

1   Television has a lot to teach us, not about actual facts, of course—learning science from *CSI* or *The Dr. Oz Show* seems about as effective as getting medical advice from a **carny**. But as a reflection of society, television can be a powerful tool, revealing our changing attitudes about gender, politics, race—and especially food. It may seem trivial, but almost every TV character eats or drinks on screen, even if it is just Dr. House washing down painkillers with pure vitriol. The way in which food is portrayed on television can tell us a lot about the shifting cultural attitudes.

carny: a person who works for a carnival

2   The tension between healthy moderation and debauched indulgence is amplified to unhealthy extremes in contemporary television, with shows either championing near-starvation or reveling in **abject gluttony**. Some reality TV takes the former approach, molding unrealistic body types by treating hunger like a disease. With their focus on dramatic weight loss, shows like *The Biggest Loser* and *Bulging Brides* are fairly overt in their treatment of food as an almost sick, shameful necessity. Rarely does a TV character eat healthily without setting up a plot point or a punchline. In *The Big Bang Theory*, whatever nutrition the characters absorb at lunch is cancelled out by the endless pizza and Chinese takeout fueling their evening arguments over *Green Lantern* villains.

abject gluttony: excessive eating

3   Someone basing his or her opinion of Western culture on prime-time programing might conclude that our insatiable hunger is matched only by our self-loathing. *The Simpsons* established many of its frequent fat gags in the 1990s, with Homer's severely disordered eating leading to everything from heart attacks to a spiritual journey. *Friends*, one of the biggest successes of the 1990s and early 2000s, was largely set in the fictional New York coffee house Central Perk, where characters rarely had anything more substantial than a latte in their hands. Their diet involved eating only once a year, preferably during a heartwarming Thanksgiving special, and otherwise smothering hunger pangs with a caffeine-induced ulcer.

4   Thankfully, a few shows take the opportunity to comment on our indulgence. The sitcom *Mike & Molly*, which follows an overweight couple who met in a weight-loss support group, deals with the often discriminatory and negative attitudes about obesity in North America. Although the mobster

drama *The Sopranos* reveled in an endless consumption of ziti, cannoli, and capicola ham, many of the characters suffered ill effects, like capo Gigi Cestone, who died of a possibly sausage-induced heart attack. *The Sopranos* also drew a connection between food and psychology. A particularly insightful arc explored Tony's subconscious association of raw meat with violence and sexuality in one of his more traumatic therapy sessions.

5   Clearly, television can provide great insight about our eating habits. Certainly, any given block of food-related programing reveals how our eating habits are defined by often chaotic, contradictory impulses. Some shows suggest our future palates will be challenged by a variety of unique flavors, such as worm-based food in *Babylon 5* or the addictive drink made from a larval creature in *Futurama*. Those items may not be popular now, but just wait until they show up on *Diners, Drive-Ins and Dives*.

PRACTICE 4

1. Highlight the thesis statement.

2. Underline the topic sentences in paragraphs 2, 3, and 4.

3. In paragraphs 2, 3, and 4, what type of examples does the writer use?

   a. a series of examples   b. an extended example

4. In paragraph 2, how are *The Biggest Loser* and *The Big Bang Theory* similar and different in their portrayals of food?

   _____

   _____

   _____

5. How does the show *Mike & Molly* differ from other shows in the way in which it treats the subject of food?

   _____

   _____

   _____

6. List at least ten examples of television shows that the author uses as examples in the essay.

   _____   _____

   _____   _____

   _____   _____

   _____   _____

   _____   _____

THE WRITER'S ROOM

MyWritingLab™

MyWritingLab™
**Complete these
writing assignments at
mywritinglab.com**

Writing Activity 1: Topics

Write an illustration essay about one of the following topics, or choose
your own topic.

General Topics

1. crazy fashions
2. endangered species
3. mistakes that newlyweds make
4. great or horrible films
5. diets

College and Work-Related Topics

6. things people should know
   about my college
7. examples of successful
   financial planning
8. qualities of an ineffective
   manager
9. mistakes students make
10. examples of obsolete jobs

**READING LINK
MORE
ILLUSTRATION
READINGS**

"Marketing New
Inventions"
by Robert
Rodriguez
(page 548)
"Can We Talk?"
by Josh Freed
(page 554)

Writing Activity 2: Media Writing

Watch a popular television
show or movie that focuses on
helping others. Examples are
movies such as *Dallas Buyers
Club, 12 Years a Slave*, and *The
Book Thief*. The television shows
The Doctors, The Biggest Loser,
and *Super Nanny* also focus
on helping others. Also look
on YouTube for videos about
people helping other people.
Write an essay and provide
examples showing how the main
characters help others.

**WRITING LINK
MORE
ILLUSTRATION
WRITING TOPICS**

Chapter 20,
Writer's
Room topic 1
(page 312)
Chapter 24,
Writer's
Room topic 1
(page 352)
Chapter 30,
Writer's
Room topic 1
(page 417)
Chapter 36,
Writer's
Room topic 1
(page 484)
Chapter 37,
Writer's
Room topic 1
(page 497)

Checklist: Illustration Essay

After you write your illustration essay, review the essay checklist at the back of the book. Also ask yourself the following questions.

☐ Does my thesis statement include a controlling idea that I can support with examples?

☐ Do I use a series of examples or an extended example in each body paragraph?

☐ Does each body paragraph support the thesis statement?

☐ Does each body paragraph focus on one idea?

☐ Do I have sufficient examples to support my thesis statement?

☐ Do I logically and smoothly connect paragraphs and supporting examples?

Narration 7

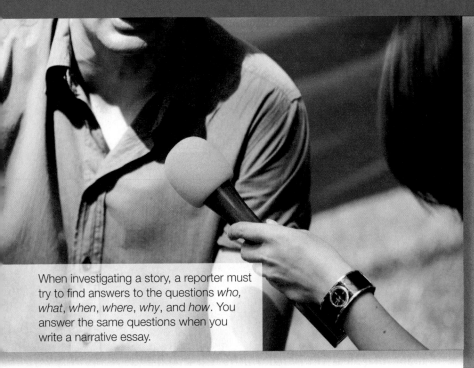

When investigating a story, a reporter must try to find answers to the questions *who, what*, *when*, *where*, *why*, and *how*. You answer the same questions when you write a narrative essay.

WRITERS' EXCHANGE

Try some nonstop talking. First, sit with a partner and come up with a television show or movie that you have both seen. Then, starting at the beginning, describe what happened in that episode or film. Remember that you must speak without stopping. If one of you stops talking, the other must jump in and continue describing the story.

▶ **EXPLORING**

L01 Define
narration.

What Is Narration?

Narrating is telling a story about what happened. You generally explain events in the order in which they occurred, and you include information about when they happened and who was involved in the incidents.

People use narration in everyday situations. For instance, at home, someone might explain how a cooking accident happened. At college, students tell stories to explain absences or lateness. At work, a salesperson might narrate what happened on a business trip.

HINT ◂ Value of Narration

Narration is useful on its own, but it also enhances other types of writing. For example, student writer Bruno Garcia had to write an argument essay about traffic laws. His essay was more compelling than it might otherwise have been because he included a story about his grandmother's eyesight and her driving accident.

Visualizing Narration

PRACTICE 1

Brainstorm supporting ideas for the following thesis statement.

THESIS STATEMENT: My first date with Calvin was a disaster.

_____   _____   _____

_____   _____   _____

_____   _____   _____

The Narrative Essay

LO2 Define the purpose of a narrative essay.

When you write a narrative essay, consider your point of view.

Use **first-person narration** to describe a personal experience. To show that you are directly involved in the story, use *I* (first-person singular) or *we* (first-person plural).

> When **we** landed in Boston, **I** was shocked by the white landscape. **I** had never seen so much snow.

Use **third-person narration** to describe what happened to somebody else. Show that you are simply an observer or storyteller by using *he, she, it* (third-person singular), or *they* (third-person plural).

> Drivers waited on the highway. **They** honked their horns and yelled in frustration. **They** did not understand what was happening.

NARRATION AT WORK

When lawyer Murray Marshall meets with clients, he records the facts and confirms those facts in writing. Here is an excerpt from one of his e-mails.

I will summarize the facts of your accident as you have related them to me. You stated that on March 10 at approximately 5 pm, you were driving your vehicle westbound on Main Street. The weather was sunny, and the road conditions were dry. In the 3000 block, after a dog darted in front of your vehicle, you strenuously applied your brakes, bringing your car to a sudden halt. Seconds later, the vehicle behind you made contact with the rear of your vehicle. You sustained a whiplash-type injury to your neck and a sprain to your right wrist. You visited a local hospital within one hour following the accident, where you were given a brace for your neck and a compression bandage for your wrist. As a result of the pain you suffered in the days following the accident, you missed five days of work, for which you received no compensation from your employer. You have requested that our office research the likelihood of your recovering damages for your pain and suffering and loss of income, and to advise what the amount of those damages might be. If I have omitted or misunderstood any salient detail, please contact our office at your convenience.

important

inertia

The **topic sentence** states the topic and controlling idea.

The **supporting sentences** provide details and examples.

The **concluding sentence** brings the paragraph to a satisfactory close.

MyWritingLab™

Access the interactive "At Work" paragraphs in MyWritingLab

A Student Essay

Read the student essay and answer the questions that follow.

Rehabilitation

Jack McKelvey

1   I am the sum of all my experiences. I take away lessons from my failures and disappointments. These memories shape my view of my existence.

Many individual experiences, from my first day of school to my first love, have changed me. However, one experience overshadows the rest: prison. Although being in prison was not pleasant, the experience has made me a much better person today.

2   Before I was convicted and shipped off to jail, I was not a good person. I sold drugs, I lied, and I stole. If I thought I could get away with something, I would try. I had no respect for anyone, including myself. I harbored no ambitions or desires. I just wanted to sell drugs, spend money, and smoke pot. In April of 2003, that would all change.

3   On April 11, I was on the return leg of my usual trip to Grand Rapids for two pounds of marijuana. Flashing lights blinded me through the rearview mirror. I pulled over, and the lights followed. I had been making this trip every week or so for almost two years without incident. That day, I didn't even hide my illegal cargo. I knew the officer was going to smell the marijuana I was smoking. I knew he would find the large black trash bag on my back seat. I thought about running, but that never seems to end up well for the people who try it on television. Resigned to my fate, I enjoyed one last cigarette before I was shoved into the back of a royal blue state police cruiser.

4   "I sentence you to twenty-four to sixty months in the Michigan Department of Corrections." I had never heard a more sinister cluster of words. My stomach turned, and a single cold drop of sweat trickled from my armpit. My ears must not have been working correctly. The judge had just used the word *prison*. The worst images from prison documentaries flashed through my mind like lightning. I am five foot nothing and a buck thirty soaking wet, so how was I going to survive incarceration?

5   The first day of prison was not as I had imagined. I was expecting to see someone running with a knife sticking out of his ribs or to hear someone screaming as he was being raped. Bad things did occur but not on that first day. What did happen was nothing—just silence—and that, I believe, was even worse. Alone, I relived every mistake I had made that led to prison. As the months progressed, I thought most often of freedom and what I wanted to do the day I was released. I also thought of odd things I came to miss: adjusting the water temperature in the shower, opening a refrigerator door, and sleeping in a dark room. I also thought of how I had spent my life so far, and how little I had accomplished. I began to feel as if my life were over, and the best years of my life were sliding by. Although most inmates considered me a short timer, I felt as if my sentence was timeless eternity.

6   Two years into my incarceration, I realized that my release was on the horizon, and I became motivated to change. I began tearing through books with a vengeance. I took every college course available at the institution, and I even enrolled in a vocational skills program. I was going to have a second chance, and soon. Although I was doing all I could intellectually to

prepare myself for my release, I was most anxious to begin repairing the relationships I had labored to destroy. I often thought of what I would say to everyone I had disappointed and hurt. I soon realized that words would not prove that I had changed from the person I was before prison. I was going to have to show them, and that is exactly what I planned to do. For the first time since my early teen years, I was optimistic about my future.

7   After three years, two months, six days, eleven hours, and twenty-two minutes, I left prison. Euphoria fails to describe the feeling, and fails miserably. After readjusting to freedom, I found work at a landscaping company, one of the few places that will hire a felon with no degree, and I stayed out of trouble. Over the next year, I would spend a great deal of time with my family. I am proud to say that our relationship now is the best it has ever been. I have come to realize that life is about those we care about. Being imprisoned was what it took for me to realize what I was truly missing in life. The time we have is fleeting, even when it appears to be standing still. I don't plan to waste another second.

PRACTICE 2

1. Highlight the thesis statement.

2. Underline the topic sentences in paragraphs 2, 5, and 6.

3. Using your own words, sum up what happened in paragraphs 3 and 4.

    Paragraph 3: _____

    _____

    Paragraph 4: _____

    _____

4. In paragraphs 3, 4, and 5, the narrative is simple: a man is arrested and jailed. Yet the power of the narrative is in the details: readers can see, hear, feel, and smell what happened. What are some of the most striking descriptions?

    Paragraph 3: _____

    _____

    Paragraph 4: _____

    _____

    Paragraph 5: _____

    _____

5. Why did Jack McKelvey write about his experience? What are some messages in this essay?

_____

_____

_____

_____

LO3 Explore topics for a narrative essay.

Explore Topics

In the Writer's Desk Warm Up, you will try an exploring strategy to generate ideas about different topics.

THE WRITER'S DESK **Warm Up**

Read the following questions, and write the first ideas that come to your mind. Think of two to three ideas for each topic.

EXAMPLE: What interesting journeys have you been on?

I walked across the city one night. I went to the Grand Canyon.

I rode my bike to the Arizona border.

1. What are some emotional ceremonies or celebrations that you have witnessed or been a part of?

_____

_____

_____

2. What significant experiences have changed you or taught you life lessons?

_____

_____

_____

3. What adventures have you had with a good friend? What happened?

_____

_____

_____

▶ **DEVELOPING**

The Thesis Statement

When you write a narrative essay, choose a topic that you personally find very interesting, and then share it with your readers. For example, very few people may be interested if you simply list what you did during your recent vacation. However, if you write about a particularly moving experience during your vacation, you can create an entertaining narrative essay.

Ensure that your narrative essay expresses a main point. Your thesis statement should have a controlling idea.

LO 4 Write the thesis statement of a narrative essay.

topic   controlling idea

The day I decided to get a new job, <u>my life took a dramatic turn</u>.

controlling idea   topic

<u>Sadie's problems began</u> **as soon as she drove her new car home**.

HINT ◂ How to Make a Point

In a narrative essay, the thesis statement should make a point. To help you find the controlling idea, you can ask yourself the following questions:

- What did I learn?
- How did I change?
- How did it make me feel?
- What is important about it?

For example:

Topic	*ran away from home*
Possible controlling idea	*learned the importance of family*

topic   controlling idea

When I ran away from home at the age of fifteen, <u>I discovered the importance of my family</u>.

PRACTICE 3

Practice writing thesis statements. Complete the following sentences by adding a controlling idea.

1. During her wedding, my sister realized _____

   _____

2. During my years with the National Guard, I learned _____

_____

3. When I graduated, I discovered _____

_____

THE WRITER'S DESK **Write Thesis Statements**

Write a thesis statement for each of the following topics. You can look for ideas in the Warm Up on page 98. Each thesis statement should mention the topic and express a controlling idea.

EXAMPLE: Topic: An interesting journey

Thesis statement: _I went on an exciting hike in the Grand Canyon._

1. Topic: An emotional ceremony

   Thesis statement: _____

   _____

2. Topic: A significant experience

   Thesis statement: _____

   _____

3. Topic: An adventure with a friend

   Thesis statement: _____

   _____

LO 5 Generate the supporting ideas of a narrative essay.

The Supporting Ideas

A narrative essay should contain specific details so that the reader understands what happened. To come up with the details, ask yourself a series of questions and then answer them as you plan your essay.

- ◆ **Who** is the essay about?
- ◆ **What** happened?
- ◆ **When** did it happen?

- ◆ **Where** did it happen?
- ◆ **Why** did it happen?
- ◆ **How** did it happen?

When you recount a story to a friend, you may go back and add details, saying, "Oh, I forgot to mention something." However, when you write, you have the opportunity to clearly plan the sequence of events so that your reader can easily follow your story. Organize events in chronological order (the order in which they occurred). You can also begin your essay with the outcome and then explain what happened that led to the outcome.

> ## HINT ◀ Narrative Essay Tips
>
> Here are some tips to remember as you develop your narrative essay.
>
> - Do not simply recount what happened. Reflect on why the event is important.
> - Consider the main source of tension in your narrative. Descriptions of conflict or tension can help engage the reader.
> - To make your essay more powerful, use descriptive language that appeals to the senses. For more information on using descriptive imagery, see pages 113–114 in Chapter 8.

THE WRITER'S DESK Develop Supporting Ideas

Choose one of your thesis statements from the previous Writer's Desk. Then generate supporting ideas. List what happened.

EXAMPLE: An interesting journey   Topic: _____

—hitchhiked to the canyon   _____

—descended five miles   _____

—met a crazy man at the ranch   _____

—saw a sheep on a narrow ledge   _____

—was worn out during the final climb   _____

The Essay Plan

LO 6 Develop a narrative essay plan.

Before you write a narrative essay, make a detailed essay plan. Write down main events in the order in which they occurred. To make your narration more complete, include details about each event.

Thesis Statement: My hike in the Grand Canyon was an exhausting adventure.

    I.   On the first day, my condition rapidly deteriorated as I walked down the trail.

         A.   The soles of my boots ripped.

         B.   I got blisters.

         C.   My backpack hurt my shoulders.

II.   Eventually, I reached Phantom Ranch at the bottom of the canyon.

   A.   A slow talker poked a piece of wood.

   B.   He described tragedies in the canyon.

   C.   His stories shocked and depressed me.

III.   On the way back up, I came face to face with trouble.

   A.   I encountered a bighorn sheep.

   B.   We were both on a narrow ledge, with room for just one of us to pass.

   C.   The sheep suddenly went straight up.

   D.   I was able to pass.

IV.   Near the end of my hike, I had no drive left.

   A.   The rock face kept getting steeper and the air significantly thinner.

   B.   Whenever I felt that I was at the top, another area opened up above me.

   C.   I didn't want to take another step.

Concluding idea: My journey showed me that there is nothing that can stop me.

THE WRITER'S DESK **Write an Essay Plan**

Refer to the information you generated in previous Writer's Desks, and prepare a detailed essay plan. Include details for each supporting idea.

LO 7 Write the first draft of a narrative essay.

The First Draft

After you outline your ideas in a plan, you are ready to write the first draft. Remember to write complete sentences and to use transitions to help readers understand the order in which events occur or occurred. Here are some transitions that are useful in narrative essays.

To show a sequence of events

after that	finally	in the end	meanwhile
afterward	first	last	next
eventually	in the beginning	later	then

Enhancing Your Essay

One effective way to enhance your narrative essay is to use dialogue. A **direct quotation** contains someone's exact words, and the quotation is set off with quotation marks. When you include the exact words of more than one person in a text, you must make a new paragraph each time the speaker changes.

> "Who did this?" my mom shrieked, as my brother and I stood frozen with fear.
>
> "Mark did it," I assured her shamelessly, as I pointed at my quivering brother.

An **indirect quotation** does not give the author's exact words, but it keeps the author's meaning. It is not set off by quotation marks.

> As Mark and I stood frozen with fear, our shrieking mother asked who had done it. I assured her shamelessly that Mark had done it, as my finger pointed at my quivering brother.

GRAMMAR HINT ◂ Using Quotations

When you insert a direct quotation into your writing, capitalize the first word of the quotation, and put the final punctuation inside the closing quotation marks.

- Place a comma after an introductory phrase.

  Zsolt Alapi said, "Everyone was terrified."

- Place a colon after an introductory sentence.

  Zsolt Alapi described the atmosphere: "Everyone was terrified."

See Chapter 37 for more information about using quotations.

THE WRITER'S DESK Write the First Draft

In the previous Writer's Desk, you developed an essay plan. Carefully review your essay plan, make any necessary changes to the details or chronology, and then write the first draft of your narrative essay.

▶ REVISING AND EDITING

Revise and Edit a Narrative Essay

LO 8 Revise and edit a narrative essay.

When you finish writing a narrative essay, carefully review your work and revise it to make the events as clear as possible to your readers. Check that you have organized events chronologically, and remove any irrelevant details. Before you revise and edit your own essay, practice revising and editing a student essay.

A Student Essay

Read the essay, and then answer the questions that follow. As you read, correct any errors that you find, and make comments in the margins.

MY JOURNEY DOWN THE GRAND CANYON

Andrew Wells

1. Twenty years old, on a break from studies, I decided to set out backpacking to see where it would take me. After staying in a youth hostel in Flagstaff, Arizona, I spontaneously decided to see the Grand Canyon. From the upper ridge to the Colorado River at the base, and back up again. I told no one of my plans, and I did not register with authorities. What I didn't realize was that this sort of hiking is not a simple test of aerobic fitness or personal desire. No, it's a type of brutal self-destruction. My hike in the Grand Canyon left me dazed and depleted.

2. After walking and hitchhiking from Flagstaff, I descended five miles into the canyon. The next morning, I set out towards the river, and my physical condition rapidly deteriorated. First, the soles of my boots gave out, partially tearing from the seams and flapping against the pads of my feet with every step I took. My feet were raw and peeling. My blisters ached continuously. The straps from my backpack tore into my shoulder blades, and pain ran down my spine. But the dull pounding of my boots against the rocky terrain drowned out my thoughts. My focus remained on the path in front of me. I knew that if I lost concentration, at any point I can trip and fall over the edge. At least the awe-inspiring surroundings made it easier to forget the pain.

3. Eventually, I reached Phantom Ranch at the bottom of the canyon. The isolated ranch serves as a rest-stop, it is so popular that people reserve years ahead of time. I spoke with the man working the canteen desk. He was a calm, slow talker in his early thirties, tall and thin, with ear-length tangled hair and a dull, emotionless expression. While poking at a block of wood with a steel pick, he droned on and on about all the people who had died in the canyon. "Once, some parents let their three-year-old girl walk alone, and she just walked right off the edge" he said. "Another time a couple tried to hike in from the far west, ran out of water, and expired." He kept tapping the wood with his pick. He continued, "Then there was the guy who was knocked off the edge by one of the sheep." In my head I screamed for him to stop!

4. On my climb back up, I encountered a bighorn sheep on a narrow ledge. I also saw a California condor gliding in the open air. The sheep wanted to go where I was, and I wanted to go where it was, but there was no room to pass. For minutes on end the sheep and I engaged in a stare-down. Then all of a sudden it got bored with me and climbed up an 85-degree sheer rock face! I was stunned. It was so smart, and as soon as I passed, it climbed back down, turned and looked at me, and walked on.

5. After several hours of nonstop hiking, I had absolutely no drive left. The rock face kept getting steeper and the air significantly thinner. Each layer of the canyon above me was hidden behind the nearest sheet of towering sandstone.

Whenever I felt that I was at the top, a hole new area opened up above me. At certain points, I felt like saying, "That's it. I'm living the rest of my life on this ledge. I'm not moving." Then I started making deals with myself, planning what I was going to do with my life once I got out, just to motivate myself to keep going.

6.   When I reached the top, I looked down into the bowels of the canyon and felt relieved that I had done it. Hiking the Grand Canyon is something that does not need to be done more than once. I can retain the knowledge of what I have accomplished. I have come out believing that there's nothing that can stop me, and there's no greater feeling.

PRACTICE 4

Revising

1. Highlight the thesis statement.

2. What type of narration is this?

    a. first person   b. third person

3. Paragraph 3 lacks a topic sentence. An appropriate topic sentence for paragraph 3 could be:

    a. Phantom Ranch is at the bottom of the canyon, and it is a very popular place.

    b. At Phantom Ranch, I met a strange man who told gruesome stories.

    c. Many people die in the Grand Canyon.

    d. Sheep can knock people off ledges in the Grand Canyon.

4. Paragraph 4 lacks unity. One sentence adds a description, but it doesn't support the paragraph's topic. Strike through that sentence.

Editing

5. A fragment is an incomplete sentence. Underline a fragment in paragraph 1, and then write the correction on the line below.

    Correction: _____

6. Paragraph 2 contains a tense shift. A verb tense changes for no logical reason. Underline the sentence with the tense shift, and write a correction on the line below.

    Correction: _____

7. Paragraph 3 contains a run-on sentence. Underline the error, and show three ways to correct the sentence.

    Corrections: _____

    _____

    _____

GRAMMAR LINK

See the following chapters for more information about these grammar topics:

Fragments, Chaapter 23

Run-Ons, Chapter 24

Verb Consistency, Chapter 29

Spelling and Commonly Confused Words, Chapter 34

Commas, Chapter 35

8. There is a missing comma in paragraph 3. Circle where the comma should be placed and write the correction here.

Correction: _____

9. Underline two spelling errors in paragraph 5. Write the corrections here.

Corrections: _____   _____

THE WRITER'S DESK Revise and Edit Your Essay

Revise and edit the essay that you wrote for the previous Writer's Desk. You can refer to the revising and editing checklists at the end of this chapter and at the end of this book.

VOCABULARY BOOST

Writers commonly overuse words. To make your writing more vivid and interesting, identify five common and overused verbs in your essay. Replace each verb with a more vivid and specific verb.

First draft   We walked to the edge of the cliff and looked at the sea.

Revision   We <u>strolled</u> to the edge of the cliff and <u>gazed</u> at the sea.

A Professional Essay

Sarah Stanfield writes and edits for publications such as *Videography Magazine* and the *New York Post*. In this essay from *Salon*, she narrates what happened while she was living in Ecuador.

Botched Tan

Sarah Stanfield

1   Baños, Ecuador, is a balmy village of waterfalls and thermal springs poised on the neck of the massive Tungurahua volcano. Normally, I would be thrilled to be there, but instead, I was half-conscious with pain. Baños was supposed to be my first stop on a trek into the Amazon rain forest. Thanks to what I would later find out were second-degree burns on my legs, it became my last stop.

2   I was living in Quito as part of my university's study abroad program, conducting anthropological fieldwork for my senior thesis. A few days before, I had accompanied my host family to its relatives' ranch just outside the city. The place had a pool, and the cloudy sky convinced me it was the perfect day to change my pale skin to brown, no sunscreen needed. Quito rises about nine

thousand feet above sea level. At this elevation, the atmosphere is thinner, making skin more vulnerable to the sun's rays. I knew this, but convinced myself the clouds in the sky would temper the intensity of the sun. As my skin is fair with pink undertones, all my previous sunbathing efforts had resulted in some shade of red blooming across my skin. Self-tanners left me orange and streaky. Yet I kept striving for the miracle day when I would achieve a bronze glow. So I stretched out next to the pool with a Toni Morrison novel. Four hours later, I arose with legs the color of smoked salmon.

3   In Ecuador, almost everyone is of mixed Spanish and indigenous ancestry, with brown eyes, thick, glossy black hair, and olive skin. Like many young and naive anthropology students out in the field for the first time, I fell in love with the beauty of the people. I envied the Ecuadorans. Looks-wise, they were everything I was not. My hair was mousy brown and lank, and my skin was too **sallow**.

sallow: an unhealthy pale color

4   I was surprised when, shortly after my arrival, Diana, my fifteen-year-old host sister, complimented me on my good skin. At first, I thought she was referring to my lack of acne. But then she ran her hand through my hair, saying that I had good hair, too. She grabbed a chunk of her own hair and made a face. I figured this to be typical teen-girl self-criticism.

5   Eventually, I realized that Ecuador has plenty of image complexes. Skin-lightening cream gets top billing on pharmacy shelves, and billboards advertising everything from cigarettes to public health messages depict smiling gringos. Matinee idols are mostly white American movie stars. Of course, Ecuadorians are not alone in aspiring to gringo beauty ideals. The most notorious example is Xuxa, the Brazilian singer and actress with the second-best-selling album in the history of Brazil. Xuxa is tall and blond, yet she presides over millions of fans in a country where almost half the citizens are of mixed African, Amerindian, and European ancestry.

6   I wasn't thinking about this as I took the bus ride from Quito to Baños, though. Before the bus trip, I had spent three days unable to walk, and now dime-size blisters were sprouting up and down my legs. I was just hoping that after all of the pain I was going through, my skin would fade from pink to brown. The bus suddenly lurched forward, causing my right leg to bump the scratchy surface of the seat in front of me. One of the blisters tore open, leaking burning fluid down my leg. Its sting convinced me that this was serious. I needed medical attention.

7   In Baños, I headed straight to the medical clinic. The waiting room was packed, mostly with young, exhausted-looking women and their numerous children. Meanwhile, my blisters were growing; they were now the size of quarters. In a tiny examination room, a young woman in a nurse's uniform greeted me. Her skin was the exact shade of caramel I yearned for. She was strikingly beautiful, except for her hair color. It was the strained yellow of a botched bleach job.

8   I lifted my skirt to my thighs, displaying my blisters and explaining in Spanish what had happened. The nurse sucked in her breath and made a little clicking sound, shaking her head. "We'll need to pop the blisters and disinfect them," she said. "Then you need to go back to Quito and go to the hospital. This looks like a second-degree burn." She took out a bottle of alcohol, a needle, and some cotton balls. With that, she got to work. I whimpered, and tears brimmed up in my eyes. Over and over I felt the sting of the needle, then the feeling of fire crawling down my legs as the fluid dribbled out, then the sting of the alcohol on open wounds, which felt like a thousand needle points battering my skin.

9   The pain alone was enough for me to swear never again to go near a beach or tanning salon. But it was the comment from the nurse, as she finished her task, which made me realize the insanity of what I had done. Screwing the cap back on the bottle of alcohol, she said, "What a pity. You had such good skin."

PRACTICE 5

1. What type of narration is this text?
   a. first person   b. third person

2. Approximately when and where do the events take place?

   _____

3. List the main events in the order in which they occur.

   _____

   _____

   _____

   _____

   _____

   _____

   _____

4. How does the writer's burn affect her plans in Ecuador?

   _____

   _____

5. The writer mentions some reasons for her decision to tan. What are her main reasons?

   _____

   _____

6. According to the writer, how do some people in Ecuador feel about their appearance? Provide some examples from the text.

_____

_____

_____

_____

7. Write down one example of a direct quotation from the essay. (See pages 102–103 for a definition of direct and indirect quotations.)

_____

_____

8. Write down one example of an indirect quotation.

_____

_____

9. Narrative writers do more than simply list a series of events. What did Stanfield learn from her experience?

_____

_____

THE WRITER'S ROOM — MyWritingLab™

MyWritingLab™

Complete these writing assignments at mywritinglab.com

Writing Activity 1: Topics

Choose any of the following topics, or choose your own topic, and write a narrative essay.

General Topics

1. a breakup
2. a lie or a mistake
3. a good encounter with a stranger
4. a thrilling or frightening moment
5. a news event that affected you

College and Work-Related Topics

6. a positive moment at college
7. a turning point in your life
8. an uncomfortable incident at work
9. a positive or negative job interview
10. a difficult lesson at work or school

READING LINK
MORE
NARRATIVE
READINGS
"My Bully, My
  Best Friend"
  by Yannick
  LeJacq
  (page 531)
"My African
  Childhood" by
  David Sedaris
  (page 539)

WRITING LINK
MORE
NARRATIVE
WRITING
TOPICS
Chapter 21,
  Writer's
  Room topic
  1 (page 323)
Chapter 27,
  Writer's
  Room topic 1
  (page 378)
Chapter 28,
  Writer's
  Room topic 1
  (page 394)

Writing Activity 2: Media Writing

Watch a popular television show or movie that describes how someone overcame an obstacle to be successful. Examples are movies such as *Precious*, *Dream Girls*, and *Milk*, or television shows such as *Grey's Anatomy*, *Parks and Recreation*, and *The Good Wife*. Also look on YouTube for videos about ordinary people who achieved surprising success. Write an essay and describe what happened to the main character(s).

Checklist: Narrative Essay

After you write your narration essay, review the checklist at the back of the book. Also ask yourself these questions.

☐ Does my thesis statement clearly express the topic of the narration?

☐ Does my thesis statement contain a controlling idea that is meaningful and interesting?

☐ Does my essay answer most of the following questions: who, what, when, where, why, how?

☐ Do I use transitional expressions that help clarify the order of events?

☐ Do I include details to make my narration more vivid?

Description 8

Painters add details in their work to express their artistic vision. Similarly, writers use the tools of descriptive writing to create images that readers can visualize in their mind's eye.

WRITERS' EXCHANGE

Choose one of the objects from the following list. Then, brainstorm a list of descriptive words about the object. Think about the shape, texture, smell, taste, color, and so on. List the first words that come to your mind.

For example: cake   *gooey, sweet, chocolate, smooth, pink icing, layered*

polar bear   school bus   tree   an older adult   lemon

111

▶ **EXPLORING**

LO 1 Define description.

What Is Description?

Description creates vivid images in the reader's mind by portraying people, places, or moments in detail. Here are some everyday situations that might call for description.

People use description every day. At home, family members might describe the style of their new apartment to a friend. At college, students could describe the results of a chemistry experiment to their classmates. At work, employees may describe a retirement party to an absent colleague.

Visualizing Description

PRACTICE 1

Brainstorm supporting ideas for the following thesis statement. Write some descriptive words or phrases on the lines.

THESIS STATEMENT: Historically, there have been some very unhealthy fashion trends.

corsets

_____

_____

_____

tall wigs

_____

_____

_____

extremely high heels

_____

_____

_____

DESCRIPTION **AT WORK**

To help hikers plan camping trips effectively, Zion National Park's Web site describes hiking trails.

Walking in the shadow of Zion Narrow's soaring walls, sandstone grottos, natural springs, and hanging gardens can be an unforgettable wilderness experience. It is not, however, a trip to be underestimated because hiking the Zion Narrows means hiking in the Virgin River. At least 60 percent of the hike is spent wading, walking, and sometimes swimming in the stream. There is no maintained trail; the route is the river. The current is swift, the water is cold, and the rocks underfoot are slippery. Flash flooding and hypothermia are constant dangers. Good planning, proper equipment, and sound judgment are essential for a safe and successful trip.

The **topic sentence** states the topic and controlling idea.

The **supporting sentences** provide details and examples.

The **concluding sentence** brings the paragraph to a satisfactory close.

The Descriptive Essay

When you write a descriptive essay, focus on three main points.

MyWritingLab™

Access the interactive "At Work" paragraphs in MyWritingLab

LO 2 Define the purpose of a descriptive essay.

1. **Create a dominant impression.** The dominant impression is the overall atmosphere that you wish to convey. It can be a strong feeling, mood, or image. For example, if you are describing a casual Sunday afternoon party, you can emphasize the relaxed ambience in the room.

2. **Express your attitude toward the subject.** Do you feel positive or negative toward the subject? For instance, if you feel pleased about your last vacation, then the details of your essay might convey the good feelings you have about it. If you feel tense during a business meeting, then your details might express how uncomfortable the situation makes you feel.

3. **Include concrete details.** Details will enable a reader to visualize the person, place, or situation that you are describing. You can use active verbs, adjectives, and adverbs so that the reader imagines the scene more clearly. You can also use **imagery**, which is description using the five senses. Review the following examples of imagery.

Sight A Western Tiger Swallowtail dipped by my face. About three inches across, its lemon yellow wings were striped improbably and fluted in black. They filliped into a long forked tail with spots of red and blue.

—Sharman Apt Russell, "Beauty on the Wing"

Sound The tree outside is full of crows and white cranes who gurgle and screech.

—Michael Ondaatje, *Running in the Family*

Smell   I think it was the smell that so intoxicated us after those dreary
months of nostril-scorching heat, the smell of dust hissing at the
touch of rain and then settling down, damply placid on the ground.

—Sara Suleri, *Meatless Days*

Touch   The straps from my backpack tore into my shoulder blades, and
pain ran down my spine.

—Andrew Wells, "My Journey Down the Grand Canyon"

Taste   Entirely and blessedly absent are the cloying sweetness, chalky
texture, and oily, gummy aftertaste that afflict many mass-
manufactured ice creams.

—R.W. Apple Jr., "Making Texas Cows Proud"

A Student Essay

Read the following student essay, and answer the questions that follow.

The House with the Brown Door

Judith Lafrance

1   In the little village of St. Lin, there is a house with a brown front door.
It has beautiful awnings on the windows and huge grounds. When I was
a child, the house was sold and a strange couple moved in. The man
and woman stayed in their house, never going outside except to work.
Furthermore, I never saw anyone visiting them. When they first moved into
my neighborhood, I thought they were malicious or unpleasant. In reality,
I have come to know them better, and everything scary that happened
behind the brown door one fateful evening was nothing but coincidence.

2   When I was seven years old, a moving van rumbled down the street. I was
excited and curious. I watched four men unload the van. They carried in a
refrigerator, a black sofa, two beds, and boxes of various sizes and shapes. As
I was looking at the movers, a woman parked her shiny green car behind the
truck. Tall and impressive, she had big blue eyes and long auburn hair, and
she was wearing a red dress. In her hands, she held a huge pink purse that I
imagined was full of cosmetics because the aging skin on her face was heavily
made up. Even so, she was beautiful. A very tall muscular man stepped out
of the driver's seat. He had blond hair and wore a gray suit. They must have
unpacked quickly because empty boxes were piled by the street two days later.

3   My friend Mary Lou and I were curious, so after school, we decided
to spy on the new neighbors. We crept behind their house. The first few
times, we had fun imagining their conversations as they gestured behind the
windows. However, one cool autumn afternoon, we were frightened by what
we heard. As we peered from behind a bush, we heard a loud bang and some
shrieking coming from inside the house. Terrified, we rushed to leave. In our

haste, we forgot to stay clear of the rose bushes, so thorns scratched our skin and snagged on our clothing. Mary Lou and I decided that we wouldn't go there anymore.

4   When I arrived home, I saw my brother Karl in the kitchen. I could smell the bacon sizzling on the stove. I told him what I had heard and said that my spying days were over. He chuckled and replied that I was so young and delicate. Feeling insulted, I shouted angrily, "I am not so young! I'll go with you to the house tonight." I hoped he wouldn't accept my idea, but he did.

5   That evening, after dinner, we snuck into our neighbors' garden. I pretended to be brave, but my skin was covered in goosebumps. As we peered at the house, we heard a loud cracking noise. Then the sounds of yelling, crying, and suffering came from the house. I turned white. Karl said we should go closer to find out what had happened. We crept up to the house and peered through the kitchen window. There was no one there, but I saw a big shadow coming from the bedroom. I tried to yell, but no sound came from my mouth. Karl saw the same shadow. We looked at each other, let go of the window sill, and turned around. A large man was standing in the darkness right behind us. My imagination went wild. I thought, "This big ugly man is going to kill us. He doesn't like children, and he thinks we are too curious." Then I fainted.

6   Parents want their children to have great lives full of love, peace, and joy. That's why, when I was a child, my mother always told me, "Don't talk to strangers." That's also why, the night that my older brother and I decided to spy on our new neighbors, my father followed us to make sure we would not get into mischief. He was the man who was standing in front of us. He wanted to punish us for our inquisitiveness, but I had briefly lost consciousness. When I opened my eyes, I saw my brother and father arguing. Hearing the commotion, the man living in the house came outside. He was surprised to see the three of us in his backyard. He asked if I was okay and then said that he was a doctor. He examined me and told my father I would be fine after a couple hours of sleep. He asked why we were in his backyard. My brother sheepishly admitted that we were spying on the man and his wife. Instead of being angry, the man laughed and said that it was normal for children to be curious.

7   The neighbor introduced himself: "By the way, my name is Martin Champagne. I am very pleased to meet you and your family." He was so gentle that my brother and I felt shy. However, I asked him about the screaming I had heard. He answered, "My wife and I love horror films. We turn the sound up high to get the full effect of the movie. Maybe that is what you heard." His wife then appeared and introduced herself.

8   This story happened ten years ago. Since then, our families have become close friends. They still live in the same house near us, and we see each other often. With time, they had a baby, and I am their babysitter. I love them as if they were my aunt and uncle. I should have gotten to know them before judging them.

PRACTICE 2

1. Highlight the thesis statement.

2. The writer recounts the story using description that appeals to the senses. Find imagery from the essay.

   a. Sight: _____

   _____

   b. Sound: _____

   _____

   c. Touch: _____

   _____

   d. Smell: _____

   _____

3. What dominant impression does the writer create in this essay? Underline examples in the essay to support your answer.

   _____

L03 Explore topics for a descriptive essay.

Explore Topics

In the Writer's Desk Warm Up, you will try an exploring strategy to generate ideas about different topics.

THE WRITER'S DESK Warm Up

Read the following questions, and write the first ideas that come to your mind. Think of two or three ideas for each topic.

EXAMPLE: List some memorable trips you have taken.

—my trip to Africa

—the time I stayed with my grandmother in Seattle

—a field trip to the Natural History Museum

1. Who are your best friends?

_____

_____

_____

2. What are some unattractive fashion trends?

   _____

   _____

   _____

3. What is your favorite food?

   _____

   _____

   _____

▶ DEVELOPING

When you write a descriptive essay, choose a subject that lends itself to description. You should be able to describe images or objects using some of the five senses. To get in the frame of mind, try thinking about the sounds, sights, tastes, smells, and feelings you would experience in certain places, such as a busy restaurant, a hospital room, a subway car, a zoo, and so on.

The Thesis Statement

LO 4 Write the thesis statement of a descriptive essay.

In the thesis statement of a descriptive essay, you should convey a dominant impression about the subject. The dominant impression is the overall impression or feeling that the topic inspires.

       topic   controlling idea

The photograph of me as a ten-year-old has an embarrassing story behind it.

controlling idea   topic

Feeling self-satisfied, **Odysseus Ramsey started his first day in public office**.

HINT ◀ How to Create a Dominant Impression

To create a dominant impression, ask yourself how or why the topic is important.

    Poor   Land developers have built homes on parkland.
                  (Why should readers care about this statement?)

    Better   The once pristine municipal park has been converted into giant estate homes that average families cannot afford.

THE WRITER'S DESK Thesis Statements

Write a thesis statement for each of the following topics. You can look for ideas in the Warm Up in the previous Writer's Desk. Each thesis statement should state what you are describing and contain a controlling idea.

EXAMPLE: Topic: a memorable trip

Thesis Statement: _My first day in Ghana left me enthralled but exhausted._

1. Topic: a close friend

   Thesis Statement: _____

   _____

2. Topic: unattractive fashion trends

   Thesis Statement: _____

   _____

3. Topic: favorite food

   Thesis Statement: _____

   _____

L05 Generate the supporting ideas of a descriptive essay.

The Supporting Ideas

After you have developed an effective thesis statement, generate supporting details.

- Use prewriting strategies such as freewriting and brainstorming to generate ideas.
- Choose the best ideas. Most descriptive essays use imagery that describes the person or scene.
- Organize your ideas. Choose the best organizational method for this essay pattern.

Show, Don't Tell

Your audience will find it more interesting to read your written work if you show an action of a person or a quality of a place rather than just state it.

Example of Telling: Laura was angry.

Example of Showing: Laura stomped down the stairs and rushed into the kitchen. With a red face, she glared at her older brother. "Where were you? I was waiting for half an hour," she hollered. Instead of waiting for his answer, she scowled at him and marched out of the kitchen, banging the door behind her.

PRACTICE 3

Choose one of the following sentences, and write a short description that shows—not tells—the quality or action.

1. Today was a perfect day.

2. I was frightened as I entered the cave.

3. The weather did not cooperate with our plans.

Use Different Figurative Devices

When writing a descriptive essay, you can use other figurative devices (besides **imagery**) to add vivid details to your writing.

- A **simile** is a comparison using *like* or *as*.

   My thoughts ran as fast as a cheetah.

   Let us go then you and I,
   When the evening is spread out against the sky
   Like a patient etherised upon a table
   —from "The Love Song of J. Alfred Prufrock" by T.S. Eliot

- A **metaphor** is a comparison that does not use *like* or *as*.

   Life is sweet-and-sour soup.

   Love is a temple.
   —from "One" by U2

- **Personification** is the act of attributing human qualities to an inanimate object or an animal.

   The chocolate cake winked invitingly at us.

   Life has a funny way of helping you out.
   —from "Ironic" by Alanis Morissette

PRACTICE 4

Practice using figurative language. Use a simile, metaphor, or personification to describe each numbered item below. If you are comparing two things, try to use an unusual comparison.

EXAMPLE: toddler: The toddler was like a monkey, climbing up and down with great agility. (simile)

1. mountain: _____

_____

2. hair: _____

_____

3. ocean: _____

_____

VOCABULARY BOOST

Use Vivid Language

When you write a descriptive essay, try to use vivid language. Use specific action verbs and adjectives to create a clear picture of what you are describing.

	livid
Use a more vivid, specific adjective.	My boss was ~~angry~~.
	whimpered
Use a more vivid, specific verb or image.	The child ~~cried~~.

Think about other words or expressions that more effectively describe these words: *laugh*, *talk*, *nice*, *walk*.

THE WRITER'S DESK   List Sensory Details

Choose one of your thesis statements from the previous Writer's Desk, and make a list of sensory details. Think about images, impressions, and feelings that the topic inspires in you.

EXAMPLE: Topic: a memorable trip

—colorful clothes

—bright, warm sand

—appetizing smell of food

—putrid odor of sewers

—a cool breeze

—powerful drumbeat of music

—bodies moving to a beat

Your topic: _____

Your list of sensory details: _____

_____

_____

_____

_____

The Essay Plan

LO 6 Develop a descriptive essay plan.

An essay plan helps you organize your thesis statement, topic sentences, and supporting details before you write a first draft. When you make an essay plan, remember to include concrete details and to organize your ideas in a logical order. If you want to emphasize some descriptive details more than others, arrange them from least affecting to most affecting. If you want your readers to envision a space (a room, a park, and so on), arrange details using spatial order.

Thesis Statement: My first day in Ghana left me enthralled but exhausted.

   I.   I was overwhelmed by my surroundings.
       A.   People wore traditional African clothing.
       B.   Some walked balancing objects on their heads.
       C.   Mothers carried babies tied to their backs.
       D.   I could smell different types of food.

  II.   The beach was unlike any other beach I'd seen.
       A.   I felt a cool breeze and saw orange sand.
       B.   I sat in the shade and had a cold beverage.
       C.   People were swimming and dancing.

 III.   The scenery of the countryside was breathtaking.
       A.   There were mud huts with straw roofs.
       B.   People were cooking on open fires.
       C.   Many animals roamed, including dogs and goats.
       D.   I saw immense anthills.

THE WRITER'S DESK   Write an Essay Plan

Choose one of the ideas that you have developed in previous Writer's Desks and prepare an essay plan. Remember to use vivid details and figurative language to help create a dominant overall impression.

LO 7 Write the first draft of a descriptive essay.

The First Draft

After you outline your ideas in a plan, you are ready to write the first draft. Remember to write complete sentences. Also, as you write, think about which transitions can effectively help you lead your readers from one idea to the next. Descriptive writing often uses space order. Here is a list of transitions that are useful for describing the details in space order.

To show place or position

above	beyond	in the distance	outside
behind	closer in	nearby	over there
below	farther out	on the left/right	under
beside	in front	on top	underneath

THE WRITER'S DESK **Write the First Draft**

In the previous Writer's Desk, you developed an essay plan. Now write the first draft of your descriptive essay. Before you write, carefully review your essay plan and make any necessary changes.

▶ **REVISING AND EDITING**

LO 8 Revise and edit a descriptive essay.

Revise and Edit a Descriptive Essay

When you finish writing a descriptive essay, review your work and revise it to make the description as vivid as possible to your readers. Check that you have organized your ideas, and remove any irrelevant details. Before you work on your own essay, practice revising and editing a student essay.

GRAMMAR HINT ◀ **Using Adjectives and Adverbs**

When you revise your descriptive essay, check that you have used adjectives and adverbs correctly. For example, many people use *real* when the adjective is actually *really*.

                              really

    My brother, Magnus, is ~~real~~ tall and powerful.

See Chapter 32 for more information about adjectives and adverbs.

A Student Essay

Read the essay, and then answer the questions that follow. As you read, correct any errors that you find and make comments in the margins.

AFRICAN ADVENTURE

Natalia MacDonald

1. My trip to Africa began with a twenty-hour journey filled with boring flights and long layovers. When I finaly arrived in Ghana, it was 9:00 P.M. local time, and I was exhausted. I went straight to my hotel to get some rest for the long day I had ahead of me. My first day in Ghana left me enthralled but exhausted.

2. Kwame, the coordinator of my volunteer program picked me up to accompany me for the day. As I left the hotel, I was overwhelmed by the surroundings. Although many people dressed in Western-style clothing, the majority wore traditional African dress. The colors were vibrant: bright blues, purples, and yellows. Men, women, and children alike walked by carrying incredible amounts of goods balanced on their heads with amazing grace and poise. Mothers also carried their babies in a way you had never seen before, tied to their backs with colorful scarves in almost a piggy-back position with the babies' little feet sticking out at either side. As we hurried through the center, I noticed the strong smells of food being cooked by street vendors, fruit being sold in baskets, and of course the not-so-pleasant smell of the open sewers lining the roads. After getting to the bank and cashing my traveler's checks, it was off to the beach.

3. Everything, from the sand to the activities people were doing, was unique. The first thing I felt was the much-needed cool breeze from the ocean brushing against my face as I approached. After the hustle and bustle of the capital, I felt relaxed as I walked on the beach. I wiggled my toes in the rich, dark orange sand. I then took a seat in the shade to enjoy a cold beverage and observe my surroundings. Some people were swimming and sunbathing, and others were dancing. There was a particular group of young boys dressed in colorful loincloths dancing to traditional music. The powerful drumbeat of the music was moving. The boys moved their bodies with such a natural fluidity along with the music that I was completely captivated. I was thoroughly enjoying myself, but it was time to catch my bus.

4. The bus was a large white van that left from a station not too far from the beach. As we drove out of the city and onto the dirt road, the scenery was breathtaking. We drove past many different types of villages along the way. Some of the villages were large and had schools, stores, and houses while others were much smaller and more basic and consisted of a circle of around twenty little mud huts with straw roofs with people cooking over an open fire in the middle of the circle. Along the road there were many animals walking around, such as dogs, mules, and small goats. A month later I went to visit a national park to see wild animals. The road itself was the same rich, dark orange color that the sand had been at the beach. One of the most incredible sights were the numerous huge anthills that were formed

from the dark orange dirt. They stood about four feet high! After driving through some rain, we finally arrived in Manya Krobo, my new home.

5.   My first full day in Ghana was one filled with new discoveries and adventure. In a mere matter of hours, I saw things that I had only read about in books and seen in movies. In one day, I had gone from the snowy minus 18-degree weather of Montreal to the humid 90 degrees of Ghana. My long-planned and awaited adventure in Africa was finally a reality.

PRACTICE 5

Revising

1. Highlight the thesis statement.

2. Highlight the topic sentences in paragraphs 2 and 4.

3. Paragraph 3 lacks a topic sentence. One possible topic sentence could be:
   a. I went to the beach that evening.
   b. La Pleasure beach was unlike any other beach I had ever seen.
   c. There were many people at La Pleasure beach.
   d. Everyone goes to La Pleasure beach in Ghana.

4. What overall dominant impression does the writer convey in the essay? Underline examples in the essay to support your answer.

   _____

5. In paragraph 4, cross out the sentence that does not support the topic sentence.

Editing

6. Paragraph 1 contains a spelling mistake. Underline and correct the mistake.

   Correction: _____

7. Paragraph 2 contains a pronoun shift. Underline and correct the error.

   Correction: _____

   _____

8. Underline and correct a comma error in paragraph 2. _____

   _____

9. Underline and correct one subject–verb agreement error in paragraph 4.

   Correction: _____

   _____

GRAMMAR LINK
See the following chapters for more information about these grammar topics:
   Subject–Verb Agreement, Chapter 27
   Pronouns, Chapter 31
   Spelling, Chapter 34
   Commas, Chapter 35

A Professional Essay

Sy Montgomery is a conservationist and award-winning writer of adult and children's books about our natural world. The next excerpt, from her book *Spell of the Tiger*, is about the tigers of the Sundarbans, a mangrove jungle on the India–Bangladesh border.

With an Open Mouth

Sy Montgomery

1   On a soft May night in West Bengal, when the sweet scent of khalsi flowers clung to the wet, warm darkness, when the moon shone round and white, and boatmen's lanterns winked at one another like fireflies up and down the river, death came with an open mouth for Malek Molla. The day's work was over. Molla and his six companions had collected five kilograms of honey from the fat combs they'd found hanging among the small, curved, downward-pointing leaves of a genwa tree. Collecting honey is one of the most dangerous jobs in Sundarbans, yet from April to June hundreds of men leave their mud and thatch houses and their rice fields and fishing nets to follow the bees into the forest.

2   In little wooden boats, they glide down the numberless channels that permeate the sodden land of Sundarbans. Barefoot, they wade through the sucking clay mud. Carefully, they step around the breathing roots of the mangroves, which spike up from the earth like bayonets. Sometimes they must pass through stands thick with hental, which is used by crocodiles to build their nests. Its stems are armored with two-inch thorns so sharp that by the time you feel one in your foot, it has already penetrated half an inch and broken off in your flesh.

3   One man always stands guard for the group because there are many dangers. Tigers hunt in these forests. Crocodiles lurk in the shallows. Vipers coil in the shade. Even the bees can kill. They are aggressive, and their sting causes muscle spasms, swelling, and fever. People who have been badly stung say that the pain can last for a year.

4   The honey itself is said to be an antidote to the bees' poison. Some who have survived attacks by bee swarms say companions saved their lives

by smearing the thin, spicy honey over the stings. Sundarbans honey is considered an elixir of sorts. Shamans say eating some each day will ensure a long life. The leaves of the khalsi, whose fragrant, white blossoms supply the pollen from which the earliest honey is made, are curative, too: a paste made from them will staunch the flow of blood.

5   The group found the first bees' nest easily, eight feet up in a genwa. One man climbed the spindly trunk. With smoke from a kerosene-soaked torch of green hental **fronds**, he drove the bees from the hive and cut loose the swollen comb with a machete. Another man below caught the comb in a ten-gallon tin that had once held mustard oil. The others waited, armed with clubs, ready in case a tiger appeared; but none did.

fronds: large leaves

6   That afternoon, they emerged from the forest safe and laden with their riches, the golden honey. In their low-bodied wooden boat, anchored in the Chamta River, beneath the palm thatch that roofed the cabin, the six tired men relaxed. Their lantern gleamed. The men talked and laughed and smoked the harsh, leaf-wrapped cigarettes called bidi. A pot of curry and India's ubiquitous dahl—lentil stew—bubbled on the boat's clay stove. One man offered a song. The notes of the Bengali melody rose and fell, full and then empty, like the tides that rise to engulf the forest every six and a half hours and then fall back, drained.

7   No one felt the boat rock. No one heard a scream. But everyone heard the splash when something very heavy hit the water beside the boat. The men pointed their flashlights into the forest, along the shore. On the far bank of the river, the light barely caught the figure of a huge, wet cat slinking into the mangroves, carrying the body of Malek Molla like a fish in its mouth. Molla had been quiet that evening; possibly, he had been asleep. The tiger may have killed him without ever waking him up. Without making a sound, without rocking the boat, a predator—possibly weighing five hundred pounds and stretching to nine feet long—had launched itself from the water, selected its victim, seized him in its jaws, and killed him instantly.

8   Molla's body was recovered the following day. The tiger had severed his spinal cord with a single bite to the back of the neck. It had eaten the soft belly first. In Sundarbans, everyone watches for the tiger. But the tiger, they say, always sees its victim first.

PRACTICE 6

1. What is the dominant impression conveyed by the author?

_____

2. Highlight the thesis statement.

3. Why is collecting honey a dangerous occupation for the men of the Sundarbans?

   _____

   _____

   _____

   _____

4. The writer uses imagery to describe the Sundarbans. Find examples of imagery for the following senses.

   Sight: _____

   Smell: _____

   Taste: _____

   Sound: _____

   Touch: _____

5. A simile is a comparison using *like* or *as*. Underline one simile in paragraph 6 and one in paragraph 7.

6. Personification is giving human traits to nonhuman objects. Underline an example of personification in paragraph 1.

7. In the Sundarbans, what can the honey collectors do to protect themselves? You will have to infer or make a guess.

   _____

   _____

THE WRITER'S ROOM   MyWritingLab™

MyWritingLab™

Complete these writing assignments at mywritinglab.com

Writing Activity 1: Topics

Write a descriptive essay about one of the following topics, or choose your own topic.

General Topics

1. a music concert
2. a public place that has a lot of odors
3. your dream house
4. a night out
5. an exciting sports event

College and Work-Related Topics

6. a beautiful building or area on campus
7. a frustrating day
8. an eccentric professor
9. a new person I have met
10. graduation day

READING LINK

MORE DESCRIPTIVE READINGS

"Into Thin Air" by Jon Krakauer, page 562

"Guy" by Maya Angelou, page 569

WRITING LINK

MORE DESCRIPTIVE WRITING TOPICS
Chapter 25,
    Writer's Room
    topic 1
    (page 359)
Chapter 27,
    Writer's Room
    topic 1
    (page 378)
Chapter 29,
    Writer's Room
    topic 1
    (page 407)
Chapter 38,
    Writer's Room
    topic 1
    (page 506)

Writing Activity 2: Media Writing

Watch a popular television show or movie that describes a past era. For example, you can watch movies such as *Lincoln*, *Les Misérables*, or *Lawless*. Some television shows such as *Mad Men* or *Downton Abbey* also describe the past. You can also check on YouTube for video clips from past eras. In an essay, describe the setting. Use imagery that appeals to the senses.

Checklist: Descriptive Essay

After you write your descriptive essay, review the essay checklist at the back of the book. Also ask yourself these questions.

☐ Does my thesis statement clearly show what I will describe in the essay?

☐ Does my thesis statement have a controlling idea that makes a point about the topic?

☐ Does my essay have a dominant impression?

☐ Does each body paragraph contain supporting details that appeal to the reader's senses?

☐ Do I use vivid language?

Process 9

Every industry uses processes. For example, to make pottery, an artist needs to shape, fire, and glaze the pot. Along similar lines, not only do writers have to follow the writing process, but sometimes they need to be able to explain processes to their readers as well.

LEARNING OBJECTIVES

LO 1 Define process. **(p. 130)**

LO 2 Define the purpose of a process essay. **(p. 131)**

LO 3 Explore topics for a process essay. **(p. 133)**

LO 4 Write the thesis statement of a process essay. **(p. 134)**

LO 5 Generate the supporting ideas of a process essay. **(p. 135)**

LO 6 Develop a process essay plan. **(p. 136)**

LO 7 Write the first draft of a process essay. **(p. 137)**

LO 8 Revise and edit a process essay. **(p. 137)**

WRITERS' EXCHANGE

Choose one of the following topics, and have a group or class discussion. Describe the steps you would take to do that process.

- how to play a card game
- how to bathe a dog
- how to play baseball
- how to plan a party

LO1 Define
process.

What Is Process?

A **process** is a series of steps usually done in chronological order. In process writing, you explain how to do something, how an incident took place, or how something works.

People explain processes every day. At home, parents might explain to their children how to cook spaghetti. At college, a professor may explain to students how they could become tutors. At work, an employer could describe to newly hired interns how to perform their daily responsibilities.

Visualizing Process

PRACTICE 1

Brainstorm supporting ideas for the following thesis statement. Write a few words to show each step.

THESIS STATEMENT: When you are traveling to a tropical destination, there are some important steps to follow.

_____   _____   _____

_____   _____   _____

_____   _____   _____

_____   _____   _____

_____   _____   _____

_____   _____

PROCESS **AT WORK**

Frank Morelli is a mechanic who specializes in repairing sports cars. In this pamphlet excerpt, he advises customers on how to buy a car.

Purchasing a car for the first time is both stressful and exciting. To ensure that you make the best choice, consider the following suggestions. First, identify your needs. For example, make a list of why you want a vehicle, how much you want to pay, and what color and model you want. Next, do some research. Many Web sites and magazines have information about the performance and reliability of different car models. For instance, the magazine *Consumer Reports* publishes reports based on laboratory tests of various vehicles. Finally, test-drive several different cars. You will know not only if the engine runs smoothly but also if you are comfortable driving the car. By following these simple steps, you will be able to make an informed decision when buying your next car.

The **topic sentence** states the topic and controlling idea.

The **supporting sentences** provide details and examples.

The **concluding sentence** brings the paragraph to a satisfactory close.

MyWritingLab™

Access the interactive "At Work" paragraphs in MyWritingLab

The Process Essay

Before planning a process essay, you need to determine your purpose. Do you want to tell readers how to complete a process or how to understand a process?

LO 2 Define the purpose of a process essay.

1. **Complete a process.** This type of essay contains directions for completing a particular task. For example, a writer might explain how to change a flat tire, how to decorate a room, or how to use a particular computer program.

2. **Understand a process.** This type of essay explains how something works or how something happens. For example, a writer might explain how the admissions process at a college works or how food goes from the farm to the table.

A Student Essay

Read the essay and answer the questions that follow.

How to Plant a Tree

Samuel Charland Larivière

1   Imagine sitting under a large leafy tree on a hot summer day. It is one of life's greatest pleasures. These gigantic umbrellas can be very pleasant and offer cool shade for rest and relaxation. But, if they are neither properly planted nor well looked after, trees might threaten your garden or your

home. By following a few simple rules, you will be able to plant the best trees to suit your needs.

2   First, decide on the type of tree that is right for your garden. Does the soil in your garden contain a large percent of clay, lime, or sand? Is it well drained? Trees are **capricious** and will not grow in every type of soil. For example, conifers such as Jack Pine prefer sandy soil whereas birches prefer soil with high lime content. Maples and elms grow well in clay. In addition, consider the size, shape, color, and type of tree that would fit best in your garden. Do you need a tree that will be tall and leafy when it matures, or would a large bush suit your needs? A fruit tree will cover your lawn with rotten fruit if it is not picked frequently. As a result, you could have problems with raccoons or other animals. Also, are there power lines or telephone lines near your property? You should avoid trees that will interfere with the various wires that are found around your house.

capricious:
unpredictable

3   Next, plant your tree the correct distance from your house. For example, if a tree is planted too close to the house, its branches and roots might cause problems. A falling branch or an invasive root system could destroy either the roof or the foundation of your house. The distance you should plant the tree from the house depends on the species of the tree. A maple will spread its roots in a large area, but a poplar will have short roots. To make the best choice, ask for guidance at a nursery. Once you have this information, you are ready to purchase your tree.

4   Finally, become informed about the best method to plant the tree. If you plant it incorrectly, your tree could either die or grow very slowly. Dig a two- or three-foot hole in the ground because at this depth the soil is wet and contains more minerals for young roots to grow. Then, fill the first foot of your hole with fertilizer. Finally, remove the sapling from the pot and place it in the hole. Fill up the rest of the hole with some earth and verify that the tree is upright.

5   In conclusion, you should not plant a tree impulsively. Planting a tree involves planning and following a few simple steps. You must choose the right tree, learn the proper distance to plant it, and plant it correctly. After the tree matures, you will enjoy its shade and beauty every day of the year.

PRACTICE 2

1. Highlight the thesis statement.

2. Underline the topic sentence in each body paragraph.

3. For body paragraphs 2 and 3, list some supporting details.

   Paragraph 2: _____

   _____

Paragraph 3: _____

_____

4. What type of process essay is this?

   a. complete a process   b. understand a process

Explore Topics

LO 3 Explore topics for a process essay.

In the Writer's Desk Warm Up, you will try an exploring strategy to generate ideas about different topics.

THE WRITER'S DESK Warm Up

Read the following questions, and write the first ideas that come to your mind. Think of two or three ideas for each topic.

EXAMPLE: Imagine that you are starting college tomorrow. What are some steps that you would take to make your first day of class successful?

—start to get organized the day before

—try to make a good first impression

—don't stress out; try to relax

1. How do you choose your major at college?

   _____

   _____

   _____

2. How do you end a relationship?

   _____

   _____

   _____

3. How can you become a better friend?

   _____

   _____

   _____

> ▶ **DEVELOPING**

When you write a process essay, choose a process that you know something about. For example, you might be able to explain how to become more environmentally conscious; however, you might not know how to reduce nuclear waste.

LO 4 Write the thesis statement of a process essay.

The Thesis Statement

In a process essay, the thesis statement states what process you will be explaining and what readers will be able to do after they have read the essay.

     topic   controlling idea
Surviving in the wilderness <u>requires some basic knowledge.</u>

    controlling idea   topic
<u>Consistency, patience, and time are essential</u> **to becoming a good parent.**

THE WRITER'S DESK   **Thesis Statements**

Write a thesis statement for each of the following topics. You can look for ideas in the Warm Up in the previous Writer's Desk. Each thesis statement should state the process and contain a controlling idea.

EXAMPLE: Topic: how to prepare for the first day of class

  Thesis Statement: <u>To have a good first day of class, follow the next</u>

  <u>steps.</u>

1. Topic: how to choose a college major

  Thesis Statement: _____

  _____

2. Topic: how to end a relationship

  Thesis Statement: _____

  _____

3. Topic: how to become a better friend

  Thesis Statement: _____

  _____

The Supporting Ideas

LO 5 Generate the supporting ideas of a process essay.

A process essay contains a series of steps. When you develop supporting ideas for a process essay, think about the main steps that are necessary to complete the process.

- Use prewriting strategies such as freewriting and brainstorming to generate ideas.
- Choose the best ideas. Clearly explain the steps of the process.
- Organize your ideas. Choose the best organizational method for this essay pattern. Process essays generally use chronological (time) order.

HINT ◀ Give Steps, Not Examples

When you explain how to complete a process, describe each step. Do not simply list examples of the process.

Topic: How to Plan an Interesting Vacation

List of Examples	Steps in the Process
• going to a tropical island	• decide what your goal is
• riding a hot air balloon	• research possible locations
• swimming with the sharks	• find out the cost
• touring an exotic city	• plan the itinerary according to budget

THE WRITER'S DESK List the Main Steps

Choose one thesis statement from the previous Writer's Desk. List the main steps to complete the process.

EXAMPLE: Thesis Statement: To have a good first day of classes, follow the next steps.

Steps:
1. Get your final preparations done the day before classes begin.
2. Make a good impression with professors and other students.
3. Remember to relax.

Thesis Statement: _____

_____

Steps: _____

                _____

                _____

                _____

                _____

                _____

LO 6 Develop
a process essay
plan.

The Essay Plan

An essay plan helps you organize your thesis statement, topic sentences, and supporting details before you write a first draft. Decide which steps and which details your reader will really need to complete the process or understand it.

Thesis Statement: To have a good first day of classes, begin preparations the day before classes start, focus on making a good first impression, and remember to relax.

    I.   Immediately get all your final preparations done.
        A. Buy remaining school supplies.
        B. Gas up your car.
        C. Find nice clothes.
        D. Get a good night's sleep.
    II. Make a good first impression.
        A. Set your alarm clock early.
        B. Get to your class on time.
        C. Impress classmates with your preparedness.
    III. Remember to relax.
        A. Relaxing will help you take everything one step at a time.
        B. If you are not relaxed, you may have a meltdown.

THE WRITER'S DESK   Write an Essay Plan

Refer to the information you generated in previous Writer's Desks, and prepare a detailed essay plan. Add details and examples that will help to explain each step.

The First Draft

LO 7 Write the first draft of a process essay.

As you write your first draft, explain the process in a way that would be clear for your audience. Address the reader directly. For example, instead of writing "You should scan the newspaper for used cars," simply write "Scan the newspaper for used cars." Also, remember to use complete sentences and transitions to smoothly string together the ideas from your essay plan. Here are some time-order transitions that are useful for explaining processes.

To begin a process	To continue a process		To end a process
(at) first	after that	later	eventually
initially	afterward	meanwhile	finally
the first step	also	second	in the end
	furthermore	then	ultimately
	in addition	third	

GRAMMAR HINT ◀ Avoid Sentence Fragments

Ensure that you do not use sentence fragments to list the steps of the process. A sentence must have a subject and a verb to express a complete idea.

                                                      check

Consider your airline's carry-on luggage requirements. First, the weight of your suitcase.

See Chapter 23 for more information about sentence fragments.

THE WRITER'S DESK Write the First Draft

In the previous Writer's Desk, you developed an essay plan. Now, carefully review your essay plan, make any necessary changes, and write the first draft of your process essay.

▶ REVISING AND EDITING

Revise and Edit a Process Essay

LO 8 Revise and edit a process essay.

When you finish writing a process essay, carefully review your work and revise it to make the process as clear as possible to your readers. Check to make sure that you have organized your steps, and remove any details that are not relevant to being able to complete or understand the process. Before you revise and edit your own essay, practice revising and editing a student essay.

A Student Essay

Read the essay, and then answer the questions that follow. As you read, correct any errors that you find and make comments in the margins.

STEPS TO HELP OUT YOUR FIRST DAY OF CLASSES

Justin Sanders

1.　　Summer vacation was fun; you played hard and saw too much sun. As soon as you realize that classes start tomorrow, the reality of summer vacation shatters instantly like a window being hit by a baseball. You begin to pull your hair out from anxiety about and anticipation for the following morning. Fear not; I have a few helpful tips to aid you through your first day of classes. To have a good first day of classes, begin preparations the day before classes begin, focus on making a good first impression, and remember to relax.

2.　　You might think that since classes do not start until tomorrow, you have one more day to play. Use today to get all your final preparations done. Otherwise, tomorrow could be a bad day. Write down all the school supplies that you have and don't have. Figure out how long it will take you to buy the remaining supplies. If you're like me, you will remember to buy at least twenty pencils so that you can end tomorrow with at least one of them. You never know who might need one or how many you will accidentally leave behind in a class as you nervously run off to your next class. Schedule time for your most expensive activity: putting a few gallons of gas in your tank. Stop by your local clothing store, and pick up something new and in style. To replace those moth-eaten rags you have been wearing over the vacation. It would be a fashion disaster to wear the same outfit twice in the first week. Think hard. Make sure that you consider every last thing you could possibly need, and make time to get it. You will need to plan for your bedtime. If you want to be alert and ready for your classes the next day, get a good night's sleep.

3.　　Tomorrow is now today. Classes begin. You should have set your alarm early enough to get ready and to make sure you get to class on time. Making a good first impression can have a big impact on the entire semester. If you are on the instructor's good side, he or she might be more lenient with due dates, offer extra credit, give extra help on assignments, and probably more. Now, granted, there are instructors that are as hard as rocks and are so indifferent that it doesn't matter what you do because it won't help. Also, during your first day, there are other areas where you will want to make a good impression. During some of your classes, you may find yourself seated next to an attractive person. Impress them with your incredible preparedness by loaning one of your pencils. In such a situation, you really hope you woke up on time, you wore a matching outfit, and you showered. If you smell like the gym socks you left in the locker room over the summer and look like a three-year-old dressed you, it might be a little hard to ask out or be asked out by this person. Impressions are important, so take your time and make a good one.

4.   Relaxation will allow you to take everything one step at a time. Not relaxing can result in a major breakdown. If you fall apart, I sincerely hope you made a really good first impression on your instructors before the meltdown, that way you will survive the semester.

5.   If you follow these simple steps, you will have a great first day of classes. You are now in with your instructors, you may have a date, and you won't fall into a bottomless hole of depression from stress and anxiety. I hope this gives you a pleasant enough outlook on the future to encourage you to repeat these steps many times for the next eternity, or at least until graduation. Good luck and remember that school does end . . . some year.

PRACTICE 3

Revising

1. Highlight the thesis statement.

2. Highlight the topic sentences for paragraphs 2 and 3. (Remember that a topic sentence may not always be the first sentence in the paragraph.)

3. Paragraph 2 lacks transitions. Add at least three transitions to link the sentences. Draw lines indicating where they should be placed.

4. In paragraph 3, cross out the sentence that does not support the topic sentence.

5. Which of the following would make an effective topic sentence for paragraph 4?
   a. With all the stress and tensions of school, remember one key thing: relax.
   b. Becoming nervous is not a good idea.
   c. All students get stressed on the first day of classes.

6. Paragraph 4 lacks adequate support. Think of a detailed example that would help flesh out the paragraph.

_____

_____

_____

GRAMMAR LINK

See the following chapters for more information about these grammar topics:

Fragments,
   Chapter 23
Run-Ons,
   Chapter 24
Pronouns,
   Chapter 31

Editing

7. Underline a sentence fragment in paragraph 2. Then correct it.

   Correction: _____

   _____

   _____

8. Underline a pronoun error in paragraph 3. Write the correction below.

   Correction: _____

   _____

9. Underline the run-on sentence in paragraph 4. Then correct it here.

   Correction: _____

   _____

   _____

THE WRITER'S DESK Revise and Edit Your Process Essay

Revise and edit the essay that you wrote for the previous Writer's Desk. You can refer to the revising and editing checklists at the end of this chapter and at the end of the book.

VOCABULARY BOOST

Look at the first draft of your process essay. Underline the verb that you use to describe each step of the process. Then, when possible, come up with a more evocative verb. Use your thesaurus for this activity.

A Professional Essay

Journalist Stacey Colino specializes in health and family issues and has written for *The Washington Post*, *Parenting*, and *Shape*. In the next essay, she writes about how to become a happier person.

Do You Have What It Takes to Be Happy?

Stacey Colino

1   If you add up money, beauty, fame and admiration, you've got the formula for a lifetime of bliss, right? Wrong. The truth is, your financial status, external circumstances, and life events account for no more than 15 percent of your happiness quotient, studies show. What elements do make a difference? Surprisingly simple internal factors such as having healthy self-esteem, a sense of optimism and hope, gratifying relationships, and meaning and purpose in your life have the most influence, according to recent studies on what researchers call "subjective well-being."

2   If that sounds like a tall order, here's the good news: Even if they don't come naturally, many of the attitudes and thought patterns that influence happiness can be cultivated, which means you can boost your capacity for happiness today—and in the future. "Studies with twins reveal that happiness is somewhat like a person's cholesterol level—it's genetically influenced, but it's also influenced by some factors that are under our control," explains David Myers, Ph.D., a social psychologist at Hope College in Holland, Michigan, and author of *The Pursuit of Happiness*. In other words, while your genetically determined temperament has a fairly strong influence on your happiness quotient, you can nudge it upward with the attitudes and approaches you bring to your life. To develop a sunnier disposition, use the simple strategies outlined below, and you'll be on your way to a richer, more satisfying life, starting now!

3   Develop an upbeat attitude. No, you don't want to become a Pollyanna who overlooks problems and thinks everything is peachy even when it isn't. But you do want to consciously focus on what's positive in your life because this can engender a sense of optimism and hope. And research has found that happy people are brimming with these key ingredients. In one study at Southern Methodist University in Dallas, happy subjects were more hopeful about their wishes than their less **sanguine** peers. It's not that their wishes came true more often, but the happy people expected them to come true. How? They do it by expecting to have a joyful summer every day, not just when they're on vacation, by identifying negative thoughts and countering them with positive or neutral ones, and by embracing challenges (such as parasailing or public speaking) instead of fearing them. Such people realize that challenges will help them grow as a person.

sanguine:
optimistic

4   Hang out with your favorite people. It's as simple as this: Carving out as much time as you can to spend with people you value gives you a sense of connection, as well as a support system for when your luck heads south.

Research at the University of Illinois at Urbana–Champaign found that people who are consistently very happy have stronger romantic and social relationships than unhappy people. "We're social creatures by nature," says Louis H. Janda, an associate professor of psychology at Old Dominion University in Norfolk, Virginia. "When you're involved with others, it gives you a sense of belonging and lets you engage in mutually enjoyable activities, all of which can buffer you from stress."

5   Infuse your life with a sense of purpose. If you want to be happy, it is important to give your life meaning: Research at Middle Tennessee State University in Murfreesboro found that having a sense of purpose is a significant predictor of happiness and life satisfaction. To create a vision of what's meaningful to you, ask yourself, "What activities make me feel excited or enthusiastic? What do I want to be remembered for? What matters most to me?" If you can articulate these desires to yourself, you can set specific goals to help you fulfill them. If you realize that your strongest desire is to become an influential teacher and role model, for example, you might set a goal of volunteering to help disadvantaged kids or of going back to school to get your teaching degree.

6   Count your blessings, not your burdens. When people keep a gratitude journal, in which they jot down a daily list of what they appreciate in their lives, they experience a heightened sense of well being, according to research at the University of California, Davis, and the University of Miami in Florida. "There's a natural tendency to take things for granted, but if you stop and think of all the ways you are blessed, it doesn't take long for the mind to use that as the new baseline for perceiving how happy you are," explains study co-author Michael E. McCullough, Ph.D., an associate professor of psychology and religious studies at the University of Miami.

R & R: rest and relaxation

7   Recharge your energy and your spirits. Sure, exercise can work wonders in keeping your mood buoyant, but so can getting some simple **R & R**. "Happy people lead active, vigorous lives yet reserve time for restorative sleep and solitude," Myers says. Short-change yourself of the shut-eye you need, and it's hard to enjoy much of anything when you're exhausted. In a recent study involving more than nine hundred women, researchers assessed how happy women were based on their daily activities and found that sleep quality had a substantial influence over how much the women enjoyed life, even when they engaged in plenty of pleasurable activities like sex and socializing.

8   Put on a happy face! If you act as if you're on cloud nine—by smiling with your mouth and eyes, speaking in a cheerful voice, and walking confidently—going through the motions can trigger the actual emotion. There's even science to prove it: A study at Fairleigh Dickinson University in Teaneck, New Jersey, found that when people forced themselves to smile or laugh, they experienced a substantial boost in mood afterward.

9   So start off by acting as if you're walking on the sunny side of the street—even if it's cloudy. Chances are, you'll begin to feel a little happier after just a few steps!

PRACTICE 4

1. What is the writer's specific purpose? _____

2. Highlight the thesis statement. It may not be in the first paragraph.

3. Find the topic sentence of each body paragraph. Highlight the verbs in each topic sentence.

4. In each topic sentence, the subject is implied but not stated. What is the subject?

   _____

5. In paragraph 5, list the examples the writer gives to support the topic sentence.

   _____

   _____

   _____

6. The writer supported her main ideas with many specific examples. Identify and underline six research studies that the writer refers to.

7. Circle the names of three experts that the writer quotes.

8. The writer uses no transitional words or phrases to link the steps of the process. Add a transitional word or expression to the beginning of at least four body paragraphs.

THE WRITER' ROOM   MyWritingLab™

MyWritingLab™
Complete these writing assignments at mywritinglab.com

Writing Activity 1: Topics

Write a process essay about one of the following topics, or choose your own topic.

General Topics

How to . . .

1. find a place to live
2. become a good leader
3. get a good night's sleep
4. find a roommate
5. do an activity or a hobby

College and Work-Related Topics

How to . . .

6. look for a new job
7. assemble a _____
8. become a better manager or supervisor
9. change a law
10. make a good impression at an interview

WRITING LINK MORE PROCESS WRITING TOPICS
Chapter 21, Writer's Room topic 2 (page 323)
Chapter 25, Writer's Room topic 2 (page 359)
Chapter 26, Writer's Room topic 1 (page 367)
Chapter 31, Writer's Room topic 1 (page 431)

**READING LINK
MORE PROCESS
READINGS**

"The Rules of
Survival" by
Laurence
Gonzales
(page 557)

"How Cults
Become
Religions" by
John D. Carl
(page 572)

Writing Activity 2: Media Writing

Watch a television show or movie about training an animal. For example, watch the television show *The Dog Whisperer*, the channel *Animal Planet*, or a movie such as *The Horse Whisperer* or *Seabiscuit*. You might also look on YouTube for videos about animal training. In an essay, explain how to train a dog, horse, cat, bird, or other animal.

Checklist: Process Essay

As you write your process essay, review the checklist at the back of the book. Also ask yourself these questions.

- ☐ Does my thesis statement make a point about the process?

- ☐ Do I include all of the steps in the process?

- ☐ Do I clearly explain each step so my reader can accomplish the process?

- ☐ Do I mention all of the supplies that my reader needs to complete the process?

- ☐ Do I use transitions to connect all of the steps in the process?

Definition 10

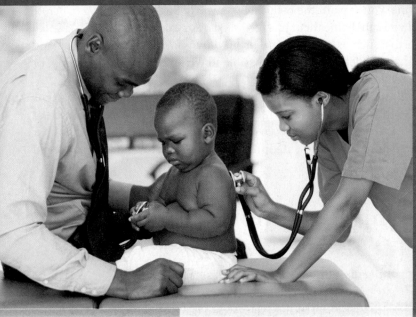

To help patients understand a diagnosis, doctors may define the illness itself or explain related medical terms. Similarly, you may write an entire essay in which you define a term.

WRITERS' EXCHANGE

Brainstorm some common slang expressions. Think about words you use to express pleasure or disgust. You can also consider words describing a specific type of person. Choose one expression and define it without using a dictionary. Make your definition clear so that a nonnative speaker will understand the word.

L01 Define
definition.

What Is Definition?

When you define, you explain the meaning of a word. Some terms have concrete meanings, and you can define them in a few words. For example, a *town* is "a small city." Other terms, such as *values*, *faith*, or *human rights*, are more abstract and require more detailed definitions. It is possible to write a paragraph, an essay, or even an entire book about such concepts.

People often try to define what they mean. For example, at home, parents might explain to their children what it means to be *reliable*. At college, a professor may ask students to define the term *poverty*. At work, a colleague could tell her coworkers that their business presentation *needs improvement*, and then she could explain what she means.

Visualizing Definition
PRACTICE 1

Brainstorm supporting ideas for the following thesis statement.

THESIS STATEMENT: A home is not just wood, plaster, and shingles; it is a place where one feels safe.

_____   _____

_____   _____

_____   _____

_____   _____

The Definition Essay

LO 2 Define the purpose of a definition essay.

When you write a definition essay, try to explain what a term means to you. For example, if someone asks you to define *overachiever*, you might give examples of overachievers and what you think those people do that goes beyond the limits. You may also explain what an overachiever is not. Also, remember the next two points.

1. **Choose a term that you know something about.** You need to understand a term to say something relevant and interesting about it.

2. **Give a clear definition.** Write a definition that your reader will easily understand, and support your definition with examples.

DEFINITION **AT WORK**

In the following excerpt, Anthony Mullen, National Teacher of the Year, defines one characteristic of an exceptional teacher.

> Passion is the noblest of the trio because it ignites a flame too bright to be ignored by students. A teacher must project passion in the classroom because this powerful emotion sparks the learning process in children and motivates them to remember key concepts and ideas. Students can feel the energy, enthusiasm, and creativity radiating from a teacher. Students will realize that what is being taught is important and worthwhile.

The **topic sentence** states the topic and controlling idea.

The **supporting sentences** provide details and examples.

The **concluding sentence** brings the paragraph to a satisfactory close.

HINT ◄ Consider Your Audience

Consider your audience when you write a definition essay. You may have to adjust your tone and vocabulary, depending on who will be reading the essay. For example, if you write a definition essay about cloning for your political science class, you may have to explain concepts using basic, nontechnical terms. If you write the same essay for your biology class, you may be able to use more technical terms.

MyWritingLab™

Access the interactive "At Work" paragraphs in MyWritingLab

A Student Essay

Read the student essay, and answer the questions that follow.

Journalists Are History's Record Keepers

Lindsey Davis

1   When you want to find research for that paper on World War II for class, you hit the books in the library, looking for the historian who summed up the

events or the political scientist who offered critical insight as to why it happened. But when you want to find out what is happening in the world right now, you pick up the *Los Angeles Times* or log on to your computer and browse the **plethora** of news sites. Journalists play multiple roles in society. From acting as a check on government and business to hosting a forum for free and open debate, the **Fourth Estate** plays a crucial role in society. But beyond this, journalists are historians. They are the note takers and storytellers who document today's activities and events and preserve them for a record of history.

plethora: a large amount

Fourth Estate: the entire press, including newspapers, television news programs, magazines, etc.

2   First, different types of media are crucial for preserving historical records. Newspapers, news Web sites, and television news programs are the only places you can find the latest developments concerning what is happening in Washington, what reforms Governor Jerry Brown is planning, the status of conflicts in the Middle East or Africa, and the crucial stats of the last NFL playoff game. Before it goes into the history books, that information goes into the newspaper. Before you can find it in the library, you can find it in the news.

3   Moreover, journalists are the record keepers for the community. They will give you the plain and simple facts. They will find out how much those tickets were selling for at the Rose Bowl. They will tell you who won the basketball games and what the upcoming baseball season looks like. But beyond simple facts, they will record the emotions of a Rose Bowl defeat. How about those new movies and DVDs that are coming out next week? They will give you the scoop of what's good and what's bad. They will tell you what you can't miss in Los Angeles. You can find the thoughts and analyses of a vast array of differing voices.

4   Furthermore, journalists are also crucial to preserving the spirit of the times. It is within the media that you'll find the record of the year's events. But this history won't be complete unless it includes your voice, your opinion, and your perspective on events. Tell the journalists what's going on and what you would like to see covered. Send them an e-mail. Talk to reporters and tell them what you think. The media will never be able to create an accurate record of history unless you help gather all the facts by saying what you know or what you saw. Do you think something was wrongly covered? Let the media know. Do you disagree with a column you have read? Send a letter to the editor, and make sure your viewpoint is printed and recorded as well.

Topic Sentence ←

5   Journalists are committed to ensuring that whatever happens is recorded forever. Some people say that journalists write the first rough draft of history. But they strive to report accurately enough that their record of history will be the final draft. Their dedication ensures that you get the news and ensures that history is recorded. All they ask is that you read to keep the history alive.

PRACTICE 2

1. This essay defines the role of journalists. What point is the writer making?

   _____

   _____

2. Highlight the thesis statement.

3. Underline the topic sentence of each body paragraph.

4. What introductory style is used? Circle the best answer.
   a. anecdote   c. contrasting position
   b. historical   d. general background

5. In your own words, list some of the specific examples in each body paragraph.

   _____

   _____

   _____

   _____

   _____

   _____

6. Circle the transitional expressions that link the body paragraphs.

Explore Topics

In the Writer's Desk Warm Up, you will try an exploring strategy to generate ideas about different topics.

LO 3 Explore topics for a definition essay.

THE WRITER'S DESK Warm Up

Read the following questions, and write the first ideas that come to your mind. Think of two or three ideas for each topic.

EXAMPLE: What is a Goth? Think of some characteristics of a Goth.

—wears black

—people stare at them

—not mainstream

—listens to Goth metal

1. What is oversharing?

     It's revealing too much information, details

2. What is the American dream?

     Opportunitty
     Free of Speech
     able to live well

3. What is a good citizen?

     — Honest

VOCABULARY BOOST

Some words have neutral, positive, or negative associations. Look at each set of words and categorize each as neutral (=), positive (+), or negative (–). Do this with a partner.

1. thin, cadaverous, lean, emaciated, wiry, skinny, slender
2. home, shack, cottage, slum, stomping ground, dump, sanctuary
3. dainty, delicate, finicky, fussy, prissy, fragile, elegant, frail
4. honest, coarse, crude, open, gross, straightforward
5. brat, child, sweetheart, cutie, munchkin, delinquent, heir, mama's boy

---

▶ DEVELOPING

LO 4 Write the thesis statement of a definition essay.

The Thesis Statement

A clear thesis statement for a definition essay introduces the term and provides a definition. There are three basic ways to define a term.

Definition by Synonym

Providing a definition by synonym is useful if the original term is difficult to understand, and the synonym is a more familiar word.

term	+	synonym
He is a neophyte,		which means he is a beginner or novice.

Definition by Category

When you define by category, you determine the larger group to which the term belongs. Then you determine what unique characteristics set the term apart from others in that category.

term	+	category	+	detail
A forest ranger		is a worker		who is trained to protect wildlife in national parks.

Definition by Negation

When you define by negation, you explain what a term does not mean. You can then include a sentence explaining what it does mean.

term	+	what it is not	+	what it is
Obsession		is not an eccentricity;		it is a mental illness.

GRAMMAR HINT ◄ Using Semicolons

You can join two related and complete ideas with a semicolon, as the writer has done in this example of a definition.

Marriage is not the end of your freedom; it is the beginning of a shared journey.

See Chapter 21 for more information about using semicolons.

Making a Point

Defining a term by synonym, category, and negation is only a guideline for writing thesis statements for a definition essay. Keep in mind that your essay will be more interesting if you express your attitude or point of view in your thesis statement.

No point	Avarice means greed.
Point	Avarice, or greed, invariably leads to tragedy.

PRACTICE 3

Write thesis statements by defining the following terms using your own words. Try to make definitions by synonym, category, and negation. Remember to indicate your controlling idea in the thesis statements.

EXAMPLE: Road rage is not a momentary lapse of judgment; it is serious criminal behavior.

1. Kindness _____

_____

2. Helicopter parents _____

_____

3. Cyberbully _____

_____

4. Avatar _____

_____

5. Viral marketing _____

_____

HINT ⟨ Be Precise!

When you write a definition essay, it is important to use precise words to define the term. Moreover, when you define a term by category, make sure that the category for your term is correct.

Anorexia nervosa is the <u>inability</u> to eat.
(Anorexia nervosa is not an ability or an inability.)

Anorexia nervosa is <u>when</u> you want to be thin.
(*When* refers to a time, but anorexia nervosa is not a time.)

Anorexia nervosa is <u>where</u> it is hard to eat properly.
(*Where* refers to a place, but anorexia nervosa is not a place.)

Now look at a better definition of this illness.

Anorexia nervosa is a tragic **eating disorder** characterized by the desire to become very thin.

PRACTICE 4

Revise each sentence using precise language.

EXAMPLE: Multitasking is when you do many activities at once.

Multitasking is doing many activities at once.

_____

1. A spin doctor is when public opinion is influenced by manipulating information.

_____

_____

2. A poor loser is the inability to accept defeat graciously.

_____

_____

3. Brain candy is someone having an enjoyable experience associated with fluffy entertainment.

_____

_____

THE WRITER'S DESK **Write Thesis Statements**

Write a thesis statement in which you define each of the following topics. You can look for ideas in the previous Writer's Desk. Remember to make a point in your thesis statement.

EXAMPLE: Topic: Goth

Thesis Statement: _Goth is a complete lifestyle that embraces attitude, culture, and fashion._

1. Topic: oversharing

Thesis statement: _____

_____

2. Topic: the American dream

Thesis statement: _____

_____

3. Topic: a good citizen

Thesis statement: _____

_____

_____

The Supporting Ideas

After you have developed an effective thesis statement, generate supporting ideas. In a definition essay, you can give examples that clarify your definition. To develop supporting ideas, follow these three steps:

LO 5 Generate the supporting ideas of a definition essay.

◆ Use prewriting strategies to generate ideas. Think about facts, anecdotes, and examples that will help define your term.

- Choose the best ideas. Use examples that clearly reveal the definition of the term.
- Organize your ideas. Choose the best organizational method for this essay pattern.

THE WRITER'S DESK **Generate Supporting Ideas**

Choose one of your thesis statements from the previous Writer's Desk. List three or four ideas that most effectively illustrate the definition.

EXAMPLE: Thesis Statement: _Goth is a complete lifestyle that_

embraces attitude, culture, and fashion.

Supports: _—must have self-confidence_

—must believe in the culture

—introspective music is important

—black colors and theatrical fashions are critical

Thesis Statement: _____

_____

Supports: _____

_____

_____

_____

_____

LO 6 Develop a definition essay plan.

The Essay Plan

An essay plan helps you organize your thesis statement and supporting details before you write the first draft. A definition essay includes a complete definition of the term and provides adequate examples to support the central definition. When creating a definition essay plan, make sure that your examples provide varied evidence and do not just repeat the definition. Organize your ideas in a logical sequence.

Thesis Statement: Goth is a complete lifestyle that embraces attitude, culture, and fashion.

   I.   What makes a real Goth is the attitude he or she shows.
        A. Confidence is key.
        B. A Goth feels outside mainstream culture.
        C. Outsiders often misunderstand Goth culture.
   II. Music is important to Goths.
        A. Goth music started in the late 1970s.
        B. Music was introspective with dark lyrics.
        C. It had elements of horror and the supernatural.
   III. Fashion is crucial to Goths' way of life.
        A. They love medieval or Victorian styles with velvet and lace.
        B. They sometimes wear religious symbols.
        C. They often wear black and dye their hair black.

THE WRITER'S DESK Write an Essay Plan

Refer to the information you generated in previous Writer's Desks and prepare a detailed essay plan.

The First Draft

Your essay plan is the backbone upon which you can build your first draft. As you write, remember to vary your sentence structure. Also include transitional words or expressions to help your ideas flow smoothly. Here are some transitional expressions that can help you show different levels of importance in a definition essay.

LO 7 Write the first draft of a definition essay.

To Show the Level of Importance

clearly	next
first	one quality . . . another quality
most important	second
most of all	undoubtedly

THE WRITER'S DESK Write the First Draft

Carefully review the essay plan you prepared in the previous Writer's Desk. Make any necessary changes to the definition or its supporting details, and then write your first draft.

L0 8 Revise and
edit a definition
essay.

Revise and Edit a Definition Essay

When you finish writing a definition essay, carefully review your work and revise it to make the definition as clear as possible to your readers. You might have to adjust your definition and supporting ideas to suit their knowledge. Also keep in mind the tone of your essay. Certain words have either negative or positive connotations. Finally, check that you have organized your ideas logically and remove any irrelevant details. Before you revise and edit your own essay, practice revising and editing a student essay.

A Student Essay

Read the student essay, and then answer the questions that follow. As you read, correct any errors that you find and make comments in the margins.

WELCOME TO MY WORLD

Marie-Pier Joly

1.   A woman passes by wearing a long black dress. Her pale face, dark eyeliner and lipstick, and jet-black hair are objects of attention. Whether its a single horror-filled glance or a full stop to stare in shock, people react to Goths in surprising ways. A Goth's appearance clearly attracts scrutiny. However, being Goth is not just about clothes; it is a complete lifestyle that embraces attitude, culture, and fashion.

2.   Be it, breathe it, live it, and believe it. What makes someone a real Goth is the attitude he or she shows. Confidence is the key. Without it, people will not remain in the Goth scene for very long. For example, if someone is extremely shy and has very low self-esteem, he will not tolerate people's stares. Also, Goths must believe in their culture. Most Goths feel that they do not fit into mainstream society, and their outsider status binds them. Being a Goth is risky because of the misconceptions that the public has, so Goths must be strong. For instance, people incorrectly believe that the Columbine killers were Goths; thus, Goths are associated with violence. The 2002 film *Bowling for Columbine* is about this tragedy. Violence is not part of the Goth **creed**, so good Goths have to trust themselves. Most importantly, they have to demonstrate that they have self-composure.

creed: belief
system

3.   Goth music culture started in the late 1970s within the punk subculture. The elder Goths appreciated bands such as Siouxsie and the banshees and Bauhaus. The music was introspective and had dark lyrics. It had elements of horror, morbidity, and the supernatural. But it was also tongue in cheek.

Performers would dress in campy outfits. Current Goths listen to a variety of music styles, including Goth metal and industrial music.

4.   Fashion is not just a passing fad for Goths it is crucial for their way of life. They have a sense of drama and love theatrical clothing. For example, romantic Goths like velvet and lace and are inspired by Victorian or medieval styles. They sometimes wear religious symbols such as crucifixes. Both males and females may dye their hair black, paint their fingernails black or dark purple, and wear dark eyeliner. People who wear dark trench coats and white face makeup are not necessarily Goths.

5.   Finaly, Goth is an entire lifestyle that may be very demanding. There is a special image to maintain and music to buy. Goths must also have the right attitude. Goths draw a lot of attention, not all of it positive. So those who plan to be Goths must believe in themselves.

PRACTICE 5

Revising

1. Highlight the thesis statement.

2. What type of definition does the thesis statement have? Circle the best answer.

   a. synonym   b. category   c. negation

3. Highlight the topic sentences in paragraphs 2 and 4.

4. Cross out one sentence in paragraph 2 that does not support the topic sentence.

5. Paragraph 3 does not have a topic sentence. Which sentence would be an effective topic sentence for that paragraph? Circle the best answer.

   a. Goths listen to punk music.

   b. Goths listen to a lot of music.

   c. Music is an important element in the Goth subculture.

   d. All Goth music has its origins in the 19th century.

6. What type of definition is the topic sentence in paragraph 4?

   a. synonym   b. category   c. negation

Editing

7. In paragraph 1, there is an apostrophe error. Underline and correct the error.

   Correction: _____

8. In paragraph 3, there is a capitalization error. Underline and correct the error.

   Correction: _____

> **GRAMMAR LINK**
> See the following chapters for more information about these grammar topics:
> Run-Ons, Chapter 24
> Spelling, Chapter 34
> Apostrophes, Chapter 36
> Capitalization, Chapter 37

9. In paragraph 4, there is a run-on sentence. Underline and correct the run-on.

   Correction: _____

   _____

10. There is a spelling mistake in paragraph 5. Underline and correct the error.

    Correction: _____

THE WRITER'S DESK **Revise and Edit Your Essay**

Revise and edit the essay that you wrote for the previous Writer's Desk. You can refer to the revising and editing checklists at the end of this chapter and at the end of the book.

A Professional Essay

Lisa Selin Davis has written about a variety of subjects such as architecture and real estate. She has also written a novel, *Belly*. She currently blogs full time.

Internet Trolls

Lisa Selin Davis

1   When I wrote for a blog about Brooklyn real estate, I was regularly plagued by "trolls"—online commentators who write inflammatory or derisive things in public forums, hoping to provoke an emotional response. These commentators called me, and one another, everything from stupid to racist, or sometimes stupid racists. And that was just when I posted the menu of a new café. The most offensive of these trolls was a man who called himself "The What." His remarks ranged from insults to threats. "I know where you live, and I'm coming for you and your family," he once wrote. The intrigue around The What's identity warranted a cover story in *New York* magazine. Internet trolls are people who spend time and energy engaging in virtual hate.

2   The consensus among sociologists and psychologists who study online behavior is that all kinds of people can become trolls—not just the unwound, the immature, or the irate. Do you see your perfectly pleasant work neighbor furiously typing next to you? He might be trolling an Internet site right now. "Most people who troll are people who are just like you and me, but just a bit more intense," says Olivier Morin, a cultural anthropologist who has written about trolling.

3   One Web site breaks trolls into categories: the hater, the moral crusader, the debunker, and the defender, but trolls might not exhibit those qualities in real life. The Internet's anonymity makes it impossible for them to resist

spewing vitriol from the protective cave of cyberspace. Psychologists call it the "disinhibition effect," in which "the frequency of self-interested unethical behavior increases among anonymous people." Nonacademics refer to it as "**John Gabriel's** Greater Internet F-wad Theory": the combination of anonymity and an audience brings out the absolute worst in people.

John Gabriel: a character in a Web comic called *Penny Arcade*

4   Online disinhibition ranges from benign oversharing of personal information to toxic virtual hit-and-runs in which writers are called stupid racists. For example, in response to the *Batman* movie shooting in Colorado, someone wrote, "What kind of idiot parents bring their three-month-old to a midnight movie. Morans." I guess mean people don't have to be good spellers. Only someone incapable of empathy or perpetually engulfed by rage would say such things in public. But people feel alone when they're typing on a computer, even if they're in a public "place" like a chat room on Facebook or the comments section of an article. MIT professor Sherry Turkle calls this "being alone together." The Internet causes "emotional dislocation," so we forget about the together part.

5   There is a movement to eradicate, or at least reduce, anonymous commenting in the hopes that it will seal up this space between our lives, online and off. Many sites require readers to log in through social media to comment, so that they are, in theory, linked to their real-life selves. Perhaps, like a lot of people, The What simply wanted to articulate his worldview. Maybe we can't ask why trolls do what they do without asking why people argue in general. The answer could be that they simply want to assert their own **rectitude**. "They really want to be right and prove a point," says Olivier Morin, "and the magic of the Internet does the rest."

rectitude: righteousness; sense of moral correctness

PRACTICE 6

1. Highlight the thesis statement of this essay.

2. What type of definition does the thesis statement have? Circle the best answer

a. synonym   b. category   c. negation

3. According to the author, what are some characteristics of an Internet troll? Give three or four characteristics.

_____

_____

_____

4. Why is the Internet such a good place to become a troll?

_____

_____

_____

5. Using your own words, define the "disinhibition effect." See paragraphs 3 and 4.

   _____

   _____

   _____

6. This essay has many types of supporting details. In which paragraphs do you find the following:

   anecdote: _____

   informed sources: _____

7. In your opinion, what can be done to prevent people from becoming Internet trolls? List some ideas.

   _____

   _____

   _____

   _____

   _____

MyWritingLab™

Complete these writing assignments at mywritinglab.com

MyWritingLab™

THE WRITER'S ROOM

Writing Activity 1: Topics

Write a definition essay about any of the following topics, or choose your own topic.

General Topics

1. a soul mate
2. a negative political campaign
3. a culture of entitlement
4. mind games
5. an adult

College and Work-Related Topics

6. a good team player
7. a hacktavist
8. equal opportunity
9. a good education
10. healthy competition

Writing Activity 2: Media Writing

Define "common sense." Watch a television show such as *Dr. Phil* or *The Dr. Oz Show*. You can also watch a movie such as *The Descendants*, *We Bought a Zoo*, or *The Great Gatsby*. In an essay, define the term "common sense" and support your definition with examples or anecdotes from the media.

READING LINK

MORE DEFINITION READINGS

"Slum Tourism" by Eric Weiner (page 565)

"Chance and Circumstance" by David Leonhardt (page 578)

WRITING LINK

MORE DEFINITION WRITING TOPICS

Chapter 23, Writer's Room topic 1 (page 342)

Chapter 29, Writer's Room topic 2 (page 407)

Chapter 33, Writer's Room topic 1 (page 452)

Chapter 36, Writer's Room topic 2 (page 484)

Checklist: Definition Essay

As you write your definition essay, review the checklist at the back of the book. Also ask yourself the following set of questions.

☐ Does my thesis statement contain a definition by synonym, category, or negation?

☐ Do I use concise language in my definition?

☐ Do I make a point in my thesis statement?

☐ Do all of my supporting paragraphs relate to the thesis statement?

☐ Do the body paragraphs contain enough supporting details that help define the term?

11 Classification

LEARNING OBJECTIVES

LO 1 Define classification. **(p. 163)**

LO 2 Define the purpose of a classification essay. **(p. 164)**

LO 3 Explore topics for a classification essay. **(p. 167)**

LO 4 Write the thesis statement for a classification essay. **(p. 172)**

LO 5 Generate the supporting ideas of a classification essay. **(p. 172)**

LO 6 Develop a classification essay plan. **(p. 174)**

LO 7 Write the first draft of a classification essay. **(p. 174)**

LO 8 Revise and edit a classification essay. **(p. 175)**

To make shopping easier for consumers, car dealerships organize vehicles according to their make, model, and size. Similarly, when writing a classification essay, you organize ideas into categories.

WRITERS' EXCHANGE

Work with a partner or group. Divide the next words into three or four different categories. What are the categories? Why did you choose those categories?

art	studio	medicine
construction	stethoscope	workshop
doctor	paintbrush	hospital
hammer	welder	sculptor

▶ **EXPLORING**

What Is Classification?

L01 Define classification.

When you classify, you divide a large group into smaller and more understandable categories. For instance, if a bookstore simply put books randomly on shelves, you would have a hard time finding the book that you need. Instead, the bookstore classifies according to subject area. In classification writing, each of the categories must be part of a larger group, yet they must also be distinct. For example, you might write an essay about the most common types of hobbies and sort those into board games, sports, and crafts.

People use classification in their everyday lives. For instance, at home you classify laundry into piles on the basis of fabric or color. At college, the administration classifies subjects into arts, sciences, and so on. A workplace such as an office might classify employees as managers, sales staff, and secretaries.

Visualizing Classification

PRACTICE 1

Brainstorm supporting ideas for the following thesis statement. Divide each category into subcategories by thinking of related activities.

THESIS STATEMENT: There are several categories of games that are good for the mind.

Board Games

_____

_____

_____

Card Games

_____

_____

_____

Puzzles

_____

_____

_____

L02 Define
the purpose of
a classification
essay.

The Classification Essay

To find a topic for a classification essay, think of something that you can sort or divide into different groups. Also, determine a reason for classifying the items. When you are planning your ideas for a classification essay, remember the following points.

1. **Use a common classification principle.**
   A **classification principle** is the overall method that you use to sort the subject into categories. To find the classification principle, think about one common characteristic that unites the different categories. For example, if your subject is "jobs," your classification principle might be any of the following:

   ◆ jobs in which people work with their hands
   ◆ dangerous jobs
   ◆ outsourced jobs

2. **Sort the subject into distinct categories.**
   A classification essay should have two or more categories.

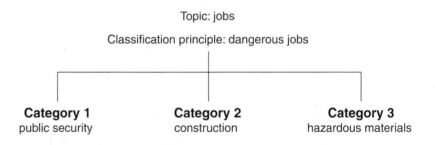

Topic: jobs

Classification principle: dangerous jobs

| **Category 1** | **Category 2** | **Category 3** |
| public security | construction | hazardous materials |

3. **Say something meaningful.**
   Your essay should not simply divide a topic into categories; it should say something meaningful. For instance, you can divide cars into small, medium, and large sizes. If you simply describe those categories, you will not be giving the reader any valuable information because everyone knows those three sizes exist. Instead, justify why each category is significant. For example, you can describe what the size of a car tells us about the owner. Or you can categorize cars according to specific life stages (the ideal dating car, family car, and retirement car). Always consider what point you are trying to make.

   In an essay about dangerous jobs, your point can be the following: "The public should express more gratitude to those people who work in dangerous fields."

MyWritingLab™

Access the interactive "At Work" paragraphs in MyWritingLab

CLASSIFICATION **AT WORK**

Ahmad Bishr is a Web design consultant. In the next excerpt from an e-mail to a client, he makes suggestions about classifying a Web site.

> The second thing you need to do is decide how to divide your site. The opening page should contain only the most pertinent information about the cottage you are trying to rent. For instance, include the number of rooms, the location, the most spectacular traits of the cottage, and so on. Each subcategory will become a link. Because you are trying to rent your cottage, I suggest that one link contain photos of the interior, with details about each room. You will also need a link that includes a rental calendar and rates. A third section might contain information about local attractions. Remember that too many categories will confuse the viewer. You'll want a simple, uncluttered site. Keep the divisions down to four or five pages at the most. Definitely, organization is a key element in a Web site.

The **topic sentence** states the topic and controlling idea.

The **supporting sentences** provide details and examples.

The **concluding sentence** brings the paragraph to a satisfactory close.

A Student Essay

Read the student essay and answer the questions that follow.

Discrimination in the 21st Century

Victoria Johnson

1 When the topic of discrimination is discussed, it is usually described in terms of racial, religious, or gender offenses. These types of discrimination are undeniable, but the disabled community is rarely mentioned. In 1990, Congress passed the Americans with Disabilities Act. The ADA mandated that buildings be accessible and job modifications be made to accommodate the disabled. Although this policy was a welcome beginning for people with disabilities, in practical terms, the disabled still face challenges. The disabled, specifically those in electric wheelchairs, are discriminated against in personal relationships, transportation options, and public venues.

2 Disabled people have more difficulties establishing relationships with others. I use an electric wheelchair, and a hard part of my life is not having a lot of friends. When I was little, I had friends because the other children thought it was cool to push me or to ride in my wheelchair. However, by the time I was ten, the situation had changed. As people grow up, they begin doing more and more activities; they no longer just want to go over to someone's house to play. For people in electric wheelchairs, this is a problem. I cannot go to a friend's house unless there is a way to get inside. During

my adolescence, I usually couldn't go to parties because there was no ramp. Because I was not able to take part in weekend activities like roller-skating or sports, the kids started to forget me. They saw me only at school and did not think to include me in the after-school activities. Unfortunately, people are uncomfortable around the disabled.

3   Transportation is another problem for people in electric wheelchairs because they need vans with ramps. Anyone can drive a van, but many hesitate to do so. The disabled cannot just get into any car and go to lunch. Friends need to make arrangements to take disabled people in a special van. This extra planning causes problems. Since many disabled people cannot drive and go where they want when they want, they become frustrated. In most localities, the bus system has only a few buses with wheelchair lifts, so people in wheelchairs are dependent on others to get where they want to go. The lack of independence can lead to a lack of self-esteem. People with disabilities feel they are bothering others when they ask for transportation help, and it becomes easier to stay at home.

4   People without disabilities think that things are so much better now because buildings are accessible. Of course, gaining access to buildings is important, but what happens once a disabled person is inside? Public venues often do not meet the needs of the handicapped. Whenever I go to a sports event or a concert, I have to sit near the top, and I cannot see a thing. For example, when the Clay Center in Charleston, West Virginia, was built, handicapped seating was placed in the back row instead of throughout the theater. Shopping malls are also a problem. Although the entrance is easily accessible, actual shopping is difficult. In some stores, the aisles are so narrow that the chair hits everything. Stores place too many clothes on the racks, and wheelchairs cannot get between them. The dressing rooms are also too small. The bigger department stores will have one handicapped dressing room, but usually it is filled with boxes. Grocery stores place items too high to reach. The clerks are helpful, but it is still annoying to have to ask for help.

5   For people in wheelchairs, doing activities for and by themselves is difficult. Whether the discrimination in personal relationships, transportation, and building accommodations is intentional or not, it still serves to divide people. It has been more the twenty years since the Americans with Disabilities Act was passed. The disabled should not be complacent about the steps that have been taken to improve their lives because discrimination is still a problem. Unfortunately, it may take years for the handicapped population to truly become a part of the community.

PRACTICE 2

1. Highlight the thesis statement.

2. Highlight the topic sentence in each body paragraph. Remember that the topic sentence is not always the first sentence in the paragraph.

3. State the three categories that the writer discusses, and list some details about each category.

   a. _____

   Details: _____

   _____

   _____

   b. _____

   Details: _____

   _____

   _____

   c. _____

   Details: _____

   _____

   _____

4. Which introductory style does this essay use? Circle your answer.

   a. anecdote   c. historical

   b. definition   d. opposing position

Explore Topics

In the Writer's Desk Warm Up, you will try an exploring strategy to generate ideas about different topics.

L0 3 Explore topics for a classification essay.

THE WRITER'S DESK **Warm Up**

Read the following questions, and write the first ideas that come to your mind. Think of two to three ideas for each topic.

EXAMPLE: How is social media useful?

—make friends

—organize events

—build workplace networking

1. What are some different categories of families?

   _____

   _____

   _____

2. What are some different types of consumers? To get ideas, think of some people you know and the way that they shop.

   _____

   _____

   _____

3. What are some types of heroes that people have at different times in their lives?

   _____

   _____

   _____

Making a Classification Chart

A **classification chart** is a visual representation of a main topic and its categories. Making a classification chart can help you to identify the categories more clearly so that you will be able to write more exact thesis statements.

When you classify items, remember to find a common classification principle. For example, you can classify sports according to their benefits, their degree of difficulty, or their costs.

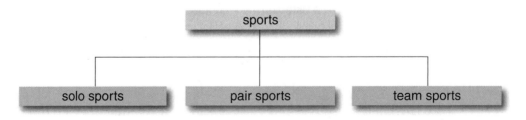

Classification Principle: psychological benefits

You can also use a pie chart to help you classify items.

Psychological Benefits of Sports

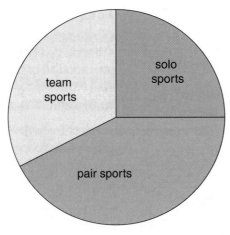

HINT ◄ **Make a Point**

To make interesting classification essays, try to express an attitude, opinion, or feeling about the topic. For example, in an essay about discipline, your classification principle might be types of discipline methods; however, the essay needs to inform readers of something specific about those methods. You could write about discipline methods that are most effective, least effective, ethical, unethical, violent, nonviolent, and so on.

PRACTICE 3

In the following classification charts, a subject has been broken down into distinct categories. The items in the group should have the same classification principle. Cross out one item in each group that does not belong. Then write down the classification principle that unites the group.

EXAMPLE:

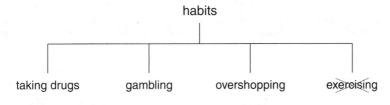

Classification principle: damaging habits _____

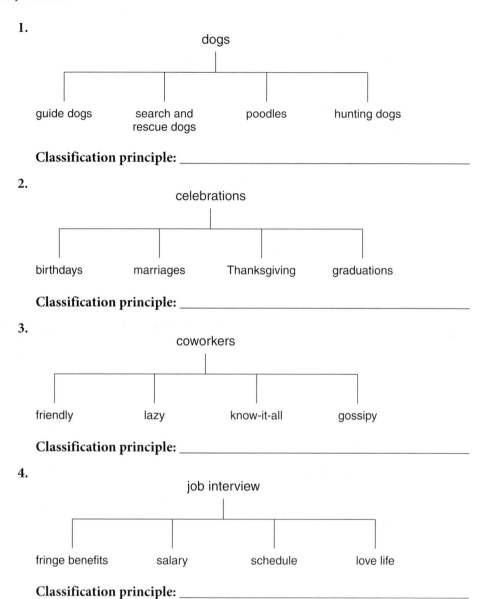

1.

dogs

guide dogs | search and rescue dogs | poodles | hunting dogs

Classification principle: _____

2.

celebrations

birthdays | marriages | Thanksgiving | graduations

Classification principle: _____

3.

coworkers

friendly | lazy | know-it-all | gossipy

Classification principle: _____

4.

job interview

fringe benefits | salary | schedule | love life

Classification principle: _____

HINT ◀ **Categories Should Not Overlap**

When sorting a topic into categories, make sure that the categories do not overlap. For example, you would not classify *roommates* into the categories *aloof*, *friendly*, and *messy* because a messy roommate could also be aloof or friendly. Although the categories share something in common, each category should be distinct.

THE WRITER'S DESK Find Distinct Categories

Break down the following topics into three distinct categories. Remember to find categories that do not overlap. You can look for ideas in the Writer's Desk Warm Up on pages 167–168.

EXAMPLE:

Events organized with online tools

flash mobs   flash robs   riots

Classification principle: _activities done with strangers_

1.

families

_____   _____   _____

Classification principle: _____

2.

consumers

_____   _____   _____

Classification principle: _____

3.

heroes

_____   _____   _____

Classification principle: _____

▶ **DEVELOPING**

LO 4 Write the thesis statement for a classification essay.

The Thesis Statement

The thesis statement in a classification essay clearly indicates what you will classify. It also includes the controlling idea, which is the classification principle.

topic   controlling idea

Several types of coworkers can completely destroy a workplace environment.

You can also mention the types of categories in your thesis statement.

topic   controlling idea

Gossipy, lazy, and know-it-all coworkers can completely destroy a workplace environment.

THE WRITER'S DESK Write Thesis Statements

Write clear thesis statements. You can refer to your ideas in previous Writer's Desks. Remember that your thesis statement can include the different categories you will be discussing.

EXAMPLE: Topic: events organized online

Thesis statement: _Three types of interesting and unexpected_

social activities are flash mobs, flash robs, and riots.

1. Topic: families

   Thesis statement: _____

   _____

2. Topic: consumers

   Thesis statement: _____

   _____

3. Topic: heroes

   Thesis statement: _____

   _____

LO 5 Generate the supporting ideas of a classification essay.

The Supporting Ideas

After you have developed an effective thesis statement, generate supporting ideas. In a classification essay, you can list details about each of your categories.

* Use prewriting strategies to generate examples for each category.
* Choose the best ideas.
* Organize your ideas. Choose the best organizational method for this essay pattern.

You can prepare a traditional essay plan. You can also illustrate your main and supporting ideas in a classification chart such as the one that follows.

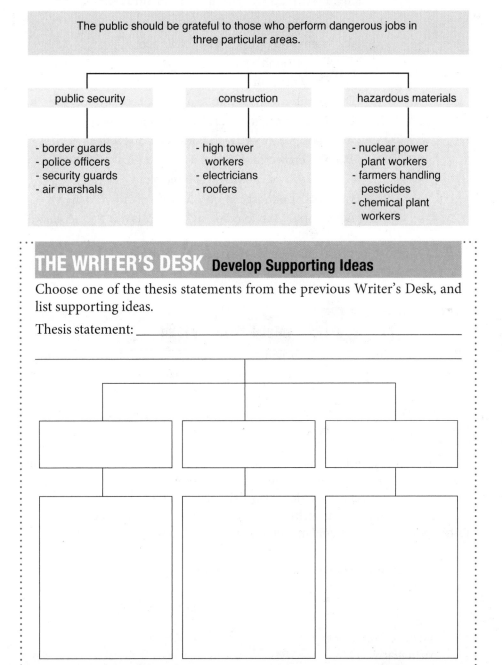

The public should be grateful to those who perform dangerous jobs in three particular areas.

public security	construction	hazardous materials
- border guards - police officers - security guards - air marshals	- high tower workers - electricians - roofers	- nuclear power plant workers - farmers handling pesticides - chemical plant workers

THE WRITER'S DESK Develop Supporting Ideas

Choose one of the thesis statements from the previous Writer's Desk, and list supporting ideas.

Thesis statement: _____

LO 6 Develop a classification essay plan.

The Essay Plan

Before you write a classification essay, make a detailed essay plan. Add supporting details for each category.

Thesis Statement: Three types of interesting and unexpected crowd activities are flash mobs, flash robs, and riots.

I.   Flash mobs are unexpected fun activities.
    A.   Someone plans a song or dance.
    B.   People sign up online.
    C.   They meet in public and do the activity.
    D.   Members of the public are shocked but may join in.

II.   Flash rob groups use crowds to commit theft.
    A.   People connect with Facebook or Twitter.
    B.   The crowd meets in a store at a particular time.
    C.   The crowd members rob the store.

III.   Riots are the most dangerous type of crowd activity.
    A.   People plan to meet after a sports game or political event.
    B.   Some people begin to break the law.
    C.   Bystanders join in to break windows and rob stores.

THE WRITER'S DESK **Make an Essay Plan**

Refer to the information you generated in previous Writer's Desks, and prepare a detailed essay plan. Arrange the supporting details in a logical order.

LO 7 Write the first draft of a classification essay.

The First Draft

After you outline your ideas in a plan, you are ready to write the first draft. Weave together the ideas you have in your essay plan. Remember to write complete sentences and to include transitional words or expressions to help your ideas flow smoothly. Here are some transitions that can help you express which category is most important and to signal movement from one category to the next.

To show importance	To show types of categories
above all	one kind . . . another kind
clearly	the first/second kind
most of all	the first/second type
the most important	the last category
particularly	

THE WRITER'S DESK **Write the First Draft**

Carefully review the classification essay plan you prepared in the previous Writer's Desk and make any necessary changes. Then, write the first draft of your classification essay.

▶ **REVISING AND EDITING**

Revise and Edit a Classification Essay

When you finish writing a classification essay, carefully review your work and revise it to make sure that the categories do not overlap. Check to make sure that you have organized your essay logically, and remove any irrelevant details. Before you work on your own essay, practice revising and editing a student essay.

LO 8 Revise and edit a classification essay.

A Student Essay

Read the essay, and then answer the questions that follow. As you read, correct any errors that you find and make comments in the margins.

FLASH MOBS, FLASH ROBS, AND RIOTS

Diego Pelaez

1.   Facebook, Twitter, and instant messaging provide people with the information necessary to gather in public places. Most citizens use social media to meet up with family and friends. However, sometimes groups of strangers congregate using such technology, and they do harmful or illegal actions. Three types of interesting and unexpected crowd activities are flash mobs, flash robs, and riots.

2.   A flash mob occurs when a group of people gather in a public place to do some type of unexpected performance. That is harmless and fun. Some credit Improv Everywhere's "Frozen Grand Central" as the clip that really ignited the flash mob revolution. Uploaded in 2008, the clip shows people who be walking around New York's Grand Central Terminal. Suddenly, about two hundred people freeze in position, looking like statues. A minute later, they walk away as if nothing has happened. The stunned expressions on the faces of onlookers helped make the video clip a Web sensation. Since then, crowds of people have gathered in public squares to have pillow fights, dance with synchronized movements, sing, and even to quack like

ducks. Although such activities involve some planning, to onlookers they appear to be spontaneous acts of mass silliness.

3.   A flash rob is a more dangerous and illegal group activity. In 2010, American police saw the first flash robs, where large groups of people descended on stores to steal items. For instance, on July 30, 2012, a Chicago clothing store was the victim of flash robbing. About twenty people entered Mildblend Supply Company and stole high-price denim jeans. Flash robs also occur in Canada. In July 2011, a thieving mob descended on an Ottawa convenience store, showing little compassion for the local merchant. Sometimes lone gunmen rob stores, and their images are captured on security cameras.

4.   Riots, which are the worse group activity, include wanton destruction and violence. In the spring of 2011, disappointed Vancouver hockey fans burned cars, broke windows, and stores were robbed. That summer, England had five days of rioting. The first riot began in Tottenham, an area in North London, where a peaceful protest about a police shooting turned violent. As the riots spread, participants in different towns took advantage of the chaos to go on destructive shopping sprees. Some people lost their homes, their businesses, and even their lives. For instance, an uninsured butcher in Tottenham lost about $50,000 worth of meat and worried that this event had destroyed his life's work. Even more seriously, sixty-eight-year-old Richard Bowes was beaten to death merely because he tried to stop rioters from burning down a building, and three people were run over as they tried to defend their neighborhood.

5.   Flash mobs are generally safe and fun events. Flash robs and riots, however, are much more destructive. Social media can contribute to all three types of gatherings, it can also be used to catch lawbreakers. After flash robs and riots, some outraged citizens have created "name and shame" Facebook pages, uploading cellphone images of lawbreakers and publicly humiliating them. Police forces also use the tools of social media, putting photos on Facebook and YouTube. In England, with the public's help, police identified close to two thousand looters. Perhaps the biggest wake-up call for flash robbers and rioters is to find out that social media can cut both ways.

PRACTICE 4

Revising

1. Highlight the thesis statement and the topic sentences in the three body paragraphs.

2. The essay is organized using what type of order?

    a. time   b. space   c. emphatic

Explain your answer: _____

_____

3. In paragraph 3, one of the examples is not a valid support. Cross it out.
   Explain why it is not valid. _____

_____

4. What does the writer mean in the conclusion when he says that social media
   "can cut both ways." _____

_____

Editing

5. A fragment lacks a subject or a verb and is an incomplete sentence. Underline
   one fragment in paragraph 2. Then write the correction in the space.

   Correction: _____

6. Paragraph 2 contains a verb-tense error. Underline the error, and write the
   correction here.

   Correction: _____

7. In paragraph 4, there is an error with the superlative form of an adjective.
   Underline the error, and write the correction here.

   Correction: _____

8. In paragraph 4, there is a parallel structure error. Underline and correct the
   error. (For more information about parallel structure, see the Grammar Hint
   below.)

_____

9. Paragraph 5 contains a run-on sentence. Underline it, and show a possible
   correction here.

   Correction: _____

_____

> **GRAMMAR LINK**
>
> See the following chapters for more information about these grammar topics:
>
> Fragments, Chapter 23
> Run-ons, Chapter 24
> Parallel Structure, Chapter 25
> Verb Tenses, Chapter 28
> Adjectives, Chapter 32

GRAMMAR HINT ◀ Parallel Structure

Use parallel structure when words or phrases are joined in a series. The groups of items should be balanced.

Some annoying sales methods include calling customers on the phone,
leaving
putting pop-up ads on the Internet, and ~~when they leave~~ text messages.

THE WRITER'S DESK **Revise and Edit Your Essay**

Revise and edit the essay that you wrote for the previous Writer's Desk. You can refer to the revising and editing checklists at the end of this chapter and at the end of the book.

VOCABULARY BOOST

Writers commonly overuse the same vocabulary. To make your writing more vivid and interesting, look at your first draft and underline at least ten repeated nouns and verbs. (Remember that a noun is a person, place, or thing.) Then add details or specific descriptions to five of the nouns and write more vivid verbs. Here is a brief example of how you might avoid repetition of nouns and verbs.

Dull, repetitive	Patrice likes cycling. Patrice often cycles to work at his bookstore. Often Patrice is reckless and cycles without a helmet.
Detailed, uses synonyms	**Patrice** likes **cycling** and **commutes** to work on his **bike**. Although **the 30-year-old bookstore owner** knows better, **he** often **recklessly rides** without a helmet.

A Professional Essay

Frank Schmalleger is director of the Justice Research Association, a private consulting firm that focuses on issues relating to crime and justice. The following excerpt is from his book *Criminal Justice Today*.

Types of Correctional Officers

Frank Schmalleger

1   Prison staff culture, in combination with naturally occurring personality types, gives rise to a diversity of officer types. Correction staff can be classified according to certain distinguishing characteristics. Among the most prevalent types are the dictator, the friend, the merchant, the turnkey, the climber, and the reformer.

The Dictator

2   Some officers go by the book; others go beyond it, using prison rules to reinforce their own brand of discipline. The guard who demands signs of inmate subservience, from constant use of the word *sir* or *ma'am* to frequent free shoeshines, is one type of dictator. Another goes beyond legality,

beating or "macing" inmates even for minor infractions or perceived insults. Dictator guards are bullies.

3   Dictator guards may have sadistic personalities and gain ego satisfaction through feelings of near omnipotence, which come from the total control of others. Some may be fundamentally insecure and employ a false bravado to hide their fear of inmates. Officers who fit the dictator category are the most likely to be targeted for vengeance should control of the institution temporarily fall into the hands of the inmates.

The Friend

4   Friendly officers try to fraternize with inmates. They approach the issue of control by trying to be "one of the guys." They seem to believe that they can win inmate cooperation by being nice. Unfortunately, such guards do not recognize that fraternization quickly leads to unending requests for special favors—from delivering mail to bending "minor" prison rules. Once a few rules have been bent, the officer may find that inmates have the upper hand through the potential for blackmail.

5   Many officers have amiable relationships with inmates. In most cases, however, affability is only a convenience that both sides recognize can quickly evaporate. "Friendly officers," as the term is being used here, are *overly* friendly. They may be young and inexperienced. On the other hand, they may simply be possessed of kind and idealistic personalities built on successful friendships in free society.

The Merchant

6   Contraband could not exist in any correctional facility without the merchant officer. The merchant participates in the inmate economy, supplying drugs, pornography, alcohol, and sometimes even weapons to inmates who can afford to pay for them.

7   Probably only a very few officers consistently perform the role of merchant, although a far larger proportion may occasionally turn a few dollars by smuggling some item through the gate. Low salaries create the potential for mercantile corruption among many otherwise "straight-arrow" officers. Until salaries rise substantially, the merchant will remain an institutionalized feature of most prisons.

The Turnkey

8   The turnkey officer cares little for what goes on in the prison setting. Officers who fit this category may be close to retirement, or they may be alienated from their jobs for various reasons. Low pay, the view that inmates are basically "worthless" and incapable of changing, and the monotonous

ethic of "doing time" all combine to numb the professional consciousness of even young officers.

9   The term *turnkey* comes from prison argot where it means a guard who is there just to open and shut doors and who cares about nothing other than getting through his or her shift. Inmates do not see the turnkey as a threat, nor is such an officer likely to challenge the status quo in institutions where merchant guards operate.

The Climber

10   The climber is apt to be a young officer with an eye for promotion. Nothing seems impossible to the climber, who probably hopes eventually to be warden or program director or to hold some high-status position within the institutional hierarchy. Climbers are likely to be involved in schooling, correspondence courses, and professional organizations. They may lead a movement toward unionization for correctional personnel and tend to see the guard's role as a profession that should receive greater social recognition.

11   Climbers have many ideas. They may be heavily involved in reading about the latest confinement or administrative technology. If so, they will suggest many ways to improve prison routine, often to the consternation of complacent staff members. Like the turnkey, climbers turn a blind eye toward inmates and their problems. They are more concerned with improving institutional procedures and with their own careers than they are with the treatment or day-to-day control of inmates.

The Reformer

12   The reformer is the "do-gooder" among officers, the person who believes that prison should offer opportunities for personal change. The reformer tends to lend a sympathetic ear to the personal needs of inmates and is apt to offer armchair counseling and suggestions. Many reformers are motivated by personal ideals, and some of them are highly religious. Inmates tend to see the reformer guard as naive but harmless. Because the reformer actually tries to help, even when help is unsolicited, he or she is the most likely of all the guard types to be accepted by prisoners.

13   Correctional officers have generally been accorded low occupational status. Historically, the role of prison guard required minimal formal education and held few opportunities for professional growth and career advancement. Such jobs were typically low paying, frustrating, and often boring. Growing problems in our nation's prisons, including emerging

issues of legal liability, however, increasingly require a well-trained and adequately equipped force of professionals. As correctional personnel have become better trained and more proficient, the old concept of guard has been supplanted by that of correctional officer. Thus, many states and a growing number of large-city correctional systems make efforts to eliminate individuals with potentially harmful personality characteristics from correctional officer applicant pools.

PRACTICE 5

1. What is the topic of this essay? _____

2. What are the main characteristics of the following types of guards?

   a. the dictator _____

   _____

   b. the friend _____

   _____

   c. the merchant _____

   _____

   d. the turnkey _____

   _____

   e. the climber _____

   _____

   f. the reformer _____

   _____

3. What is the writer's purpose? Circle your answer.

   a. to entertain   b. to persuade   c. to inform

4. Consider the order in which the guards are listed. Think of another effective way to organize the guards, and list them in order here.

   Organizational method: _____

   a. _____   c. _____   e. _____

   b. _____   d. _____   f. _____

READING LINK MORE CLASSIFICATION READINGS

"Types of Rioters" by David Locher (page 525)

"Living Environments" by Avi Friedman (page 535)

**WRITING LINK
MORE
CLASSIFICATION
WRITING TOPICS**

Chapter 22,
    Writer's Room
    topic 1
    (page 333)
Chapter 26,
    Writer's Room
    topic 2
    (page 367)
Chapter 29,
    Writer's Room
    topic 2
    (page 407)
Chapter 34,
    Writer's Room
    topic 1
    (page 465)
Chapter 37,
    Writer's Room
    topic 2
    (page 497)

MyWritingLab™

THE WRITER'S ROOM

Writing Activity 1: Topics

Choose any of the following topics, or choose your own topic, and write
a classification essay. Determine your classification principle, and make
sure that your categories do not overlap.

General Topics

Categories of . . .

1. computer users
2. useful Web sites
3. weight-loss methods
4. neighbors
5. reality shows

College and Work-Related Topics

Categories of . . .

6. electronic modes of
   communication
7. help professions
8. success
9. work environments
10. customers

Writing Activity 2: Media Writing

Watch a television show or movie that
deals with crime. There are many possible
television programs, such as *Law & Order:
SVU*, *Castle*, or *Dexter*. Examples of crime
movies are *When Corruption Was King*,
Michael Clayton, and *The Godfather*. In
an essay, divide crime fighters or criminals
into categories or describe different types of
crimes. Use examples to support your ideas.

Checklist: Classification Essay

After you write your classification essay, review the checklist at the back of the book. Also, ask yourself these questions.

- [ ] Does my thesis statement explain the categories that I will discuss?
- [ ] Do I use a common classification principle to unite the various items?
- [ ] Do I offer sufficient details to explain each category?
- [ ] Do I arrange the categories in a logical manner?
- [ ] Does all of the supporting information relate to the categories that I am discussing?
- [ ] Do I include categories that do not overlap?
- [ ] Does my essay make a point and say something meaningful?

12 Comparison and Contrast

When you plan to move to a new place, you compare the features of different houses or apartments to help you make a decision. When you write a comparison and contrast essay, you examine two or more items and make conclusions about them.

WRITERS' EXCHANGE

What were your goals as a child? What are your goals as an adult? Think about work, money, and family. Compare your answers with those of a partner, and discuss how childhood goals are different from adult goals.

▶ **EXPLORING**

What Is Comparison and Contrast?

LO1 Define comparison and contrast.

When you want to decide between options, you compare and contrast. You **compare** to find similarities and **contrast** to find differences. The exercise of comparing and contrasting can help you make judgments about things. It can also help you to better understand familiar things.

People use comparison and contrast in their daily lives. For instance, at home, you might explain to your father why a laptop is more useful than a desktop computer. At college, students often compare two courses. In workplaces, salespeople compare their new products with competing products to highlight the differences.

Visualizing Comparison and Contrast

PRACTICE 1

Brainstorm supporting ideas for the following thesis statement. Write some benefits of each type of sport on the lines provided.

THESIS STATEMENT: Team sports provide different benefits than solo sports.

Team sports   Solo sports

_____   _____

_____   _____

_____   _____

LO2 Define the purpose of the comparison and contrast essay.

The Comparison and Contrast Essay

In a comparison and contrast essay, you can compare and contrast two different subjects, or you can compare and contrast different aspects of a single subject. When you write using this essay pattern, remember to think about your specific purpose.

* Your purpose could be to make judgments about two items. For example, you might compare and contrast two cars to convince your readers that one is preferable.

* Your purpose could be to describe or understand two familiar things. For example, you might compare two movies to help your readers understand their thematic similarities.

MyWritingLab™

Access the interactive "At Work" paragraphs in MyWritingLab

The **topic sentence** states the topic and controlling idea.

The **supporting sentences** provide details and examples.

The **concluding sentence** brings the paragraph to a satisfactory close.

COMPARISON AND CONTRAST **AT WORK**

Eric Hollymead works in public relations. In the next memo, he compares two job candidates. To respect each person's privacy, he has numbered the candidates.

Topic-by-topic

> Although both candidates have the required education, Candidate 1 has qualities that will make her a better fit for this company. Her sales experience is more relevant to our industry. She also has good social skills, so the clients will like her. In her reference letters, notice that she is called a good "team player," which is what we need. Candidate 2 has worked in sales, but in the garment industry, not in high tech. He was quite nervous, and he may not be at ease with clients. On the other hand, he was thoughtful, and his questions showed that he is learning about the business. I also appreciate his sense of humor. Perhaps we should keep his résumé on file in case a second position opens up. Both candidates were good, but right now we should go with Candidate 1.

Comparison and Contrast Patterns

Comparison and contrast essays follow two common patterns.

Point by Point Present one point about Topic A and then present the same point about Topic B. Keep following this pattern until you have a few points for each topic. Go back and forth from one side to the other like tennis players hitting a ball back and forth across a net.

Topic by Topic Present all of your points about one topic, and then present all of your points about the second topic. Offer one side and then the other side, just as opposing lawyers would do in the closing arguments of a court case.

Marina's Example

Marina is trying to decide whether she would prefer a part-time job in a clothing store or in a restaurant. Marina can organize her information using a topic-by-topic pattern or a point-by-point method.

Thesis Statement: The clothing store is a better place to work than the restaurant.

Point-by-Point Comparison	**Topic-by-Topic Comparison** *Everything*
Topic sentence: Salaries	Topic sentence: Job A
Job A	◆ salary
Job B	◆ hours
Topic sentence: Working hours	◆ working environment
Job A	Topic sentence: Job B
Job B	◆ salary
Topic sentence: Working environments	◆ hours
Job A	◆ working environment
Job B	

A Student Essay

Read the student essay, and answer the questions that follow.

Swamps and Pesticides

Corey Kaminska

1   Having had many jobs in my twenty-two years, I have realized some jobs are a good experience, but many jobs turn into a horrible nightmare. I have also realized that every job has some good points. My favorite all-time job was working as a mosquito abater, and my worst was being a Crystal Hot Springs campground janitor.

2   In my best job, I worked for the Box Elder Mosquito Abatement District, and I had a very exciting routine. This may sound like an odd job, and I would not blame anyone for thinking so. I began my day by walking into the modern abatement building. I drooled over the fancy trucks and four-wheelers that would be mine for the summer. Each morning, the abatement crew met in the conference room to discuss the day's duties. We were then set free to protect the citizens of Box Elder County.

3   Being a mosquito abater was a laid-back and pleasant job. I could work alone while enjoying the outdoors and having fun at the same time. Each day, I gathered my pesticides and supplies. I tossed the chemicals into my 2005 Chevy extended cab, and then I traveled the vast countryside for the

day. Pulling my new Honda Rancher on the trailer behind, I searched for a spot where mosquito larvae might be. Then I unloaded my four-wheeler off the trailer and drove through the mucky swamp looking for the perfect spot to start treating the unpleasant larvae-infested water. When I finally found the tiny worm-like creatures swimming on top of the water, the fun began. I turned on my hopper, which spread sand-like granules into the water and killed the larvae. Bogging through the swampy water on the four-wheeler was something I would have done for fun, but now I was getting paid for it.

4   On the other hand, my job as a Crystal Springs campground janitor was horrible in almost every way. As a janitor, I would begin my day by waking up exceptionally early. Arriving at Crystal Springs, the first thing I had to do was clean out the empty pools and hot tubs. That was a nasty experience. Cleaning up human filth that lingers in the pools until evening and then sticks to the walls as the pool drains is not an appealing task. Scrubbing the walls of the pool for hours is a boring nightmare. The only thing that made it worse was the constant smell from the dairy farm directly across the street. After cleaning out the pools and refilling them with fresh water, I was required to clean out the men's and women's locker rooms. During the cleaning, I often found disgusting items. The work was boring, and the pay was horrible.

5   Although there were drastic differences between my best and my worst job, I discovered some surprising similarities. Both jobs taught me that work is work and money is money. In each job, I helped other people and made their lives just a little bit more enjoyable. I also learned that life is not always about me. Although I was not really appreciated in either job, I learned to recognize my own value. If the job had not been done, people would have suffered the consequences. They would have lived with more mosquitoes, and they would have seen the filth in the pool, hot tubs, and locker rooms.

PRACTICE 2

1. Highlight the thesis statement.

2. Highlight the topic sentences in paragraphs 2, 3, and 4.

3. What pattern of comparison does the writer follow in the entire essay?
   a. point by point   b. topic by topic

4. In paragraphs 2, 3, and 4, what does the writer focus on?
   a. similarities   b. differences

5. List the main advantages of the mosquito abater job.

   _____

   _____

6. List reasons why the janitor job was horrible.

_____

_____

_____

7. In the conclusion, the writer mentions some similarities. Use your own words to list the main similarities.

_____

_____

Explore Topics

In the Writer's Desk Warm Up, you will try an exploring strategy to generate ideas about different topics.

LO 3 Explore topics for a comparison and contrast essay.

THE WRITER'S DESK **Warm Up**

Read the following questions, and write the first ideas that come to your mind. Think of two to three ideas for each topic.

EXAMPLE: What are some key differences between girls' and boys' toys?

girls' toys	boys' toys
—pastel colors	—noisy
—stuffed animals	—toy cars, trucks, fire engines
—dolls with clothes	—action figures

1. What are some key features of high school and college?

high school	college

2. What are the key features of your generation and your parents' generation?

your generation	your parents' generation

3. What are some key features of a celebrity and a hero?

celebrity   hero

_____   _____

_____   _____

_____   _____

LO 4 Write the
thesis statement
of a comparison
and contrast
statement.

The Thesis Statement

In a comparison and contrast essay, the thesis statement indicates what you are comparing and contrasting, and it expresses a controlling idea. For example, the following thesis statement indicates that the essay will compare the myths and reality of mold to prove that it does not seriously threaten human health.

Common household mold is not as dangerous as many people believe.

PRACTICE 3

Read each thesis statement, and then answer the questions that follow. State whether the essay would focus on similarities or differences.

1. The weather in our region is more extreme than it was in the past.

    a. What is being compared? _____

    b. What is the controlling idea? _____

    c. What will the essay focus on?   _____ similarities   _____ differences

2. In our city, the newcomers and the older inhabitants share similar values.

    a. What is being compared? _____

    b. What is the controlling idea? _____

    c. What will the essay focus on?   _____ similarities   _____ differences

3. Before marriage, people expect to feel eternally lustful toward their "soul mate," but the reality of married life is quite different.

    a. What is being compared? _____

    b. What is the controlling idea? _____

    _____

    c. What will the essay focus on?   _____ similarities   _____ differences

VOCABULARY BOOST

Some prefixes mean "not" and give words opposite meanings. Examples are *il-*, *im-*, *in-*, *dis-*, *un-*, *non-*, and *ir-*. Create opposites by adding prefixes to the following words.

EXAMPLE: ___un___ available

1. _____ legal
2. _____ polite
3. _____ toxic
4. _____ appropriate
5. _____ approve
6. _____ considerate
7. _____ reliable
8. _____ harmed
9. _____ reversible
10. _____ necessary
11. _____ patient
12. _____ agree

THE WRITER'S DESK Write Thesis Statements

For each topic, write a thesis statement that includes what you are comparing and contrasting and a controlling idea.

EXAMPLE: Topic: girls' and boys' toys

Thesis statement: *Both girls' and boys' toys reinforce gender stereotypes.*

1. Topic: key features of high school and college

Thesis statement: _____

_____

_____

2. Topic: two generations

Thesis statement: _____

_____

_____

3. Topic: a celebrity versus a hero

Thesis statement: _____

_____

_____

LO 5 Generate the supporting ideas of a comparison and contrast essay.

The Supporting Ideas

After you have developed an effective thesis statement, generate supporting ideas. In a comparison and contrast essay, think of examples that help to clarify the similarities or differences, and then incorporate some ideas in your final essay plan.

To generate supporting ideas, you might try using a Venn diagram. In this example, you can see how the writer draws two circles to compare traditional boys' and girls' toys and how some ideas fall into both categories.

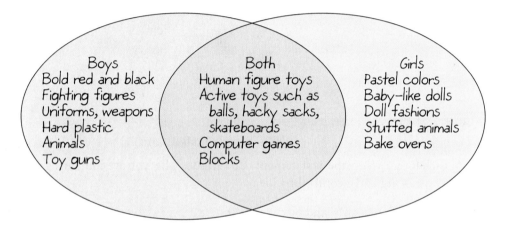

Boys
Bold red and black
Fighting figures
Uniforms, weapons
Hard plastic
Animals
Toy guns

Both
Human figure toys
Active toys such as
  balls, hacky sacks,
  skateboards
Computer games
Blocks

Girls
Pastel colors
Baby-like dolls
Doll fashions
Stuffed animals
Bake ovens

THE WRITER'S DESK **Develop Supporting Ideas**

Choose one of your thesis statements from the previous Writer's Desk. List some similarities and differences.

The Essay Plan

LO 6 Develop a comparison and contrast essay plan.

Before you write a comparison and contrast essay, make a detailed essay plan. Decide which pattern you will follow: point by point or topic by topic. Then add supporting details. Make sure that each detail supports the thesis statement. Also think about the best way to organize your ideas.

Thesis Statement: Both girls' and boys' toys reinforce gender stereotypes.

Point by Point

A/B Girls' toys focus on activities in the home, whereas boys' toys focus on outside activities. Details: Girls have dollhouses and baking ovens whereas boys have carpenter sets and racecars.

A/B Girls' toys focus on physical appearance, and boys' toys focus on heroic fighters. Details: Girls dress their Barbie dolls, and they put on child-friendly makeup. Boys have action figures such as GI Joes and superheroes.

Topic by Topic

A Girls' toys reinforce the importance of looks, body image, and fashion. Details: They receive fashion dolls with clothing, shoes, and other accessories.

A Girls' toys encourage nurturing by focusing on home and family. Details: They have dolls with baby bottles, baking ovens, toy vacuums, and shopping carts.

B Boys' toys prepare them for creative careers and activities outside the home. Details: Boys have little workshops, Lego sets, and toy cars and trucks.

B Boys' toys encourage boys to be heroes in their fantasy games. Details: Boys receive action figures such as GI Joe, X-Men, and Superman.

THE WRITER'S DESK **Write an Essay Plan**

Refer to the information you generated in previous Writer's Desks, and prepare a detailed essay plan using a point-by-point or topic-by-topic pattern. You can use the letters A and B to indicate which side you are discussing in your plan. Include details about each supporting idea.

LO 7 Write the first draft of a comparison and contrast essay.

The First Draft

After you outline your ideas in an essay plan, you are ready to write the first draft. Remember to follow the topic-by-topic or the point-by-point pattern you used in your plan. Write complete sentences and use transitions to help your ideas flow smoothly. The following transitions can be helpful for guiding readers through a comparison and contrast essay.

To show similarities		To show differences	
additionally	in addition	conversely	nevertheless
at the same time	in the same way	however	on the contrary
equally	similarly	in contrast	then again

THE WRITER'S DESK Write the First Draft

Write the first draft of your comparison and contrast essay. Before you write, carefully review your essay plan to see if you have enough support for your points and topics. Flesh out each body paragraph with specific details.

▶ REVISING AND EDITING

LO 8 Revise and edit a comparison and contrast essay.

Revise and Edit a Comparison and Contrast Essay

When you finish writing a comparison and contrast essay, carefully review your work and revise it to make sure that the comparison or contrast is as clear as possible to your readers. Check that you have organized your essay logically, and remove any irrelevant details. Before you work on your own essay, practice revising and editing a student essay.

A Student Essay

Read the essay, and then answer the questions that follow. As you read, correct any errors that you find, and make comments in the margins.

GENDER AND TOYS

Ashley Lincoln

1.　　As a young mother, I try to avoid gender stereotyping my children. I encourage my five-year-old daughter to play sports, and I bought my son a baby doll when he asked for one. My friends been saying they have the same concerns about gender roles. But insulating children from male or female role expectations is almost impossible. Most parents, in spite of their best efforts, reinforce gender stereotypes every time they shop for toys.

2.   Girls' toys reinforce the importance of looks, body image, and fashion. Parents can buy their daughters makeup sets that include child-friendly lipstick, blush, and eye shadow. Barbies and other fashion dolls fill store shelves. Hanging next to the dolls are packages with tiny clothing. Of course, none of the dolls are pudgy, pimply, large-boned, or just plain unattractive. When girls play with these toys, they are taught that beauty and the right clothes and makeup are very important.

3.   If a little girl does not like fashion toys, they will surely enjoy baby dolls with their fake bottles of milk, soft little blankets, and strollers. Girls' toys encourage nurturing by focusing on the home and the family. At a very young age, girls learn to be competent mothers when they change the little diapers of their dolls. Girls can learn to cook with their Easy-Bake ovens, and they learn to shop with tiny shopping carts and cash registers. My daughter and her friends love playing "house" with one child acting as the mother. They shop for toy groceries and feed their "babies." Girls learn about the importance of parenting quicker than boys do.

4.   Boys' toys, on the other hand, stress jobs and activities outside the home. My son begged for, and received, a miniature workshop complete with a plastic saw, drill, screwdriver, and wrench. Lego sets prepare boys for creative occupations such as architecture and auto design. Computer and video games prepare boys for jobs in the high-tech industries. Finally, there is a lot of toy cars, trucks, and racetracks to remind boys that cars are very important to their identities.

5.   Toys aimed at young males also permit boys to be the heroes in their fantasy games. In the boys' aisle of the toy store, there are rows of action figures. The GI Joes fight soldiers from other armies. Batman, Superman, and the X-Men fight fantasy villains. Curiously, the X-Men figures include female characters such as Storm, but the toys are not call "X-People." Aimed predominantly at boys, fighting action figures bolster ideas boys have about rescuing others. In their fantasy lives, boys learn early on that they are the heroes and the saviors.

6.   Some suggest that it is useless to fight against the male and female roles. They point out that girls in previous centuries made their own dolls out of straw and rags, and boys made weapons out of tin cans and wood. While that is true, toy stores take the stereotyping to extremes. One solution is to try to buy gender-neutral toys such as modeling clay, painting supplies, or balls and other sporting equipment.

PRACTICE 4

Revising

1. Highlight the thesis statement.

2. Highlight the topic sentence in each body paragraph.

3. Circle a transitional word or phrase in the topic sentence of paragraph 4. Then add transitional words or phrases to the other topic sentences.

4. What pattern does the writer use to organize this essay? Circle your response.

    a. point by point   b. topic by topic

5. The student writer uses the word "reinforce" at the end of the introduction and in the first sentence of the second paragraph. To avoid repeating the same word, what synonym could the student use?

    _____

GRAMMAR LINK
See the following chapters for more information about these grammar topics:

Subject–Verb Agreement, Chapter 27
Passive Voice, Chapter 28
Verbs, Chapter 29
Pronouns, Chapter 31
Adjectives and Adverbs, Chapter 32

Editing

6. Underline the verb error in the introduction. Write the correction on the line.

    Correction: _____

7. Underline and correct the pronoun–antecedent error in paragraph 3.

    Correction: _____
    _____

8. Underline and correct a comparative form error in paragraph 3. (For more information about comparative errors, see the Grammar Hint on the next page.)

    Correction: _____
    _____

9. Underline and correct the subject–verb agreement error in paragraph 4.

    Correction: _____

10. Underline and correct the passive verb that has been incorrectly formed in paragraph 5. (See page 388 in Chapter 28 for a definition of passive verbs.)

    Correction: _____

GRAMMAR HINT ◄ Comparing Adjectives and Adverbs

When comparing or contrasting two items, ensure that you have correctly written your comparative forms. For instance, never put *more* with an adjective ending in *-er*.

City life is ~~more~~ better than country life.

If you are comparing two actions, remember to use an adverb instead of an adjective.

more easily

Children learn lessons ~~easier~~ when they are treated with respect.

THE WRITER'S DESK   Revise and Edit Your Essay

Revise and edit the essay that you wrote for the previous Writer's Desk. You can refer to the revising and editing checklists at the end of this chapter and at the end of the book.

A Professional Essay

Matthew Fraser, a professor at the American University of Paris, is also an author of several books and a blogger. In this next essay, he uses the comparison and contrast writing pattern. Read the essay, and answer the questions that follow.

Viral Vigilantes

Matthew Fraser

1   In August 2010, Mary Bale, a dowdy middle-aged English woman, committed a baffling and senseless act. While walking down a residential street in Coventry, she saw a cat. After caressing it and picking it up, she flung the animal inside a large plastic garbage can, closing the lid on the tabby. Fifteen hours later, Darryl Mann—the cat's owner—heard his pet's distressed meows and rescued it. Mann had two closed-circuit cameras in front of his house that captured Bale's gesture on video. Soon, the video was viral, and Bale had been named and shamed. In the past, "Big Brother" surveillance was done by states and institutions, but today, digitally mediated "Little Brother" surveillance puts everyone on a level playing field.

Kafkaesque: nightmarish and surreal (from the writing of Franz Kafka)

2   In past centuries, only states, corporations, and large **Kafkaesque** bureaucracies were able to marshal the resources needed to monitor the actions of individuals. The function of surveillance was to encourage people to behave according to established expectations because they always imagined that they were being watched. Historically, rulers relied on paid snitches to spy on the population. Later, espionage networks were highly developed in the former Soviet Union and Eastern European nations. Under constant scrutiny, citizens learned to passively accept that government-controlled surveillance was in place. It was never a two-way process: individuals had no capacity to monitor states and corporations.

3   In the twentieth century, states adopted high-tech surveillance, which was a more subtle method of enforcement aimed at controlling people's minds and habits. In 1960, authorities installed one of the first public security cameras in London's Trafalgar Square. Later, in the 1970s and 1980s, nations expanded the usage of closed-circuit television cameras to spy on lawbreakers and possible terrorists. Great Britain is the country with the most surveillance cameras in the world. Thus, even in free and democratic societies, it is impossible to escape some form of video detection—in parking lots, office corridors, at bank machines—during the banal course of a normal day. Most of us have watched television news footage from a CCTV video taken of a traffic accident or a bank robbery. Until the 1990s, even such high-tech surveillance was largely unidirectional, with the powerful spying on the powerless.

4   Today states and institutions no longer possess a monopoly on surveillance as a form of coercion. Social media like Google, YouTube, Facebook, and Twitter offer radically new, and efficient, techniques of surveillance. Ordinary citizens are able to look into spheres that once were opaque or impenetrable; thus, surveillance now occurs in both directions: from the top down and from the bottom up. Employers, teachers, and politicians have been publically humiliated because misconduct was caught on a cell phone camera. Furthermore, social media played a pivotal role during the Arab uprisings of early 2011, when citizens captured police or army misconduct on cell phones. Thanks to the Web, citizens can now monitor and hold to account the states that govern their lives.

5   Today, citizens can also spy on each other. Online social networks make everything and everyone visible—from our "likes" on Facebook to photos posted on Flickr. What's more, the viral distribution dynamics of the Web—notably on YouTube—can make everything visible instantly and globally. Online social networks function to enforce social norms—not by top-down institutional surveillance but through horizontally networked monitoring.

6   Digitally mediated surveillance can lead to a troubling form of viral vigilantism. Anyone with a mobile device can report—and even film—deviant actions in real time. In the Mary Bale case, the feedback was

explosive. The video of her act instantly went viral on YouTube, and almost immediately, Bale was recognized and shamed. Questioned by a TV reporter on the pavement as she was fleeing the media, Bale made the mistake of retorting, "It's just a cat." Within days, Darryl Mann's video was being played on TV newscasts around the world. The Royal Society for the Prevention of Cruelty to Animals became involved. Bale was dubbed the "the most evil woman in Britain," and an anti-Bale page on Facebook rapidly attracted twenty thousand fans. While the tabby cat's ordeal lasted only fifteen hours, Mary Bale isn't likely to recover from the explosive reaction to the YouTube video that turned her into one of the most hated people in Britain.

7   The strange story of the Cat-Bin Lady provides an alarming illustration of how the dynamics of surveillance have been radically transformed by social media. We will never know why Mary Bale flung Lola into the **rubbish bin**, but the Cat-Bin Lady saga has demonstrated the coercive power of "Little Brother" and its role in the enforcement of social norms. Today we must accept that everything we do, including our smallest gestures, risks being exposed by some form of intrusive surveillance. As Mary Bale discovered, nobody can hide; someone is watching.

rubbish bin: British term for garbage can

PRACTICE 5

1. Highlight the thesis statement.

2. Underline the topic sentences in paragraphs 2 through 6.

3. The author compares and contrasts several things in this essay. List some of them.

_____

_____

_____

4. This essay refers to "Big Brother" and "Little Brother." The term "Big Brother," which was first used by George Orwell in his book *1984*, refers to a state or organization that can monitor and control citizens' lives. What does "Little Brother" refer to? Make a guess based on the information in the essay.

_____

_____

5. Why was the reaction to Mary Bale's act so intense? Make two or three inferences or guesses.

_____

_____

_____

_____

6. Define the following three types of surveillance. For each definition, provide a specific example.

Top down: _____

_____

_____

Bottom up: _____

_____

_____

Horizontal: _____

_____

_____

7. This essay compares and contrasts two things, but it also presents an argument in paragraphs 6 and 7. What is the argument?

_____

_____

_____

_____

MyWritingLab™

Complete these writing assignments at mywritinglab.com

READING LINK

MORE COMPARISON AND CONTRAST READINGS

"The Untranslatable Word 'Macho'" by Rose del Castillo Guilbault (page 575)

"The Happiness Factor" by David Brooks (page 582)

MyWritingLab™

THE WRITER'S ROOM

Writing Activity 1: Topics

Choose any of the following topics, or choose your own topic, and write a comparison and contrast essay.

General Topics

Compare or contrast . . .

1. two types of music
2. an early bird and a night owl
3. a male and a female friend
4. two characters from film or fiction
5. two common phobias

College and Work-Related Topics

Compare or contrast . . .

6. courage versus recklessness
7. living on campus versus living off campus
8. being self-employed versus working for others
9. online classes and traditional classes
10. expectations about a job versus the reality of the job

Writing Activity 2: Media Writing

Compare and contrast two characters or two life stages. Watch a television soap opera or a drama such as *House of Cards* or *Parenthood* or a movie such as *An Education*, *The Namesake*, or *Winter's Bone*. In an essay, you can compare and contrast two life stages, such as childhood and adulthood or adolescence and old age. You can also choose to compare and contrast two characters in the television show or movie.

WRITING LINK

MORE COMPARISON AND CONTRAST WRITING TOPICS
Chapter 20, Writer's Room topic 2 (page 312)
Chapter 23, Writer's Room topic 2 (page 342)
Chapter 27, Writer's Room topic 2 (page 378)
Chapter 32, Writer's Room topic 1 (page 443)
Chapter 38, Writer's Room topic 2 (page 506)

Checklist: Comparison and Contrast

After you write your comparison and contrast essay, review the checklist at the end of the book. Also, ask yourself the following set of questions.

☐ Does my thesis statement explain what I am comparing and contrasting?

☐ Does my thesis statement make a point about the comparison?

☐ Does my essay have a point-by-point or topic-by-topic pattern?

☐ Does my essay focus on similarities or on differences?

☐ Do all of my supporting examples clearly relate to the topics that I am comparing or contrasting?

13 Cause and Effect

When a flood occurs, people ask themselves, "How did this happen?" and "What is the extent of the damage?" Writers use the cause and effect pattern to explain the answers to these types of questions.

WRITERS' EXCHANGE

Work with a group of students. Each group has two minutes to brainstorm as many reasons as possible to explain why people follow fashion fads. Then, each team will have two minutes to explain the effects of following fashion fads. The team with the most causes and effects wins.

What Is Cause and Effect?

LO 1 Define cause and effect.

Cause and effect writing explains why an event happened or what the consequences of such an event were. A cause and effect essay can focus on causes, effects, or both.

People often analyze the causes or effects of something. At home, a teenager might explain to her parents why she had a car accident. At college, an administrator may be asked to give reasons for the lack of student housing on campus. At work, a boss might clarify the reasons for company downsizing to employees.

Visualizing Cause and Effect

PRACTICE 1

Brainstorm supporting ideas for the following thesis statement. Write some details on the lines provided.

THESIS STATEMENT: A shopping addiction has some serious effects.

_____   _____   _____

_____   _____   _____

_____   _____   _____

_____   _____   _____

L02 Define
the purpose of a
cause and effect
essay.

The Cause and Effect Essay

When you write a cause and effect essay, focus on two main tasks.

1. **Indicate whether you are focusing on causes, effects, or both.** If you do decide to focus on both causes and effects, make sure that your thesis statement indicates your purpose to the reader.
2. **Make sure that your causes and effects are valid.** You should determine real causes and effects and not simply list things that happened before or after the event. Also, verify that your assumptions are logical.

Illogical	Our furnace stopped working because the weather was too cold. (This is illogical; cold weather cannot stop a furnace from working.)
Better	Our furnace stopped working because the filters needed replacing and the gas burners needed adjusting.

MyWritingLab™

**Access the interactive
"At Work" paragraphs
in MyWritingLab**

The **topic
sentence**
states the topic
and controlling
idea.

The **supporting
sentences**
provide details
and examples.

The
**concluding
sentence**
brings the
paragraph to
a satisfactory
close.

CAUSE AND EFFECT **AT WORK**

In a petition to stop the expansion of an airport, Green Hills townspeople explain the effects of noise pollution on their quality of life.

   If the airport expands, increasing noise pollution would significantly alter the quality of life for our community. First, we may not be able to enjoy daily activities, such as outdoor barbecues, garden parties, or relaxing in our yards if noise increases. Next, excessive noise may affect our health. Research has shown that noise pollution can in some instances lead to hypertension, hearing loss, and sleep disruption. In addition, we may also suffer psychological effects such as stress and annoyance. Therefore, we must ensure that the expansion of the airport is stopped.

A Student Essay

Read the student essay, and answer the questions that follow.

College Students and the Challenge of Credit Card Debt

Katie Earnest

1   Did you know that most college students carry credit card debt? In fact, according to a Nelli Mae study, three out of four students have an outstanding balance of $2,200. My son maxed out three different credit cards by the time he was in the second semester of his junior year. He couldn't keep up with his monthly payments to the credit card companies

anymore, even though he had a part-time job on campus and a part-time job off campus. Students get into credit card debt for a variety of reasons.

2   Credit card companies have clever ways to promote their products to students. Anyone who is at least eighteen years old can get a credit card without parental consent or any source of income. According to the *Daily Emerald*, one of the many ways that major credit card companies take advantage of this situation is to offer universities generous monetary donations in exchange for the full rights to market their cards on campus. Credit card companies distribute brochures or flyers around campus, and set up a booth offering free gifts to college students if they fill out a card application. Another way that credit card companies target college students is by calling them four to five times a month or continuously mailing them card applications.

3   While most college students obtain a credit card with the intention of using it only for emergencies, it doesn't always work out that way. Students start off using their credit card to buy gas, purchase a few groceries, catch a movie, or grab a late night pizza. However, before they know it, they have reached their credit card limit. College students don't realize that fees or penalties will grow because of high interest rates. After maxing out the first credit card, many people will sign up for another credit card, still telling themselves that it will be for emergencies only. The credit card debt spirals out of control. There have been two widely reported cases of college students who took their lives because of their excessive accumulation of credit card debt. According to the *College Student Journal*, one of the students was a twenty-year-old with a debt of $10,000, and the other was a nineteen-year-old with a debt of $2,500.

4   Furthermore, students don't realize how difficult it can be to pay credit card bills. A part-time job may result in a lower than expected salary. Living expenses may be higher than expected. Thus, it is challenging for students to make their monthly payments on time. For example, my son could not keep up with his monthly payments even though he had two part-time jobs. His debt accumulated quickly.

5   In conclusion, credit cards have become a fact of life on college campuses, and they continue to be a temptation for students. College students who carry a high level of credit card debt face financial stress just as my son did. If I had known that card companies solicited students on campus, I would have educated my son about credit card usage, and I would have warned him about the challenges that he would face if he accumulated a large amount of debt.

PRACTICE 2

1. What introductory style does the writer use?

a. general background

b. anecdote

c. definition

d. contrasting position

2. Highlight the thesis statement.

3. Does the thesis statement express causes, effects, or both?

   a. causes   b. effects   c. both

4. Highlight the topic sentences in paragraphs 2, 3, and 4.

5. Using your own words, sum up the causes for student credit card debt.

   _____

   _____

   _____

   _____

   _____

6. What does the writer think she should have done to help her son?

   _____

   _____

LO 3 Explore topics for a cause and effect essay.

Explore Topics

In the Writer's Desk Warm Up, you will try an exploring strategy to generate ideas about different topics.

THE WRITER'S DESK **Warm Up**

Read the following questions, and write the first ideas that come to your mind. Think of two or three ideas for each topic.

EXAMPLE: What are some causes and effects of workplace hostility?

    —jealousy and competition

    —demanding bosses

    —employee burnout

1. What are some causes and effects of workplace romances?

   _____

   _____

   _____

2. What are some causes and effects of bullying?

_____

_____

_____

3. What are causes and effects of being homeless?

_____

_____

_____

▶ DEVELOPING

The Thesis Statement

L0 4 Write the thesis statement of a cause and effect essay.

When writing a thesis statement for a cause and effect essay, clearly demonstrate whether the focus is on causes, effects, or both. Also, make sure that you state a controlling idea that expresses your point of view or attitude.

controlling idea (causes)   topic
There are many reasons for **global warming**.

topic   controlling idea (effects)
Global warming may have a profound influence on our lifestyles.

topic   controlling idea (causes and effects)
Global warming, which has developed for many reasons, may have a profound → very important
influence on our lifestyles.

PRACTICE 3

Look carefully at the following thesis statements. Decide if each sentence focuses on the causes, effects, or both. Look at the key words that give you the clues, and circle the best answer.

1. Poverty persists in developing countries because of lack of education, scarcity of jobs, and corruption of politicians.
   a. causes   b. effects   c. both

2. In our college, the high student dropout rate, which is triggered by the tourist industry, results in long-term problems for the community.
   a. causes   b. effects   c. both

3. The Japanese tsunami has created many problems for the environment.

    a. causes   (b.) effects   c. both

GRAMMAR HINT   *Affect* and *Effect*

Use *affect* as a verb and *effect* as a noun. *Affect* means "to influence or change" and *effect* means "the result."

                                                    verb

How does the ban on fast food in public schools <u>affect</u> children's health?

        noun

What <u>effects</u> will the ban on fast food in public schools have on children's health?

You can also use *effect* as a verb that means "to cause or to bring about a change or implement a plan."

                                       verb

Health care professionals lobbied to <u>effect</u> changes in public school lunch menus.

See Chapter 34 for more information about commonly confused words.

THE WRITER'S DESK   Write Thesis Statements

Write a thesis statement for each of the following topics. You can look for ideas in the previous Writer's Desk. Determine if you will focus on the causes, effects, or both in your essay.

EXAMPLE: Topic: hostile work environment

    Thesis Statement: *A hostile workplace, which can lead to several*
    problems, is often triggered by jealousy or an unpleasant boss.

1. Topic: workplace romance

    Thesis Statement: _____

    _____

2. Topic: bullying

    Thesis Statement: _____

    _____

3. Topic: being homeless

    Thesis Statement: *Has many negative effect*
    on society.

[handwritten: affect – verb / effect – noun]

The Supporting Ideas

After you have developed an effective thesis statement, generate supporting ideas. In a cause and effect essay, think of examples that clearly show the causes or effects. To develop supporting ideas, follow these three steps:

- ◆ Use prewriting strategies such as freewriting and brainstorming to generate ideas.
- ◆ Choose the best ideas. Use examples that clearly reveal the causes and effects.
- ◆ Organize your ideas. Choose the best organizational method for this essay pattern.

HINT ◀ Do Not Oversimplify

Avoid attributing a simple or general cause to a very complex issue. When you use expressions such as *it appears that* or *a possible cause is*, it shows that you are aware of the complex factors involved in the situation.

Oversimplification	Global warming is caused by cars.
Better	One possible cause of global warming is the CO_2 emissions from cars.

[handwritten: Emissions fossil fuel]

Identifying Causes and Effects

Imagine that you had to write a cause and effect essay on gambling. You could brainstorm and think of as many causes and effects as possible.

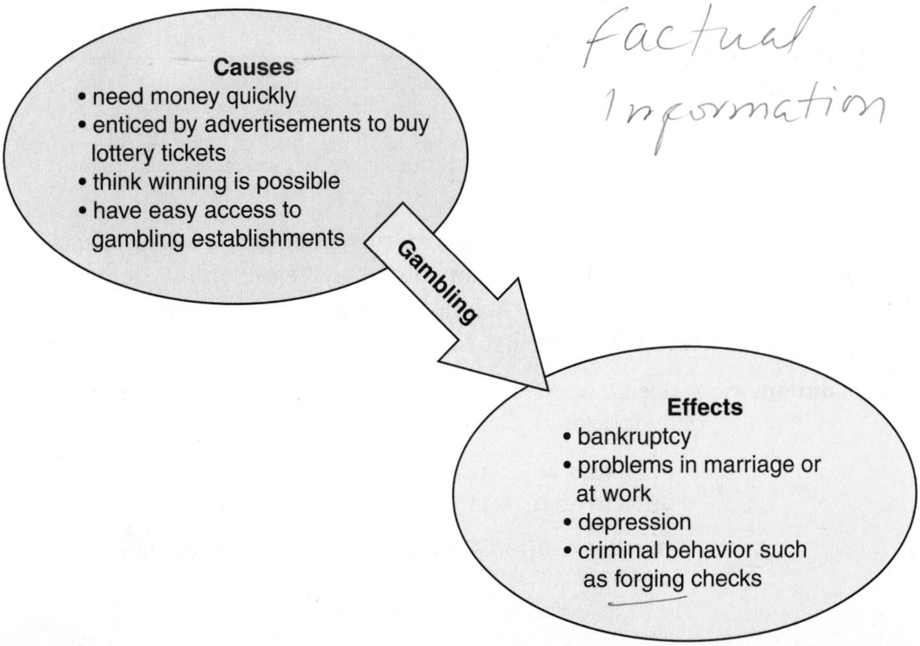

[handwritten: factual Information]

Causes
- need money quickly
- enticed by advertisements to buy lottery tickets
- think winning is possible
- have easy access to gambling establishments

Gambling

Effects
- bankruptcy
- problems in marriage or at work
- depression
- criminal behavior such as forging checks

THE WRITER'S DESK Identify Causes and Effects

Choose the topic of one of the thesis statements from the previous Writer's Desk. Then write some possible causes and effects.

EXAMPLE: Topic: hostile work environment

Causes	Effects
-arrogant employees	-physical problems such as insomnia
-too much work	-psychological problems such as
-jealous coworker	low self-esteem or burnout
-a very strict and demanding boss	-depression
	-diminished quality of life

Focus on: causes

Topic: Global Warming

Causes	Effects
- Pollution	
- Cutting down trees	
-Emissions fossils fuels	
Charcoals	
Carbo monoxide	

Focus on:

LO 6 Develop a cause and effect essay plan.

The Essay Plan

In many courses, instructors ask students to write about the causes or effects of a particular subject. Take the time to plan your essay before you write your first draft. Also, think about how you would logically arrange the order of ideas. As you develop your plan, make sure that you focus on causes, effects, or both.

Thesis Statement: A hostile workplace, which can lead to several problems, is often triggered by employee jealousy or an unpleasant boss.

    I.   A hostile work environment is often caused by employee arrogance or envy.

        A.   Some groups are tight-knit and don't easily accept newcomers.

   B.   Some employees have high opinions of themselves.

   C.   Coworkers may feel jealous of a new employee's expertise.

II.   Another reason for a hostile workplace is a strict boss.

   A.   Some employees may be frightened of a difficult boss.

   B.   Some bosses may overreact if an employee makes a mistake.

   C.   A strict boss generates a lot of stress for employees.

III.   People in stressful workplaces may experience physical and psychological stress.

   A.   Some people may suffer from insomnia.

   B.   Some employees may develop burnout or depression.

THE WRITER'S DESK Write an Essay Plan

Choose one of the ideas that you have developed in previous Writer's Desks, and prepare an essay plan. If you think of new details that will explain your point more effectively, include them in your plan.

The First Draft

LO 7 Write the first draft of a cause and effect essay.

After you have developed and organized your ideas in your essay plan, write the first draft. Remember to write complete sentences and to use transitional words or expressions to help your ideas flow smoothly. Most writers arrange cause and effect essays using emphatic order, which means that they place examples from the most to the least important or from the least to the most important. The following transitional expressions are useful for showing causes and effects.

To show causes	To show effects
for this reason	accordingly
the first cause	as a result
the most important cause	consequently

THE WRITER'S DESK Write the First Draft

Carefully review and, if necessary, revise your essay plan from the previous Writer's Desk, and then write the first draft of your cause and effect essay.

VOCABULARY BOOST

Using inappropriate vocabulary in a particular context can affect the way people respond to you. For example, you would not use street language in a business meeting. Replace the following words with terms that can be used in academic or professional writing.

buddy   guy   kid   chill   stuff   crook

▶ REVISING AND EDITING

LO 8 Revise and edit a cause and effect essay.

Revise and Edit a Cause and Effect Essay

When you finish writing a cause and effect essay, review your work and revise it to make the examples as clear as possible to your readers. Check that you have organized your ideas logically, and remove any irrelevant details. Before you work on your own essay, practice revising and editing a student essay.

A Student Essay

Read the essay, and then answer the questions that follow. As you read, correct any errors that you find, and make comments in the margins.

WORKPLACE HOSTILITY

Emily Dubois

causes.   *Both*

1.   I will always remember the very first day I went to work. I was a little nervous, and I wondered if I would like working in a kitchen. What I dreaded the most was to meet my colleagues. Fortunately, they turned out to be very amiable. However, many people are unlucky because they have uncaring coworkers. A hostile workplace, which can lead to several problems, is often triggered by employee jealousy or an unpleasant boss.

2.   First, a hostile work environment is often caused by arrogance or envy. When a person joins a working team that has been together for a long time, it is normal for that person to initially feel left out. Some groups are tight-knit and don't easily accept a new coworker. For example, my mother once started a new job where everyone was very close. Her coworkers never really tried to

interact with her, and when they did, it was only to criticize. The situation made my mother very uncomfortable, and she quit after two months. Also, some workers have a high opinion of themselves and want to show the new person that they deserve respect because of their superior experience. They may snub newcomers. Additionally, if the new employee has a lot of expertise, a higher salary, and better benefits, then coworkers may feel jealous. Such situations create a negative atmosphere.

3.   Another reason for a hostile workplace is a very strict boss. Some employees are justifiably frightened of their superiors. Of course, employers do not tolerate major mistakes and are bothered when deadlines are not met. However, some bosses overreact because their expectations are too high. For example, in the movie *The Devil Wears Prada*, Meryl Streep acts as Miranda, a terrifying boss. The movie is based on a real-life mean boss, Anna Wintour, the editor of *Vogue*. I have also worked under a nasty boss. At my second job, my manager was frequently in a foul mood and would scream even when I simply dropped a spoon. An angry superior generates a lot of stress for the workers. Colleagues tend to snap at each other instead of working together, and then they start a silent competition to see who can please the boss the most. In the end, employees don't enjoy going to work.

4.   A hostile workplace may cause physical and psychological problems in employees. People in stressful workplaces can experience health problems such as insomnia. A hostile workplace can also impact a worker's self-esteem and lead to burnout. When my mother had spiteful colleagues, she lost her confidence and became depressed. In today's difficult economy, people sometimes remain in hostile workplaces for years simply because they have no choice and cannot find another job. But such people have a diminished quality of life. However, some people in a hostile work environment benefit from doing stress relieving activities. At my work, many of my colleagues take yoga courses.

5.   In conclusion, hostile workplaces are usually caused by peer envy and nightmarish employers. The work experience becomes physically and emotionally draining. Every working environment should be calm and respectful. Perhaps everyone should follow the footsteps of Anne Hathaway's character in *The Devil Wears Prada*, and they should quit if a workplace is too hostile.

PRACTICE 4

Revising

1. Does this essay focus on causes, effects, or both? _____

2. Highlight the thesis statement of the essay.

3. Underline the topic sentences of the body paragraphs 2, 3, and 4.

4. What are some of the causes for workplace hostility?

_____

_____

5. What are some effects of workplace hostility?

Insommia, Depressed

_____

6. Paragraph 4 lacks unity. Cross out any sentences that do not support the topic sentence of the paragraph.

7. What is the introductory style of this essay?

a. historical background   c. an anecdote

b. a definition   d. a contrasting position

GRAMMAR LINK
See the following chapters for more information about these grammar topics:

Subject–Verb Agreement, Chapter 27

Spelling, Chapter 34

Titles, Chapter 37

Editing

8. Circle and correct the misspelled word in paragraph 2.
   Correction: _Environment_____

9. In paragraph 3, the movie title is incorrectly written. Write the title correctly here.
   Correction: _____

10. There is a subject–verb agreement error in paragraph 5. Underline and correct the mistake.
    Correction: _____

THE WRITER'S DESK Revise and Edit Your Essay

Revise and edit the essay that you wrote for the previous Writer's Desk. You can refer to the revising and editing checklists at the end of this chapter and at the end of the book.

A Professional Essay

Ellen Goodman is a Pulitzer Prize–winning columnist for the *Boston Globe*, and her articles appear in more than 370 newspapers. She has also written several books, including *Value Judgments* and *Keeping in Touch*. In the next essay, she examines why North Americans are becoming more isolated socially.

Friendless in North America

Ellen Goodman

1   Lynn Smith-Lovin was listening in the back seat of a taxi when a woman called the radio talk-show hosts to confess her affairs with a new boyfriend and a not-yet-former husband. The hosts, in their best therapeutic voices, offered their on-air opinion, "Give me an S, give me an L, give me a U." You can spell the rest. It was the sort of exchange that would leave most of us wondering why anyone would share her intimate life story with a radio host. Didn't she have anyone else to talk with? Smith-Lovin might have been the only one in the audience with an answer to the question: maybe not.

2   The Duke University sociologist is co-author of one of those blockbuster studies that makes us look at ourselves. This one is labeled "Friendless in America." A face-to-face study of 1,467 adults turned up some disheartening news. One-fourth reported that they have nobody to talk to about "important matters." Another quarter reported they are just one person away from nobody. But this was the most startling fact. The study is a replica of one done twenty years ago. In only two decades, from 1985 to 2004, the number of people who have no one to talk to has doubled. And the number of confidants of the average person has gone down from three to two.

3   The people to whom we are closest form our own informal safety net. They're the ones who see us through a life crisis, lend us their spare bedroom, or pick up our kids at school in a pinch. Social isolation is as big a risk factor for premature death as smoking. Robert Putnam has already chronicled the erosion of the ties that bind in *Bowling Alone*. But we've paid less attention to "coping alone" or "suffering alone." Imagine if some other piece of the social safety net had frayed that furiously. Imagine if income had gone down by a third or divorce doubled or the medical system halved. We would be setting up commissions and organizing rallies.

4   Not everything in the study was gloomy. Deep in the data is the suggestion that families—husbands and wives, parents and adult children—might be closer. Spouses who call each other "my best friend" might be right. We might have fewer intimates, but we're more intimate with them. On average, we see them more than once a week and have known them seven years. Nevertheless, the big news is that circles have tightened, shrunk, and gone nuclear. As Smith-Lovin says, "Literally nothing takes the place of family." The greatest loss has been in neighbors and friends who will provide help, support, advice, and connections to a wider world.

5   There is no shortage of speculation about why our circle of friends is eroding. The usual suspect is the time crunch. It's knocked friendship off the balancing beam of life as we attend to work and family. It's left less time for the groups and associations that bind us. But in the past twenty years, technology has changed the way we use our "relationship time." Walk along any city street and people talking on cell phones are more common than pigeons. Go into Starbucks and a third of the customers are having coffee dates with their laptops. "It could be that talking to people close to us on cell phones has caused our social circle to shrink," says Smith-Lovin. It could be that we are both increasingly in-touch and isolated. It's become easier to keep extensive relationships over time and distance but harder to build the deep ones in our backyard. In the virtual neighborhood, how many have substituted e-mail for intimacy, contacts for confidants, and Facebook for face to face?

6   A few years ago, when my friend Patricia O'Brien and I wrote a book on the power of friendship in women's lives, we noted that there was no official status for friends, no pro-friendship movement, and no cultural or political support system for friends. Yet this voluntary relationship can be the most sustaining one of life.

7   Now we are living in smaller, tighter circles. We are ten degrees of separation from each other and one or two people away from loneliness. And many now outsource intimacy from friends to professional therapists and *gawd* help us, talk shows. Who can we talk to about important matters? Who can we count on? As we search for tools to repair this frayed safety net, we can take poor, paradoxical comfort from the fact that if we are feeling isolated, we are not alone.

PRACTICE 5

1. Who is the audience for this essay? _____

2. The thesis of this essay is not stated directly, but it is implied. Using your own words, write the thesis of this essay.

   _____

   _____

3. Circle the type of introduction Goodman uses.
   a. historical background   b. anecdote   c. general background

4. According to Goodman, why are friends important?

   _____

   _____

   _____

5. In your own words, how have the socialization habits of North Americans changed in the past twenty years?

_____

_____

_____

6. What specific reasons does Goodman give for this social change?

_____

_____

_____

7. Goodman writes, "It could be that we are both increasingly in-touch and isolated." What does she mean?

_____

_____

_____

_____

> **READING LINK**
> **MORE CAUSE AND EFFECT READINGS**
>
> "The *CSI* Effect" by Richard Willing (page 522)
> "Nature Returns to the Cities" by John Roach (page 545)

THE WRITER'S ROOM — MyWritingLab™

MyWritingLab™

Complete these writing assignments at mywritinglab.com

Writing Activity 1: Topics

Write a cause and effect essay about one of the following topics, or choose your own topic.

General Topics

Causes and/or effects of . . .

1. playing a sport
2. getting married
3. a fear of _____
4. road rage
5. a natural phenomenon

College and Work-Related Topics

Causes and/or effects of . . .

6. changing a career
7. becoming successful
8. workplace discrimination
9. learning a skill
10. unemployment

> **WRITING LINK**
> **MORE CAUSE AND EFFECT WRITING TOPICS**
>
> Chapter 22, Writer's Room topic 2 (page 333)
> Chapter 28, Writer's Room topic 2 (page 394)
> Chapter 33, Writer's Room topic 2 (page 452)
> Chapter 35, Writer's Room topic 1 (page 477)

Writing Activity 2: Media Writing

Watch a medical show or movie that deals with health issues. You could watch *House, Nip/Tuck,* or *The Big C.* You can also watch movies such as *Dallas Buyers Club, Erin Brockovich, Angels in America, The Elephant Man,* or *Philadelphia.* Write an essay describing the causes or effects of a physical or mental ailment, and use examples to support your point.

Checklist: Cause and Effect Essay

As you write your cause and effect essay, review the checklist at the end of the book. Also, ask yourself the following questions.

☐ Does my thesis statement indicate clearly that my essay focuses on causes, effects, or both?

☐ Do I have adequate supporting examples of causes and/or effects?

☐ Do I make logical and valid points?

☐ Do I use the terms *effect* and/or *affect* correctly?

Argument 14

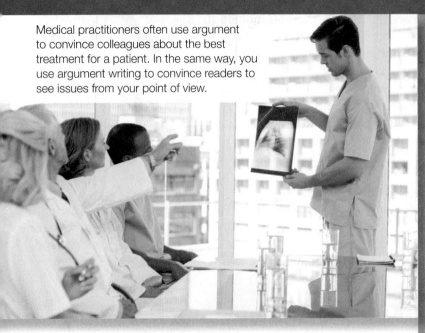

Medical practitioners often use argument to convince colleagues about the best treatment for a patient. In the same way, you use argument writing to convince readers to see issues from your point of view.

WRITERS' EXCHANGE

For this activity, you and a partner will take turns debating an issue. To start, choose which one of you will begin speaking. The first speaker chooses one side of any issue listed below, and then argues about that issue without stopping. When your instructor makes a signal, switch speakers. The second speaker talks nonstop about the opposing view. If you run out of ideas, you can switch topics when it is your turn to speak.

Debate Topics:

The United States should build walls on its northern and southern borders.

It is better to be an only child.

Adolescence is the best time of life.

LO 1 Define argument.

What Is Argument?

When you use **argument**, you take a position on an issue, and you try to prove or defend your position. Using effective argument strategies can help you convince somebody that your point of view is a valid one.

Argument is both a writing pattern and a purpose for writing. In fact, it is one of the most common aims, or purposes, in most college and work-related writing. For example, in Chapter 10, there is an essay called "Journalists Are History's Record Keepers," in which the writer uses definition as the predominant pattern. At the same time, the author uses argument to convince the reader that in addition to reporting the news, journalists have the important role of recording history. Therefore, in most of your college and work-related writing, your purpose is to persuade the reader that your ideas are compelling and legitimate.

People use argument in their daily lives. For instance, at home, you might argue about the distribution of housework, providing examples to support your point. At college, students argue for better equipment in the computer lab or art department. At work, salespeople make well-planned arguments to convince customers to buy a product or service.

Visualizing Argument

PRACTICE 1

Brainstorm supporting ideas for the following thesis statement. Write some details on the lines provided.

THESIS STATEMENT: All college students should learn a second language.

_____   _____   _____

_____   _____   _____

_____   _____   _____

The Argument Essay

LO2 Define the purpose of an argument essay.

When you write an argument essay, remember four key points.

1. **Consider your readers.** What do your readers already know about the topic? Will they be likely to agree or disagree with you? Do they have specific concerns? Consider what kind of evidence would be most effective with your audience.

2. **Know your purpose.** In argument writing, your main purpose is to persuade the reader to agree with you. Your specific purpose is more focused. You may want the reader to take action, you may want to support a viewpoint, you may want to counter somebody else's argument, or you may want to offer a solution to a problem. Ask yourself what your specific purpose is.

3. **Take a strong position, and provide persuasive evidence.** Your thesis statement and your topic sentences should clearly show your point of view. Then back up your point of view with a combination of facts, statistics, examples, and informed opinions.

4. **Show that you are trustworthy.** Respect your readers by making a serious argument. If you are condescending, or if you try to joke about the topic, your readers may be less inclined to accept your argument. You can also help your readers have more respect for your ideas when you choose a topic that you know something about. For example, if you have been in the military or know people in the military, you might be able to make a very convincing argument about the lack of proper equipment for soldiers.

ARGUMENT **AT WORK**

MyWritingLab™

Access the interactive "At Work" paragraphs in MyWritingLab

Network administrator Octavio Pelaez uses argument writing in this excerpt from a memo to his director.

> We need to invest in a new e-mail server. First, the slow speed and unreliability of the present equipment is becoming a serious inconvenience. While the cost of replacing the server and the accompanying software will be very high, the cost of not doing so is going to be much higher in lost time and productivity. It would not be an exaggeration to say that for the last three months, we have lost more than a thousand billable hours as a result of the poor condition of our equipment. The average hourly rate per user is $30; thus, those lost hours of productivity have cost the company more than $30,000. Also, consider the impact on our company's reputation when the clients have problems communicating with us. We cannot afford to wait any longer to invest in new equipment and technology. In fact, over the long term, replacing the e-mail server will actually increase productivity and profitability.

The **topic sentence** states the topic and controlling idea.

The **supporting sentences** provide details and examples.

The **concluding sentence** brings the paragraph to a satisfactory close.

A Student Essay

Read the student essay, and answer the questions that follow.

Graffiti as Art

Jordan Foster

1   Long ago—about 30,000 B.C.E.—people made markings on cave walls, depicting great hunts and travels. Those handprints and rough figures can still be seen today. They have withstood the test of time and give us a better idea of who our ancestors were. That ancient graffiti was the voice of early humans and their way of saying, "I exist." Today, graffiti should be accepted and celebrated.

2   First, graffiti—or street art—is a treasure trove of self-expression. There are seven billion people on this planet and counting. Cities are crowded, and a lot of people feel invisible and powerless. Graffiti is a way for some of them to proclaim, "I exist, and this is what I have to say." Some street artists feel validated when their images and words appear on public walls. Self-expression and art should belong to the world regardless of medium, not just to those who can afford $1,500 for space on a billboard. If advertisers can use the public spaces to spread their messages, then graffiti artists should be allowed to use those spaces as well.

3   Furthermore, a lot of graffiti art conveys powerful messages and makes us think. Banksy, a world-famous street artist, has risen to rock-star fame, and his politically subversive messages are in cities around the world. For instance, in England, a wall portrays a rioter throwing a bouquet of flowers. In 2005, he decorated Israel's controversial West Bank wall with images of children escaping with helium balloons and a man holding back a curtain to expose a paradise on the other side.

4   Most importantly, graffiti can also serve to decorate or beautify something ugly or plain. For sure, people's homes and places of worship and burial should remain sacred and shouldn't be touched. But a lot of graffiti is in neighborhoods and locations that nobody really cares about. Old rail cars or a train underpass might have graffiti. The explosion of colors in an otherwise drab gray landscape beautifies the area, especially if the artist has some talent. Many street artists are recognized for the esthetic quality of their work. Shepard Fairey, for instance, is most famous for his stenciled blue and red image of President Obama, but his street art appears all over the country.

5   Graffiti is one of the oldest forms of self-expression. Regardless of its message, it should remain as one of the public forms of expression and art. People should have the right to convey who they are, regardless of the surface they use for their self-expression.

Convey =

April 21 2016

PRACTICE 2

LO3 Explore topics for an argument essay.

1. Highlight the thesis statement.

2. What introduction style does the writer use?
   a. an anecdote
   b. a definition
   c. a contrasting position
   d. historical background

3. Underline the topic sentences in body paragraphs 2, 3, and 4.

4. Circle the transitional expressions in the three topic sentences.

5. How does the writer organize his arguments?
   a. time   b. space   c. emphatic
   Explain your answer?

Explore Topics

In the Writer's Desk Warm Up, you will try an exploring strategy to generate ideas about different topics.

THE WRITER'S DESK Warm Up

Read the following questions, and write the first ideas that come to your mind. Think of two or three ideas for each topic.

EXAMPLE: Does age matter in a relationship?

 I don't know. Love is love, but there could be problems.

 What if the older person doesn't want children?

1. What should children learn about cell phone, e-mail, and online etiquette?

   _____

   _____

   _____

2. Should college students be permitted to carry concealed weapons on campus? Why or why not?

   _____

   _____

   _____

3. What are some of the major controversial issues in your neighborhood, workplace, college, state, or country? List some issues.

_____

_____

_____

▶ DEVELOPING

LO 4 Write the thesis statement of an argument essay.

The Thesis Statement

In the thesis statement of an argument essay, state your position on the issue.

topic   controlling idea (the writer's position)

Many corporate executives are overpaid for very substandard work.

A thesis statement should be debatable; it should not simply be a fact or a statement of opinion.

Fact   In American restaurants, people generally tip for service.
(This is a fact. It cannot be debated.)

Opinion   I think that tipping for service should be abolished in US restaurants.
(This is a statement of opinion. Nobody can deny that you feel this way. Therefore, do not use phrases such as *In my opinion, I think,* or *I believe* in your thesis statement.)

Argument   Tipping for service should be abolished in US restaurants.
(This is a debatable statement.)

HINT ◀ Be Direct

Many students feel reluctant to take a stand on an issue. They may feel that it is too personal or impolite to do so. However, in academic writing, it is perfectly acceptable, and even desirable, to state an argument in a direct manner and then support it.

PRACTICE 3

Evaluate the following statements. Write *F* for a fact, *O* for an opinion, or *A* for an argument.

1. In our state, many youths drop out of school.

2. I think that our town needs more police officers.

3. There are three effective strategies to reduce the high school dropout rate. _A_

4. Oil companies should not be permitted to drill in deep oceans. _A_

5. I don't think it is safe to drill in deep ocean waters. _O_

6. Many Internet sites have pop-up advertising. _F_

7. In my opinion, country music is predictable and repetitive. _O_

8. Our mayor should resign for three reasons. _A_

HINT ◀ Making a Guided Thesis Statement

Your instructor may want you to guide the reader through your main points.
To do this, mention your main and supporting ideas in your thesis statement.
In other words, your thesis statement provides a map for the readers to
follow.

> High school students should receive art education because it
> promotes their creativity, enhances their cultural knowledge, and
> develops their analytical skills.

THE WRITER'S DESK   Write Thesis Statements

Write a thesis statement for the next topics. You can look for ideas in the
Warm Up on page 223. Make sure that each thesis statement clearly expresses
your position on the issue.

EXAMPLE: Topic: age in relationships

Thesis statement: _Age matters in relationships._

1. Topic: etiquette in our technological age

   Thesis statement: _____

   this person is way _in political_

   _____

2. Topic: concealed weapons on campus

   Thesis statement: _____

   _____

3. Topic: a controversial issue

   Thesis statement: _____

   _____

LO5 Generate the supporting details of an argument essay.

The Supporting Ideas

To make a logical and reasoned argument, support your main point with facts, examples, and statistics. (For details about adding facts, examples, and statistics, see page 46 in Chapter 4.)

You can also include the following types of support.

- **Quote informed sources.** Sometimes experts in a field express an informed opinion about an issue. An expert's thoughts and ideas can add weight to your argument. For example, if you want to argue that people are becoming complacent about AIDS, you might quote an article published by a respected national health organization.
- **Consider logical consequences.** When you plan an argument, think about long-term consequences of a proposed solution to a problem. For instance, maybe you oppose a decision to drill for oil off the coast of California. A long-term consequence could be an environmental disaster if there is an earthquake near the rig.
- **Acknowledge opposing viewpoints.** Anticipating and responding to opposing views can strengthen your position. For instance, if you argue that school uniforms should be mandatory, you might address those who feel that students need freedom to express themselves. Try to refute some of the strongest arguments of the opposition.

Making an Emotional Appeal

Generally, an effective argument appeals to the reader's reason, but it can also appeal to his or her emotion. For example, you could use certain words or descriptions to encourage a reader's sense of justice, humanity, or pride. However, use emotional appeals sparingly. If you use **emotionally charged words** such as *wimp* or *thug*, or if you appeal to base instincts such as fear or prejudice, then you may seriously undermine your argument. Review the next examples of emotional appeals.

Overemotional	Crazy women such as the "Octomom" go to fertility clinics, have multiple births, and then feed off the state like leeches. The innocent premature infants, facing chronic illness and blindness, can end up needing lifelong medical care.
Reasonable and more neutral	Women visiting fertility clinics may underestimate potential problems. If a multiple birth results, the parents can face financial difficulties. Additionally, premature infants can suffer from a variety of long-term medical problems.

HINT ◄ Avoid Common Errors

When you write your argument essay, avoid the following pitfalls.

Do not make generalizations. If you begin a statement with *Everyone knows* or *It is common knowledge*, then the reader may mistrust what you say. You cannot possibly know what everyone else knows or does not know. It is better to refer to specific sources.

Generalization	American children are spoiled brats.
Better	Parents should not overindulge their children for several reasons.

Do not make exaggerated claims. Make sure that your arguments are plausible.

Exaggerated	If marijuana is legalized, drug use will soar in schools across the nation.
Better	If marijuana is legalized, drug use may increase in schools across the nation.

PRACTICE 4

You have learned about different methods to support a topic. Read each of the following thesis statements, and think of a supporting idea for each item. Use the type of support suggested in parentheses.

1. Volunteer work should be mandatory in all high schools.

   (Logical consequence) _____
   _____ *Being more responsible, learn to suppor community*

2. Online dating is a great way to meet a potential mate.

   (Acknowledge an opposing view) _____
   _____

3. Children should not be spanked.

   (Emotional appeal) _____
   _____

4. The college dropout rate is too high in our state.

   (Logical consequence) _____
   _____

VOCABULARY BOOST

Some words can influence readers because they have positive or negative connotations, which are implied or associated meanings. The meaning often carries a cultural value judgment with it. For example, *macho* may have negative connotations in one country and positive connotations in another country. For the word *thin*, synonyms like *skinny* or *skeletal* have negative connotations, while *slender* and *svelte* have positive ones.

Using a thesaurus, try to come up with related terms or descriptions that have either positive or negative connotations for the words in bold.

Gloria is **large**.

Calvin is **not assertive**.

Mr. Wayne **expresses his opinion**.

Franklin is a **liberal**.

Identify terms you chose that might be too emotionally loaded for an argument essay.

Consider Both Sides of the Issue

Once you have decided what issue you want to write about, try to think about both sides of the issue. Then you can predict arguments that your opponents might make, and you can plan your answer to the opposition. Here are examples.

Topic: Age matters in relationships

For	Against
◆ People have different levels of maturity.	◆ Love is love, and age doesn't matter.
◆ The desire to have children is strong at certain ages.	◆ People can adapt to each other.
◆ Such relationships will probably not last when one person gets ill.	◆ Other factors (finances, culture) may be more important than age.
◆ Society condemns couples with large age differences.	◆ People must be free to choose their own partners.

THE WRITER'S DESK   Consider Both Sides of the Issue

Choose one of the topics from the previous Writer's Desk, and write arguments showing both sides of the issue.

Topic: _____

For	Against
_____	_____
_____	_____
_____	_____
_____	_____
_____	_____

HINT ◀ Strengthening an Essay with Research

In some courses, your instructors may ask you to include supporting ideas from informed sources to strengthen your essays. You can find information in a variety of resources, including textbooks, journals, newspapers, magazines, or the Internet. When researching, make sure that your sources are from legitimate organizations. For example, for information about the spread of AIDS, you might find statistics on the World Health Organization Web site. You would not go to someone's personal rant or conspiracy theory site.

For more information about evaluating and documenting sources, refer to Chapter 17, The Research Essay.

The Essay Plan

LO 6 Develop an argument essay plan.

Before you write your argument essay, outline your ideas in a plan. Include details that can help illustrate each argument. Make sure that every example is valid and relates to the thesis statement. Also think about your organization. Many argument essays use emphatic order and list ideas from the least to the most important.

Thesis Statement: Age matters in a relationship.

I. Two people with a large age difference may have conflicting values and cultural experiences.

    A. Music, movies, politics, etc. change over time.

    B. People raised in different generations may see gender roles differently.

    C. Such differences can lead to breakups (Rick and Barbara example).

II. People's goals change as they age.

    A. One person may want to retire when the other doesn't.

    B. The younger partner may want children, but the older partner already has kids.

    C. The younger partner might still want to party when the older partner is more career oriented.

III.   Other people judge such couples.
   A.   Young wives are called "trophy wives" and "gold diggers."
   B.   Older men are called "sugar daddies."
   C.   Older women are called "cougars."
   D.   Demi Moore was judged harshly when she married a younger man.

IV.   Couples break up when the older one starts getting frail.
   A.   People get more fragile and unhealthy as they age.
   B.   The younger partner may not want to become a nursemaid.
   C.   Barbara and Rick broke up after Rick had a stroke.

Concluding idea: People should look for age-appropriate partners.

THE WRITER'S DESK Write an Essay Plan

Choose one of the ideas that you have developed in the previous Writer's Desk, and write a detailed essay plan.

LO7 Write the first draft of an argument essay.

The First Draft

Now that you have a refined thesis statement, solid supporting details, and a roadmap of your arguments and the order in which you will present them, you are ready to write the first draft. Remember to write complete sentences and to include transitional words or expressions to lead readers from one idea to the next. Here are some transitions that introduce an answer to the opposition or the supporting ideas for an argument.

To answer the opposition		To support your argument	
admittedly	of course	certainly	in fact
however	on one hand/other hand	consequently	obviously
nevertheless	undoubtedly	furthermore	of course

THE WRITER'S DESK Write the First Draft

Write the first draft of your argument essay. Include an interesting introduction. Also, add specific details to flesh out each body paragraph.

Revise and Edit an Argument Essay

L08 Revise and edit an argument essay.

When you finish writing an argument essay, carefully review your work and revise it to make the supporting examples as clear as possible to your readers. Check that the order of ideas is logical, and remove any irrelevant details. Before you revise and edit your own essay, practice revising and editing a student essay.

A Student Essay

Read the essay, and then answer the questions that follow. As you read, correct any errors that you find and make comments in the margins.

AGE MATTERS

Chloe Vallieres

1. In 2003, the American Association of Retired Persons (AARP) published a study revealing that 34 percent of women over forty were dating younger men. Having a younger spouse is becoming more and more popular. However, statistics also demonstrate that couples separate more often when the age gap between the two lovers exceeds ten years. Important age gaps in relationships can lead to considerable conflicts; therefore, age matters in a relationship.

2. Two people with a large age difference may have conflicting values and cultural experiences. Your views about religion and gender roles may differ. Also, politics, music, and movies change with time, so it may be hard to find topics to talk about if partners grew up in different eras. They might not have none of the same tastes. Imagine that a forty-year-old woman is dating a sixty-year-old man. The woman loves hip hop. She was raised to believe that her job is as important as her spouse's job and that childrearing should be shared. Her older partner might hate her musical tastes, and he could assume that his wife should be the primary caretaker of their children. Our family friends Rick and Barbara had this experience. Barbara, who is much younger than Rick, often complained about Rick's chauvinism. He hated her clothing styles and music. Their fifteen-year relationship ended last year.

3. Partners with an age gap are likely to have different goals. When Rick turned sixty-two, he retired, but Barbara still had professional ambitions. He wanted to travel every winter, she hoped to build her career. Damon and Sherrie, another May–December couple, disagree about having children. Damon, who is in his fifties, already has three adult children, but Sherrie, who is just thirty-five, wants to have a baby. Even younger couples can have

problems. A twenty-five-year-old woman who has finished university might want to settle down and focus on her career, but her younger partner might still want to party.

4. Couples with age differences have to face other people's bad opinions. "Cougar" and "dirty old man" are common negative terms. There are other unflattering stereotypes: The girl dates the older man (her "sugar daddy") to get her hands on his money, and the mature man marries his young girlfriend (his "trophy wife") to have sexual favors and to appear virile. For example, Demi Moore. She was judged harshly when she married Ashton Kutcher, who was fifteen years her junior. Then she was humiliated when he cheated on her with younger women. People pitied her, and some bloggers said that it was "inevitable" that Kutcher would find a more age-appropriate partner.

5. Finally, some couples break up when the older partner develops health problems. Bone injuries or a weak heart. For example, Rick has high blood pressure, and, three years ago, he suffered a minor stroke. Barbara recently left the marriage, confiding to my mother that she did not want to spend the next years being a nursemaid for an old man.

6. Those who proclaim that love can overcome everything are naïve airheads. Age matters, and people should look for age-appropriate partners. When spouses have huge age differences, the relationship is doomed. Dave, a popular blogger on the Intro2u Web site, writes, "It's elements like maturity and life experience, which tend to correlate with age, that can make or break a relationship's long-term potential."

PRACTICE 5

Revising

1. Highlight the thesis statement.

2. Highlight the topic sentences in paragraphs 2, 3, 4, and 5.

3. In the margins next to the essay, add transitional words or expressions to each topic sentence in paragraphs 2 to 4.

4. In the concluding paragraph, the writer uses emotionally charged words and exaggerates. Give examples of these two problems.

Emotionally charged language: _____

Exaggeration: _____

_____

Editing

5. Paragraph 2 contains a pronoun shift error. (See the explanation in the Grammar Hint below.) Circle the incorrect pronoun, and write your correction here.

_____

6. Paragraph 2 contains a double negative. Underline it and correct it here.

_____

7. Paragraph 3 contains a run-on sentence. Two complete ideas are incorrectly joined. Underline the run-on sentence, and correct it on the lines provided.

_____

_____

8. Underline fragments in paragraphs 4 and 5 and correct them here.

Paragraph 4: _____

Paragraph 5: _____

GRAMMAR LINK

See the following chapters for more information about these topics:

Fragments, Chapter 23
Run-Ons, Chapter 24
Double Negatives, Chapter 29
Pronouns, Chapter 31

GRAMMAR HINT ◄ Keeping Pronouns Consistent

In argument writing, make sure that your pronouns do not switch between *they*, *we*, and *you*. If you are writing about specific groups of people, use *they* to refer to those people. Change pronouns only when the switch is logical.

Many hunters argue that they need large collections and varieties of guns.

                    they
Yet why would ~~you~~ need a semi-automatic to go hunting?

See Chapter 31 for more information about pronoun usage.

THE WRITER'S DESK Revise and Edit Your Essay

Revise and edit the essay that you wrote for the previous Writer's Desk. You can refer to the revising and editing checklists at the end of this chapter and at the back of the book.

A Professional Essay

Melonyce McAfee is an editorial assistant at *Slate* magazine. She has written for a variety of publications including the *San Diego Union-Tribune*. In this essay, she argues for the abolition of Administrative Professionals Day. Read the essay and answer the questions that follow.

Keep Your Roses

Melonyce McAfee

1   Here's a plot line for the writers at NBC's *The Office*: It's April 26. Paper salesman Jim presents a bouquet of tulips to his office crush, Pam, the receptionist. The accompanying card reads, "For all you do. Happy Secretaries Day." Competitive and cringe-inducing boss Michael, until now oblivious to the holiday, sees the card and orders a garish bouquet, large enough to blot out Pam's head and overshadow Jim's arrangement. The bouquet arrives at 4:49 p.m. Eyes roll. Administrative Professionals Day is the Hallmark holiday that leads to interoffice jealousy, discomfort, and not much else.

2   The National Secretaries Association got the ball rolling with Professional Secretaries Week in 1952. The holiday was renamed Administrative Professionals Week in 2000, but I prefer the tell-it-like-it-is Secretaries Day. The **NSA** (now, naturally, the International Association of Administrative Professionals) claims the day is meant to enhance the image of administrative workers, promote career development, and encourage people to enter the field. But does it really do any of the above?

3   In my first job out of college, I worked as a typist at a title company, a job akin to cryptography. I pecked my way toward carpal tunnel syndrome to turn chicken scratch into property reports. Typists served the entire office, but title officers also had personal secretaries. On Secretaries Day, we typists sucked our teeth at the bouquets on the secretaries' desks. At my next corporate job, I had gained an "assistant" title. But along with the other assistants, I was still left empty-handed. The office professionals chipped in for a bouquet for the division secretary, who regularly pawned off duties on us assistants and huffed when asked to, well, work. "I can't believe they got *her* flowers," we hissed.

4   My mother, a former hospital administrative assistant, was surprised with three greeting cards and a gorgeous scarf last Secretaries Day. She wasn't aware of the holiday and was touched that the nurses in her department took the opportunity to thank her for working hard on special projects. But she also had to listen to a chorus of "*I* didn't get anything" from other administrators. She says that didn't diminish her pleasure, but it does prove my point. When the holiday makes someone feel appreciated, it almost invariably leaves others out in the cold.

5   Maybe part of the problem is that in the fifty years since the holiday began, the duties of a secretary have been farmed out across the office,

NSA: National Secretaries Association

and the job definition is no longer clear. A secretary used to be the woman who answered phones, took dictation, typed, picked up dry cleaning, and stole the boss's husband, if she was really good. Now she (or he) might give PowerPoint presentations or build a Web site. Meanwhile, someone else might do the typing and filing.

6   The confusion over who qualifies as a secretary creates social anxiety about either overcelebrating the holiday or undercelebrating it. One Secretaries Day, a former advertising-sales assistant and co-worker of mine got lovely plants from colleagues who rushed to point out that they'd gotten her a gift even though she wasn't really a secretary. She got the impression they thought she might be offended by being lumped in with the administrative staff. The holiday forces workers, like it or not, to evaluate how they stack up. Mail-room guy, copy clerk, typist, receptionist, administrative secretary, executive assistant—are they low enough on the totem pole to merit a gift? Or are they too low?

7   Perhaps my impatience with Secretaries Day springs from job dissatisfaction, as an executive assistant at a New York–based magazine suggested when we mused about why the holiday creates bitterness. True—in my mind, I should be the boss. And I resent being reminded of my slow progress up the chain of command every April 26. Those of us who yearn to be professionals, not administrative professionals, tend to bristle at the idea that we're just boosters for the big boys and girls.

8   Some bosses feel compelled to take their secretary, assistant, or whoever out to lunch on Secretaries Day. It's a nice gesture, but who wants to sit through that awkward meal? Anyone who has seen the *Curb Your Enthusiasm* episode in which Larry David takes his maid on a squirm-worthy lunch date at his country club knows the potential disaster of forced boss–employee **conviviality**. Instead of Secretaries Day, why not just chip in for a big cake on the Friday before Labor Day and toast everyone in the office. Wouldn't that be kinder, not to mention easier? I'd much prefer that to a holiday that's a catch-all for "attagirl," "I'm sorry for being an insufferable employer," and "we should talk about that raise."

conviviality: friendliness

PRACTICE 6

1. Highlight the thesis statement.

2. What technique does the writer use to introduce the topic?

     a. historical background   b. anecdote   c. a definition

3. What synonyms does McAfee use for "secretary" in this essay?

_____

_____

4. In which paragraphs does the writer acknowledge an opposing viewpoint? _____

5. Which sentence best sums up the writer's implied argument in paragraph 3?

   a. Typists and assistants are secretaries.

   b. The writer worked as a typist in a small company for many years, and then she became an executive.

   c. Typists do a lot of hard work but are not appreciated.

   d. Many people in offices, such as typists and assistants, feel resentful when they are not rewarded on Secretaries Day.

6. Underline the topic sentence in paragraph 5.

7. Which sentence best sums up the writer's implied argument in paragraph 7?

   a. Administrative assistants really do the work of the bosses.

   b. Honestly, most administrative assistants dislike their jobs.

   c. Secretaries Day reminds administrative assistants that they have not advanced on the career ladder.

   d. Most administrative assistants want to be professionals.

8. Using your own words, sum up McAfee's main supporting arguments.

   _____

   _____

   _____

READING LINK ARGUMENT

"Brands R Us" by Stephen Garey (page 551)

"Medicating Ourselves" by Robyn Sarah (page 585)

MyWritingLab™

Complete these writing assignments at mywritinglab.com

MyWritingLab™ **THE WRITER'S ROOM**

Writing Activity 1: Topics

Choose any of the following topics, or choose your own topic, and write an argument essay. Remember to narrow your topic and to follow the writing process.

General Topics

1. Should online gambling be banned?

2. Should children be spanked?

3. Should voting be compulsory?

4. Should tipping for service be abolished?

5. What is the biggest problem in your town or city?

College and Work-Related Topics

6. Should students work while going to college?

7. Should all college disciplines include apprenticeship or intern programs?

8. Should service workers create unions?

9. Should some college courses be removed from the curriculum?

10. What is the most underappreciated profession?

Writing Activity 2: Media Writing

Watch a television show or movie that deals with war. You can watch television shows such as *Homeland* or movies such as *Zero Dark Thirty*, *Les Miserables*, or *Schindler's List*. Find a controversial issue online or in a program or movie, and write an argument essay.

WRITING LINK
See the next grammar sections for more argument writing topics.
Chapter 24,
    Writer's
    Room topic 2
    (page 352)
Chapter 30,
    Writer's
    Room topic 2
    (page 417)
Chapter 31,
    Writer's
    Room topic 2
    (page 431)
Chapter 32,
    Writer's
    Room topic 2
    (page 443)
Chapter 34,
    Writer's
    Room topic 2
    (page 465)
Chapter 35,
    Writer's
    Room topic 2
    (page 477)

Checklist: Argument Essay

After you write your argument essay, review the checklist at the end of the book. Also, ask yourself the following set of questions.

☐ Does my thesis statement clearly state my position on the issue?

☐ Do I make strong supporting arguments?

☐ Do I include facts, examples, statistics, and logical consequences?

☐ Do my supporting arguments provide evidence that directly supports the thesis statement?

☐ Do I acknowledge and counter opposing arguments?

☐ Do I use valid arguments? (Do I avoid making broad generalizations? Do I restrain any emotional appeals?)

☐ Do I use a courteous tone?

Part III

More College and Workplace Writing

In the next chapters, you will learn about college and workplace writing. Chapter 15 provides valuable information about writing essay exams. Chapters 16 and 17 guide you through the process of synthesizing material and writing a research essay. Chapter 18 focuses on the response essay, and Chapter 19 gives you some important workplace writing strategies.

The Essay Exam 15

LEARNING OBJECTIVES

LO 1 Prepare for exams. (p. 240)

LO 2 Write essay exams. (p. 241)

Just as athletes rigorously train to win an important race, successful students follow specific strategies to ace exams.

WRITERS' EXCHANGE

Tell a partner about your study habits. Discuss the following questions.

1. When you are given an assignment, how do you react? Do you procrastinate or start working right away?

2. When you are told about a test, what do you do? Do you panic? Do you plan study times? Do you give yourself enough time to study?

3. How do you balance your college, home, and work lives? Do you put too much emphasis on your social life? Do you spend too much time at a part-time job?

After you discuss the questions, brainstorm a list of steps students can take to become successful at college.

LO 1 Prepare for exams.

Preparing for Exams

In many of your college courses, you will be asked to write essay exams. You will be expected to show what you know in an organized and logical manner. To be better prepared for such exams, try the following strategies.

Take meaningful notes. In class, listen carefully and take notes about key points. Your instructor might signal important ideas with phrases such as "and most importantly." Also, remember to date your notes. You will want a record of when you wrote them during the semester. The dates might help you to know what to focus on while you are studying.

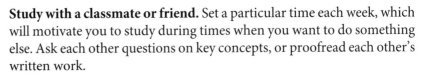

HINT ◂ Using Abbreviations

Many abbreviations we use in English derive from Latin terms. Here are some abbreviations to help you take notes more efficiently.

Abbreviation	English	Latin
e.g.	for example	exempli gratia
etc.	and so on	et cetera
i.e.	that is	id est
N.B.	important	nota bene
vs., v.	against	versus

Keep in mind that these abbreviations are useful for note taking. When you write an essay, use the complete English words, not the abbreviations.

Review course material. Cramming is an ineffective, short-term strategy for college success. Instead, reviewing your course material *regularly*, perhaps every second day or each week, will ensure that you know your subjects well.

Study with a classmate or friend. Set a particular time each week, which will motivate you to study during times when you want to do something else. Ask each other questions on key concepts, or proofread each other's written work.

Ask questions. When you don't understand something in class, speak up. Chances are great that others in the class also have problems understanding the material. Also consider speaking with your instructors during their office hours. Prepare questions about concepts that you do not understand. Waiting until the day before your exam will be too late.

Predict exam questions. Look for important themes in your course outline. Also review your notes and identify what information is of particular importance. Look over previous exams and answer those questions. Finally, predict what types of questions will be on the exam. Write down possible questions, and practice answering them.

PRACTICE 1

Imagine that your English instructor will give you an exam next week. The exam will cover material from the past three weeks. What types of questions might your instructor ask? Brainstorm some ideas here.

_____

_____

_____

_____

_____

_____

Writing Essay Exams

LO2 Write essay exams.

In many of your courses, you will have to answer exam questions with a paragraph or essay to reveal how well you understand information. Although taking any exam can be stressful, you can reduce exam anxiety and increase your chances of doing well by following some of the preparation and exam-writing strategies outlined in this chapter.

Schedule Your Time

Before you write the exam, find out exactly how much time you have, and then plan how much time you will need to answer the questions. For example, if you have a one-hour exam, and you have three questions worth the same value, try to spend no more than twenty minutes on each question.

Determine Point Values

As soon as you get an exam, scan the questions and determine which questions have a larger value. For example, you might respond to the questions with the largest point value first, or you might begin with those that you understand well. Then go to the more difficult questions. If you are blocked on a certain answer, skip to another question, and then go back to that question later.

Carefully Read the Exam Questions

In an exam question, every word counts. Here are two ways you can read actively.

1. **Identify key words and phrases.** When you read an exam question, underline or circle key words and phrases to understand exactly what you are supposed to do. In the next example of an essay question, the underlined words highlight two different tasks.

1. Define the term.

2. Explain why it is important.

Discuss cost-plus pricing, and analyze its importance to a company.

2. **Pay attention to common question words.** Directions for exam questions often use specific verbs (action words). The following chart gives you several common words that you will find in essay-style questions.

Verb	Meaning
describe discuss review	Examine a subject as thoroughly as possible. Focus on the main points.
narrate trace	Describe the development or progress of something using time order.
evaluate explain your point of view interpret justify take a stand	State your opinion and give reasons to support your opinion. In other words, write an argument essay.
analyze criticize classify	Explain something carefully by breaking it down into smaller parts.
enumerate list outline	Go through important facts one by one.
compare contrast distinguish	Discuss important similarities and/or differences.
define explain what is meant by	Give a complete and accurate definition that demonstrates your understanding of the concept.
explain causes	Analyze the reasons for an event.
explain effects	Analyze the consequences or results of an event.
explain a process	Give the steps needed to do a task.
illustrate	Demonstrate your understanding by giving examples.
summarize	Write down the main points from a larger piece of work.

PRACTICE 2

What tasks are students expected to do in each essay exam? Choose the best key words.

Topic

1. Explain how the gross domestic product (GDP) of a country is calculated. _____
2. Explain the reasons for the economic crash of 2008. _____
3. Illustrate alternative energy sources. _____
4. Distinguish between universal health care and privatized medicine. _____
5. Discuss whether capital punishment should be abolished. _____
6. Explain what guerilla marketing is. _____

Key Word

a. compare and contrast
b. define
c. explain a process
d. argue
e. explain causes
f. give examples

PRACTICE 3

The following is an exam from a sociology course. Read the instructions, and then answer the questions that follow the sample.

Answer both parts A and B. You will have two hours to complete the evaluation.

Part A Define two of the following terms. (5 points each)
1. democracy
2. theocracy
3. fascism
4. communism

Part B Write a 300-word essay about one of the following topics. (40 points)

1. How will economic development in low-income countries improve if women are given a higher social status? Explain your answer.
2. How does poverty in poor nations compare with poverty in the United States?
3. Some consider the United States a "middle-class society." Explain how true you believe this claim to be.
4. Explain the causes of homelessness in this nation.

1. What is the total point value of the exam? _____
2. How many definitions should you write? _____
3. How many essays should you write? _____

4. Which part of the exam would you do first? Explain why.

_____

_____

5. How much time would you spend on Part A and Part B? Explain why.

_____

_____

Follow the Writing Process

Treat an essay exam as you would any other writing assignment by following the three main steps of the writing process.

Explore	Jot down any ideas that you think can help you answer the question. Try the prewriting activities suggested in Chapter 1 of this book, such as brainstorming or clustering. Prewriting will help you generate some ideas for your essay.
Develop	Use the exam question to guide your thesis statement and topic sentences. List supporting ideas, organize your ideas using an essay plan or outline, and then write an essay. Remember to include an introduction with a clear thesis statement and to use transitions such as *first*, *moreover*, or *in addition* to link your ideas.
Revise and Edit	Read over your essay to verify that all ideas support the thesis statement and to ensure that you have adequate details to support your topic sentences. Also check your spelling, punctuation, and mechanics.

HINT ◂ **Writing a Thesis Statement**

In an essay exam, your thesis statement should be very clear. A good strategy is to write a guided thesis statement that includes details you will cover in the essay. Review the essay topic and sample thesis statement.

Essay topic	Explain the key pricing strategies that companies use.
Thesis statement	The most common pricing strategies are **cost-plus pricing**, **target pricing**, and **yield-management pricing**.

PRACTICE 4

Write thesis statements for the following exam questions. Remember that your thesis must have a controlling idea.

EXAMPLE: Discuss the influences of the industrial revolution on class structure.

Thesis statement: _The industrial revolution caused a dramatic change_
in traditional class structure.

1. Compare viral marketing with traditional print marketing. Point out the advantages and disadvantages of each type.

_____

_____

_____

2. Explain the steps needed to convince a consumer to buy a product.

_____

_____

_____

3. What is the most efficient marketing method? Defend your viewpoint.

_____

_____

_____

PRACTICE 5

College student Seokman Chang wrote the following essay for an exam. Read the essay, and answer the questions that follow.

1   Throughout human history, there have been migratory movements of people all over the world. The Polynesians journeyed to and stayed in the Hawaiian Islands, the Vikings found homes in Great Britain and Ireland, and the Moguls settled in India. Today, the migration trend continues. People migrate to different parts of the world for many reasons and often bring benefits to the host region or country.

2   First, many people go to different countries searching for better work opportunities. For example, many groups of professionals migrate to get higher-paying jobs. There are engineers, teachers, lawyers, and computer specialists who have come to this country to broaden their skills and work experience. One day, in a supermarket line, I had a conversation with a woman from China. She and her husband had just arrived in this country. They were both doctors and were preparing to take the qualifying exams. Unskilled laborers also come to North America because the pay for such jobs is higher than in their homeland. A factory worker usually earns more per hour in an

industrialized country than in a developing country. Most skilled and unskilled economic migrants go to new lands seeking a better quality of life.

3   Second, sometimes immigrants leave their homelands unwillingly. They may be forced to leave their homes because of famine or war. For example, there are droughts in some nations and wars in Congo, Darfur, Somalia, and other areas. Furthermore, sometimes people are expelled from their homeland. In 1972, the Ugandan dictator Idi Amin expelled the Indian community. They had very little time to pack up and leave. China and other countries have expelled some political activists, while other activists have fled for their lives, claiming political refugee status.

4   Moreover, some people leave their native lands to join family members who have already emigrated. Such cases are especially true of new immigrants. Often new immigrants arrive in the new country alone. When they have settled, they send for their immediate family members. My neighbor came from Vietnam about ten years ago. For the first few years, he was in this country alone. He worked during the day and took night courses. As soon as he got settled, he sent for his parents because they were getting older and had no one to take care of them in Vietnam. Now the family is together again.

5   The receiving country gains many advantages from immigrants. New groups add to the cultural diversity of the country. North American cities have a variety of ethnic restaurants, grocery stores, and cultural festivals. In addition, Western countries need immigrants to maintain or increase the population. The birthrates of most developed countries are falling, and immigrants are needed to maintain population rates. New immigrants also bring skills that are advantageous to the host country. New immigrants perform many varied jobs, from fruit pickers and waiters to doctors and engineers. Immigrants contribute to the economy of the host country.

6   People leave their homelands for a variety of reasons, and their adopted countries gain tremendously from migration. The immigrant usually finds a more stable and prosperous life. The adopted countries of new immigrants gain tremendously in social and economic areas. So the next time you eat at your favorite Italian restaurant, dance to Carlos Santana, or debate the political influence of former governor of California Arnold Schwarzenegger, remember that immigration made it all possible.

1.   This student essay is an answer to which of the following questions? Circle the best possible answer.

   a.   Distinguish the periods of immigration to North America, and describe the migrant groups.

   b.   Evaluate the current immigration policy of the nation.

   c.   Explain why people leave their countries, and describe some consequences of their migration.

2. Highlight the thesis statement in the introduction. Also highlight the topic sentences in body paragraphs 2 through 5.

3. On a separate sheet of paper or on the computer, create a plan for this essay. For the details, just use words or phrases.

MyWritingLab™

THE WRITER'S ROOM Essay Exam Topics

MyWritingLab™
Complete these writing assignments at mywritinglab.com

1. Predict at least three essay exam questions for one of your courses. Then develop an informal essay plan for one of the questions.

2. Look at an exam that you completed previously. Write a paragraph explaining what you could have done to receive a higher mark.

Checklist: An Essay Exam

As you prepare for your essay exam, ask yourself the following questions.

- ☐ Have I taken clear notes during lectures?
- ☐ Have I reviewed my notes on a regular basis?
- ☐ Have I organized study time?
- ☐ Have I asked my instructor questions when I didn't understand a concept?
- ☐ Have I asked my instructor what material the exam will cover?

16 Summarizing

When a stylist cuts hair, the excess is trimmed away, and the essential style is revealed. In the same way, when you summarize, you write about key points and discard the details.

WRITERS' EXCHANGE

Work with a partner. In a couple of minutes, describe the contents of an article or essay that you have read for this course. What were the key points?

LO 1 Define summary.

What Is a Summary?

A summary is a logical shortened form of a longer reading. It provides a clear and precise snapshot of an author's ideas and arguments. Writing a summary is not as simple as it seems. First, there is a discovery phase: You must thoroughly understand what an author wishes to convey. Then, after you have a clear understanding of the key points, you must express the author's ideas in a fair and unbiased way. When writing a summary, it is essential to put aside your own reactions and opinions.

Summaries matter: They demonstrate to instructors that you can convey another person's ideas accurately and fairly and without plagiarizing or copying that person's exact words. In college courses, you often write summaries. An instructor may ask you to show your understanding of a concept by summarizing an article or book. In response and analysis reports, a summary can provide background information before you make your own arguments. And in research essays, brief summaries of other people's ideas can add weight to your arguments.

Additionally, people in many professions are asked to write summaries. For instance, politicians and CEOs hire assistants to read articles and to compress detailed information into its basic components so that the leader can identify what action to take. Science labs summarize important findings. Even the minutes of a meeting are essentially summaries of the key ideas that were discussed. Thus, the ability to summarize properly is useful in many contexts.

A summary is a snapshot of a more complete work.

How to Write a Summary

LO 2 Write a summary.

When you summarize, you condense a message to its basic elements. Do the following:

- Read the original text carefully because you will need a complete picture before you begin to write.
- Underline, highlight, or write notes beside any key ideas. In a summary, you will only present the main ideas of a text.
- Take notes. Ask yourself *who*, *what*, *when*, *where*, *why*, and *how* questions. These questions will help you identify the central ideas.
- Mention the author and title of the original source near the beginning of your summary.
- Restate the main ideas using your own words. You can keep specialized words, common words, and the names of people or places. However, find synonyms for other words and use your own sentence structure. Use a dictionary or thesaurus, if necessary, to find synonyms.
- To ensure that you do not unintentionally plagiarize, set aside the original work and write your summary from memory and with the help of your notes.
- Maintain the original author's meaning and intent. Put aside your own beliefs and feelings. Focus on the author's ideas, not your own.
- Keep your summary to a maximum of 30 percent of the original work's length.
- Reread your summary. Verify that you have explained the critical messages, and ensure that you have restated the ideas in your own words.

In written summaries, readers should be able to understand the essential message. The complete document would contain more details and examples, but readers would not require the original to make sense of the central ideas.

SAMPLE SUMMARY

Review this summary of an essay that appears in Chapter 12 on page 197.

Mention the source (author, title).

Using your own words, explain the writer's main ideas.

Conclude your summary. Mention the page number (when available).

In his essay "Viral Vigilantes," which appears in *The Writer's World*, Matthew Fraser describes the expansion of surveillance from governments and institutions to private citizens. In past eras, governments and large organizations had the means to spy on others. Later, surveillance methods became more technologically based, and concealed cameras were installed in public places. These days, surveillance is no longer done exclusively by the powerful. In fact, regular people can take cell phone images of their instructors, bosses, and political leaders and, using social media, rapidly spread proof of authority figures' transgressions. But nowadays, ordinary people also snoop on each other, so viral vigilantism is on the rise. The author provides the example of British citizen Mary Bale, who put someone's cat into a large garbage bin. A hidden camera filmed the action, and the video was then posted on YouTube. Soon, Bale's reputation was shattered, and she became an object of hatred and scorn. Fraser ends his essay by pointing out that we can all be seen and exposed at any time (198).

HINT ◀ Citing the Source in a Summary

In a summary, you can cite the source in the opening sentence. Mention the author and title of the work. If you are summarizing from a print source, then you can include the page number in the first sentence, or you can place the page number, in parentheses, at the end of the summary. If you are summarizing a large work such as a novel, or if the source is Web-based, generally no page numbers are necessary. For more detailed information about citing sources, see Chapter 17, "The Research Essay."

PRACTICE 1

Summarize the next selections. Your summary should be much shorter than the original selection. Remember to cite the source and to use your own words.

1. Developing a friendship with a co-worker who has a work ethic and who can "keep it zipped" is a must-have. No matter how great your significant other, friends, and neighbors are at solving problems or listening to your work concerns, they are not your best option. Why? Because they don't work where you do. Only a co-worker can completely understand the personalities and culture of your workplace.

—Goddard, Stephanie. "Top Ten Ways to Beat Stress at Work." *Work-Stress-Solutions.com*. N.p., n.d. Web. 14 May 2010.

Summary

Having a good friednship with a co-worker is mandatory. Even if you have a strong friendship with another person outside of work, It does not matter. A coworker is your best option, because they know how everything works at your work place.

2. And credit-card companies have changed their lending policies in ways that make credit more accessible—but also more complicated. . . . Instead of charging everyone the same, companies adjust the interest rates according to customers' credit scores. They also charge special fees for late payments, purchases that exceed a credit limit, foreign-currency transactions, phone payments, and so forth. This structure makes it profitable to extend credit to high-risk borrowers, including those with low incomes.

—Postrel, Virginia. "The Case for Debt." *Atlantic* Nov. 2008: 44–47. Print.

Summary

_____

_____

_____

_____

_____

3. The progression of skateboarding went from a cult-like activity with rebellious undertones to a mainstream hobby. The originators of skateboarding in 1970s Southern California, who were portrayed in the popular documentary *Dogtown and Z-Boys*, wouldn't recognize the sport today. At that time, boarders were outlaws; as one of the main characters in the film says, "We get the beat-down from all over. Everywhere we go, man, people hate us." Nowadays, skateboarding is about as countercultural as *The Simpsons*. More kids ride skateboards than play basketball, and many of them snap up pricey T-shirts, skate shoes, helmets, and other accessories. In fact, boarders spend almost six times as much on "soft goods," such as T-shirts, shorts, and sunglasses (about $4.4 billion in a year), than on hard-core equipment, including the boards themselves.

—Solomon, Michael R. *Consumer Behavior.* 10th Ed. Boston: Pearson, 2013. Print. p. 557.

Summary

_____

_____

_____

_____

LO3 Summarize a longer text.

Summarizing a Longer Text

You may think that summarizing a longer text is difficult, but it is very manageable if you focus on the essential ideas. Follow the next steps.

- First, scan the article or book, looking for chapter titles, headings, illustrations, and photos. This will provide you with a preliminary idea of the work's focus.
- Read the text, and take notes of key points. Remember that main ideas are facts, not questions.
- To identify central ideas and to consolidate your thoughts, ask yourself *who*, *what*, *when*, *where*, *why*, and *how* questions.
- Use your notes to write a first draft of the summary.
- Remove any unnecessary details.
- Ensure that you have not used the exact words or phrases from the original text.
- Reduce your writing to only a paragraph by revising and condensing your draft.
- Reread your summary to verify that you have stated the essential ideas of the text.

PRACTICE 2

The following adapted essay appeared on page 534 of *Sociology* by John J. Macionis. Read the essay and then write a one-paragraph summary. Remember to follow the summary-writing guidelines in this chapter.

The Twenty-First-Century Campus: Where Are the Men?

1   A century ago, the campuses of colleges and universities across the United States might as well have hung out a sign that read "Men Only." Almost all of the students and faculty were male. There were a small number of women's colleges, but many more schools—including some of the best known U.S. universities such as Yale, Harvard, and Princeton—barred women outright. Since then, women have won greater social equality.

By 1980, the number of women enrolled at U.S. colleges finally matched the number of men.

2   In a surprising trend, however, the share of women on campus has continued to increase. As a result, in 2005, men accounted for only 43 percent of all U.S. undergraduates. The gender gap is evident in all racial and ethnic categories and at all class levels. Among African Americans on campus, only 33 percent are men. The lower the income level, the greater the gender gap in college attendance.

3   Meg DeLong noticed the gender imbalance right away when she moved into her dorm at the University of Georgia at Athens; she soon learned that just 39 percent of her first-year classmates were men. In some classes, there were few men, and women usually dominated discussions. Out of class, DeLong and many other women soon complained that having so few men on campus hurt their social life. Not surprisingly, most of the men felt otherwise.

4   What accounts for the shifting gender balance on U.S. campuses? One theory is that many young men are drawn away from college by the lure of jobs, especially in high technology. This pattern is sometimes termed the "Bill Gates syndrome," after the man who dropped out of college and soon became the world's richest person by helping to found Microsoft. Thus, many boys have unrealistic expectations about their earning power if they don't have an education.

5   In addition, analysts point to an anti-intellectual male culture. More young women are drawn to learning and seek to do well in school, whereas some young men attach less importance to studying. According to Judith Kleinfeld, in the journal *Gender Issues*, stereotyping is also holding boys back. Because girls generally have more developed social skills and are better behaved than boys, they perform better in school, which then prepares them for college. Boys, on the other hand, are often labeled as less cooperative and more likely to act out in classrooms, which can affect their grades. Rightly or wrongly, more men seem to think they can get a good job without investing years of their lives and a considerable amount of money in getting a college degree.

6   Many college officials are concerned about the lack of men on campus. In an effort to attract more balanced enrollments, some colleges are adopting what amounts to affirmative action programs for males. But courts in several states have already ruled such policies illegal. Many colleges, therefore, are turning to more active recruitment; admissions officers are paying special attention to male applicants and stressing a college's strength in mathematics and science—areas traditionally popular with men. In the same way that colleges across the country are striving to increase their share of minority students, the hope is that they can also succeed in attracting a larger share of men.

MyWritingLab™ / **THE WRITER'S ROOM**

Writing Activity

Choose one of the following topics, and write a summary.

1. Summarize a paragraph from a newspaper or magazine article.

2. Summarize the essay "Discrimination in the 21st Century" from Chapter 11 (page 165).

3. Summarize Chapter 15, The Essay Exam.

4. Summarize the plot of a television program or movie.

5. Summarize a text that you have read for another course.

6. Choose an essay from Chapter 40 of this book, and summarize it.

Checklist: Summarizing

When you paraphrase or summarize, ask yourself these questions.

☐ Have I kept the original intent of the author?

☐ Have I kept only the key ideas?

☐ Have I used my own words when summarizing?

☐ Have I mentioned the source when summarizing?

When cooking, you combine small amounts of specific ingredients to create an appetizing meal. When writing a research-supported essay, you cite other people's ideas and combine them with your own to make a more convincing paper.

LEARNING OBJECTIVES

LO 1 Plan a research essay. **(p. 256)**

LO 2 Gather information. **(p. 256)**

LO 3 Evaluate sources. **(p. 260)**

LO 4 Take notes. **(p. 263)**

LO 5 Organize your first draft. **(p. 267)**

LO 6 Incorporate visuals. **(p. 268)**

LO 7 Avoid plagiarism. **(p. 269)**

LO 8 Integrate paraphrases, summaries, and quotations. **(p. 270)**

LO 9 Use MLA style. **(p. 272)**

LO 10 Review a sample research essay. **(p. 282)**

WRITERS' EXCHANGE

Work with a partner. Match the word in Column A with a word that has a similar meaning in Column B. Then discuss the different meanings of each pair of words.

A	B
MLA	Footnote
Works Cited	Plagiarism
Copying	Indirect quotation
Parenthetical documentation	APA
Paraphrase	Bibliography

LO 1 Plan a research essay.

Planning a Research Essay

Conducting **research** means looking for information that will help you better understand a subject. Knowing how to locate, evaluate, and use information from other sources is valuable in your work and day-to-day activities. It is also crucial in college writing because, in many of your assignments, you are expected to include information from outside sources. In this chapter, you will learn some strategies for writing a research paper.

Determining Your Topic

In some courses, your instructor will ask you to write a research paper about a specific topic. However, if you are not assigned one, then you will need to think about issues related to your field of study or to your personal interests.

The scope of your topic should match the size of the assignment. Longer essays may have a broader topic, but a short research essay (of three or four pages) must have a rather narrow focus. If you have a very specific focus, you will be able to delve more thoroughly into the topic. To help find and develop a topic, you can try exploring strategies such as freewriting, questioning, or brainstorming. (See Chapter 1 for more information about prewriting strategies.)

Finding a Guiding Research Question

The point of a research essay is not simply to collect information and summarize it; the idea is to gather information that relates directly to your guiding research question. To help you determine your central question, brainstorm a list of questions that you would like your research to answer. For example, Karyne Maheu wants to write about energy drinks, so she asks herself some questions to narrow her topic.

How are energy drinks marketed?

What are the health effects of energy drinks?

How popular are energy drinks?

Who are the main consumers of energy drinks?

Karyne's next step is to find a guiding research question that can become the focus of her essay.

What are the health effects of energy drinks?

LO 2 Gather information.

Gathering Information

Once you know what information you seek, you can begin gathering ideas, facts, quotations, anecdotes, and examples about the research topic you have chosen. Before you begin to gather information, consider how to find it and how to sort the valid information from the questionable information.

THE WRITER'S DESK Find a Research Topic

Choose a general topic that you might like to write about.

Topic: _____

Now ask five or six questions to help you narrow the topic.

_____

_____

_____

_____

_____

Decide which question will become your guiding research question, and write it here.

_____

_____

_____

Consulting Library-Based Sources

Today's technological advances in both print and electronic publishing make it easier than ever to access information. For sources, you can consult encyclopedias, online catalogues in libraries, periodicals, and the Internet. Here are some tips for finding information about your topic through library resources.

- **Ask a reference librarian** to help you locate information using various research tools, such as online catalogues, CD-ROMs, and microfiches. Before meeting with the librarian, write down some questions that you would like the answers to. Possible questions might be *Can I access the library's online databases from my home computer?* and *Can you recommend a particular online database?*

- **Search the library's online holdings.** You can search by keyword, author, title, or subject. Using an online catalogue, student Karyne Maheu typed in the key words *addiction* and *biology* and found the following book.

Author	Goldstein, Avram
Title	Addiction: from biology to drug policy
Imprint	New York: Oxford University Press, 2001
Call Number	RC564.G66 2001
Location	NRG – Book Shelves
Status	Available
Description	353 p.; 24 cm.
ISBN	0195146638

Notice that the listing gives the call number, which helps you locate the book on the library shelves. If the catalogue is part of a library network, the online listing explains which library to visit. Because books are organized by topic, chances are good that you will find other relevant books near the one you have chosen.

♦ **Use online periodicals in libraries.** Your library may have access to EBSCOhost® or INFOtrac. By typing keywords into EBSCO, you can search through national or international newspapers, magazines, or reference books. When you find an article that you need, print it or cut and paste it into a word processing file, and then e-mail the document to yourself. Remember to print or copy the publication data because you will need that information when you cite your source.

Searching the Internet

Search engines such as Google and Yahoo! can rapidly retrieve thousands of documents from the Internet. However, most people do not need as many documents as those engines can generate. Here are some tips to help make your Internet searches focused and efficient.

♦ **Choose your keywords with care.** Imagine you want information about new fuel sources for automobiles. If you type the words *alternative energy* in Google's keyword search space, you will come up with ten million entries (also known as "hits"). Think about more precise terms that could help you limit your search. For instance, if you are really interested in fuel sources for automobiles, you might change your search request to *alternative car fuel*. If you do not find information on your topic, think about synonyms or alternative ways to describe it.

♦ **Use quotation marks to limit the search.** Remember that you are driving the search, and you can control how many hits you get. By putting quotation marks around your search query, you limit the number of sites to those that contain all of the words that you requested. For example, when you input the words *alternative car fuel* into Google, you will have more than three million hits. When the same words are enclosed within quotation marks, the number of hits is reduced significantly.

◆ **Use bookmarks.** When you find information that might be useful, create a folder where you can store the information in a "bookmark" or "favorites" list. Then you can easily find it later. (The bookmark icon appears on the toolbar of your search engine.)

◆ **Use academic search engines.** Sites such as *Google Scholar* or *Virtual Learning Resources Center* help you look through academic publications such as theses, peer-reviewed papers, books, and articles. To find more academic sites, simply do a search for "academic search engines."

Conducting Interviews or Surveys

You can support your research essay with information from an interview. Speak to an expert in the field or someone who is directly affected by an issue. If you record the interview, ensure that your subject gives you permission to do so. Remember to plan the interview before you meet the person and list key questions that you would like answered. Include the person's complete name and qualifications in your research notes.

Another source of information can be a **survey**, which is an assessment of the views of many people. For example, if you are writing about a tuition fee increase, you can survey students to gather their opinions. When you plan your survey, follow some basic guidelines:

◆ **Determine your goal.** What do you want to discover?

◆ **Determine the age, gender, and status of the respondents** (people you will survey). For example, you might decide to survey equal-sized groups of males and females or those over and under twenty-five years of age.

◆ **Decide how many people you will survey.** Survey at least ten people (or a number determined by your instructor).

◆ **Determine the type of survey you will do.** Will you survey people using the phone, e-mail, or written forms? Keep in mind that people are more likely to obscure the truth when asked questions directly, especially if the questions are embarrassing or very personal. For example, if you ask someone whether he agrees or disagrees with legalized abortion, he might present a viewpoint that he thinks you or nearby listeners will accept. The same person might be more honest in an anonymous written survey.

◆ **Plan your survey questions.** If gender, age, marital status, or job status are important, place questions about those items at the beginning of your survey. When you form your questions, do not ask open-ended, essay-type questions because it will be difficult to compile the results. Instead, ask yes/no questions or provide a choice of answers. Sample questions:

What is your gender?   male _____ female _____

How often do you use the public transit system (the bus, subway, or train)?

_____ weekdays   _____ about once a week

_____ rarely or never   _____ about once a month

If you want to determine your respondents' knowledge about a topic, include an "I don't know" response. Otherwise, people will make selections that could skew your survey results.

Has Jackson Monroe done a good job as student union leader?

_____ yes   _____ no   _____ I don't know

L03 Evaluate sources.

Evaluating Sources

When you see sources published in print or online, especially when they are attention-grabbing with color or graphics, you may forget to question whether those sources are reliable. For instance, a company's Web site advertising an alternative cancer therapy might be less reliable than an article in a scientific journal by a team of oncologists (doctors who treat cancer).

HINT ◄ Questions for Evaluating a Source

Each time you find a source, ask yourself the following questions:

- Will the information support the point that I want to make?
- Is the information current? When was the site last updated? Ask yourself if the date is appropriate for your topic.
- Is the site reliable and highly regarded? For instance, is it from a well-respected newspaper, magazine, or journal? Is the English grammatically correct?
- Is the author an expert on the subject? (Many sites provide biographical information about the author.)
- Does the writer present a balanced view, or does he or she clearly favor one viewpoint over another? Ask yourself if the writer has a political or financial interest in the issue.
- Is there advertising on the site? Consider how advertising might influence the site's content.
- Do different writers supply the same information on various sites? Information is more likely to be reliable if multiple sources cite the same facts.

PRACTICE 1

Imagine that you are conducting research about the safety of bottled water. Answer the questions by referring to the list of Web entries that follows the questions.

1. Write the letters of three Web hits that are **not** useful for your essay. For each one you choose, explain why.

   _____

   _____

   _____

2. Write the letters of the three Web hits that you should investigate further. Briefly explain how each one could be useful.

   _____

   _____

   _____

A. Is Bottled Really Better? The NRDC Takes A Look At The Pros And . . .
http://www.cbsnews.com/stories...shtml
The Natural Resources Defense Council (NRDC) Takes A Look At
The Pros And Cons Of Bottled Water. July 25, 2007 | by Erin Petrun.

B. There Can Be Dangers Of Drinking Bottled Water | Water Purifiers
http://www.home-water-distiller.com/waterpurifiers/drinkingwater/
there-can-be-dangers...62/
22 Aug 2008 . . . Water is an excellent way to keep your mind sharp
and your body in excellent shape as most everyone in the world
already knows.

C. Healthy Diet Info Zone: BOTTLED WATER - DANGER!!!
http://health-diet-info.blogspot.com/2008/05...html
BOTTLED WATER - DANGER!!! Posted by Martin | 6:55 AM.
Healthy Drinks · 0 comments. Bottled water in your car . . .
very dangerous, woman! . . .

D. Bottled vs. Tap
http://pediatrics.about.com...a/080702_ask_3.htm
Is the extra cost of bottled water vs. tap water worth it? . . . "consumers
should feel confident of the safety of their water," says Stew Thornley,
a water quality health educator with the Minnesota Department
of Health. . . .

E. City still in shock over water danger
   http://www.chinadaily.com.cn/china/2009-02/23...htm
   City still in shock over water danger. By Qian Yanfeng (China Daily)
   "... but I'm still drinking bottled water and only use tap water for
   washing," he said. ...

F. ABC News: Study: Bottled Water No Safer Than Tap Water
   http://abcnews.go.com...id=87558&page=
   Bottled water users were twice as likely as others to cite health for
   their choice of beverage, the study found. Fifty-six percent of
   bottled water users ...

HINT ◄ **Do Not Pay for Online Articles**

Ignore Web sites that offer to sell articles or essays. There are many free
online journals, magazines, and newspapers that contain articles suitable
for a research project. Also find out if your college has access to extensive
online databases such as EBSCO.

THE WRITER'S DESK **Research Your Topic**

Using the guiding research question that you developed in the previous
Writer's Desk, list some keywords that you can use to research your
topic.

_____

_____

_____

_____

Using the library and the Internet, find some sources that you can use
for your research essay. You might also conduct interviews or prepare a
survey. Print out relevant online sources, and keep track of your source
information.

Taking Notes

LO 4 Take notes.

As you research your topic, keep careful notes on paper, on note cards, or in computer files. Do not rely on your memory! You would not want to spend several weeks researching, only to accidentally plagiarize because you had not adequately acknowledged some sources.

Look for sources that support your thesis statement. Each time you find a source that seems relevant, keep a detailed record of its publication information so that you can easily cite the source when you begin to write your research essay. You will find important information about preparing in-text citations and a Works Cited (MLA) list later in this chapter.

For example, Karyne Maheu created the following note card after finding source material in the library.

> Source: *Psychology* by Scott O. Lilienfeld et al., Upper Saddle River: Pearson, 2009. Print.
>
> Page 432: Although most brain maturation occurs prenatally and in the first few years of life, the frontal lobes don't mature fully until late adolescence or early adulthood.

Finding Complete Source Information

Source information is easy to find in most print publications. It is usually on the copyright page, which is often the second or third page of the book, magazine, or newspaper. On many Internet sites, however, finding the same information can take more investigative work. When you research on the Internet, look for the home page to find the site's title, publication date, and so on. Record as much information from the site as possible.

Book, Magazine, Newspaper	**Web Site**
author's full name	author's full name
title of article or chapter	title of article
title of book, magazine, or newspaper	title of site
	publisher of site
publishing information (name of publisher, city, and date of publication)	date of publication or update
	date that you accessed the site
page numbers used	complete Web site address

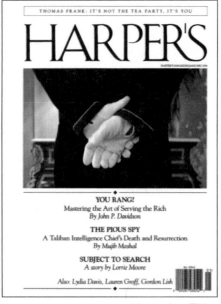

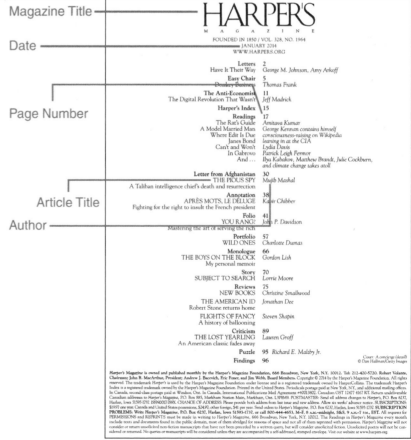

Magazine Title

Date

Page Number

Article Title

Author

Cover: A concierge (detail)
© Dan Hallman/Getty Images

Harper's Magazine is owned and published monthly by the Harper's Magazine Foundation, 666 Broadway, New York, N.Y. 10012. Tel: 212-420-5720. Robert Volante, Chairman; John R. MacArthur, President; Andrew J. Bacevich, Eric Foner, and Jim Webb, Board Members. Copyright © 2014 by the Harper's Magazine Foundation. All rights reserved. The trademark *Harper's* is used by the Harper's Magazine Foundation under license and is a registered trademark owned by HarperCollins. The trademark Harper's Index is a registered trademark owned by the Harper's Magazine Foundation. Printed in the United States. Periodicals postage paid at New York, N.Y., and additional mailing offices. In Canada, second-class postage paid at Windsor, Ont. In Canada, International Publications Mail Agreement #40013802. Canadian GST 12477 4167 RT. Return undeliverable Canadian addresses to *Harper's Magazine*, P.O. Box 885, Markham Station Main, Markham, Ont. L3P9M9. POSTMASTER: Send all address changes to *Harper's*, P.O. Box 6237, Harlan, Iowa 51593-1737. ISSN0017-789X. CHANGE OF ADDRESS: Please provide both address from last issue and new address. Allow six weeks' advance notice. SUBSCRIPTIONS: $19.97 one year. Canada and United States possessions, $24.97, other foreign, $41 per year. Send orders to *Harper's Magazine*, P.O. Box 6237, Harlan, Iowa 51593-1737. SUBSCRIPTION PROBLEMS: Write: *Harper's Magazine*, P.O. Box 6237, Harlan, Iowa 51593-1737, or call 800-444-4653, M–F, 8 A.M.–midnight, S&S, 9 A.M.–7 P.M., EST. All requests for PERMISSIONS and REPRINTS must be made in writing to *Harper's Magazine*, 666 Broadway, New York, N.Y. 10012. The Readings in *Harper's Magazine* every month include texts and documents found in the public domain, most of them abridged for reasons of space and not all of them reprinted with permission. *Harper's Magazine* will not consider or return unsolicited non-fiction manuscripts that have not been preceded by a written query, but will consider unsolicited fiction. Unsolicited poetry will not be considered or returned. No queries or manuscripts will be considered unless they are accompanied by a self-addressed, stamped envelope. Visit our website at www.harpers.org.

Newspaper Title

Edition

Date

Page Number

Article Title

Author

Title of Site

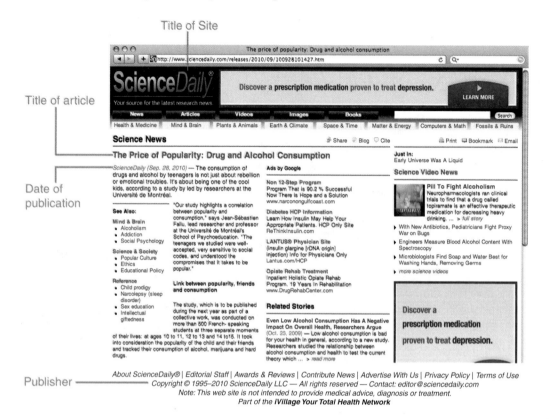

Title of article

Date of publication

Publisher

HINT ◁ Avoid Plagiarism

Do not plagiarize. Plagiarism is using someone else's work without giving that person credit. Such an act is considered stealing and is a very serious offense. To eliminate your chances of inadvertently plagiarizing, ensure that your notes contain detailed and clear source information. Then, when you later quote, paraphrase, or summarize another's work, you can cite the source. For more information about summarizing, see Chapter 16.

THE WRITER'S DESK Take Notes

Use your topic from the previous Writer's Desk. Take notes from the sources that you have found. In your notes, include direct quotations, paraphrases, and summaries. Organize your sources, and keep a record of them. For more information about quoting, paraphrasing, and summarizing, see pages 270–275 in this chapter.

Organizing Your First Draft

LO 5 Organize your first draft.

For research essays, as for any other type of essay, planning is essential. After you have evaluated the material that you have gathered, decide how you will organize your material. Group your notes under the main points that you would like to develop. Then arrange your ideas in a logical order. You might choose to use spatial, chronological, or emphatic order.

Writing a Thesis Statement

After taking notes, plan your thesis statement. Your thesis statement expresses the main focus of your essay. You can convert your guiding research question into a thesis statement. For instance, Karyne Maheu wrote the guiding research question *What are the health effects of energy drinks?* After researching and gathering material, she reworked her question to create a thesis statement.

> Energy drinks have serious side effects and are harmful when overused.

Creating an Outline

An **outline** or **plan** will help you organize your ideas. Write your main points, and list supporting details and examples. You can mention the sources you intend to use to support specific points. After looking at your preliminary outline, check if there are any holes in your research. If necessary, do more research to fill in those holes before writing your first draft. (For more samples of essay plans and for reminders about the writing process, see Chapters 1–5.)

Karyne's Preliminary Outline

Thesis: Energy drinks have serious side effects and are harmful when overused.

1. The stimulants in energy drinks can be potentially harmful when consumed with alcoholic drinks.
   —Wake Forest University study about alcohol and energy drinks
   —Energy drinks contain alcohol (Cloud 47)

2. If taken in excess, energy drinks can cause cardiovascular problems.
   —Blood pressure and energy drinks (Doheny)
   —Heart disease link (Tedmanson)

3. An ingredient in energy drinks called taurine might affect the brain.
   —Taurine can cause seizures (Merriman)
   —Age of consumers and developing brain (Lilienfeld 432)
   —Taurine's sedative properties ("Scientists")

> **THE WRITER'S DESK** **Make a Preliminary Plan**
>
> Write a thesis statement for your essay. Then organize your topic and make a plan. In your preliminary plan, include source information. Remember that this is not a final plan. You can add or remove information afterward.

LO 6 Incorporate visuals.

Incorporating Visuals

Visuals—such as charts, maps, graphs, photos, or diagrams—can help to clarify, summarize, emphasize, or illustrate certain concepts in research essays. For example, a graph showing the falling crime rate can be an effective way to support an argument that policing methods have become increasingly successful. Remember to use visuals sparingly and to cite them properly.

Most word processing programs offer templates for many visuals. For example, the toolbar in MS Word allows you to select *Chart* under *Insert* to create line, bar, pie, and other types of charts. Simply input your own data, and the program will create the chart for you. The following charts are standard templates from MS Word.

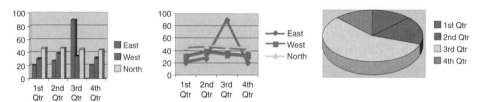

Other visuals can also be useful for illustrating concepts. Often, readers prefer seeing an object or idea in context rather than trying to understand it in writing. Basic diagrams, like the one shown here, can be especially useful for scientific and technical writing.

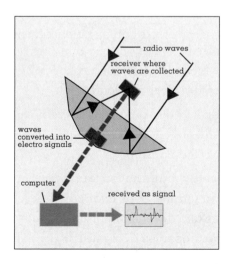

HINT ◄ Using Visuals

Here are some recommendations for using visuals in an academic research essay:

- Ask your instructor whether you are permitted to use visuals in your essay and, if so, where you need to insert them (in the body of your essay or in an appendix).
- Include a label above each visual to clearly identify it. For example, you can number figures and tables sequentially: *Figure 1, Figure 2,* or *Table 1, Table 2,* and so on.
- Place a caption alongside or under the visual to help the reader understand it.
- Acknowledge the source of any visual that you borrow.
- Explain in the text how the visual supports a specific point. For example, in the body of your paper, you might write *Figure 2 illustrates how the crime rate has fallen steadily since the 1990s.*

Citing Sources

Each time you borrow someone's words, ideas, or images, you must **cite** or credit the source to avoid plagiarizing. There are two places you need to cite sources in your research essays—in the essay and at the end of it. Use **in-text citations** (also known as **parenthetical citations**) as you incorporate quotations, paraphrases, or summaries. Then, cite the sources in an alphabetized list at the end of your essay. The title of this source list depends on the documentation style you choose. For example, the Modern Language Association (MLA) refers to the list as Works Cited and the American Psychological Association (APA) refers to it as References. This chapter presents MLA guidelines. For information about APA guidelines, see Appendix 5 (pages 609–613). You can also check each organization's Web site.

HINT ◄ Choose a Documentation Style

A **documentation style** is a method of presenting the material that you have researched. Three common sources for documenting style are the Modern Language Association (MLA), the American Psychological Association (APA), and the *Chicago Manual of Style* (CMS). Before writing a research essay, check with your instructor about which documentation style you should use and where you can find more information about it.

Avoid Plagiarism

LO7 Avoid plagiarism.

Plagiarism is the act of using someone else's **words** or **ideas** without giving that person credit. Plagiarism is a very serious offense and can result in expulsion from a course or termination from work. Always acknowledge the source when you borrow material.

The following actions are examples of plagiarism.

* copying and pasting text from an Internet source without using quotation marks to properly set off the author's words
* using ideas from another source without citing that source
* making slight modifications to an author's sentences but presenting the work as your own
* buying another work and presenting it as your own
* using another student's work and presenting it as your own

HINT ◂ Be Careful

The Internet has made it easier to plagiarize, but it is also easier for instructors to catch cheaters. To avoid plagiarism, always cite the source when you borrow words or ideas.

LO 8 Integrate paraphrases, summaries, and quotations.

Integrating Paraphrases, Summaries, and Quotations

In a research essay, you can support your main points with paraphrases, summaries, and integrated quotations. They strengthen your research paper and make it more forceful and convincing.

* A **paraphrase** is an indirect quotation. It is roughly the same length as the author's original words. When you paraphrase, restate someone's ideas using your own words.
* A **summary** is another type of indirect quotation. It is shorter than a paraphrase and includes only the main ideas of the original work.
* A **direct quotation** contains the exact words of the speaker or writer, and it is set off with quotation marks.

All of these strategies are valid ways to incorporate research into your writing, as long as you give credit to the author or speaker. Review examples of a paraphrase, summary, and quotation.

Original Selection

Identity marketing is a promotional strategy whereby consumers alter some aspects of themselves to advertise for a branded product. A British marketing firm paid five people to legally change their names for one year to "Turok," the hero of a video game series about a time-traveling Native American who slays bionically enhanced dinosaurs. In another case, the Internet Underground Music Archive (IUMA) paid a Kansas couple $5,000 to name their baby boy Iuma. Body art is the most common form of identity advertising. Air New Zealand created "cranial billboards" in exchange for a round-trip ticket to New Zealand; thirty Los Angeles participants shaved their heads and walked around with an ad for the airline on their skulls. Some companies pay people to display more permanent body art. The Casa Sanchez restaurant in San Francisco gives free lunches for life to anyone who gets its logo tattooed on his or her body. The Daytona Cubs baseball team awards free season tickets for life to anyone who will tattoo the Cubs logo on his or her body.

—Solomon, Michael R. *Consumer Behavior*. 10th ed. Boston: Pearson, 2013. Print. 557.

Paraphrase

In his book *Consumer Behavior*, Michael R. Solomon discusses a marketing trend called identity marketing. Citizens receive a financial incentive to promote a company in some way. For example, an advertising company paid people to briefly rename themselves after a popular game's lead character. An online music archive offered cash to parents who would name their baby after the company. The most widespread form of identity marketing occurs when people agree to have their head shaved or their body tattooed in exchange for some reward, such as a free flight, a lifetime supply of baseball tickets, or unlimited free lunches (557).

Summary

Michael R. Solomon, in his book *Consumer Behavior*, discusses a marketing trend called identity marketing. Examples include some firms who pay people to adopt the company's name and companies who give rewards such as free lunches or sports tickets to those who agree to be tattooed with the business's name (557).

Quotation

In his book *Consumer Behavior*, Michael R. Solomon discusses identity marketing, which is "a promotional strategy whereby consumers alter some aspects of themselves to advertise for a branded product" (557).

> Mention source

> **GRAMMAR LINK**
> To find out more about using quotations, see Chapter 37.

How to Summarize and Paraphrase

When you paraphrase or summarize, you restate someone's ideas using your own words. The main difference between a paraphrase and a summary is the length. A paraphrase can be close to the same length as the original selection, but a summary is much shorter.

To paraphrase or summarize, do the following:

* Paraphrase if your audience needs detailed information about the subject.
* Summarize if the audience needs to know only general information. A summary is generally a maximum of 30 percent of the length of the original selection.

◆ Restate the main ideas using your own words. You can keep specialized words, common words, and names of people or places. However, find synonyms for other words, and use your own sentence structure.

◆ Maintain the original author's ideas and intent.

◆ Acknowledge the source. Mention the author or title of the work. When available, also include the page number.

◆ Proofread your writing to ensure that you have expressed the message in your own words.

Note: Chapter 16 contains more information about summary writing.

HINT ◀ **Should I Paraphrase, Summarize, or Quote?**

In a research essay, include some quotations, but do not overwhelm your reader with other people's direct speech. Instead, sprinkle in very short paraphrases, summaries, and quotations, when needed, to back up your arguments.

LO 9 Use MLA style.

MLA Style: In-Text Citations

When you paraphrase, summarize, or quote, you must cite the source in the body of the essay. You must also cite the source in a Works Cited page at the end of your essay. See the Hint on page 277 to view the Works Cited page for the following quotations.

You can do in-text citations in two different ways. Note that these methods must be used with paraphrases, summaries, and quotations.

1. **Cite the source in the sentence.**
   Mention the author's last name in the sentence. If you are using a print source, then put the page number in the sentence or in parentheses at the end of the sentence.

   Author's name   page number in parentheses

   Postrel mentions that the crisis became a national obsession (**44**).

   For online sources, just mention the author's name. No page number is necessary.

   Michelle Singletary mentions the misconception: "If you have a federal student loan, it can't be discharged in bankruptcy."

   If an online source does not provide an author's name, mention the article's title or the Web site title in the sentence.

   According to **"Student Debt Assistance,"** too many students have extremely high credit card balances.

2. **Cite the source in parentheses following the sentence.**
    In parentheses after the selection, put the author's last name and the page number, with no punctuation in between.

    The crisis was on everyone's mind: "On the subject of credit, bad news sells"
    Name and page number
    (Postrel 44).

    For online sources, just put the author's last name in parentheses.

    Students cannot simply refuse to pay a student loan from the federal government (**Singletary**).

    If the online source does not provide an author's name, write a short form of the title in parentheses.

    The student debt load is worrisome: "Undergraduates are carrying record-high credit card balances" (**"Student"**).

HINT ◀ **Quoting from a Secondary Source**

Some works include quotations from other people. If an author is quoted in a secondary source, then put the abbreviation **_qtd. in_**, meaning "quoted in," in parentheses.

> Hillel Black describes a "consumer credit explosion that makes the population explosion seem small" (qtd. in Postrel).

See Chapter 37 for more information about using quotations.

> **GRAMMAR LINK**
> To find out more about writing titles, see page 494 in Chapter 37.

PRACTICE 2

Read the next selection and then write a paraphrase, a summary, and a direct quotation. Remember to acknowledge the source. If you are unsure about how to punctuate a quotation, refer to pages 486–487 in Chapter 37.

Original Selection
     Although fewer Americans are smoking (down to about 25 percent from over 40 percent in the sixties), women and teenagers are actually smoking more than before. This is alarming news when one considers the toxic nature of nicotine: In the 1920s and 1930s, it was used as an insecticide and is considered to be highly toxic and fast acting. Although the amount of nicotine in a cigarette is low, first-time smokers often experience nausea as a result of the toxic effects after just a few puffs.

                    —Ciccarelli, Saundra K. *Psychology*. Upper Saddle River:
                                       Pearson, 2009. Print. 148–149.

1. Write a paraphrase.

_____

_____

_____

_____

_____

_____

2. Write a summary.

_____

_____

_____

_____

3. Write a direct quotation.

_____

_____

_____

PRACTICE 3

Practice identifying plagiarism. Read the following selection, and then determine if the paraphrase and summaries contain plagiarized information. Check for copied words or phrases, and also determine if the source is properly mentioned.

Original Selection

Having children can affect marital satisfaction. Studies show that parents report lower levels of satisfaction compared to nonparents. Mothers of infants, however, show the greatest difference in marital contentment when compared to women with no children at all. In general, the data show that satisfaction for both men and women decreases after the birth of the first child. Researchers suggest that this is, in large part, due to conflicts that come about from parenting and decreased levels of personal freedom. Children demand attention and force a shift in roles from husband/wife to father/mother. Regardless of the form of the study, parents exhibit lower levels of a sense of well-being while expressing more frequent negative emotions than do peers who are without children.

—Carl, John D. *Think: Social Problems*. Boston: Pearson, 2013. Print. 219.

1. **Paraphrase**

   In *Think: Social Problems*, John D. Carl writes that parents have a lower rate of marital happiness than couples without children. Mothers of infants show the greatest difference in marital happiness, perhaps because there are many conflicts that are caused by the presence of children. For instance, children demand attention and couples experience a shift in roles from spouses to parents. Also, parents have decreased levels of personal freedom. They express more frequent negative emotions than nonparents (219).

   Is this an example of plagiarism?   yes _____   no _____

   Why? _____

2. **Summary**

   According to John D. Carl, on page 219 of *Think: Social Problems*, childless couples are actually more satisfied than those with children. The decline in happiness may partially be due to the stresses involved in parenting. Mothers and fathers see their liberty eroded as they expend a lot of time and energy taking care of their offspring.

   Is this an example of plagiarism?   yes _____   no _____

   Why? _____

   _____

3. **Summary**

   Studies show that parents do not feel as content as nonparents, mainly because there are many stresses involved in raising children. Mothers and fathers have a lot of restrictions on their personal time, and their role as spouse is taken over by the role of caretaker. Thus, they have a more pessimistic outlook than child-free couples.

   Is this an example of plagiarism?   yes _____   no _____

   Why? _____

MLA: Preparing a Works Cited List

An MLA-style Works Cited list appears at the end of a research essay. It gives readers details about each source from which you have borrowed material to write your essay. Works Cited is not the same as a running bibliography, which lists all of the sources you consulted while you were researching your essay topic. In a Works Cited list, include only works that you have quoted, paraphrased, or summarized.

To prepare a Works Cited list, follow these basic guidelines.

1. A Works Cited list always starts on a new page. Put your name and page number in the upper right-hand corner, as you do on all other pages of the essay.
2. Write "Works Cited" at the top of the page and center it. Do not italicize it, underline it, or put quotation marks around it.
3. List each source alphabetically, using the author's last name.
4. Indent the second line and all subsequent lines of each entry five spaces.
5. Double-space all lines.

Parts of a Works Cited Reference

A Works Cited reference generally has the following parts, with the order and punctuation shown below.

1.	**Author(s)**	Complete last name, first name. Coauthor's first name last name.
2.	**Title of short work**	"Article." or "Short Story."
3.	**Title of long work**	*Book.* or *Magazine.* or *Web site Name.*
4.	**Edition (if applicable)**	2nd ed.
		For second, third, or subsequent editions, write the abbreviated form: 8th ed.
5.	**Place of publication**	City:
6.	**Publisher's name**	Company,
		Omit *A*, *An*, or *The* and words such as *Co.*, *Corp.*, *Books*, *Press*, and *Publishers*. The short form for University Press is UP. On Internet sites, look for the publisher's or sponsor's name.
7.	**Date of publication**	Day Month Year.
		Provide as specific a date as is available. For instance, book citations require just the publication year. Periodicals generally have just the month and year.
8.	**Medium of publication**	Print. or Web.
		For paper sources, write *Print.* For Internet content, write *Web.* Other sources might be *CD*, *Performance*, *Television*, or *Film*.
9.	**Page numbers (if applicable)**	B13. or 112–115.
10.	**Date of Access (Web sources)**	Day Month Year.

EXAMPLE

Bonvillain, Nancy. "Making a Living." *Cultural Anthropology.* 3rd Ed. Upper Saddle River: Pearson, 2013. Print. 210–245.

HINT ◄ Placement and Order of Works Cited

The Works Cited list should be at the end of the research paper. List sources in alphabetical order of the authors' last names. If there is no author, put the title in the alphabetized list. The example is a Works Cited page for the quotations listed on pages 272–273.

Works Cited

Postrel, Virginia. "The Case for Debt." *Atlantic* Nov. 2008: 44–47. Print.

Singletary, Michelle. "The Color of Money." *Washington Post.* The Washington Post Company, 24 Sept. 2006. Web. 14 May 2014.

"Student Debt Statistics." *American Student Assistance.* American Student Assistance, 2009. Web. 15 May 2014.

Sample MLA-Style Works Cited Entries

The following are a few sample entries for various publications. The *MLA Handbook for Writers of Research Papers* has a complete list of sample entries. As you look at the samples, notice how they are punctuated.

Model Entries
Books

comma	period	period	period	colon

Last name, First name. *Title of the Book.* edition. Place of Publication:

comma period period

Publisher, Year. Print.

One author

Carl, John D. *Think: Social Problems*. Boston: Pearson, 2013. Print.

Two or more authors

After the first author's last and first name, write the first and last name of the subsequent authors. Write *and* before the last author name.

Robinson, Richard D., Michael McKenna, and Kristin Conradi. *Issues and Trends in Literacy Education*. 5th ed. Boston: Pearson, 2012. Print.

Four or more authors

Put the first author's name followed by *et al.*, which means "and others."

Goldfield, David, et al. *The American Journey*. Upper Saddle River: Prentice Hall, 2002. Print.

Editor instead of an author

Write the editor's name followed by *ed.*

> Gansworth, Eric, ed. *Sovereign Bones: New Native American Writing*.
> New York: Nation, 2007. Print.

Two or more books by the same author

Write the author's name in the first entry only. In subsequent entries, type three hyphens followed by a period. Then add the title.

> Angelou, Maya. *I Know Why the Caged Bird Sings*. New York: Random
> House, 1969. Print.
> ---. *Mother: A Cradle to Hold Me*. New York: Random House, 2006. Print.

A work in an anthology

For articles or essays taken from an anthology or edited collection, mention the author and title of the article first. Then write the anthology's title followed by *Ed.* and the editor's name. End with the page numbers of the piece you are citing followed by *Print*.

> Weaskus, Jeanette. "A Ghost Dance for Words." *Sovereign Bones: New
> Native American Writing*. Ed. Eric Gansworth. New York: Nation,
> 2007. 129–134. Print.

A previously published article in a collection

Some collections give information about a previously published article on the page where the article appears. When citing such sources, include information about the previous publication, and then add *Rpt. in* (which means "Reprinted in"). Then include the title of the collection.

> Buchwald, Art. "The Hydrogen Bomb Lobby." *Laid Back in Washington*.
> New York: G.P. Putman. 1981. Rpt. in *Controversy: Issues for Reading
> and Writing*. Ed. Judith J. Pula, Audrey T. Edwards, and R. Allan
> Dermott. 3rd ed. Upper Saddle River: Pearson, 2005. 178–180. Print.

A book in a series

If the book is part of a series, then end your citation with the series name (but do not italicize it or set it off in any way).

> Fiorina, Morris P., Samuel J. Abrams, and Jeremy C. Pope, eds. *Culture
> War?*, 3rd ed. New York: Longman, 2011. Print. Great Questions in
> Politics.

Encyclopedia and dictionary

When encyclopedias and dictionaries list items alphabetically, you can omit volume and page numbers. It is sufficient to list the edition and year of publication.

> "Democracy." *Columbia Encyclopedia*. 6th ed. 2005. Print.

"Legitimate." *New American Webster Handy College Dictionary.* 3rd
    ed. 2003. Print.

Periodicals

Last name, First name. "Title of Article." *Title of Magazine* or
    Newspaper Date: Pages. Print.

Note: If the pages are not consecutive, put the first page number and a plus sign (81+).

Newspaper article

Fulford, Robert. "Feeding the Illness Industry Machine." *National Post*
    18 Aug. 2012: A17. Print.

Magazine article

Lepore, Jill. "Battleground America." *New Yorker* 23 Apr. 2012: 39–47. Print.

Editorial

Put the editor's name first. If the editorial is unsigned, begin with the title. Put
"Editorial" after the title.

"The Thin Blue Line." Editorial. *National Post* 18 Aug. 2012: A14. Print.

Journal article

Seligman, Martin. "The American Way of Blame." *APA Monitor* 29.7
    (1998): 97. Print.

Electronic (Internet) Sources

When using a source published on the Internet, include as much of the following
information as you can find. Keep in mind that some sites do not contain complete
information. Put a comma after the publisher or sponsor, and put periods after all
other parts of the citation. **Do not include the complete URL address unless the
site is difficult to find or your teacher requires it.**

Last name, First name. "Title of Article." *Title of Site* or *Online
    Publication.* Publisher or sponsor, Date of publication or recent
    update. Web. Date you accessed the site.

Note: If there is no clear publisher or sponsor, write N.p. If there is no clear publication date, write N.d.

Personal Web site article

Sacks, Oliver. "Uncle Tungsten." *Oliver Sacks.* Oliver Sacks, 2008. Web.
    10 Apr. 2010.

E-Book

Format the book reference like you would if it were a print version. For the
medium of publication, mention the type of file, such as *Nook file, Kindle file,
PDF file,* etc. If you cannot identify the file, write *Digital file.* Note: You don't need
to mention the date you accessed the file.

> McKenna, Christina. *The Misremembered Man*. Las Vegas:
> AmazonEncore, 2008. Kindle file.

Online newspaper article

> Llewellyn Smith, Julia. "The Truth About Lying." *The Telegraph*.
> Telegraph Media Group, 15 Aug. 2012. Web. 14 May 2014.

Online magazine article

> Frances, Allen, M.D. "Fighting the Wrong War on Drugs." *Psychology
> Today*. Sussex, 28 Aug. 2012. Web. 15 May 2014.

Online dictionary

> "Prescient." *Dictionary.com*. 2013. Web. 22 Aug. 2014.

Web-only article

> Leonard, Andrew. "America Favors the Rich." *Salon*. Salon Media
> Group, 28 Aug. 2012. Web. 14 May 2014.

No listed author

If the site does not list an author's name, begin with the title of the article.

> "Mass Layoff Statistics." *Bureau of Labor Statistics*. US Bureau of Labor,
> 23 Aug. 2012. Web. 28 May 2014.
>
> "How to Maintain a Healthy Relationship." *Truth About Deception*. Truth
> About Deception, 2012. Web. 14 Sept. 2014.

Other Types of Sources

Interview that you conducted

> Kumar, Nantha. Personal interview. 14 Aug. 2014.

Film or DVD

Include the name of the film, the director, the studio, and the year of release. You
can include other data that you consider relevant such as the names of the main
performers or screenwriters. End with *Film* or *DVD*.

> *The Hunger Games*. Dir. Gary Ross. Perf. Jennifer Lawrence. Lion's
> Gate, 2012. Film.

Radio or television program

Include the segment title, the narrator (if applicable), the program name, the
station, and the broadcast date. End with *Television* or *Radio*.

> "The Case Against Lehman Brothers." Narr. Steve Kroft. *Sixty Minutes*.
> CBS. 19 Aug. 2012. Television.

Sound recording

Include the name of the performer or band, the title of the song, the title of the
CD, the name of the recording company, and the year of release.

> Nirvana. "About a Girl." *Unplugged in New York*. Geffen, 1994. CD.

PRACTICE 4

Imagine that you are using the following sources in a research paper. Arrange the sources for a Works Cited list using MLA style. Remember to place the items in alphabetical order.

- You use a definition of "amnesia" from the online dictionary *Merriam-Webster*. The year of publication is 2012. You accessed the site today.
- You quote from a book by Jeffrey Moore called *The Memory Artists*. The publisher is St. Martin's, and the publication date is 2006. The publisher's city is New York.
- You use statistics from an online article called "Honesty/Ethics in Professions." The Web site is *Gallup*, and the publisher is Gallup. The publication date is December 1, 2011. There is no author. You accessed the site today.
- You quote from the textbook *Anthropology* by Carol R. Ember, Melvin Ember, and Peter N. Peregrine. The publisher is Pearson, and the publication date is 2007. The publisher's city is Upper Saddle River.
- You quote from the article "Still Cuckoo After All These Years" by James Wolcott. It appeared in a magazine called *Vanity Fair*, which was published in December 2011. Your quote was from page 134.
- You quote from an online magazine called *Salon*. "The Neuroscience of Happiness" was written by Lucy McKeon and published on January 28, 2012. The online publisher is Salon Media Group. You accessed the site today.

Works Cited

_____

_____

_____

_____

_____

_____

_____

_____

_____

_____

LO 10 Review a sample research essay.

Sample Research Essay
Title Pages and Outlines

Although MLA does not insist on an outline for a research essay, your instructor may request one.

Outline

Thesis: Energy drinks have serious side effects and are harmful when overused.

I.   The stimulants in energy drinks can be potentially harmful when consumed with alcoholic drinks.

   A. Wake Forest University studied alcohol and energy drinks.

   B. Energy drinks can mask a person's level of intoxication.

   C. Some companies mix energy drinks and alcohol.

II.   Furthermore, if taken in excess, energy drinks can cause cardiovascular problems.

   A. The drinks can increase blood pressure.

   B. Heart disease is linked to energy drinks.

III. Taurine, an ingredient in energy drinks, might affect the brain.

   A. Taurine increases alertness but can cause seizures.

   B. Youths have developing brains.

   C. Taurine may act as a sedative.

The Research Essay

Maheu 1

Karyne Maheu

Professor Slater

English 102B

May 8, 2014

The Dangers of Energy Drinks

Red Bull, Monster, Rockstar, Burn, and Energy are all popular energy drinks. These products are an effective way to get coffee-like stimulation. People consume these products to wake up in the morning, to perform at work or school, to stay up late in clubs, and to perform in sports. Manufacturers point out that energy drinks contain natural ingredients such as herbs and vitamins. However, energy drinks also contain a lot of sugar and a high concentration of caffeine. Some people have experienced illness and even death after consuming such drinks. Energy drinks have serious side effects and are harmful when overused.

The stimulants in energy drinks can be potentially harmful, especially when consumed with alcohol. Scientists at Wake Forest University discovered that "students who consumed alcohol mixed with energy drinks were twice as likely to be hurt or injured . . . as were students who did not consume alcohol mixed with energy drinks" (Nauert). Another danger of mixing alcohol with energy drinks is that the stimulant can make intoxicated students feel awake enough to drive (Doheny). In *Time* magazine, John Cloud reports that "a new generation of malt beverages also contains stimulants" (47).

Write your last name and page number in the top right corner of each page.

Double-space your identification information.

Center the title without underlining, italics, quotation marks, or boldface type.

Double-space throughout the body of the essay.

It is not necessary to document your common knowledge.

End your introduction with your thesis statement.

Identify the source in parentheses.

Acknowledge sources of summary.

Include the page number of a print source.

Maheu 2

Furthermore, if taken in excess, energy drinks can cause cardiovascular problems. According to *WebMD*, many people report increased blood pressure after consuming the drinks. In Australia, researchers gave energy drinks to thirty university students. Sophie Tedmanson and David Rose report that the consequences on the heart were serious: "Australian researchers said that after drinking one can, participants had shown a cardiovascular profile similar to that of someone with heart disease." Scott Willoughby, who works at the Cardiovascular Research Center at the Royal Adelaide Hospital, says, "People who have existing cardiovascular disease may want to talk to their physician before they drink Red Bull" (qtd. in Tedmanson). Thus, energy drinks, which can boost blood pressure and the pulse rate, should be used with care.

Finally, taurine, a key ingredient in energy drinks, might affect the brain. Taurine increases intellectual alertness, so it's active in the brain area. Researchers at St. Joseph's Hospital and Medical Center in Phoenix found that energy drink consumption was related to seizures: "One patient, a previously healthy 25-year-old male, had been admitted to the emergency room for two seizure episodes four months apart. . . . The patient reported that he had consumed two 24-oz bottles of the energy drink Rockstar on an empty stomach approximately thirty to sixty minutes prior to both seizures" (Merriman). Although only four people had related seizures, the possible link between energy drinks and brain injury is worrisome. Furthermore, most energy drink consumers are youths with undeveloped frontal lobes (Lilienfeld 432). Thus, young people might suffer long-term effects when exposed to the stimulants

Acknowledge sources of borrowed ideas.

Indentify the source in the phrase introducing the quotation.

Use "qtd. in" to show that the quotation appeared in a secondary source.

Place ellipses after the period to show where irrelevant material has been removed.

Cite the source of summarized information.

Maheu 3

and taurine in energy drinks. Also, taurine can have a "sedative effect" on the brain and "may play a role in the 'crash' people report after drinking these highly caffeinated beverages" ("Scientists").

In conclusion, energy drink ingredients such as caffeine, sugar, herbs, vitamins, and taurine have possibly dangerous side effects. These drinks, promoted heavily to youths, are not closely regulated for their medicinal qualities. Manufacturers of Red Bull and similar products should be forced to provide warnings. Consumers should use such drinks with moderation, and those with heart problems should avoid energy drinks completely.

If the author is not known, write the first words of the title in parentheses.

End with a quotation, prediction, or recommendation.

Works Cited   Maheu 4

Cloud, John. "Alcoholic Energy Drinks: A Risky Mix." *Time* 30 May 2008: 47. Print.

Doheny, Kathleen. "Energy Drinks: Hazardous to Your Health?" *WebMD*. WebMD, 24 Sept. 2008. Web. 4 May 2014.

Lilienfeld, Scott O., et al. *Psychology*. Upper Saddle River: Pearson, 2009. Print.

Merriman, John. "Do Stimulants in Energy Drinks Provoke Seizures?" *NeurologyReviews.com*. Quadrant HealthCom, June 2007. Web. 4 May 2014.

Nauert, Rick. "Energy Drinks + Alcohol = Danger." *PsychCentral*. Psych Central, 5 Nov. 2007. Web. 4 May 2014.

"Scientists Close in on Taurine's Activity in the Brain." *Medical News Today*. MediLexicon International Ltd., 18 Jan. 2008. Web. 4 May 2014.

Tedmanson, Sophie, and David Rose. "Red Bull Gives You Wings—and Heart Trouble?" *TimesOnline*. Times Newspapers, 15 Aug. 2008. Web. 5 May 2014.

Double-space sources.

Place sources in alphabetical order.

Indent the second and subsequent lines when an entry runs over one line.

PRACTICE 5

Answer the following questions by referring to the research essay.

1. How many magazines or books were used as sources? _____

2. How many Internet articles were used as sources? _____

3. When the student used a quotation that appeared as a quotation in another source, how did she show that fact? (See the third paragraph.)

   _____

4. In the Works Cited page, how many sources do not mention an author? _____

5. On the Works Cited page, are the sources listed in alphabetical order?

   yes _____   no _____

Indicate if the following sentences are true (T) or false (F). Look at the Works Cited page to answer each question. If the sentence is false, write a true statement under it.

6. The second row of each citation should be indented.

   T   F

   _____

7. The title of articles should be set off with italics.

   T   F

   _____

8. Place periods after the author's first name and the title of the work.

   T   F

   _____

9. For Internet sources, no dates are necessary.

   T   F

   _____

10. For Internet sources, always put "Web" at the very end.

    T   F

    _____

HINT ◄ APA Web Site

To get some general information about some basic style questions, you can view the APA's Web site. Use the menu on the left side of the page to direct you to specific style questions and answers.

On the same Web site, there is a link to information about online or "electronic" sources. Because the information about online sources is continually being updated, the site has comprehensive information about the latest citation methods.

MyWritingLab™

THE WRITER'S ROOM

MyWritingLab™

Complete these writing assignments at mywritinglab.com

Writing Activity 1

Write a research paper about one of the following topics. Ask your instructor what reference style you should use. Put a Works Cited page at the end of your assignment.

1. Write about a contemporary issue that is in the news.

2. Write about any issue in your career choice or field of study.

Writing Activity 2

Write a research paper about one of the following topics. First, brainstorm questions about your topic and find a guiding research question. Then follow the process of writing a research essay.

Abortion	Fast food
Affirmative action	Foreign adoptions
Assisted suicide	Gambling
Attention-deficit disorder	Genetically modified food
Body image	Government-sponsored gambling
Censorship of the Internet	Health-care reform
Childhood obesity	Holistic healing
Consequences of war	Home schooling
Date rape	Immigration
Executive salaries	Legalization of marijuana

continued

Mandatory drug testing   Teen pregnancy
Prison reform   Tobacco industry
Privacy and the Internet   Violence in the media
Same-sex marriage   Volunteer work
Technology and pollution (e-waste)   Youth gangs

Checklist: Research Essay

When you plan a research essay, ask yourself these questions.

☐ Have I narrowed my topic?

☐ Have I created a guiding research question?

☐ Are my sources reliable?

☐ Have I organized my notes?

☐ Have I integrated source information using quotations, paraphrases, and summaries?

☐ Have I correctly documented my in-text or parenthetical citations?

☐ Have I correctly prepared and punctuated my Works Cited page?

The Response Essay 18

LEARNING OBJECTIVES

LO 1 Respond to film and literature. **(p. 289)**

Critics who review musical performances are influenced by many factors. They consider the skill of the performer and the quality of the acoustics. They also notice the concert venue and the costumes. You take similar elements into consideration when you interpret works of film and literature.

WRITERS' EXCHANGE

Work with a partner. Discuss films or stories that you love. Make a "top-five" list.

Writing a Response Essay

LO 1 Respond to film and literature.

As a college student, you are often asked to state your opinion, to interpret issues, and to support your ideas. In some of your courses, your instructor may ask you to respond to another work with a **response essay**, which can also be called a **report**.

In such an essay, you include a brief summary of the original work, showing that you have a clear understanding of it. Then you explain your reactions to the work. Review the four parts of a response essay.

Introduction

In your introductory paragraph, identify the source of the work you are analyzing. For instance, if you are writing about a written work, identify the author, title, and publication date. If you are responding to a film, identify the title, director, and date of release. You can complete your introduction with general background information about the work. End your introduction with your thesis, which includes the topic and your controlling idea.

Summary

Write a **brief synopsis** of the work. Include the main points, and do not go into great detail about the work. Summarize the work so that readers can clearly understand the main storyline. At this point, do not make any personal value judgments about the work. Simply state what happened. (To learn more about summary writing, see Chapter 16: Summarizing.)

Reactions

After the summary, include several reaction paragraphs. Remember that each body paragraph should develop one main point. (Review the model response essays on the next pages and notice that each body paragraph has a single focus.) To find ideas for your reaction paragraphs, you can ask yourself the following questions.

- Is the subject relevant to any of my academic studies? Does it relate to topics we have discussed in this class or in another course?
- Does the work give accurate, complete, or unbiased information about a subject? Does the author or filmmaker present the information in a balanced or a slanted way?
- Can I relate to the characters? What do they tell me about human nature?
- Does the work have technical merits? Does the author have a vivid writing style? Does the film have beautiful camera work or impressive special effects?
- What is the work's message? Has it changed my understanding about an issue? Is it related to a real-world problem?
- Would I recommend the work to other people? If so, why?

Note: Always support your reactions with specific examples.

Conclusion

Sum up your main points. End with a recommendation or a final thought.

Follow the Writing Process

When preparing your response essay, remember to follow the writing process.

* Use exploring strategies to generate ideas.
* Organize your ideas in distinct paragraphs that each have a central focus. Ensure that each body paragraph has unity, adequate support, and coherence.
* Back up your reactions with specific details from the work. Avoid vague statements such as *I like the movie* or *The book is interesting*. Instead, explain why you like the work or find it interesting, and support your point with details and examples.
* Edit your work, and correct any errors.

Include Quotations

You may decide to include direct quotations in your summary and your reaction paragraphs. Ensure that your quotations include a page reference, if available. Also ensure that you punctuate your quotations correctly. (For more information about using quotations, see pages 489–492 in Chapter 37.)

HINT ◄ Citing the Work

Your instructor might ask you to cite the work at the end of your response essay. For instance, the two response essays in this chapter would have the following MLA "Works Cited" information.

Works Cited

Avatar. Dir. James Cameron. Perf. Sam Worthington and Zoe Saldana. 2009. Fox. DVD.

Hemingway, Ernest. *For Whom the Bell Tolls*. 1940. New York: Scribner, 1995. Print.

For more information about MLA guidelines, see Chapter 17. For information about APA Guidelines, see Appendix 5 on pages 609–613.

A Sample Response to a Film

College student Matt Fiorentino wrote the following response to one of his favorite films. Notice how he structured his response.

The World of *Avatar*

"They've sent us a message that they can take whatever they want. Well, we will send them a message. That this—this is our land!" cries Jake Sully at the height of a climactic battle scene in James Cameron's 2009 blockbuster *Avatar*. Using 3D technology, Cameron presents an ordinary

Introduction

The writer begins with general background information. He identifies the film's title, release date, and director.

man in a strange land and includes a heart-warming romance. *Avatar* reminds viewers about the dangers of uncontrolled greed and exploitation of the environment.

As the films opens, we are introduced to the hero of the story, a paraplegic former Marine named Jake Sully. Sully decides to sign up for a paramilitary mission on the distant world of Pandora. He learns that greedy corporate figurehead Parker Selfridge intends to remove the native humanoid "Na'vi" from their homeland. The corporation wants the precious material known as unobtainium, which is scattered throughout the Na'vi's woodland. Selfridge states, "This is why we're here: because this little gray rock sells for twenty million a kilo." In exchange for the spinal surgery that will fix his legs, Jake gathers intelligence for a special military unit headed by Colonel Quaritch. Using an avatar identity, Jake infiltrates the Na'vi people. While Jake is bonding with the native tribe and falling in love with the beautiful alien Neytiri, the restless colonel prepares to invade Na'vi lands. Jake must take a stand and fight back in an epic battle for the fate of Pandora.

James Cameron's avatars are impressive. The director found a way for audiences to sympathize with the Na'vi, tall blue creatures with spotted faces. Young viewers like me are already familiar with avatars. We make graphic depictions of ourselves and pretend to be those characters in videogames or in online worlds such as Second Life. In the movie, the avatars are alien bodies that are controlled by human minds. Scenes of the floating avatar in a large tank are powerful and surprisingly realistic. Viewers believe that the sleeping Jake enters the alien's body and moves easily on a distant planet.

The planet Pandora is beautiful. Cameron's use of 3D technology completely immerses the viewer in the alien landscape. Many animals on Pandora, such as the pterodactyl-like creatures that inhabit the skies, are a shocking neon blue. Another quality we do not expect from most living things is light. Yet on Pandora, light glows from bright ferns and from the pulsating white moss floating among the trees. Although Pandora is a fantasy world, it makes us realize that there is beauty in our own planet that we have not noticed or valued.

An important message in the film is that we need to show greater appreciation for the ecological world. One of the most impressive sequences in the film shows Jake Sully training among the Na'vi for three months. Jake learns to let himself fall from great heights, trusting that trees and bushes will save him. Jake also creates relationships with magnificent flying lizards. Most importantly, he learns about a sacred tree and its importance to the planet's inhabitants. After learning Na'vi customs and rituals, he understands the tribe's reverence for the living, breathing forest that surrounds them. Near the end of the film, viewers recoil when they see tanks destroy the sacred tree and burn the forest. After watching the film, I took a closer look at the natural world near my home, and I wished I understood more about nature. I don't know the names of trees, and I don't know what plants are edible. I feel horrible when I think of the ways humans are destroying our planet.

Avatar is a remarkable film that brilliantly depicts aliens in a distant land, and it makes us reflect on our environment. It also shows how wars are often fought for economic reasons. I would highly recommend the film especially because the message is very relevant. In the film, as we watch ignorant and greedy humans destroy Pandora, we remember how our Earth's forests, water, and mineral resources are being plundered. But as Jake Sully quietly says, "Eventually, you always have to wake up."

◄ Conclusion

The writer sums up the film's strongest points and makes a recommendation.

A Sample Response to a Novel

College student Diego Pelaez responded to the novel *For Whom the Bell Tolls*. Review how he structured his response.

Introduction

The writer begins with general background

◄ information about the novel. He identifies the title and date of publication.

Lessons from *For Whom the Bell Tolls*

Robert Jordan says to himself, "You have only one thing to do, and you must do it" (45). He plans the strategic destruction of a bridge in Ernest Hemingway's novel *For Whom the Bell Tolls*. The story, published in 1940, contains a relevant message. The novel follows Robert Jordan, an American university teacher and weapons expert, as he fights with Spanish republican forces against the fascist army led by Francisco Franco. *For Whom the Bell Tolls* asks difficult, relevant questions about the necessity of war, and it graphically depicts the consequences.

◄ Thesis statement

He expresses the main focus of the essay.

The novel opens with Jordan planning a strategic demolition of a bridge. The rest of the novel explains the preparations required for the risky operation. Jordan is a cold military strategist. He falls in love with Maria, a beautiful young woman. She had been brutalized by fascist forces and was then rescued and nurtured back to health by the guerrilla band. Pablo, the previous leader of the band, makes it clear that he wants nothing to do with the blowing up of the bridge, and his refusal is considered a sign of cowardice. In the meantime, Jordan's love for Maria and his growing loyalty to the guerrillas make his mission more difficult. Knowing that the enemy forces are too numerous, Jordan's attack on the bridge becomes more and more doomed as the story progresses.

◄ Summary

The writer briefly describes the book's main events. Notice that he uses the present tense to narrate actions that happen within the story.

I was greatly moved and at times horrified by the honest depictions of war in the novel. For example, there is a description of an earlier attack by Pablo's band. Pablo orders all the fascists to be brutally whipped, and members of his band make fun of their fascist captives. "Should we send to the house for thy spectacles?" (115) the crowd asks Don Guillermo, one of the fascist sympathizers. Then they attack him with flails (instruments used for cutting down grain), and they throw him over a cliff. The scene shows the excessive brutality involved in war, even wars that can be justified.

◄ Reaction

The writer responds to the book's depiction of war. The page of each direct quotation is indicated in parentheses.

Reaction ➤

The writer responds to the characters.

I sympathized greatly with the characters in the novel, particularly the main character, Robert Jordan. At first, Jordan views the guerrilla band at his disposal as means to an end. His priority is the mission more than the well-being of the guerrillas. However, as the story progresses, Jordan becomes conflicted. His love for Maria grows, and he realizes that he has something to live for. While lying beside Maria, "he held her, feeling she was all of life there was" (253).

Support ➤

The writer provides specific examples to show that the characters are varied and interesting.

The other characters are also diverse and fascinating. Pablo's wife, Pilar, is a voice of conscience, and she strongly condemns the treatment Don Guillermo receives. She says, "Nobody can tell me that such things as the killing of Don Guillermo in that fashion will not bring bad luck" (117). Also, the guerrilla band is a very likeable group, with a wise-cracking gypsy and the honorable old Anselmo, among others. Pledging allegiance to the cause, Anselmo says, "I am an old man who will live until I die" (19). Despite Jordan's growing affection for the group, he keeps planning the dangerous mission knowing that a lot of his new friends could die while carrying it out.

Reaction ➤

The writer responds to one of the book's messages.

For Whom the Bell Tolls shows the horrors of war. The desire to drive the fascists out is seen as a worthy goal, even if there will be many deaths. However, the futility of war is also shown. Robert Jordan's single-minded determination becomes eroded by his newfound love and desire for life. As his death approaches, Jordan thinks, "The world is a fine place and worth fighting for, and I hate very much to leave it" (440).

Conclusion ➤

The writer ends with a final insight about the book.

In the end, war is presented as neither good nor bad, but rather as a simple fact of life. In the final scene of the novel, after the attack on the bridge, Jordan falls and critically injures himself. He tells the rest of the group to move on. Jordan waits for the fascists to come up the path and tries to remain conscious long enough to go out in a blaze of glory. Jordan can "feel his heart beating against the pine needle floor of the forest" (444). Ultimately, this excitement is as much a reason for war as any ideals.

MyWritingLab™

Complete these writing assignments at mywritinglab.com

MyWritingLab™   **THE WRITER'S ROOM**   Responding to Film and Literature

Write a response essay (or "report") about one of the following topics. Remember to include an introduction, a summary, and several paragraphs explaining your reaction to the work.

1. In an essay, discuss "The Veldt" on page 589.

2. Write about a short story, novel, or film of your choice.

Checklist: Response to a Literary Work or a Film

After you write your response, review the checklist at the end of the book. Also, ask yourself these questions:

- ☐ Have I considered my audience and purpose?
- ☐ In the introduction, have I identified the title, author, and date?
- ☐ Have I given a short summary of the work?
- ☐ Have I described my reactions to the work?
- ☐ Have I integrated specific quotations and examples?
- ☐ Have I summed up my main arguments in the conclusion?
- ☐ Have I properly cited my sources?

19 The Résumé and Letter of Application

LEARNING OBJECTIVES

LO 1 Prepare a résumé. **(p. 297)**

LO 2 Write a letter of application. **(p. 298)**

When you apply for a job, you generally send a résumé and a letter of application. A résumé is like a professional version of your personal photo album. Each line is a snapshot of your education and work experience.

WRITERS' EXCHANGE

Work with a partner and discuss your past work experience. Write down your job titles. Then brainstorm your duties, skills you developed, or accomplishments you achieved. You can use the list of action verbs to get ideas.

EXAMPLE: Waiter—handled cash, interacted with customers, developed autonomy

Some action verbs

advertised	collaborated	facilitated	inspected	overhauled
assembled	compiled	forecasted	interacted	oversaw
assisted	coordinated	handled	managed	resolved
budgeted	evaluated	implemented	negotiated	served

Preparing a Résumé

The word *résumé* comes from a French word meaning "to summarize." Essentially, a résumé is a short summary of your work-related experience. Your résumé should be customized for each employer. Review the following example of a skills-focused résumé.

A Sample Résumé

TEANA BUTLER
9001 Naples Drive
Jacksonville, Florida 32211
Telephone: (904) 555-4567
E-mail: teana27@gmail.com

OBJECTIVE   Position as a respiratory therapist in a long-term care facility

QUALIFICATIONS SUMMARY
Experience with senior citizens
Knowledge of hospitality management
Strong teamwork and leadership skills
Computer skills (Word and Excel)

EDUCATION
Respiratory Therapy Diploma   **Complete this June**
Concorde Career Institute, Jacksonville, Florida
Relevant courses: Ventilator and Airway Management / Home Respiratory Care

EXPERIENCE
Sunrise Care Facility, Jacksonville, FL   **2012 to present**
Cafeteria Manager

- Handle cash and calculate end-of-day sales
- Work well under high pressure
- Negotiate patiently with elderly residents
- Manage a team of three coworkers

Gray's Children's Camp, Orlando, FL   **Summer 2011**
Activities Coordinator

- Organized a variety of summer sports activities for ten-year-olds
- Settled disagreements and led children with gentle authority
- Provided one-on-one help to a child with special needs

Meals on Wheels, Jacksonville, FL   **April–June 2010**
Volunteer

- Helped prepare meals and delivered meals to seniors

Include contact information but not your birthplace, birth date, nationality, or a personal photo.

Summarize your most pertinent qualifications and skills.

Put the most recent schooling first. If you have more than a high school education, it is not necessary to list your high school.

Outline your most recent job experience. If you have not had any paying jobs, you could mention any volunteer work that you have done. For each job that you list, mention the tasks that you completed and the aptitudes you developed.

Ideally, your résumé should be only one page long. If you have extra space, you can end with Awards, Volunteer Work, or Activities.

It is not necessary to list references. Most employers ask for references at the interview stage.

HINT ◀ Use Parallel Structure

When you describe your work experience, begin with parallel action verbs.

Not parallel	**Parallel verbs**
-greet customers	**-greeted** customers
-I took inventory	**-took** inventory
-handling cash	**-handled** cash

PRACTICE 1

Refer to the sample résumé to answer the questions.

1. Should you write *Résumé* at the top of your résumé?

   yes _____ no _____

2. In the résumé, where should you mention your strongest skills?

   _____

   _____

3. In what order should you list your work experience?

   a. from past to present

   b. from present to past

4. In the Experience section, should you use the word *I*?

   yes _____ no _____

5. What information should you include in the Experience section? Choose the best answers.

   a. job title

   b. boss's phone number

   c. job dates (when you worked)

   d. salary

   e. skills and accomplishments

   f. all of the above

LO2 Write a letter of application.

Writing a Letter of Application

A letter of application accompanies a résumé. It explains how you learned about the position and why you are right for the job. It complements your résumé and doesn't repeat it. In your letter, include specific examples to demonstrate why you are right for the job. Maintain a direct and confident tone. Remember that the letter provides you with a chance to demonstrate your communication skills.

Sample Letter of Application

Review the parts of the next letter.

Teana Butler
9001 Naples Drive
Jacksonville, FL 32211
(904) 555-4567
teana27@gmail.com

July 5, 2014

Alexia Anders
Cedars Long-Term Care Facility
225 Meadowland Boulevard
Jacksonville, FL 32101

Subject: Position as a respiratory therapist

Dear Ms. Anders:

I am applying for the position of respiratory therapist that was posted in the *Florida Times-Union*. I am completing my diploma in Respiratory Therapy and am very enthusiastic about a career in this field.

I have heard about your facility's strong reputation in elder care, and I believe I could be a valuable asset to your team. In my recently completed courses at the Concorde Career Institute, I learned about ECGs, arterial blood gas analysis, pulmonary function testing, and NICU monitoring. In addition, my experience at a nursing home has taught me to show patience and empathy when communicating with elderly patients. Furthermore, I have strong teamwork skills. For example, in a protracted dispute over shifts, I was able to negotiate an agreement between my colleagues and defuse an unhappy workplace atmosphere. Within months of being hired, I was rewarded with the manager's position.

I would appreciate the opportunity to speak with you in detail about my qualifications. I am available for an interview at your convenience and could start work immediately. Thank you for your consideration.

Sincerely yours,

Teana Butler

Teana Butler

Sender's address
Capitalize street names. Put a comma between the city and state or country. Do not put a comma before the zip code.

Date
Put a comma between the full date and the year.

Recipient's address
Capitalize each word in a company name.

Subject line (optional)
Briefly state your reason for writing.

Salutation
Find the name of the recruiter or write the following:

♦ Dear Sir or Madam:

♦ Attention: Human Resources Manager

Introductory paragraph
Explain the position you are applying for. Also mention where you heard about the job.

Body
Sell yourself! Do not just repeat what is in your résumé. Explain how you meet or exceed the job's requirements, and highlight your strongest skills.

Conclusion
Mention the interview and end with polite thanks.

Closings
Some possible closings are Yours truly or Respectfully yours.

Letter Basics

When you write a letter of application, remember the following points:

* Be brief! Employers may receive large numbers of applications. They will not appreciate long, detailed letters of application. Your letter should be no longer than four short paragraphs.

* Follow the standard business letter format. Most businesses use full block style, in which all elements of the letter are aligned with the left margin. Do not indent any paragraphs. Instead, leave an extra space between paragraphs.

* To make a favorable impression, ensure that your letter is free of grammar, spelling, or punctuation errors. Proofread your letter very carefully before you send it. If possible, ask someone else to look it over for you, too.

* If you e-mail your cover letter, you can send it as an attachment. You can also shorten it and then cut and paste it directly into your e-mail.

HINT ◀ **Abbreviations for States**

The following two-letter abbreviations are the standard ones used by the U.S. Postal Service.

* Ten states have two-part names and are abbreviated by the first letter of each word.

    NC, ND, NH, NJ, NM, NY, RI, SC, SD, WV

* Nineteen states are abbreviated by their first two letters.

    AL, AR, CA, CO, DE, FL, ID, IL, IN, MA, MI, NE, OH, OK, OR, UT, WA, WI, WY

* Twelve states are abbreviated by the first and last letter in the state's name.

    CT, GA, HI, IA, KS, KY, LA, MD, ME, PA, VA, VT

* Nine states are abbreviated with two major letters.

    AK, AZ, MN, MO, MS, MT, NV, TN, TX

PRACTICE 2

Answer the following questions. Refer to the sample letter of application on page 299.

1. Where should the date be placed? Circle your response.

   a. above the recipient's address

   b. below the recipient's address

2. If you do not know the name of the person in human resources, how should you address your letter of application?

   _____

   _____

3. Should you place a comma at the end of each line in the recipient's address?

   yes _____ no _____

4. In a letter of application, why are the next closings inappropriate?

   a. Bye for now.   _____

   b. Please accept my most gracious sentiments.   _____

5. In the sample application letter, why would Teana avoid mentioning her job at the children's camp?

   _____

   _____

   _____

6. Write the two-letter postal abbreviations for each state.

   a. Ohio   _____   d. West Virginia   _____

   b. Maine   _____   e. Texas   _____

   c. Vermont   _____   f. Kentucky   _____

PRACTICE 3

The next letter contains ten errors. Correct six punctuation errors and four capitalization errors.

Dr. Bakar Rahim

33 Winestead road,

Cincinnati, OH 45001

May 6 2013

Fernanda Martinez

965 Slater street

Chicago IL 65002

Subject, Project Assistant Position

Dear Ms. Martinez

I have received your application for a position as a project assistant. Unfortunately, as a result of unforeseen circumstances, I did not receive the budget to fund this position. Please accept my apologies. Your education and experience appear exemplary.

On a brighter note, next january, I am hoping to receive the funding, which will allow me to begin accepting applications again. At that time, if you are still available, please contact me for a project assistant's position.

Respectfully Yours

Dr. B. Rahim

Dr. Bakar Rahim

THE WRITER'S ROOM MyWritingLab™

Résumé and Letter

Find a job listing in the newspaper, at an employment center, or on the Internet. (Some Web sites are *Monster*, *USAJOBS*, or *CareerBuilder*. Also check your state's labor department Web site for job listings.) Look for a job that you feel qualified for, or find a job that you hope to have one day. Write a résumé and a letter of application.

Checklist: The Résumé and the Letter of Application

When you write a résumé or letter of application, ask yourself these questions:

☐ Have I used correct spelling and punctuation?

☐ In my résumé, have I included my work experience and my education beginning with the most recent?

☐ In my letter of application, have I indicated the position for which I am applying and where or how I heard about the job?

☐ Is my letter concise?

☐ Have I used standard English?

Part IV

Editing Handbook

When you speak, you have tools such as tone of voice and body language to help you express your ideas. When you write, however, you have only words and punctuation to get your message across. If your writing includes errors in style, grammar, and punctuation, you may distract readers from your message, and they may focus on your inability to communicate clearly. You increase your chances of succeeding in your academic and professional life when you write in clear, standard English.

This Editing Handbook will help you understand important grammar concepts, and the samples and practices in each chapter offer interesting information about many themes. Before you begin working with these chapters, review the contents and themes shown here.

SECTION 1 Effective Sentences
THEME: Conflict

Identifying Subjects and Verbs in Simple Sentences

SECTION THEME: Conflict

LEARNING OBJECTIVES

LO 1 Identify subjects. **(p. 306)**

LO 2 Identify verbs. **(p. 309)**

Is behavior learned or genetic? In this chapter, you will learn about the sources of aggressive behavior.

LO 1 Identify subjects.

Identifying Subjects

A **sentence** contains one or more subjects and verbs, and it expresses a complete thought. The **subject** tells you who or what the sentence is about.

♦ Subjects may be **singular** or **plural**. A subject can also be a **pronoun**.

> **Detective Marcos** will interview the suspects.
> Many **factors** cause people to break laws.
> **It** is an important case.

♦ A **compound subject** contains two or more subjects joined by *and*, *or*, or *nor*.

> **Reporters** and **photographers** were outside the prison gates.

♦ Sometimes a **gerund** (*-ing* form of the verb) is the subject of a sentence.

> **Listening** is an important skill.

HINT ◄ *Here* and *There*

Here and *There* are not subjects. In sentences that begin with *Here* or *There*, the subject follows the verb.

There are several **ways** to find a criminal.

Here is an interesting **brochure** about the police academy.

How to Find the Subject

To find the subject, ask yourself *who* or *what* the sentence is about. The subject is the noun or pronoun or the complete name of a person or organization.

The **Federal Bureau of Investigation** is a large organization. **It** has branches in every state.

When identifying the subject, you can ignore words that describe the noun.

       adjectives   subject

The pompous and rude **sergeant** left the room.

PRACTICE 1

Circle the subject in each sentence. Be careful because sometimes there is more than one subject.

EXAMPLE: A behavioral (study) examines genetics and behavior.

1. Research psychiatrist Carl E. Schwartz works in the Department of Psychiatry at Massachusetts General Hospital.

2. He conducted a study to determine hereditary factors in behavior.

3. There were more than one hundred children in his study.

4. Infants and toddlers were classed into two groups.

5. Objects, strange people, and unfamiliar settings were used to test the children.

6. Talking was not permitted.

Prepositional Phrases

A **preposition** is a word that links nouns, pronouns, and phrases to other words in a sentence. It expresses a relationship based on movement or position. A **prepositional phrase** is made up of a preposition and its object (a noun or a pronoun).

Because the object of a preposition is a noun, it may look like a subject. **However, the object in a prepositional phrase is never the subject of the sentence**.

<u>prepositional phrase</u>   subject
<u>With the parents' approval</u>, the **experiment** began.

Common Prepositions

about	among	beside	during	into	onto	toward
above	around	between	except	like	out	under
across	at	beyond	for	near	outside	until
after	before	by	from	of	over	up
against	behind	despite	in	off	through	with
along	below	down	inside	on	to	within

To help you identify the subject, put parentheses around prepositional phrases, as shown below. Notice that a sentence can contain more than one prepositional phrase.

(Without considering the consequences), **Adam** punched another man.

The **courthouse**, (an imposing building), was in the city center.

(In 2013), (after several months of waiting), **he** appeared before a judge.

HINT ‹ **Using *of the***

In most expressions containing *of the*, the subject appears before *of the*.

subject
Each (of the parents) has agreed to participate.

One (of the fathers) was uncomfortable with the process.

PRACTICE 2

Circle the subject in each sentence. Also add parentheses around any prepositional phrases that are near the subject.

EXAMPLE: (For many years), Schwartz has studied genetics and behavior.

1.   In Schwartz's study, half of the babies were classified as shy. The others in the group were classified as outgoing. In unfamiliar surroundings, the

shy and outgoing children reacted differently. For example, in the presence of a stranger, the shy toddlers would freeze. The outgoing toddlers would approach the stranger and interact.

2.   One of the main differences in reactions was in the heart rate. Also, each of the shy children had higher levels of stress hormones than the outgoing children. Generally, the differences in the temperament of children persisted into adulthood.

Identifying Verbs

LO 2 Identify verbs.

Every sentence must contain a verb. The **verb** expresses what the subject does, or it links the subject to other descriptive words.

+ An **action verb** describes an action that a subject performs.

   Detective Rowland <u>attended</u> a seminar. He <u>spoke</u> to some officials.

+ A **linking verb** connects a subject with words that describe it, and it does not show an action. The most common linking verb is *be*, but other common linking verbs are *appear*, *become*, *look*, and *seem*.

   Kim Rossmo <u>is</u> a former detective. His methods <u>seem</u> reliable.

+ When a subject performs more than one action, the verbs are called **compound verbs**.

   In 2003, Rossmo <u>wrote</u> and <u>spoke</u> about his methods.

Helping Verbs

The **helping verb** combines with the main verb to indicate tense, negative structure, or question structure. The most common helping verbs are forms of *be*, *have*, and *do*. **Modal auxiliaries** are another type of helping verb, and they indicate ability (*can*), obligation (*must*), and so on. For example, here are different forms of the verb *ask*, and the helping verbs are underlined.

<u>is</u> asking	<u>had</u> asked	<u>will</u> ask	<u>should have</u> asked
<u>was</u> asked	<u>had been</u> asking	<u>can</u> ask	<u>might be</u> asked
<u>has been</u> asking	<u>would</u> ask	<u>could be</u> asking	<u>could have been</u> asked

The **complete verb** is the helping verb and the main verb. In the following examples, the main verb is double underlined. In **question forms**, the first helping verb usually appears before the subject.

Criminal profiling techniques <u>have been</u> <u>spreading</u> across the continent.

<u>Should</u> the detective <u>have</u> <u>studied</u> the files? <u>Do</u> you <u>agree</u>?

Interrupting words such as *often*, *always*, *ever*, and *actually* are not part of the verb.

Rossmo <u>has</u> often <u>returned</u> to Vancouver.

HINT ◀ **Infinitives Are Not the Main Verb**

Infinitives are verbs preceded by *to*, such as *to fly*, *to speak*, and *to go*. An infinitive is never the main verb in a sentence.

verb   infinitive

The network <u>wanted</u> **to produce** a show about geographic profiling.

PRACTICE 3

In each sentence, circle the subject and underline the complete verb. Hint: You can cross out prepositional phrases that are near the subject.

EXAMPLE: (According to Professor Saundra K. Ciccarelli,) many (factors) <u>contribute</u> to aggressive behavior.

1. Should teen offenders be treated like adults? Why are some teenagers aggressive? Experts in brain development have discovered interesting facts about the teen brain. First, changes in hormone levels can have profound effects on a teen's behavior. Testosterone is linked with aggressive behavior. According to *Scientific American* magazine, an injection of testosterone motivated study participants to want to dominate others.

2. Furthermore, experts in brain development have discovered new information about the frontal lobe. That part of the brain is crucial in decision making and impulse control. In teenagers, the frontal lobe is not fully connected to the rest of the brain. Thus, teens are more likely to act

without consideration of consequences. In a *CBS News* article, Temple University professor Laurence Steinberg compares the teen brain to "a car with a good accelerator but a weak brake." Thus, treating a juvenile in the same way as an adult offender is unfair and unjust.

FINAL REVIEW

Circle the subjects and underline the complete verbs in the following sentences.

EXAMPLE: The (study) (about role models) is fascinating.

1.   There are many ways to modify a person's behavior. Young children can be influenced by aggressive characters on television. Young adults may be pressured or manipulated by peers. One of the most interesting influences on behavior is social roles.

2.   In the autumn of 1971, psychologist Philip Zimbardo conducted an experiment at Stanford University. Seventy healthy middle-class students were recruited. Each of the young men was given the role of a prison guard or a prisoner. Volunteers with the role of prisoner were kept in cells. The student guards wore uniforms and were given batons.

3.   Very quickly, students in both roles modified their behavior. The prisoners became meek and resentful. There were also noticeable differences in the guards' attitudes. On the second day, the prisoners revolted. The guards aggressively crushed the rebellion. Then, with increasing intensity, the guards humiliated and physically restrained the prisoners. The behavior of the young men had changed.

4.   Zimbardo was forced to end the experiment early. Why did the guards act so cruelly? According to psychologists, a uniform and a specific social role can have powerful influences on people's behavior.

MyWritingLab™
**Complete these
writing assignments at
mywritinglab.com**

MyWritingLab™

THE WRITER'S ROOM

Topics for Writing

Write about one of the following topics. When you finish writing, identify your subjects and verbs.

1. List various ways in which social roles influence people's behavior. Support your points with specific examples.

2. Some experts suggest that personality traits are partly inherited. Are your character traits similar to a family member's traits? Compare and contrast yourself with someone else in your family.

Checklist: Subjects and Verbs

Review this chapter's main points.

☐ To identify **subjects**, look for words that tell you who or what the sentence is about.

☐ To identify **verbs**, look for words that do the following:

–**Action verbs** describe the actions that the subject performs.
–**Linking verbs** describe a state of being or link the subject with descriptive words.
–**Helping verbs** combine with the main verb to indicate tense, negative structure, or question structure.

☐ To identify **prepositional phrases**, look for words that consist of a preposition and its object. Note: The object of a prepositional phrase cannot be the subject of the sentence.

helping
verb

prepositional phrase   subject ↓   verb

In spite of criticism, the police chief has released the suspect.

Sentence Combining 21

SECTION THEME: Conflict

In this chapter, you will read about eyewitness testimony, profiling techniques, and wrongful convictions.

LEARNING OBJECTIVES

LO 1 Identify parts of a sentence and sentence types. **(p. 313)**

LO 2 Make compound sentences. **(p. 315)**

LO 3 Make complex sentences. **(p. 319)**

LO 1 Identify parts of a sentence and sentence types.

Understanding the Parts of a Sentence and Sentence Types

When you use sentences of varying lengths and types, your writing flows more smoothly and appears more interesting. You can vary sentences and create relationships between ideas by combining sentences. Before you learn about the types of sentences, it is important to understand some key terms.

A **phrase** is a group of words that is missing a subject, a verb, or both, and is not a complete sentence.

> in the morning   acting on her own   the excited witness

A **clause** is a group of words that contains a subject and a verb. There are two types of clauses.

- ♦ An **independent clause** is also called a simple sentence. It stands alone and expresses one complete idea.

> The victims asked for compensation.

♦ A **dependent clause** has a subject and a verb, but it cannot stand alone. It "depends" on another clause to be complete. A dependent clause usually begins with a subordinator such as *after*, *although*, *because*, *unless*, and *when*.

... because they had lost a lot of money.

PRACTICE 1

Write *S* next to each complete sentence. If the group of words is not a complete sentence—perhaps it is a phrase or a dependent clause—then write *X* in the blank.

EXAMPLE: Circumstantial evidence is discounted.   _S_

Although it may be reliable.   _X_

1. Circumstantial evidence is often very reliable.   _____

2. Blood, for example.   _____

3. It may match with the DNA of the victim.   _____

4. Pieces of clothing, hair fibers, and other types of evidence.   _____

5. Unless somebody altered it.   _____

6. Such evidence is usually very good.   _____

7. A credit card may place a criminal at the crime scene.   _____

8. Although the suspect may have an alibi.   _____

Types of Sentences

Review the types of sentences. Note that Chapter 20 focuses on simple sentences. This chapter contains details about compound and complex sentences.

A **simple sentence** contains one independent clause that expresses a complete idea.

independent clause
The trial lasted for three months.

A **compound sentence** contains two or more independent clauses.

independent clause   independent clause
[The trial was long], and [the jurors became bored.]

A **complex sentence** contains at least one dependent clause joined with one independent clause.

dependent clause   independent clause
After the crime occurred, [reporters visited the town.]

Making Compound Sentences
Use a Coordinating Conjunction

LO 2 Make compound sentences.

There are several ways to create compound sentences. One method is to use a **coordinating conjunction**, which joins two complete ideas and indicates the connection between them. The most common coordinating conjunctions are *for, and, nor, but, or, yet,* and *so.*

| Complete idea | **, coordinating conjunction** | complete idea. |

The detective collected the evidence, **and** the lab analyzed it.

Review the following chart showing coordinating conjunctions and their functions.

Conjunction	Function	Example
and	to join two ideas	Anna went to school, **and** she became a forensics expert.
but	to contrast two ideas	The courses were difficult, **but** she passed them all.
for	to indicate a reason	She worked very hard, **for** she was extremely motivated.
nor	to indicate a negative idea	The work was not easy, **nor** was it pleasant.
or	to offer an alternative	She will work for a police department, **or** she will work for a private lab.
so	to indicate a cause and effect relationship	She has recently graduated, **so** she is looking for work now.
yet	to introduce a surprising choice	She wants to stay in her town, **yet** the best jobs are in a nearby city.

HINT ◀ Recognizing Compound Sentences

To be sure that a sentence is compound, place your finger over the coordinator, and then ask yourself if the two clauses are complete sentences. In compound sentences, always place a comma before the coordinator.

Simple   The witness was nervous **but** very convincing.

Compound   The witness was nervous, **but** she was very convincing.

PRACTICE 2

Insert coordinating conjunctions in the blanks. Choose from the following list, and try to use a variety of coordinators. (Some sentences may have more than one answer.)

but   or   yet   so   for   and   nor

EXAMPLE: In 1969, the FBI introduced criminal profiling as an investigative strategy, _____*and*_____ it has been quite successful.

1.   Kim Rossmo is a renowned geographic profiler, _____ he is also an excellent detective. Rossmo examines the movements of criminals, _____ he searches for specific patterns. According to Rossmo, criminals attack in places they know, _____ they generally don't work in their own neighborhoods. Most people don't want to travel long distances for their jobs, _____ they are lazy. Criminals work the same way, _____ they stay relatively close to home.

2.   Rossmo developed a fascinating mathematical formula, _____ many police departments were skeptical about his ideas. Basically, he inputs the addresses of suspects into a computer, _____ he also inputs details about the crime scenes. His program looks for a "hot" area. Suspects may live directly in the center of the hot area, _____ they may live within a few blocks. For example, in the late 1990s, there were several sexual assaults in a town in Ontario, Canada, _____ Rossmo and his associates created a profile map. One particular suspect's home was compared with the location of the crime scenes, _____ it was placed in Rossmo's computer program. Originally, the main offender's name was low on a list of 316 suspects, _____ it rose to number 6 on the list after the profiling. The suspect was eventually tried and convicted for the crimes, _____ he went to prison.

GRAMMAR LINK
For more practice using semicolons, see Chapter 24, Run-Ons.

Use a Semicolon (;)

Another way to form a compound sentence is to join two complete ideas with a semicolon. The semicolon replaces a coordinating conjunction.

| Complete idea | ; | complete idea. |

The eyewitness was certain; she pointed at the suspect.

HINT ◀ Use a Semicolon to Join Related Ideas

Use a semicolon to link two sentences when the ideas are equally important and closely related. Do not use a semicolon to join two unrelated sentences.

Incorrect   Some eyewitnesses make mistakes; I like to watch criminal trials.
(The second idea has no clear relationship with the first idea.)

Correct   One eyewitness misidentified a suspect; the witness was not wearing contact lenses that day.
(The second idea gives further information about the first idea.)

PRACTICE 3

Make compound sentences by adding a semicolon and another complete sentence to each simple sentence. Remember that the two sentences must have related ideas.

EXAMPLE: Last year, Eric joined a gang ; he regretted his decision.

1. Eric rebelled against his parents _____

   _____

2. At age fifteen, he acted like other teens _____

   _____

3. His friends tried to influence him _____

   _____

4. Some people don't have supportive families _____

   _____

Use a Semicolon and a Transitional Expression

You can also create compound sentences by joining two complete ideas with a semicolon and a transitional expression. A **transitional expression** links the two ideas and shows how they are related. Most transitional expressions are **conjunctive adverbs** such as *however* or *furthermore*.

Some Transitional Expressions

Addition	Alternative	Contrast	Time	Example or Emphasis	Result or Consequence
additionally	in fact	however	eventually	for example	consequently
also	instead	nevertheless	finally	for instance	hence
besides	on the contrary	nonetheless	frequently	namely	therefore
furthermore	on the other hand	still	later	of course	thus
in addition	otherwise		meanwhile	undoubtedly	
moreover			subsequently		

If the second clause begins with a transitional expression, put a semicolon before it and a comma after it.

Complete idea   **; transitional expression,**   complete idea

Stephen Truscott was not guilty; **nevertheless,** he was convicted.

PRACTICE 4

Combine sentences using the following transitional expressions. Choose an expression from the list, and try to use a different expression in each sentence.

in fact   ~~frequently~~   however   thus
therefore   moreover   nevertheless   eventually

; frequently, it

EXAMPLE: DNA evidence is useful. ~~It~~ has helped clear innocent people.

1. In the early 1990s, a comparison of hair samples could deliver a

   conviction. Scientists developed more sophisticated techniques.

2. Dr. Edward Blake is a leading authority on DNA evidence. He often testifies

   at trials.

3. According to Dr. Blake, microscopic hair analysis is not precise. It has

   secured convictions in many cases.

4. Billy Gregory's hair matched a hair found at a crime scene. Both strands of

   hair appeared identical.

5. The strands of hair had exactly the same color and width. They were genetically different.

6. Today, conventional hair comparison evidence is no longer allowed in most courtrooms. It may become an obsolete science.

Making Complex Sentences

LO 3 Make complex sentences.

When you combine a dependent and an independent clause, you create a **complex sentence**. An effective way to create complex sentences is to join clauses with a **subordinating conjunction**. "Subordinate" means secondary, so subordinating conjunctions—or subordinators—are words that introduce secondary ideas.

If you use a subordinator at the beginning of a sentence, put a comma after the dependent clause. Generally, if you use a subordinator in the middle of the sentence, you do not need to use a comma.

Main idea	**subordinating conjunction**	secondary idea
The police arrived	**because**	the alarm was ringing.

Subordinating conjunction	secondary idea,	main idea
Because	the alarm was ringing,	the police arrived.

Meanings of Subordinating Conjunctions

Subordinating conjunctions create a relationship between the clauses in a sentence.

Subordinating Conjunction	Indicates	Example
as, because, since, so that	a reason, cause, or effect	He paid a lot **because** he wanted a reliable alarm system.
after, before, since, until, when, whenever, while	a time	**After** he drove home, he parked on the street.
as long as, even if, if, provided that, so that, unless	a condition	The alarm won't ring **unless** someone touches the car.
although, even though, though	a contrast	**Although** the alarm began to wail, nobody looked at the car.
where, wherever	a location	**Wherever** you go, you will hear annoying car alarms.

HINT ◀ More About Complex Sentences

Complex sentences can have more than two clauses.

                               1   2

Although males commit most violent crimes, more and more females engage

                               3

in violent acts after they have joined gangs.

You can also combine compound and complex sentences. The next example is a **compound-complex sentence**.

                       complex

Although Alicia is tiny, she is strong, and she is a dedicated police officer.

                                                               compound

PRACTICE 5

Add a missing subordinating conjunction to each sentence. Use each subordinating conjunction only once. The first one is done for you.

although	when	because	since
even though	if	after	~~whenever~~

1.   _____Whenever_____ DNA evidence does not match a suspect's DNA, that person is usually released from custody. However, some people can have more than one type of DNA in their bodies. Chimeras are people with two types of DNA. _____ chimeras are rare, they do exist.

2.   Lydia Fairchild separated from her partner _____ they fought too much. To receive financial help from the government, Fairchild had to prove that she was the biological mother of her children. _____ she had given birth to her two children, her DNA showed no link to them. Eventually, scientists discovered matching DNA _____ they tested her internal organs.

3.   Chimerism occurs _____ two separate eggs fuse during the first few days of pregnancy. The judge in the Fairchild case expressed concern

_____ he often denies paternity rights to fathers based on DNA evidence. Also, _____ a criminal is a chimera, his or her DNA will not necessarily match the evidence in a crime scene.

PRACTICE 6

Combine the sentences by adding a subordinating conjunction. Use a different subordinating conjunction in each sentence. Properly punctuate your sentences.

EXAMPLE: He entered the courthouse. Photographers snapped photos.

As he entered the courthouse, photographers snapped photos.

Or The photographers snapped photos as he entered the courthouse.

1. Stephen was fourteen years old. He was arrested.

_____

_____

2. He proclaimed his innocence. The police refused to believe him.

_____

_____

3. He was extremely nervous. He appeared to be guilty.

_____

_____

4. He was in jail. He finished high school.

_____

_____

5. New evidence surfaced. He was released.

_____

_____

FINAL REVIEW

The following paragraphs contain only simple sentences. When sentences are not varied, the essay is boring to read. To give the paragraphs more sentence variety, combine at least ten sentences. You will have to add some words and delete others.

EXAMPLE: *When the* ~~The~~ witness is traumatized~~. She~~ *, she* might not remember her assailant's face.

1. James Bain spent thirty-five years in prison. He had been convicted of rape. In 2009, he was freed. DNA testing proved his innocence. The victim had mistakenly identified Bain as the culprit. Faulty eyewitness testimony has been the cause of up to 75 percent of wrongful convictions, according to data from The Innocence Project.

2. A witness's memory is not like a videotape. People continually fill in gaps in their recollections. They often remember details that did not occur. Elizabeth Loftus is a memory researcher. According to her, false information can easily become part of a subject's memory. In an experiment, subjects viewed an image of a car next to a yield sign. A researcher asked a question. She included the words "stop sign." Subjects had not seen a stop sign. They remembered seeing one rather than a yield sign. Similarly, memories can be influenced by a photograph. They can also be influenced by the words of a police officer.

3. Dr. Rod Lindsay is an eyewitness-testimony expert. He is worried. He does not trust the methods used to collect eyewitness testimony. In the Bain case, the police showed the rape victim a page with six small photos. The victim felt compelled to choose one of the six suspects. According to Dr. Lindsay, all crime scene photos should be shown sequentially. The witness examines each photo. It can be compared to his or her memory. A witness may choose none of the photos. That option is preferable to a

misidentification. Also, the investigating officer should not question the witness. He or she might accidentally influence the witness's memory of events. It is unfortunate. Eyewitness testimony can be seriously flawed.

THE WRITER'S ROOM

My WritingLab™

MyWritingLab™

Complete these writing assignments at mywritinglab.com

Write about one of the following topics. Include some compound and some complex sentences.

1. Do you watch crime shows or read about crime? Narrate what happened in your favorite crime show, movie, or book.

2. What can people do to reduce the risk of being robbed? List several steps that people can take.

Checklist: Combining Sentences

When you edit your writing, ask yourself these questions.

☐ Are my compound and complex sentences complete?

> He was arrested because
> ~~Because~~ of the scandal.

☐ Are my sentences correctly punctuated?

–In compound sentences, place a comma before the coordinator.

–In complex sentences, place a comma after a dependent introductory clause.

Comma	The case was dismissed, and the suspect was freed.
Comma	After she was released, she tried to find a job.
No comma	She tried to find a job after she was released.

22 Sentence Variety

SECTION THEME: Conflict

In this chapter, you will read about revolutionaries and rule breakers.

LO 1 Vary your sentences.

What Is Sentence Variety?

In Chapter 21, you learned to write different types of sentences. In this chapter, you will learn to vary your sentences by consciously considering the length of sentences, by altering the opening words, and by joining sentences using different methods.

Consider the following example. The first passage sounds choppy because the sentences are short and uniform in length. When the passage is rewritten with sentence variety, it flows more smoothly.

No Sentence Variety

It was 1789. France was in crisis. Grain prices rose. Bread became more expensive. Many French citizens were hungry. They began to complain publicly. They were frustrated. They protested in the streets.

Sentence Variety

In 1789, France was in crisis. As grain prices rose, bread became more expensive. Feeling hungry, many French citizens began to complain publicly. Frustrated, they protested in the streets.

HINT ◄ Be Careful with Long Sentences

If your sentence is too long, it may be difficult for the reader to understand. Also, you may accidentally write run-on sentences. If you have any doubts, break up a longer sentence into shorter ones.

Long and complicated	In France, at the time of the revolution, Marie Antoinette was the queen, and she lived a life of wealth and consumption and had very little contact with ordinary people and did not know or care about the poor, so when a journalist complained about her, everyone believed the journalist.
Better	In France, at the time of the revolution, Marie Antoinette was the queen. Living a life of wealth and consumption, she had very little contact with ordinary people. Additionally, she did not know or care about the poor. Thus, when a journalist complained about her, everyone believed the journalist.

PRACTICE 1

Combine the following sentences to provide sentence variety. Create some short and some long sentences.

Marie Antoinette was twelve years old. Her family made a decision. The girl would marry her second cousin. His name was Louis Auguste. He was fourteen years old. He would be king of France. Marie Antoinette moved from Austria to France. She had to adapt to a new culture. She lived in a palace. Excessive luxury was evident. She became one of the most famous queens in history. It was not for a good reason. She was quoted as saying, "Let them eat cake." Some historians don't believe that she said it. The phrase appeared in a book eight years before her birth. She could not have said the phrase first.

LO 2 Vary your opening words.

Varying the Opening Words

An effective way to make your sentences more vivid is to vary the opening words. Instead of beginning each sentence with the subject, you could try the following strategies.

Begin with an Adverb (*-ly* Word)

An **adverb** is a word that modifies a verb, and it often (but not always) ends in *-ly. Quickly* and *frequently* are adverbs. Non *-ly* adverbs include words such as *sometimes* and *often.*

> <u>Quickly</u>, the crowd grew.

Begin with a Prepositional Phrase

A **prepositional phrase** is a group of words made up of a preposition and its object. *In the morning* and *at dawn* are prepositional phrases.

> <u>On state television</u>, the president addressed the nation.

Begin with a Present Participle (*-ing* Verb)

You can begin your sentence with a **present participle**, or *-ing* word. Combine sentences using an *-ing* modifier only when the two actions happen at the same time.

> <u>Posting</u> information on Facebook, Karim organized a protest.

Begin with a Past Participle (*-ed* Verb)

GRAMMAR LINK
For a list of irregular past participles, see Appendix 2.

You can begin your sentence with a **past participle**, which is a verb that has an *-ed* ending. There are also many irregular past participles such as *gone, seen*, and *known.*

> <u>Raised</u> in luxury, the king did not understand the people's complaints.

PRACTICE 2

Combine the sets of sentences. Begin your new sentence using the type of word indicated in parentheses.

EXAMPLE: (-*ly* word) The Tunisian street vendor sold some produce. He was anxious.

Anxiously, the Tunisian street vendor sold some produce.

1. (-*ed* verb) Bouazizi was tired of the corruption in Tunisia. He did a desperate act.

_____

_____

2. (-*ing* verb) The vendor set himself on fire. The vendor was the catalyst for street riots.

_____

_____

3. (prepositional phrase) Protestors demanded their dictator's resignation. They did it with determination.

_____

_____

4. (-*ly* word) President Ben Ali was quick. President Ben Ali fled the country.

_____

_____

5. (prepositional phrase) The Tunisian vendor's act led to the Arab Spring. It was to everyone's surprise.

_____

_____

Combining Sentences with an Appositive

LO3 Combine sentences with an appositive.

An **appositive** is a word or phrase that gives further information about a noun or pronoun. You can combine two sentences by using an appositive. In the example, the italicized phrase could become an appositive because it describes the noun *Wael Ghonim*.

Two sentences Wael Ghonim was a *young Egyptian*. He worked at Google.

You can place the appositive directly before the word that it refers to or directly after that word. Notice that the appositives are set off with commas.

appositive

Combined   A young Egyptian, **Wael Ghonim** worked at Google.

appositive

Wael Ghonim, a young Egyptian, worked at Google.

PRACTICE 3

Combine the following pairs of sentences. In each pair, make one of the sentences an appositive. Try to vary the position of the appositive.

EXAMPLE: The man ~~was an Egyptian.~~ ^,^ ~~He~~ started a revolutionary Facebook page.

1. Wael Ghonim is an Internet technician. He works for Google.

2. On June 6, 2010, four Egyptian police officers beat Khaled Said to death. Said was a twenty-eight-year-old man.

3. To commemorate the young man's death, Ghonim turned to Facebook. It is a social networking site.

4. Ghonim's Facebook page went viral. It was called, "We are all Khaled Said."

5. Young tech-savvy Egyptians planned demonstrations using Facebook. The site is an efficient organizing tool.

6. Egypt has had a difficult transition to democracy. Egypt is a complex nation.

LO 4 Combine sentences with relative clauses.

Combining Sentences with Relative Clauses

A **relative pronoun** describes a noun or pronoun. You can form complex sentences by using relative pronouns to introduce dependent clauses. Review the most common relative pronouns.

which that who whom whomever whose

Which

Use *which* to add nonessential information about a thing. Generally use commas to set off clauses that begin with *which*.

The crime rate, **which** peaked in the 1980s, has fallen in recent years.

That

Use *that* to add information about a thing. Do not use commas to set off clauses that begin with *that*.

The car **that** was stolen belonged to a police officer.

GRAMMAR LINK
For more information about punctuating relative clauses, refer to Chapter 35.

Who

Use *who* (*whom, whomever, whose*) to add information about a person. When a clause begins with *who*, you may or may not need a comma. Put commas around the clause if it adds nonessential information. If the clause is essential to the meaning of the sentence, do not add commas. To decide if a clause is essential or not, ask yourself if the sentence still makes sense without the *who* clause. If it does, the clause is not essential.

> Many of the youths **who** protested in the streets were arrested.
>
> (The clause is essential. The sentence needs the "who" clause to make sense.)

> Dr. Hassein, **who** was a kind man, saved the wounded child.
>
> (The clause is not essential.)

HINT ◀ Using *That* or *Which*

Both *which* and *that* refer to things, but *which* refers to nonessential ideas. Also, *which* can imply that you are referring to the entire subject and not just a part of it. Compare the next two sentences.

> The shirts **that** had stains provided DNA evidence.
> (This sentence suggests that some shirts had no stains.)

> The shirts, **which** had stains, provided DNA evidence.
> (This sentence suggests that all of the shirts had stains.)

PRACTICE 4

Using a relative pronoun, combine each pair of sentences. Read both sentences before you combine them. Having the full context will help you figure out which relative pronoun to use.

EXAMPLE: Crime varies from culture to culture. ~~It~~ can force societies to change.
（, which）

1. Sociologist Emile Durkheim was from France. He believed that deviant

   behavior can sometimes help societies.

2. Definitions of criminal behavior are agreed on by citizens. The definitions

   can change over time.

3. In many countries, people express their opinions about the government. These

   people are breaking the law.

4. Last year, some citizens in Iran criticized government policies. They were imprisoned.

5. In the 1960s, Americans broke Jim Crow laws. They were arrested.

6. Sometimes activists are treated as criminals. They actually help change society.

PRACTICE 5

Add dependent clauses to each sentence. Begin each clause with a relative pronoun (*who*, *which*, or *that*). Add any necessary commas.

EXAMPLE: The story _that was about the American revolution_ was made into a documentary.

1. The boy _____
   wanted to join the soldiers and fight in the American Revolutionary War.

2. The gun _____
   was on his front porch.

3. The boy did something _____

4. The neighbors _____
   heard a loud bang.

5. The large crabapple tree _____
   was hit by the shotgun blast.

LO 5 Write embedded questions.

Writing Embedded Questions

It is possible to combine a question with a statement or to combine two questions. An **embedded question** is a question that is set within a larger sentence.

Question	**Embedded question**
How old was the victim?	The detectives wondered <u>how old the victim was</u>.

In questions, there is generally a helping verb before the subject. However, when a question is embedded in a larger sentence, remove the helping verb or place it after the subject. As you read the following examples, pay attention to the word order in the embedded questions.

1. **Combine two questions**.

   Separate Why **do** people take risks? Do you know?
   (In both questions, the helping verb is *do*.)

   Combined Do you know <u>why people take risks</u>?
   (The helping verb *do* is removed from the embedded question.)

2. **Combine a question and a statement.**

    Separate   How **should** society treat young offenders? I wonder about it.
                        (In the question, the helping verb *should* appears before the subject.)

    Combined   I wonder <u>how society should treat young offenders</u>.
                        (In the embedded question, *should* is placed after the subject.)

HINT ‹ Use the Correct Word Order

When you edit your writing, ensure that you have formed your embedded questions properly.

Dr. Alvarez wonders why **do** people commit crimes. I asked her what
she thought
~~did she think~~ about the issue.

PRACTICE 6

Correct six errors involving embedded questions.

EXAMPLE: The writer explains how ~~can~~ people *can* hold on to power for so long.

1.   Around the world, citizens wonder why are so many nations run by dictators and authoritarian regimes. They also question how were certain leaders able to accumulate their wealth. For example, people want to know how did former Egyptian president Hosni Mubarak become so wealthy.

2.   To understand the former Egyptian president's wealth, people should consider why was Mubarak admired and supported by the international political community during his reign. Around the world, democratic Western nations tend to support undemocratic regimes when it is good for international business. For example, if someone wonders how could Mubarak remain in power for eighteen years, he or she should evaluate the situation. About 4 percent of the world's oil supply must pass by boat

READING LINK

The following essays contain more information about law, order, and conflict.

"Rehabilitation" by Jack McKelvey (page 95)

"Discrimination in the 21st Century" by Victoria Johnson (page 165)

"Types of Correctional Officers" by Frank Schmalleger (page 178)

"Viral Vigilantes" by Matthew Fraser (page 197)

"The *CSI* Effect" by Richard Willing (page 522)

"Types of Rioters" by David Locher (page 525)

"My Bully, My Best Friend" by Yannick LeJacq (page 531)

through the Suez Canal in Egypt. Perhaps that explains why did Mubarak make sure business went smoothly for the companies and nations that needed to use the canal.

FINAL REVIEW

The next essay lacks sentence variety. Use the strategies that you have learned in this chapter, and create at least ten varied sentences.

EXAMPLE: ~~People have~~ *Having* a lot of Facebook friends. ~~It~~ is not a sign of popularity.

1.   I sometimes wonder. How do revolutions begin? Malcolm Gladwell is a respected author. He wrote an article called "Small Change" for the *New Yorker*. According to Gladwell, Facebook and Twitter are important. They do not have a significant impact on revolutions. He believes the following idea. Social media sites were given too much credit for uprisings in Egypt, Libya, and other nations.

2.   Gladwell gives examples. Something happened on February 1, 1960. Four black college students sat at a counter in a North Carolina Woolworth's. They ordered coffee. They were not served because of their skin color. They were determined. They sat at the counter all day. A crowd gathered eventually. Thirty-one protestors sat in the coffee shop the next day. Then the protest grew. It was to everyone's surprise. Soon neighboring cities had sit-ins. About seventy thousand students were protesting at the end of the month. People organized without Facebook or Twitter.

3.   Gladwell has a theory. Revolutions require sacrifice and strong ties.

People form "weak ties" with social media. Most Twitter and Facebook users

don't know their online friends. Such Web sites make communication

easier. The sites don't create social change.

MyWritingLab™
**Complete these
writing assignments at
mywritinglab.com**

THE WRITER'S ROOM   MyWritingLab™

Write about one of the following topics. Use a variety of sentence lengths.

1. What are some categories of criminals? Classify criminals into different types.

2. Why does criminal life seem exciting to some people? What factors contribute to make crime appealing?

Checklist: Sentence Variety

When you edit your writing, ask yourself the following questions.

☐ Are my sentences varied? Check for problems in these areas:
    –too many short sentences
    –long sentences that are difficult to follow

☐ Do I have any embedded questions? Check for problems in these areas:
    –word order
    –unnecessary helping verbs

    I don't know why ~~do~~ people break the law.

23 Fragments

SECTION THEME: Urban Development

In this chapter, you will read about the development of suburbs and cities.

LEARNING OBJECTIVES

LO 1 Define fragments. (p. 334)

LO 2 Identify phrase fragments. (p. 334)

LO 3 Correct fragments with *-ing* and *to*. (p. 336)

LO 4 Identify explanatory fragments. (p. 337)

LO 5 Identify dependent-clause fragments. (p. 339)

LO 1 Define fragments.

What Are Fragments?

A **fragment** is an incomplete sentence. It lacks either a subject or a verb, or it fails to express a complete thought. You may see fragments in newspaper headlines and advertisements (e.g., "Overnight Weight Loss"). You may also use fragments to save space when you are writing a text message. However, in college writing, it is unacceptable to write fragments.

Sentence More and more people are moving to urban centers.

Fragment In developing countries.

LO 2 Identify phrase fragments.

Phrase Fragments

Phrase fragments are missing a subject or a verb. In each example, the fragment is underlined.

No verb <u>The history of cities.</u> It is quite interesting.

No subject Ancient civilizations usually had one major city. <u>Specialized in trades.</u>

How to Correct Phrase Fragments

To correct phrase fragments, add the missing subject or verb, or join the fragment to another sentence. The following examples show how to correct the previous phrase fragments.

Join sentences   The history of cities is quite interesting.

Add words   Ancient civilizations usually had one major city. **The citizens in that city** specialized in trades.

HINT ◀ **Incomplete Verbs**

The following example is a phrase fragment because it is missing a helping verb. To make this sentence complete, you must add the helping verb.

Fragment   Modern cities growing rapidly.

Sentence   Modern cities <u>are</u> growing rapidly.

PRACTICE 1

Underline and correct eight phrase fragments.

It was founded

EXAMPLE: Damascus is one of the world's oldest cities. <u>Founded in the third millennium B.C.E.</u>

1.   The first cities began in ancient civilizations. Mesopotamia, the Indus Valley, and China. Those were large ancient civilizations. Early cities had only around 150,000 people. Eventually, ancient cities grew. Rome reached a population of one million. Baghdad. It exceeded that number. London became the largest city in the world. During the Middle Ages.

2.   The Industrial Revolution was an important phenomenon. For the growth of cities. Many people migrated from the countryside to urban centers. In the eighteenth and nineteenth centuries. Urbanization led to many social troubles. Some common problems were child labor. And low wages.

3.   During the Great Depression. People lost jobs and moved to the cities.

Economic prosperity increased. After World War II. Today, most cities are

prospering.

L0 3 Correct fragments with *-ing* and *to*.

Fragments with *-ing* and *to*

A fragment may begin with a **present participle**, which is the form of the verb that ends in *-ing* (*running, talking*). It may also begin with an **infinitive**, which is *to* plus the base form of the verb (*to run, to talk*). These fragments generally appear next to another sentence that contains the subject. In the examples, the fragments are underlined.

-ing fragment	Reacting to urban sprawl. City planners started a new movement in the 1980s and 1990s.
to fragment	Urban designers believe in the new urbanism. To help people live better lives.

How to Correct *-ing* and *to* Fragments

To correct an *-ing* or *to* fragment, add the missing words or join the fragment to another sentence. The following examples show how to correct the two previous fragments.

Join sentences	Reacting to urban sprawl, city planners started a new movement in the 1980s and 1990s.
Add words	Urban designers believe in the new urbanism. **They want** to help people live better lives.

HINT ◖ **When the *-ing* Word Is the Subject**

Sometimes a gerund (*-ing* form of the verb) is the subject of a sentence. In the example, *cycling* is the subject of the sentence.

Correct sentence Cycling is a great form of exercise in urban areas.

A sentence fragment occurs when the *-ing* word is part of an incomplete verb string or when you mention the subject in a previous sentence. In the example, the fragment is underlined.

Fragment Many city dwellers get exercise. Cycling on bike paths.

PRACTICE 2

Underline and correct eight *-ing* and *to* fragments.

One principle is designing

EXAMPLE: The new urbanism movement has many principles. ~~Designing~~ walkways in neighborhoods.

1. New urbanism is a suburban planning movement. To create people-friendly neighborhoods. Urban planners design self-contained neighborhoods. To limit the use of cars. Believing in the need to curtail urban sprawl. Architects plan areas where people can walk to work.

2. The new urbanism movement is a reaction against older suburban areas. After World War II, architects designed suburbs that relied heavily on cars. Living in traditional suburbs. Most people must drive to the city centers to go to work. The commute causes traffic congestion and air pollution. Suburban dwellers waste a lot of time. Traveling in their cars. Urban sprawl also creates problems for people who do not drive. Limiting their daily activities. Nondrivers must find other means of transport. To do errands downtown or at the mall.

3. Since 1990, the new urbanism movement has become very popular. City planners design beautiful and functional areas. To improve the quality of suburban life.

Explanatory Fragments

LO 4 Identify explanatory fragments.

An **explanatory fragment** provides an explanation about a previous sentence and is missing a subject, a complete verb, or both. These types of fragments begin with one of the following words.

also	especially	for example	including	particularly
as well as	except	for instance	like	such as

In the examples, the explanatory fragment is underlined.

Fragment　Planners in the 1960s influenced the new urbanism movement. <u>For example, Jane Jacobs.</u>

Fragment　New urbanism planners take into consideration many factors. <u>Especially reducing the use of the automobile.</u>

How to Correct Explanatory Fragments

To correct explanatory fragments, add the missing words, or join the explanation or example to another sentence. The following examples show how to correct the previous explanatory fragments.

Add words　Planners in the 1960s influenced the new urbanism movement. For example, Jane Jacobs **was an important authority on urban planning**.

Join sentences　New urbanism planners take into consideration many factors**,** especially reducing the use of the automobile.

PRACTICE 3

Underline and correct eight explanatory fragments. You may need to add or remove words.

EXAMPLE: Some new urbanism towns are famous<u>. Such as Celebration.</u> ，s

1.　Seaside, Florida, became the first community built using new urbanism principles. The town started in 1981 and became very famous. For example, *The Atlantic Monthly*. It featured Seaside on its cover. The developer Robert Davis hired experts in new urban planning. Such as architects and designers.

2.　Seaside was easy to build because the area did not have traditional rules for developing land. For instance, no zoning regulations. The buildings in the town have uniform designs. Particularly the houses. They all have certain features. Porches, for example, must be sixteen feet from the sidewalk.

Also, the streets. They must be made of bricks so cars cannot speed. Other

towns are based on the same principles. Especially, Celebration, Florida.

3.   Many people criticize such communities. Particularly the conformity

of design. On the other hand, some people hope to live in an ideal locale.

For instance, no crime. However, critics point out that all communities have

some social problems. In fact, in 2010, Celebration had its first murder.

Dependent-Clause Fragments

LO 5 Identify dependent-clause fragments.

A **dependent clause** has a subject and a verb, but it cannot stand alone. It depends on another clause to be a complete sentence. Dependent clauses may begin with subordinating conjunctions or relative pronouns. The following list contains some of the most common words that begin dependent clauses.

Common Subordinating Conjunctions				Relative Pronouns
after	before	though	whenever	that
although	even though	unless	where	which
as	if	until	whereas	who(m)
because	since	what	whether	whose

In each example, the fragment is underlined.

Fragment	In the city, houses are close together. Whereas in the suburbs, houses have large yards.
Fragment	Before William Levitt built Levittown. Many people lived in congested neighborhoods.

How to Correct Dependent-Clause Fragments

To correct dependent-clause fragments, join the fragment to a complete sentence, or add the necessary words to make it a complete idea. You could also delete the subordinating conjunction. The following examples show how to correct the previous dependent-clause fragments.

Delete subordinator	In the city, houses are close together. In the suburbs, houses have large yards.
Join sentences	Before William Levitt built Levittown, many people lived in congested neighborhoods.

Chapter 23

PRACTICE 4

Underline and correct eight dependent-clause fragments.

EXAMPLE: William Levitt and his brother built Levittown. ~~B~~ecause of a
shortage of affordable housing.

1. In 1948, developer William Levitt built a community on Long
Island. That has been designated the first traditional suburb. Levitt wanted
to give returning soldiers the opportunity to participate in the American
dream. He called his community Levittown. The town consisted of
similarly built single-family homes. That attracted young families. People
wanted to escape the crowds of big cities like New York and Philadelphia.
The community grew to approximately 17,000 houses. Which led to the
beginning of urban sprawl. Eventually, the Levitts built three more Levittowns.

2. Some people criticized the idea of Levittown. Because all of the houses
looked similar. There were only four different house styles. Although it
began with the premise of affordable housing for everyone. Levittown
initially did not permit nonwhites to buy houses in the community.
Eventually, Levittown abandoned its "whites-only" policy. In 1957, the first
African Americans to buy a house in Levittown, Pennsylvania, were Bill and
Daisy Myers. Who had rocks thrown at them by the other residents.

3. Because Levittown is getting older. It has become a more attractive
suburb. Many homeowners have remodeled their homes, and the saplings
have grown into mature trees. Although many other suburbs have
developed. Levittown remains a model of traditional suburban living.

FINAL REVIEW

The following text contains the four types of fragments: phrase, -*ing* and *to*, explanatory, and dependent clause. Correct twelve fragment errors. You may need to add or delete words to make the sentences logical.

EXAMPLE: Slums lack basic services. , s Such as electricity, sewage systems, or
numbered houses.

1.   During the nineteenth and twentieth

centuries. Great numbers of people moved

from rural regions to urban areas. To look for

work. Governments failed to provide affordable

housing. For the migrants. Although they moved

to the cities to improve their lives. People were

forced to live in slums. Therefore, shantytowns

grew at an alarming rate. Today, over one billion

people live. In slums.

2.   Dharavi. It is located in Mumbai. It was originally an island. In the

nineteenth century, the water around the island was filled in. Causing the

area to become a part of Mumbai. Presently, around one million residents

live in the Dharavi slum. People come to the shantytown. Because they can

find cheap housing. Dharavi also has thousands of small businesses. Such

as pottery shops and leather goods stores. Dharavi is really a city within

a city.

3.   Politicians want to transform Mumbai into a modern city. Like Shanghai

or Hong Kong. Thus, the government intends to convert the slum into a modern subdivision. For instance, business complexes, high rises, shopping malls, schools, and parks. Wanting to remain in their homes. Dharavi residents are fighting government plans to relocate them.

MyWritingLab™
Complete these writing assignments at mywritinglab.com

MyWritingLab™

THE WRITER'S ROOM

Topics for Writing

Write about one of the following topics. Check that there are no sentence fragments.

1. Define your ideal town. What characteristics would it have?
2. What are some similarities and differences between living in a city and living in a suburb?

Checklist: Sentence Fragments

When you edit your writing, ask yourself this question.

☐ Are my sentences complete? Check for the next types of fragments.

–phrase fragments

––*ing* and *to* fragments

–explanatory fragments

–dependent-clause fragments

Los Angeles and San Francisco are moving closer together. ~~Because of~~ ᵇ

the San Andreas Fault. The two cities will make the largest urban area

in the world. ~~If~~ ⁱ the movement continues.

Run-Ons

SECTION THEME: Urban Development

In this chapter, you will read about architects and architecture.

LO 1 Identify run-ons.

What Are Run-Ons?

A **run-on sentence** occurs when two or more complete sentences are incorrectly joined. In other words, the sentence runs on without stopping.

There are two types of run-on sentences.

1. A **fused sentence** has no punctuation to mark the break between ideas.

   Incorrect   Skyscrapers are unusually tall buildings the Taipei 101 tower is among the tallest.

2. A **comma splice** uses a comma incorrectly to connect two complete ideas.

   Incorrect   The CN Tower is located in Toronto, it is the world's tallest communication structure.

PRACTICE 1

Write *C* beside correct sentences, *FS* beside fused sentences, and *CS* beside comma splices.

EXAMPLE: The White House contains 132 rooms and 35 bathrooms, it also has a tennis court and a jogging track. _____CS_____

1. The White House is the official residence of the American president, the first president, George Washington, never lived in it. _____

2. In 1790, George Washington moved the capital from New York to the District of Columbia he chose Pierre L'Enfant to plan the city. _____

3. Washington and L'Enfant chose a site for the presidential residence, they held a competition for the best design. _____

4. A young architect, James Hoban, won the competition he was inspired by a villa in Dublin, Ireland. _____

5. The corner stone was laid in 1792, and many people came to watch the construction. _____

6. John Adams was the first president to live in the house he and his wife took up residence in 1800. _____

7. During the War of 1812, the British set fire to the house, it was painted white to hide the damage. _____

8. Originally, the residence was called the President's Palace, but Theodore Roosevelt called it the White House in 1901. _____

Correcting Run-Ons

LO 2 Correct run-ons.

You can correct both fused sentences and comma splices in a variety of ways. Read the following run-on sentence, and then review the four ways to correct it.

> **Run-On** Antoni Gaudí began his career as a secular architect he eventually became very religious.

1. Make two separate sentences by adding end punctuation, such as a period.

   Antoni Gaudí began his career as a secular architect. **He** eventually became very religious.

2. Add a semicolon (;).

   Antoni Gaudí began his career as a secular architect; he eventually became very religious.

3. Add a coordinating conjunction such as *for, and, nor, but, or, yet,* or *so*.

   Antoni Gaudí began his career as a secular architect, **but** he eventually became very religious.

4. Add a subordinating conjunction such as *although, because, when, before, while, since,* or *after*.

   Although Antoni Gaudí began his career as a secular architect, he eventually became very religious.

PRACTICE 2

Correct the run-ons by making two complete sentences.

EXAMPLE: Antoni Gaudí designed very interesting works, he is considered to be a genius.

1. Antoni Gaudí was born in 1852 in Tarragona, Spain he is Catalonia's greatest architect.

2. Gaudí designed the Sagrada Familia he wanted to express his Catholic faith in his work.

3. Nature fascinated Gaudí, he incorporated nature's images into his creations.

4. Classical design used geometric shapes Gaudí's designs mimicked shapes from nature.

5. Gaudí's style evolved from Gothic influences, he created intricate, flowing, asymmetrical shapes.

6. Businessmen in Barcelona commissioned Gaudí to design a modern neighborhood, he constructed many buildings such as the Casa Milà.

7. His work used the *trencadis* style this style involves the use of broken tiles to decorate surfaces.

8. Many people initially laughed at Gaudí's vision eight of his creations are now recognized as World Heritage Sites.

HINT ⟨ **Semicolons and Transitional Expressions** ⟩

Another way to correct run-ons is to connect sentences with a transitional expression. Place a semicolon before the expression and a comma after it.

EXAMPLE: The construction costs were too high**; therefore,** the town abandoned plans to build city hall.

The design was beautiful**; nevertheless,** it was rejected.

Some common transitional expressions are the following:

additionally	meanwhile	of course
furthermore	moreover	therefore
however	nevertheless	thus

To practice combining sentences with transitional expressions, see Chapter 21.

PRACTICE 3

Correct the run-ons by joining the two sentences with a semicolon.

EXAMPLE: In January 2010, the Burj Khalifa was officially opened; the opening ceremony included ten thousand fireworks.

1. The Burj Khalifa is located in Dubai, United Arab Emirates currently, it is the tallest manmade building in the world.

2. An American architectural firm designed the tower, the building was constructed between 2004 and 2010.

3. Construction workers for the Burj Khalifa came from South Asian countries, skilled and unskilled laborers were paid only a few dollars a day.

4. According to Human Rights Watch, Burj Khalifa employers did not provide safe working conditions for construction workers therefore, many laborers died on the construction site.

5. The tower stands at 2,717 feet it cost over $1.5 billion to build.

6. Rents are over $4,000 per square foot unfortunately, some of the rentals remain empty.

7. A few base jumpers have used the tower to jump off the balconies, for example, Hervé Le Gallou made an illegal jump off the 158th floor in 2008 and lived.

8. In March 2011, French climber Alain Robert ("Spiderman") climbed the Burj Khalifa, he used a harness and rope to prevent injuries.

PRACTICE 4

Correct the run-ons by joining the two sentences with a comma and a coordinator (*for, and, nor, but, or, yet, so*).

EXAMPLE: Maya Lin's most famous design is the Vietnam Veterans
Memorial Wall she has also created many other projects.
        , but
(insert ", but" at caret after "Wall")

1. American soldiers fought courageously in the Vietnam War the war was controversial.

2. A Vietnam War veteran, Jan Scruggs, pressured Congress to build a memorial he wanted to recognize the valor of American soldiers.

3. A competition for the best design was held in 1980 more than 2,500 people submitted ideas for the memorial.

4. The competitors could not be under eighteen could they be foreign citizens.

5. Maya Lin was only an undergraduate architect student she won the competition.

6. Lin's parents came from China she was born in Ohio.

7. Her design was a wall made of polished black granite the names of soldiers who lost their lives are etched on the wall.

8. The wall, which juts out of the earth, is an unconventional memorial it initially caused controversy.

PRACTICE 5

Correct the run-ons by joining the two sentences with a subordinator. Use one
of the following subordinators: *because, before, although, when, even though,* and
after. If the dependent clause comes at the beginning of the sentence, remember
to add a comma after it.

EXAMPLE: You may have heard of Le Corbusier ^because he is one of the most famous
architects of the twentieth century.

1. Charles-Edouard Jenneret was born into a business family, he wanted to
   become an architect.

2. Jenneret changed his name to Le Corbusier he wanted to reinvent
   himself.

3. Art Nouveau and Art Deco styles were very popular in the early 1900s Le
   Corbusier wanted to design in a bold new approach.

4. Le Corbusier became known as the leader of the International Style
   he expressed his views on architecture in pamphlets, articles,
   and books.

5. Le Corbusier designed open-air white villas he wanted buildings with a lot
   of space.

6. He gained fame as an architect, Le Corbusier became interested in urban
   planning.

7. Le Corbusier planned many sections of the Indian city of Chandigarh his
   designs were impractical.

8. Le Corbusier had greatly influenced the architectural world with his vision
   he died in 1965.

PRACTICE 6

Use a variety of methods to correct eight run-on errors. Add commas when necessary.

EXAMPLE: Many new buildings are being erected all over China, modern
building designs are very popular.

and (inserted above the comma)

1. The Chinese Revolution dominated politics China's government developed policies to minimize class differences. As a result, new buildings were designed for utility with no regard for beauty.

2. Now, China is industrializing at a great rate businesses are asking architects to design practical but beautiful buildings. The National Theatre building, for example, is controversial, it is also intriguing. It was designed by French architect Paul Andreu, many people have criticized its design. It is shaped like an egg. It has three halls and a lake, it has a bridge. Another highly discussed building in Beijing is the CCTV tower. It looks like the letter Z, many Chinese think it is an eyesore.

The CCTV tower in Beijing

3. The Beijing skyline has changed, not everybody has liked the changes. In China, some people complain about the ugly architecture, others believe the new buildings are beautiful. Average citizens are eager for Beijing to join the ranks of the most beautiful cities in the world.

FINAL REVIEW

Correct ten run-on errors.

EXAMPLE: The construction industry is the largest in the world, public and private buildings consume a lot of energy.

and (inserted above the comma)

1. When most people envision cities, they think about houses, roads, and skyscrapers built above ground they do not think about subterranean cities.

However, many people use underground public and private buildings every day. In North America, there are at least five hundred public and private underground buildings for example, the Engineering Library at the University of Berkeley and the Vietnam Veterans Memorial Education Center are only two such subterranean structures. More underground structures are being built every day.

Entrance to tunnels in Cappadocia

2. Some of the oldest underground cities are located in Cappadocia, Turkey the first underground city in that area was constructed around 2000 B.C.E. Archaeologists believe that at one time, up to twenty thousand people lived in those underground Turkish cities the early Christians used them as a means to escape persecution.

3. Montreal, Canada, contains an extremely large underground city. It was designed by I. M. Pei in the 1960s other architects have contributed to its expansion. It is located downtown and has around 26 miles of tunnels with about 120 exterior access points. More than 500,000 people use the underground city each day they want to avoid Montreal's very cold temperatures in the winter.

4. There are many reasons to build underground. First, underground buildings benefit from better climate control architects say that such buildings can be heated and cooled more efficiently than aboveground buildings. Also, building underground reduces the impact on the environment, forests and fields do not have to be cleared. Moreover, the wind, snow, and rain do not erode the walls, well-constructed underground buildings are resistant to fire and earthquakes.

5.   Perhaps in the future, there will be more underground public and private buildings, they are more environmentally friendly and more energy efficient. Certainly it is time to rethink how urban planners design cities.

MyWritingLab™
Complete these writing assignments at mywritinglab.com

MyWritingLab™   **THE WRITER'S ROOM**   Topics for Writing

Write about one of the following topics. Edit your writing, and ensure that there are no run-ons.

1.   Give examples of any buildings or areas in your neighborhood, town, or country that you find attractive or unattractive. Describe these buildings, and explain why you believe they are beautiful or unsightly.

2.   Are there any changes or additions that you would make to the town or city where you live, such as adding a new park or a museum? What suggestions would you make to city planners?

Checklist: Run-Ons

When you edit your writing, ask yourself this question.

☐ Are my sentences correctly formed and punctuated? Check for and correct any fused sentences and comma splices.

One of the most successful architects in the world is Frank Lloyd Wright. O
one famous house he designed, Fallingwater, is a national monument.

Faulty Parallel Structure **25**

In this chapter, you will read about landscapes and gardens.

LEARNING OBJECTIVES

LO 1 Define parallel structure. **(p. 353)**

LO 2 Correct faulty parallel structure. **(p. 354)**

LO 1 Define parallel structure.

What Is Parallel Structure?

Parallel structure occurs when pairs or groups of items in a sentence are balanced. Notice how the following sentences repeat grammatical structures but not ideas.

Parallel Nouns	Books, stores, and catalogs give gardeners information.
Parallel Tenses	Gardeners dig and plant in the soil.
Parallel Adjectives	Kew Garden is large, colorful, and breathtaking.
Parallel Phrases	You will find the public garden down the road, over the bridge, and through the field.
Parallel Clauses	There are some gardens that have just trees, and some that have only flowers and plants.

LO2 Correct faulty parallel structure.

Correcting Faulty Parallel Structure

Use parallel structure for a series of words or phrases, for paired clauses, for comparisons, and for two-part constructions. If you see "//" or simply "faulty parallelism" on one of your marked essays, try the following tips for correcting those errors.

Series of Words or Phrases

Use parallel structure when words or phrases are joined in a series.

Not Parallel	The English, the Chinese, and people from Japan create luxurious gardens.
Parallel Nouns	The English, the Chinese, and the Japanese create luxurious gardens.
Not Parallel	I like to read books about gardens, to attend lectures about gardening, and buying plants for my garden.
Parallel Verbs	I like to read books about gardens, to attend lectures about gardening, and to buy plants for my garden.

Paired Clauses

Use parallel structure with a series of dependent clauses.

Not Parallel	He designed a garden that was beautiful, that was well planned, and was unique.
Parallel *That* Clause	He designed a garden that was beautiful, that was well planned, and that was unique.
Not Parallel	We met a designer who was friendly, who had a lot of experience, and was available.
Parallel *Who* Clause	We met a designer who was friendly, who had a lot of experience, and who was available.

HINT ◄ Use Consistent Voice

When joining two independent clauses with a coordinating conjunction, use a consistent voice. For example, if the first part of the sentence uses the active voice, the other part should also use the active voice.

	active
Not parallel	The bees flew to the flowers, and then the
	passive
	nectar was tasted by them.

> active
> **Parallel active voice** The bees <u>flew</u> to the flowers, and then they
> active
> <u>tasted</u> the nectar.

PRACTICE 1

Underline and correct the faulty parallel structure in each
sentence.

EXAMPLE: City officials want to design gardens, to plant trees,
to develop
and ~~should be developing~~ parks.

1. City planners look for ways to beautify urban landscapes, to
to
reduce building temperatures, and minimize water use.

2. Patrick Blanc is a botanist, a landscape designer, and ~~he is~~ an
environmentalist.

3. He designs walls with growing plants that are practical, that
are
are enchanting, and ~~must be~~ unique.

4. Green walls are found on outer walls of government buildings,
stations
~~stations used for~~ subways, and office high-rises.

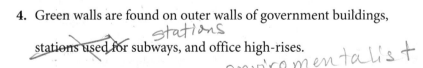

5. Chinese bureaucrats, people ~~who study the environment~~, *enviromentalist* and ordinary
citizens construct green walls of living trees.

6. Ecologists who study deserts, who gather climate statistics, and *who* ^advise the
Ministry of Forestry state that the Gobi Desert is advancing.

7. Each spring, sand blowing from the Gobi Desert covers city surfaces,
damages machinery, and ^schools and offices are shut down.

8. The Chinese government wants a huge "Green Great Wall" of trees that will
   that will
   stop desertification, that will prevent sand storms, and ~~to~~ encourage
   reforestation.

9. Chinese workers are planting trees across farmers' fields, over mountains,
   and ~~transplanting~~ through the valleys to prevent desertification.

Comparisons

Use parallel structure in comparisons containing *than* or *as*.

Not Parallel	Designing an interesting garden is easier than to ~~take~~ *taking* care of it.
Parallel -*ing* Forms	<u>Designing an interesting garden</u> is easier than <u>taking care of it.</u>
Not Parallel	The rock garden looks as colorful as ~~planting~~ roses. *garden*
Parallel Noun Phrases	<u>The rock garden</u> looks as colorful as <u>the rose garden.</u>

Two-Part Constructions

Use parallel structure for the following paired items.

either . . . or	not . . . but	both . . . and
neither . . . nor	not only . . . but also	rather . . . than

Not Parallel	The lecture on landscaping was both enlightening and of use. *useful*
Parallel Adjectives	The lecture on landscaping was both <u>enlightening</u> and <u>useful.</u>
Not Parallel	I could either see the bonsai exhibit or going to a film. *go to*
Parallel Verbs	I could either <u>see</u> the bonsai exhibit or <u>go</u> to a film.

HINT ◂ Keep Lists Parallel

After a colon, ensure that your lists of words and phrases are parallel.

We completed the following assignment: learn about a plant species,
take
~~taking~~ photographs of the plant, and create a poster.

PRACTICE 2

Underline and correct ten errors in parallel construction.

EXAMPLE: City planners build parks to create green areas, to prevent

overcrowding, and ~~people can use them for recreation.~~ *to develop recreational facilities*

1. During the Industrial Revolution, urban life changed rapidly and ~~with~~ *Complethly*

    comple~~ti~~on. City planners realized that more people were moving to the

    cities. Planners, politicians, and ~~people who~~ immigrated saw city life *Immigrants*

    changing. Urban designers wanted to create green space rather than ~~filling~~ *to fill*

    cities with concrete buildings.

2. One of the most important advocates of city beautification was Frederick

    Law Olmsted. He was born in 1822, in Hartford, Connecticut. He not only

    promoted urban planning, but he also ~~was designing~~ beautiful city gardens. *designed*

    He and his collaborator Calvert Vaux designed New York's Central Park.

    Olmsted wanted the park to have the following elements: open spaces,

    beautiful views, and ~~paths that are winding.~~ *winded*

3. Olmsted and Vaux designed many other projects. An important design

    was the Niagara Falls project. At that time, the falls were not completely

    visible to tourists. Olmsted wanted to create a harmonious landscape, to

    allow greater tourist accessibility, and ~~conservation of the area was important~~ *to greated* *to conservate*

    to him. Such a park required a great deal of planning. Goat Island separates

    Canada from the United States. Either the landscapers could buy Goat

    Island, or Goat Island ~~was~~ continuing to be an eyesore. Olmsted and Vaux *could continue*

    bought the island and restored it.

4. For Olmsted, contributing to the community was more important than
~~to have~~ *having* fame. He wanted not only the rich but also ~~the~~ people ~~who were~~ poor

to enjoy the tranquility of nature. He was known as much for his sense of

beauty as ~~respecting~~ *for his respect of* the environment. Olmsted died in 1903, but thousands

of people continue to enjoy his legacy.

FINAL REVIEW

Underline and correct ten errors in parallel construction.

EXAMPLE: Walking through a garden is more relaxing than ~~to read~~ *reading* a book.

1. *Ikebana* is the ancient tradition of Japanese flower arrangement. During

the seventh century, Chinese diplomats, monks, and people ~~who were~~

merchants came to Japan. They brought with them the idea of offering

arranged flowers to Buddha. The Japanese adopted this tradition quickly,

joyfully, and ~~with~~ *sincerely* ~~sincerity~~. Worshippers offered flowers to Buddha

because they desired tranquility, because they wanted to show their faith,

and ~~they~~ *because they* valued nature.

2. Ono no Imoko was a courtier, a sculptor, and ~~he also painted~~ *a painter*. He

became both a devout Buddhist and ~~achieved~~ *expert* expertise on Ikebana.

He decided to leave the court to devote himself to Buddha. He

traveled from the city, through the hills, and ~~he went~~ *into* a forest. He

found a lake. He remained there for the rest of his life. Many artisans,

soldiers, and people ~~who were~~ aristocrats came to learn Ikebana

from him. His lessons on flower arrangement not only delighted the

Japanese people but ~~Japanese culture was also influenced~~ *influenced Japanese culture*.

3.   Over the centuries, different Ikebana schools have developed. Poets,

essayists, and people who write novels have praised this form of flower
           novelist ~~who write~~

arrangement. Today there are about three thousand schools of Ikebana.

People who study Ikebana find it inspiring, educational, and it ~~also~~ satisfies
                                                                          satifiying

them.

THE WRITER'S ROOM   MyWritingLab™

MyWritingLab™
**Complete these
writing assignments at
mywritinglab.com**

Choose one of the following topics, and write a paragraph. Make sure your
nouns, verbs, and sentence structures are parallel.

1. If you could be anywhere right now, where would you be? Describe
    that place. Include details that appeal to the senses.

2. What do you do to relax? List some steps.

Checklist: Parallel Structure

When you edit your writing, ask yourself this question.

☐   Are my grammatical structures balanced? Check for errors in these
    cases:

    –when words or phrases are joined in a series

    –when you write a series of dependent clauses

    –when you make comparisons

                                                    English gardens
        We saw Chinese gardens, Japanese gardens, and ~~gardens from England~~.

26 Mistakes with Modifiers

SECTION THEME: Urban Development

LEARNING OBJECTIVES

LO 1 Avoid misplaced modifiers. **(p. 360)**

LO 2 Avoid dangling modifiers. **(p. 363)**

In this chapter, you will read about pollution and other urban issues.

LO 1 Avoid misplaced modifiers.

Misplaced Modifiers

A **modifier** is a word, a phrase, or a clause that describes or modifies nouns or verbs in a sentence. To use a modifier correctly, place it next to the word(s) that you want to modify.

       modifier   words that are modified

<u>Trying to combat pollution</u>, **city planners** have launched an anti-littering campaign.

A **misplaced modifier** is a word, a phrase, or a clause that is not placed next to the word that it modifies. When a modifier is too far from the word that it is describing, the meaning of the sentence can become confusing or unintentionally funny.

I saw a pamphlet about littering waiting in the mayor's office.

(How could a pamphlet wait in the mayor's office?)

I, waiting in the Mayor Office,
Waiting in the Mayor's Office, I saw a pamphlet

Commonly Misplaced Modifiers

As you read the sample sentences for each type of modifier, notice how the meaning of the sentence changes depending on where the modifier is placed.

Prepositional Phrase Modifiers

A prepositional phrase is made of a preposition and its object.

> **Confusing**   Helen read an article on electric cars <u>in a cafe</u>.
> (Who was in the cafe: Helen or the cars?)
>
> **Clear**   <u>In a cafe</u>, Helen read an article on electric cars.

Participle Modifiers

A participle modifier is a phrase that contains an *-ing* verb or an *-ed* verb.

> **Confusing**   Jamal Reed learned about anti-littering laws <u>touring Singapore</u>.
> (Can laws tour Singapore?)
>
> **Clear**   While <u>touring Singapore</u>, Jamal Reed learned about anti-littering laws.

Relative Clause Modifiers

A modifier can be a relative clause or phrase beginning with *who*, *whose*, *which*, or *that*.

> **Confusing**   The woman received a $1,000 fine from the officer <u>who dropped a candy wrapper</u>.
> (Who dropped the candy wrapper: the woman or the officer?)
>
> **Clear**   The woman who dropped a candy wrapper received a $1,000 fine from the officer.

Limiting Modifiers

Limiting modifiers are words such as *almost*, *nearly*, *only*, *merely*, *just*, and *even*. In the examples, notice how the placement of *almost* changes the meaning of each sentence.

> **Almost** all of the citizens took the steps that solved the littering problem.
> (Some of the citizens did not take the steps, but most did.)

> All of the citizens **almost** took the steps that solved the littering problem.
> (The citizens did not take the steps.)

> All of the citizens took the steps that **almost** solved the littering problem.
> (The steps did not solve the littering problem.)

Chapter 26

HINT ◀ **Correcting Misplaced Modifiers**

To correct misplaced modifiers, follow these steps:

1. First, identify the modifier.

   Armando saw the oil slick **standing on the pier**.

2. Then, identify the word or words being modified.

   Armando

3. Finally, move the modifier next to the word(s) being modified.

   Standing on the pier, Armando saw the oil slick.

PRACTICE 1

Underline and correct the misplaced modifier in each sentence.

who was fined $500
EXAMPLE: The man ^forgot to flush the public toilet ~~who was fined $500~~.

from the United Nations
1. Experts ^recognize Singapore as the cleanest city in the world ~~from the United Nations~~.

who patrol city streets
2. Singaporean police officers ^will immediately arrest litterbugs ~~who patrol city streets~~.

Polluters recieve a $1,000 fine
3. After littering, officers ~~give a $1,000 fine to polluters~~.

wearing a bright yellow vest
4. For a second littering offense, a polluter ^must clean a public area such as a park or school yard wearing a bright yellow vest.

In parliament,
5. In 1992, Singapore politicians debated a new law that prohibited the importation, selling, or chewing of gum in Parliament. ⟶ modifier

6. Because gum was stuck on them, passengers could not close the doors to the subway trains.

7. In 2004, the law was revised to allow gum ~~into the country~~ that has

   medicinal purposes. *into the country ,*

8. Singaporeans ~~with no litter~~ are proud of their city. *with no litter.*

Dangling Modifiers

L0 2 Avoid dangling modifiers.

A **dangling modifier** opens a sentence but does not modify any words in the sentence. It "dangles" or hangs loosely because it is not connected to any other part of the sentence. To avoid having a dangling modifier, make sure that the modifier and the first noun that follows it have a logical connection.

Confusing	While eating a candy bar, the wrapper fell on the ground.
	(Can a wrapper eat a candy bar?)
Clear	While eating a candy bar, **Zena dropped** the wrapper on the ground.
Confusing	To attend the conference, a background in environmental work is necessary.
	(Can a background attend a conference?)
Clear	To attend the conference, **participants need** a background in environmental work.

HINT ◀ Correcting Dangling Modifiers

To correct dangling modifiers, follow these steps:

1. First, identify the modifier.

   When traveling, public transportation should be used.

2. Then, decide who or what the writer aims to modify.

   Who is traveling? **People**

3. Finally, add the missing subject (and in some cases, also add or remove words) so that the sentence makes sense.

   When traveling, people should use public transportation.

PRACTICE 2

Underline the dangling modifier in each sentence. Then, rewrite the sentence keeping the meaning of the modifier. You may have to add or remove words to make the sentence logical.

Chapter 26

EXAMPLE: <u>Enjoying parks</u>, it is difficult when there is a lot of litter.

<u>It is difficult for people to enjoy parks when there is a lot</u>

<u>of litter.</u>

1. Believing it is not garbage, cigarette butts are left on city streets.

   Believing it is not garbage, ~~people~~ people left cigarette
   butts on the street.

2. With an unconcerned attitude, the hamburger wrapper ended up on the ground.

   With an unconcerned attitude, he dropped the
   hamburger wrapper on the ground.

3. Unhappy with the garbage in the park, a major cleanup took place.

   Because people were unhappy with the garbage
   in the park, a major cleanup took place.

4. Playing in the sand, there were pieces of glass from broken bottles.

   While playing in the sand, people found
   pieces of glass from broken bottles.

5. To understand the effects of littering, the cleanup costs must be examined.

   To understand the effect of littering, people must
   examine the cleanup costs.

6. Seeing no available trash can, the cigarette butt can be wrapped up and carried.

7. While walking barefoot on the grass, a piece of glass cut Pablo's foot.

   While Pablo was walking barefoot on the grass,
   a piece of glass cut his foot.

8. By thinking about litter, parks can be kept clean.

   People can keep parks clean, by thinking
   about litter ✗

   Parks can be kept clean by thinking
   about littering. ✓

PRACTICE 3

Correct the dangling or misplaced modifiers. If the sentence is correct, write *C* next to it.

Keisha saw that

EXAMPLE: Walking by the sea, plastic bags were caught in the rocks.

is creating a lot of pollution

1. Using plastic bags, a lot of pollution is created.

2. ~~Blown by the wind,~~ sidewalks are frequently littered with plastic bags *that are blown by the wind*

3. Clogging drains, plastic bags often cause sewage to overflow.

4. Choking on plastic, harm is caused to birds.

5. DeShawn Bertrand teaches the public about composting garbage with enthusiasm.

6. Taking public transportation, gas costs and parking fees are saved.

7. Environmental activists lobby oil industry managers who promote the green movement.

By

8. Following a few rules, communities can reduce pollution.

Communities can reduce pollution by following a few rules.

FINAL REVIEW

Identify fifteen dangling or misplaced modifier errors in this selection. Then correct each error. You may need to add or remove words to ensure that the sentence makes sense.

we encountered different issues

EXAMPLE: While studying new fuel sources, ~~different issues came up~~.

1. We discovered that there is a huge controversy about the development of natural shale gas in ecology class. People are searching for solutions who worry about the country's reliance on foreign energy sources. Many states have huge shale gas fields, so companies are exploiting those fields that want to make a profit.

2. Called fracking, oil and gas companies use a method to pump liquid into holes in shale rock to obtain natural gas. Companies have kept knowledge about shale gas extraction hidden from the public wanting to make huge profits. Containing hazardous chemicals, people's health can be affected by fracking liquids that leak into drinking wells. Also, fracking fluid can lubricate underground fault lines.

3. After enduring drilling for several years, many problems have been experienced by citizens. Showing concern, a connection between fracking and earth tremors has been confirmed by scientists. For example, near Youngstown, Ohio, fracking methods have been linked to over one hundred earthquakes. Drilling has also caused problems near Dimock, Pennsylvania. Floating upside down, fishers saw many fish. Polluted, the townspeople could not use the water. Then in 2009, a water well caused damage to a resident's property exploding suddenly. All of the homeowners almost became upset because property values have fallen.

4. Since 2011, facing hostility from citizens, access to information about fracking has been mandated. Shale gas production continues in many states by fracking. Clearly, the government needs to commission more studies on how fracking affects the environment.

READING LINK
The following essays contain more information about urban issues.
"The House with the Brown Door" by Judith Lafrance (page 114)
"Friendless in North America" by Ellen Goodman (page 215)
"Graffiti as Art" by Jordan Foster (page 222)
"Keep Your Roses" by Melonyce McAfee (page 234)
"Living Environments" by Avi Friedman (page 535)
"Nature Returns to the Cities" by John Roach (page 545)
"Slum Tourism" by Eric Weiner (page 565)

Chapter 26

MyWritingLab™

Complete these writing assignments at mywritinglab.com

THE WRITER'S ROOM

My WritingLab™

Write about one of the following topics. Proofread your text to ensure that there are no modifier errors.

1. What are some steps that your neighborhood or town could take to combat a littering or pollution problem?

2. What are some types of polluters? Write about three categories of polluters.

Checklist: Modifiers

When you edit your writing, ask yourself these questions.

☐ Are my modifiers in the correct position? Check for errors with the following:

  –prepositional phrase modifiers

  –participle modifiers

  –relative clause modifiers

  –limiting modifiers

  Wearing overalls, the
  ~~The~~ urban planner surveyed the garbage ~~wearing overalls~~.

☐ Do my modifiers modify something in the sentence? Check for dangling modifiers.

  the children dropped
  Walking down the street, food wrappers ~~were dropped~~.

27 Subject–Verb Agreement

SECTION THEME: Travel and Survival

LEARNING OBJECTIVES

LO 1 Practice basic subject–verb agreement rules. **(p. 368)**

LO 2 Maintain subject–verb agreement with more than one subject. **(p. 370)**

LO 3 Review special subject forms. **(p. 371)**

LO 4 Maintain subject–verb agreement when the verb comes before the subject. **(p. 373)**

LO 5 Maintain subject–verb agreement when there are interrupting words and phrases. **(p. 374)**

In this chapter, you will read about cultural differences, travel etiquette, and safety tips.

LO 1 Practice basic subject–verb agreement rules.

Basic Subject–Verb Agreement Rules

Subject–verb agreement simply means that a subject and verb agree in number. A singular subject needs a singular verb, and a plural subject needs a plural verb.

Simple Present Tense Agreement

Writers use **simple present tense** to indicate that an action is habitual or factual. Review the following rules for simple present tense agreement.

Third-person singular form: When the subject is *he*, *she*, *it*, or the equivalent (*Mark*, *Carol*, *Miami*), add an *-s* or *-es* ending to the verb.

Maria Orlon <u>works</u> as a marketing researcher.

> **GRAMMAR LINK**
> For more information about the present tense, see Chapter 28.

Base form: When the subject is *I, you, we, they,* or the equivalent (*women, the Rocky Mountains*), do not add an ending to the verb.

Many **businesses** <u>rely</u> on marketing research.

HINT ◄ Gerunds Are Singular Subjects

Sometimes a gerund (*-ing* form of the verb) is the singular subject of a sentence.

Fishing <u>is</u> a popular activity.

Agreement in Other Tenses

GRAMMAR LINK
For more information about using the present perfect tense, see Chapter 28.

In the past tense, almost all verbs have one past form. The only past tense verb requiring subject–verb agreement is the verb *be*, which has two past forms: *was* and *were*.

I <u>was</u> tired. **Edward** <u>was</u> also tired. That day, **we** <u>were</u> very lazy.

In the present perfect tense, which is formed with *have* or *has* and the past participle, use *has* when the subject is third-person singular and *have* for all other forms.

The **travel service** <u>has raised</u> its booking fees. Other **agencies** <u>have not raised</u> their fees.

Note: In the future tense and with modal forms (*can, could, would, may, might, must,* and *should*), use the base form of the verb with every subject.

I <u>will work</u>. **She** <u>should work</u> with me. **We** <u>can work</u> together.

HINT ◄ Use Standard English

In casual conversations and in movies, you may hear people misuse the verbs *be, have,* and *do*. In professional and academic situations, use the standard forms of these verbs.

     is   has   doesn't
Karim ~~be~~ busy. He ~~have~~ a large family. He ~~don't~~ have free time.

PRACTICE 1

Underline the correct form of the verbs in parentheses.

EXAMPLE: Travelers (<u>need</u> / needs) to learn about cultural differences.

1.   Although several countries (share / shares) the English language, some linguistic details (be / is / are) different. For example, Americans and Canadians (put / puts) gas in their cars, whereas British citizens (use / uses) petrol. In

Chapter 27

England, you (do / does) not phone people, you ring them. Australians also (use / uses) interesting expressions. A "chalkie" (is / are) a teacher, and a "mozzie" (is / are) a mosquito. Using proper terms (is / are) important.

2. Spelling also (differ / differs) among English-speaking nations. The word "flavor" (have / has) an *our* ending in Canada and Great Britain. Also, the word "theater" (become / becomes) *theatre* in England and Australia.

3. Business travelers should (learn / learns) about such differences. For example, Jeremiah Brown (do / does) the marketing for an American company. He (have / has) been with the company for two years. Last year, he visited London, England. One day, he (was / were) with a client. They (was / were) unable to agree on a price. When the client said, "That is too much dosh," Jeremiah (was / were) confused. Then he learned that *dosh* (is / are) a British slang word for "money."

LO 2 Maintain subject–verb agreement with more than one subject.

Chapter 27

More Than One Subject

There are special agreement rules when there is more than one subject in a sentence.

And

When two or more subjects are joined by *and*, use the plural form of the verb.

<u>Colleges</u>, <u>universities</u>, and <u>trade schools</u> **prepare** students for the job market.

Or / Nor

When two subjects are joined by *or* or *nor*, the verb agrees with the subject that is the closest to it.

singular
The layout artists or the <u>editor</u> **decides** how the cover will look.

plural
Neither the artist nor her <u>assistants</u> **make** changes to the design.

HINT ◀ *As Well As and Along With*

The phrases *as well as* and *along with* are not the same as *and*. They do not form a compound subject. The real subject is before the interrupting expression.

<u>Japan</u>, <u>China</u>, and <u>South Korea</u> **develop** high-tech computer products.

<u>Japan</u>, as well as China and South Korea, **develops** high-tech computer products.

PRACTICE 2

Underline the correct verb in each sentence. Make sure the verb agrees with the subject.

EXAMPLE: Ramon and Alicia (<u>take</u> / takes) many risks.

1. Ramon and Alicia Cruz (go / goes) to interesting places.

2. Right now, Ramon, along with his wife, (is / are) in a Turkish tea shop.

3. Generally, the owner or her son (greet / greets) the customers.

4. Neither Ramon nor Alicia (drink / drinks) coffee.

5. Strong black tea or herbal mountain tea (come / comes) on a special tray.

6. Sometimes, guitarists or singers (entertain / entertains) the customers.

7. The guests, along with the host, (sing / sings) Turkish songs.

8. Turkey, as well as Iran and Iraq, (have / has) a lot of tea shops.

Special Subject Forms

LO 3 Review special subject forms.

Some subjects are not easy to identify as singular or plural. Two common types are indefinite pronouns and collective nouns.

Indefinite Pronouns

Indefinite pronouns refer to a general person, place, or thing. Carefully review the following list of indefinite pronouns.

Indefinite Pronouns

Singular	another	each	no one	other
	anybody	everybody	nobody	somebody
	anyone	everyone	nothing	someone
	anything	everything	one	something
Plural	both, few, many, others, several			

Singular Indefinite Pronouns

In the following sentences, the verbs require the third-person singular form because the subjects are singular.

Almost <u>everyone</u> **knows** about tsunamis.

You can put one or more singular nouns (joined by *and*) after *each* and *every*. The verb is still singular.

<u>Every</u> passenger **likes** the new rule. <u>Each</u> man and woman **knows** about it.

Plural Indefinite Pronouns

Both, few, many, others, and *several* are all plural subjects. The verb is always plural.

A representative from the United States and another from Mexico are sitting at a table. Both **want** to compromise.

Collective Nouns

Collective nouns refer to groups of people or things. Review the following list of common collective nouns.

army	class	crowd	group	population
association	club	family	jury	public
audience	committee	gang	mob	society
band	company	government	organization	team

Generally, each group acts as a unit, so you must use the singular form of the verb.

The team **is** ready to travel to London.

HINT ◄ **Police Is Plural**

Treat the word *police* as a plural noun because the word "officers" is implied but not stated.

The police **have** a protester in custody.

PRACTICE 3

Underline the correct verb in each sentence.

EXAMPLE: The Executive Planet Web site (have / has) tips for business travelers.

1. Each large and small nation (have / has) its own gift-giving rules. For example, Singapore (have / has) strict rules against bribery, and the government (pride / prides) itself on being corruption-free. The police (arrest / arrests) officials who accept a bribe.

2. Specific rules (apply / applies) to gift-giving in Singapore. Certainly, everyone (love / loves) to receive a gift. Nobody (like / likes) to be left out while somebody else (open / opens) a present, so in Singapore, every businessman or businesswoman (know / knows) that gifts must be presented to a group. For example, if somebody (want / wants) to thank a receptionist, he or she (give / gives) a gift to the entire department. The group (accept / accepts) the gift graciously.

3.   To be polite, most individuals (refuse / refuses) a gift initially. Some (believe / believes) that a refusal (make / makes) them appear less greedy. If the gift-giver (continue / continues) to insist, the recipient will accept the gift.

4.   Singaporeans (do / does) not unwrap gifts in front of the giver. Such an act (imply / implies) that the receiver is impatient and greedy. Everyone (thank / thanks) the gift-giver and (wait / waits) to open the gift in private. To avoid insulting their hosts, business travelers should learn about gift-giving rules in other nations.

Verb Before the Subject

Usually the verb comes after the subject, but in some sentences, the verb is before the subject. In such cases, you must still ensure that the subject and verb agree.

LO 4 Maintain subject–verb agreement when the verb comes before the subject.

There or *Here*

When a sentence begins with *there* or *here*, the subject always follows the verb. *There* and *here* are not subjects.

           V   S   V   S
      Here **is** the <u>menu</u>. There **are** many different <u>sandwiches</u>.

Questions

In questions, word order is usually reversed, and the main or helping verb is placed before the subject. In the following example, the main verb is *be*.

            V   S   V   S
      Where **is** the nearest <u>restaurant</u>? **Is** the <u>food</u> good?

In questions in which the main verb is not *be*, the subject agrees with the helping verb.

           HV   S   V   HV   S   V
      When **does** the <u>café</u> **close**? **Do** <u>students</u> **work** there?

PRACTICE 4

Correct any subject–verb agreement errors. If there are no errors, write *C* for "correct" in the space.

EXAMPLE: ~~Has~~ *Have* you ever visited Turkey?   _____

1. Is there etiquette rules about greetings?   _____

2. Do each nation have its own rules?   _____

3. There be specific rules in each country. _____

4. In Turkey, if someone enters a room, he or she greet the oldest person first. _____

5. There be tremendous respect for elders. _____

6. Why the two women are holding hands? _____

7. In Turkey, handholding is a sign of respect and friendship. _____

8. In many companies, there have not been enough attention given to business etiquette. _____

LO5 Maintain subject–verb agreement when there are interrupting words and phrases.

Interrupting Words and Phrases

Words that come between the subject and the verb can cause confusion. In such cases, look for the subject and then make sure that the verb agrees with it.

S   interrupting phrase   V

Some travel <u>companies</u> that advertise online **are** very reliable.

Be particularly careful with interrupting phrases that contain *of the*. In the next examples, the subject appears before *of the*.

<u>One</u> of the most common travel-related ailments **is** dysentery.

<u>Each</u> of the travelers **has** a backpack.

Exception: Expressions of Quantity

Expressions of quantity don't follow the preceding *of the* rule. When the subject is an expression of quantity—*the majority of, one-third of, a part of, 10 percent of, the rest of*—the verb agrees with the noun that follows *of the*.

The majority of the <u>audience</u> **likes** the dance show.

About 70 percent of <u>tourists</u> **buy** flight tickets online.

HINT ◂ Identify Interrupting Phrases

When you revise your writing, place words that separate the subject and the verb in parentheses. Then you can check to see if your subjects and verbs agree.

S   interrupting phrase   V

An <u>employee</u> (in my brother's company) **annoys** his coworkers.

PRACTICE 5

Circle the subject and place any words that come between each subject and verb in parentheses. Then underline the correct form of the verb. (Two possible verb choices are in bold.)

EXAMPLE: Most (people)(in my class) **like** / **likes** to visit other places.

1.   Almost everybody in the world **want** / **wants** to experience an airline flight. Being above the clouds **is** / **are** exciting. But one of a traveler's biggest fears **is** / **are** a plane crash. In fact, there **is** / **are** many incorrect beliefs about air travel. According to George Bibel's book *Beyond the Black Box*, the odds of being in a crash **is** / **are** extremely low.

2.   A graph about air travel statistics **appear** / **appears** in Bibel's book. The majority of crashes **happen** / **happens** during takeoff or landing. For example, about 45 percent of accidents **occur** / **occurs** on landing, but only 2 percent of passengers **die** / **dies** during such events. The worst catastrophes in aviation **occur** / **occurs** when the plane is climbing or cruising. Each of Bibel's examples **is** / **are** interesting. Apparently, an aisle seat **is** / **are** not safer than any other seat in the event of a plane crash. However, according to *Popular Mechanics* editors, the back of an airplane **is** / **are** the safest place to sit. Passengers in the rear of the plane **have** / **has** a 40 percent better chance of surviving.

3.   One of the biggest myths about plane crashes **is** / **are** that they are usually deadly. In fact, plane crashes **have** / **has** very high survival rates. For example, in a recent fifty-year period, 53,000 people **was** / **were** in plane accidents, and 51,000 survived. The majority of the population **don't** / **doesn't** know that fact.

Interrupting Words — *Who, Which, That*

If a sentence contains a clause beginning with *who*, *which*, or *that*, then the verb agrees with the subject preceding *who*, *which*, or *that*.

A woman who **lives** in my neighborhood loves BMX cycling.

Sometimes a complete dependent clause appears between the subject and the verb.

interrupting clause

The <u>problem</u>, which we discussed, **needs** to be solved.

PRACTICE 6

Underline and correct ten subject–verb agreement errors.

EXAMPLE: Some travel information that <u>appear</u> online is not useful.
appears

1.   A Web site that I frequently visit provide a lot of travel information. TripAdvisor, which have millions of viewers, has been online since 2000. It provides reviews of hotels, B&Bs, restaurants, and airlines. TripAdvisor notifies any establishment that receive a negative review. Average people who live in different parts of the world also shares ideas in travel forums.

2.   One of TripAdvisor's most popular and controversial features are the ratings. Critics argue that a minority of hotels pays tourists to provide positive reviews. For example, a hotel that is in Cornwall, England, bribe guests to write positive comments online, according to the British site *The Mirror*. Also, many businesses that work in hospitality complains about biased and unedited reviews. Any person who is having a bad day have the opportunity to ruin a hotel's reputation.

3.   TripAdvisor, which is in many countries, have changed its slogan on the United Kingdom site. This change occurred because of complaints to the Advertising Standards Authority. The slogan, which used to be "Reviews you can trust," is now "Reviews from our community."

FINAL REVIEW

Underline and correct twenty errors in subject–verb agreement.

EXAMPLE: Traveling ~~include~~ *includes* certain dangers.

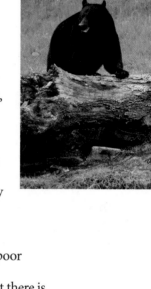

1.   Different regions in our nation has particular dangers. There is many interesting survival facts that everyone should know. For example, in the Rockies, if someone encounter a black bear, one of the worst things to do are to play dead. The black bear is predatory and welcomes easy prey. Running away are also a bad idea because a hungry bear enjoy chasing its prey and can reach speeds of up to 30 miles per hour. The best solution is to speak slowly and back away calmly. Black bears have poor eyesight and usually retreats if they hear people speaking and realize that there is humans nearby. The majority of the population don't know that fact.

2.   Travelers on unfamiliar roads sometimes panics if their car enters a body of water. Annually, there is over ten thousand car-immersion accidents. Many people, while the car is sinking, forgets to remove their seatbelts. Generally, either the driver or a passenger try to open the car door, but once the lower part of the door is under water, it is almost impossible to open. One of the biggest mistakes occur when the car's occupants wait too long to open the electric window. After the car hits the water, the electric motors that operates the windows can stop working.

3.   According to various experts, someone in a submerged car should wait until the car hits the bottom before he or she try to open the door. However, neither Andy Zhang nor his colleagues agrees. Zhang says, "What if someone don't know the depth of the water?" In such a situation, if the electric window

doesn't open, what is the options? Typically, there is just a few seconds to make a decision. It is best to break a side window with any tool or push the window with your feet, and then get out of the car.

MyWritingLab™
Complete these writing assignments at mywritinglab.com

MyWritingLab™   **THE WRITER'S ROOM**

Write about one of the following topics. Proofread your text to ensure that your subjects and verbs agree.

1. Describe a visit that you made to a culturally different restaurant. What happened? Use language that appeals to the senses.

2. Compare two cities that you have visited. How are they similar or different?

Checklist: Subject–Verb Agreement

When you edit your writing, ask yourself these questions.

☐ Do my subjects and verbs agree? Check for errors with the following:
  –present tense verbs
  –*was* and *were*
  –interrupting phrases

   takes
  That tourist, who lives in Boston, ~~take~~ great photos.

☐ Do I use the correct verb form with indefinite pronouns? Check for errors with singular indefinite pronouns such as *everybody, nobody,* or *somebody.*

   has
  Somebody ~~have~~ to modify the photograph.

☐ Do my subjects and verbs agree when the subject is after the verb? Check for errors with the following:
  –sentences with *here* and *there* before the verb
  –question forms

   Does   are
  ~~Do~~ she book tickets online? There ~~is~~ many great travel sites.

In this chapter, you will learn about survival facts and stories.

LEARNING OBJECTIVES

LO 1 Define verb tense. **(p. 379)**

LO 2 Define present and past tenses. **(p. 380)**

LO 3 Identify past participles. **(p. 383)**

LO 4 Define present perfect tense. **(p. 385)**

LO 5 Define past perfect tense. **(p. 387)**

LO 6 Define passive voice. **(p. 388)**

LO 7 Identify progressive forms. **(p. 390)**

What Is Verb Tense?

LO 1 Define verb tense.

Verb tense indicates when an action occurred. Review the various tenses of the verb *work*. (Progressive, or *-ing*, forms of these verbs appear at the end of this chapter.)

Simple Forms

Present	I <u>work</u> in a large company. My sister <u>works</u> with me.
Past	We <u>worked</u> in Cancun last summer.
Future	My sister <u>will work</u> in the Middle East next year.
Present perfect	We <u>have worked</u> together since 2001.
Past perfect	When Maria lost her job, she <u>had worked</u> there for six years.
Future perfect	By 2020, I <u>will have worked</u> here for twenty years.

HINT ◀ Use Standard Verb Forms

Nonstandard English is used in everyday conversation and may differ according to the region in which you live. **Standard American English** is the common language generally used and expected in schools, businesses, and government institutions in the United States. In college, you should write using standard American English.

Nonstandard	He don't have no money.	She be real tired.
Standard	He <u>does not have any</u> money.	She <u>is really</u> tired.

L0 2 Define present and past tenses.

Present and Past Tenses

Present Tense Verbs

The simple present tense indicates that an action is a general fact or habitual activity. Remember to add -*s* or -*es* to verbs that follow third-person singular forms.

Fact	Our fee **includes** transportation and hotel costs.
Habitual Activity	Carmen Cruz **teaches** Spanish every Saturday.

PAST	Saturday	Saturday	Saturday	Saturday	FUTURE
	She teaches.	She teaches.	She teaches.	She teaches.	

GRAMMAR LINK
For more information about subject–verb agreement, see Chapter 27.

Past Tense Verbs

The past tense indicates that an action occurred at a specific past time. Regular past tense verbs have a standard -*d* or -*ed* ending. Use the same form for both singular and plural past tense verbs.

Yesterday morning, we **discussed** the cruise.

Yesterday morning	Today
We discussed the cruise.	

PRACTICE 1

Write the present or past form of each verb in parentheses.

EXAMPLE: The tsunami (occur) __*occurred*__ several years ago.

1.   Many people (have) ___*had*___ very little knowledge about the natural world. When an earthquake (occur) ___*occured*___ underwater, it may result in a tsunami, or tidal wave. Tsunamis (be) ___*are*___ extremely dangerous. For example, in 2011, a catastrophic tsunami (destroy) ___*destroyed*___ parts of Japan.

2.   In 2004, a ten-year-old girl, Tilly Smith, (study) ___*studied*___ geography at school. One day in December, her teacher, Andrew Kearney, (describe) ___*descri*___ a tsunami. Tilly (listen) ___*listened*___ intently. Two weeks later, Tilly and her family (visit) ___*visited*___ Thailand. On December 26, 2004, over one hundred tourists were enjoying their time at the beach in Phuket, Thailand. Suddenly, the ocean water (start) ___*started*___ to churn and recede. Many people were curious, and they (walk) ___*walked*___ farther out onto the sand. Only one person (realize) ___*realized*___ what was happening at that moment. Tilly Smith (notice) ___*noticed*___ the early warning signs of a tsunami. What (happen) ___*happened*___ next?

Irregular Past Tense Verbs

Irregular verbs change internally. Because their spellings change from the present to the past tense, these verbs can be challenging to remember. For example, the irregular verb *go* becomes *went* when you convert it to the past tense.

> The hotel **sold** its furniture. (*sold* = past tense of *sell*)

> Consumers **bought** the product. (*bought* = past tense of *buy*)

Be (*Was* or *Were*)

Most past tense verbs have one form that you can use with all subjects. However, the verb *be* has two past forms: *was* and *were*. Use *was* with *I*, *he*, *she*, and *it*. Use *were* with *you*, *we*, and *they*.

> The packing box **was** not sturdy enough. The plates **were** fragile.

GRAMMAR LINK
See Appendix 2 for a list of common irregular verbs.

Chapter 28

PRACTICE 2

Write the correct past form of each verb in parentheses. Some verbs are regular, and some are irregular.

EXAMPLE: In 2004, Tilly Smith (know) _____ knew _____ about tsunamis.

1. On that December day in 2004, in Phuket, Tilly Smith (be) ___ was ___ the only person at her hotel to recognize the warning signs of a tsunami. In a panic, she (tell) ___ told ___ her parents that a giant wave was approaching. They (think) ___ thought ___ that their daughter was exaggerating, and they (be, not) ___ were not ___ worried. Tilly's mother (choose) ___ chose ___ to ignore her daughter, and she continued to walk along the beach. Mr. Smith, however, (make) ___ made ___ the decision to bring his daughter back to the hotel.

2. At the steps to the hotel, Tilly and her father (meet) ___ met ___ a security guard. Tilly (mention) ___ mentioned ___ the word "tsunami." A Japanese guest nearby (hear) ___ heard ___ the conversation and then (say) ___ said ___ that a large earthquake had just occurred in the ocean. Tilly, who (feel) ___ felt ___ certain a giant wave would come, convinced the guard. Several guards then evacuated the beach. In Thailand, roughly 230,000 people (die) ___ died ___ during the tsunami. But at Mai Khao Beach on Phuket, everyone (survive) ___ survived ___ because of a ten-year-old schoolgirl. There (be, not) ___ was not ___ one casualty!

HINT ⟨ **Use the Base Form After *Did* and *To*** ⟩

Remember to use the base form:
- of verbs that follow *did* in question and negative forms.
- of verbs that follow the word *to* (infinitive form).

          have   *survive*
The guests wanted to **had** a nice vacation. Did everyone **survived**?

PRACTICE 3

Underline and correct nine verb tense and spelling errors.

                                   capsize
EXAMPLE: The strong winds managed to <u>capsized</u> the boat.

1.   An incredible canine survival story occurred near

Queensland, Australia. In 2009, Jan Griffith decided to

take
<u>took</u> a boat ride with her dog Sophie. The weather <u>turned</u>

stormy. Far from the shore, in choppy seas, the dog slipped

fell
and <u>falled</u> overboard. Jan <u>didn't knew</u> if the dog was dead

or alive. She searched for her dog unsuccessfully.

                      was   *swang*
2.   Sophie, however, <u>be</u> a good swimmer. The dog <u>swum</u>

five nautical miles, through shark-infested water, to St. Bees Island. Sophie

then managed to <u>survived</u> for several months by eating baby goats.

                                          saw
3.   Four months later, a ranger on St. Bees Island <u>seen</u> the dog. At first, the

thought
ranger <u>thinked</u> that Sophie was wild. Then he noticed that the dog obeyed

                                                met
commands and was tame. A week after that, Sophie <u>meeted</u> her master

again. According to Jan Griffith, the dog quickly readjusted to a life of ease.

Past Participles

LO 3 Identify past participles.

A **past participle** is a verb form, not a verb tense. The past tense and the past participle of regular verbs are the same. The past tense and the past participle of irregular verbs may be different.

	Base Form	**Past Tense**	**Past Participle**
Regular verb	talk	talked	talked
Irregular verb	begin	began	begun

HINT ‹ Using Past Participles

You cannot use a past participle as the only verb in a sentence. You must use it with a helping verb such as *have*, *has*, *had*, *is*, *was*, or *were*.

	helping verb	past participle	
TripAdvisor	**was**	**founded**	in 2000.
Tourists	**have**	**rated**	thousands of hotels.

GRAMMAR LINK
For a list of irregular past participles, see Appendix 2.

PRACTICE 4

In the next selection, the past participles are underlined. Correct ten past participle errors, and write *C* above four correct past participles.

EXAMPLE: Top athletes have often <u>try</u> to break speed records.
           tried

1.   The human body is capable of much more than we have previously <u>thinked</u>. *thought*

   Over the years, athletes have <u>broke</u> many world records. For instance, in *broken*

   1954, Sir Roger Bannister ran a mile in just under four minutes, a feat that

   doctors had <u>proclaimed</u> was impossible. By 1999, Moroccan runner Hicham

   El Guerrouj had <u>did</u> it in 3 minutes and 43 seconds. Since then, athletes have *done*

   beaten the record over and over. In life and death situations, survivors have

   also <u>teached</u> experts about the body's limits. *Taught*

2.   Some survival specialists have <u>quote</u> the rule of three—the principle that *d*

   a person can survive about three minutes without air, three days without

   water, and three weeks without food. However, over the years, many true-life

   cases have <u>demonstrate</u> that human bodies can surpass expectations. For *d*

   instance, in 2009, after Haiti's earthquake, Evans Monsigrace was <u>trapped</u>

under a market for twenty-seven days with nothing but some fruit to sustain

him. When he was remove*d* from the rubble, he was <u>dehydrated</u> but alive.

3.   Dr. John Leach has <u>be<s>ing</s></u> *been* in charge of survival research for the Norwegian

military for many years. He has <u>find<s>ed</s></u> *Found* that the brain has a major role in

survival. If people cannot adapt to their new environment during a disaster,

the brain may start shutting the body down. Psychological trauma is

<u>consider</u>*ed* the biggest problem for disaster victims.

LO 4 Define present perfect tense.

Present Perfect Tense
(*have* or *has* + past participle)

A past participle combines with *have* or *has* to form the **present perfect tense**.

Kate **has been** a tourist guide for six years.

Since 2001, adventure tourism **has been** popular.

You can use this tense in two different circumstances.

1. Use the present perfect to show that an action began in the past and continues to the present time. You will often use *since* and *for* with this tense.

PAST
(The Web site
began in 2000.)   NOW

TripAdvisor **has been** popular since 2000.

2. Use the present perfect to show that one or more completed actions occurred at unspecified past times.

PAST   NOW
?   ?   ?   ?

Anton **has visited** Cambodia four times.
(The time of the four visits is not specified.)

HINT ⟨ Use Time Markers ⟩

When you try to identify which tense to use, look for time markers. **Time markers** are words such as *since*, *for*, or *ago* that indicate when an action occurred.

Simple past	Three weeks **ago**, Parker launched her new adventure magazine.
Present perfect	**Since then**, her adventure magazine has been selling very well.

Choosing the Simple Past or the Present Perfect

Look at the difference between the past and the present perfect tenses.

Simple past	In 2002, Kumar Jain **went** to Shanghai.
	(This event occurred at a known past time.)
Present perfect	Since 2002, Jain **has owned** a factory in China.
	(The action began in the past and continues to the present.)
	He **has made** many business contacts.
	(Making business contacts occurred at unknown past times.)

HINT ⟨ Simple Past or Present Perfect? ⟩

Use the past tense when referring to someone who is no longer living or to something that no longer exists. Only use the present perfect tense when the action has a relationship to someone or something that still exists.

wrote

Jules Verne **has written** many adventure novels.

PRACTICE 5

Write the simple past or present perfect form of the verb in parentheses.

EXAMPLE: For the past few years, I (be) _____*have been*_____ very careful at the beach.

1. Rip currents are narrow channels of fast-moving water. Over the years, rip

    currents (occur) ___*has occured*___ in many different lakes

    and oceans. Since 2000, lifeguards (rescue) ___*have rescued*___

    thousands of swimmers from rip tides. In previous centuries, most people (know, not) ___*did not know*___ what to do when a current

pulled them out to sea. But for the last fifty years, safety experts (teach)

___*have taught*___ people about water safety. Even so, since

2000, rip currents (cause) ___*have caused*___ over one

thousand fatalities in American coastal communities.

2.   If you are caught in a rip current, remain calm and do not try

to swim directly to shore. According to the National Ocean Service,

a rip tide can move faster than an Olympic swimmer. In 2013,

Melanie Hayes was swimming with her sons when a rip current

(pull) ___*pulled*___ them out to sea. Luckily, they

(know) ___*knew*___ what do to. They (remain)

___*remained*___ calm as the current pulled them away

from the beach, and then they (swim) ___*swam*___

parallel to the shore. After a short distance, the current (lose)

___*lost*___ strength, so they could return to the beach.

Since the incident, Hayes (speak) ___*has spoken*___ to others

about rip current safety.

Past Perfect Tense
(*had* + past participle)

L0 5 Define past perfect tense.

The **past perfect tense** indicates that one or more past actions happened before another past action. It is formed with *had* and the past participle.

PAST PERFECT   PAST   NOW

A thief **had snatched** my purse, so I bought a new one.

Chapter 28

Notice the differences between the simple past, the present perfect, and the past perfect tenses.

Simple past	In 2007, Taiwan **introduced** a high-speed rail service.
	(The action occurred at a known past time.)
Present perfect	Taiwan **has had** high-speed trains since 2007.
	(The action began in the past and continues to the present.)
Past perfect	The train **had left** the station by the time we arrived.
	(The action happened in the past, but the train left before we arrived.)

PRACTICE 6

Underline the correct verb form in each sentence. You may choose the simple past tense or the past perfect tense.

EXAMPLE: The 2004 bus accident (<u>occurred</u> / had occurred) several years ago.

1. In 2004, bus driver Edward Jones had to drive a group of students to George Washington's house, a trip he (made / <u>had made</u>) many times.

2. On the route, there (<u>was</u> / had been) a bridge on Alexandria Avenue that (survive / <u>had survived</u>) since the early 1930s.

3. Jones (<u>drove</u> / had driven) right past the large yellow warning sign that he (saw / <u>had seen</u>) on several previous occasions.

4. In the right lane, the arched bridge was only 10 feet high, but it (<u>was</u> / had been) 13 feet high in the center lane.

5. Another bus in front of Jones (already moved / <u>had already moved</u>) to the middle lane when Jones (<u>arrived</u> / had arrived) at the bridge.

6. Jones's bus (<u>smashed</u> / had smashed) forcefully into the bridge, and the collision (<u>destroyed</u> / had destroyed) the roof of the bus.

7. Glass and metal (<u>rained</u> / had rained) down on students, but luckily nobody was killed.

8. Later, investigators determined that Jones (tried / <u>had tried</u>) to multitask by driving and speaking on a cellphone at the same time.

L0 6 Define passive voice.

Passive Voice
(*be* + past participle)

In sentences with the **passive voice**, the subject receives the action and does not perform the action. To form the passive voice, use the appropriate tense of the verb *be* plus the past participle. Look carefully at the following two sentences.

Active   The boss **gave** documents to her assistant.

> (This is active because the subject, *boss*, performed the action.)

Passive   Several documents **were given** to the assistant.

> (This is passive because the subject, *documents*, was affected by the action and did not perform the action.)

HINT ◀ Avoid Overusing the Passive Voice

Generally, try to use the active voice instead of the passive voice. The active voice is more direct and friendly than the passive voice. For example, read two versions of the same message.

Passive voice	No more than two pills per day should be ingested. This medication should be taken with meals. It should not be continued if headaches or nausea are experienced.
Active voice	Do not ingest more than two pills per day. Take this medication with meals. Do not continue taking it if you experience headache or nausea.

PRACTICE 7

Complete the following sentences by changing the passive verb to the active form. Do not alter the verb tense. Sometimes you must determine who or what is doing the action.

EXAMPLE: The vaccine is given by a nurse.

A nurse gives the vaccine.

1. The trip was planned by us three months ago.

   We planned the trip three months ago

2. Free food is not provided by the airline on the flight.

   The airline do not provide free food on the flight

3. Complaints about the service are often ignored by airline companies.

   Airline companies often ignore complaits about the service.

4. Our hotel reservation was made in January.

   We made our hotel reservation in January

5. The hotel has been renovated several times by skilled workers.

   Skilled workers have renovated the hotel many times.

> **HINT** ◀ When *Be* Is Suggested, Not Written
>
> In the passive voice, sometimes the verb *be* is suggested but not written. The following sentence contains the passive voice.
>
> A book **written** in 2006 describes the adventure.
> (that was)

PRACTICE 8

Underline and correct ten errors with past participles.

EXAMPLE: The snake was <u>find</u> under a rock.   *found*

1.   Last summer, Maya was invite on a camping trip to the Arizona desert. The eighteen-year-old city girl, force to sleep in a tent, was not happy. Then, on her second day, her ankle was <u>bit</u> by a rattlesnake. *bitten* What should people do if they are attack by a poisonous snake?

2.   Many people are <u>teached</u> that venom should be suck out, but that is not *taught* a good strategy. First, if there is an open wound in the rescuer's mouth, the venom can enter the bloodstream. Also, a human mouth is fill with germs that can infect the wound. Luckily, Maya's friend Alex knew what <u>do to</u>. *to do.* First, the limb was immobilize. A small piece of wood was tie to Maya's lower leg, but not too tightly. Then Alex told Maya to keep the area of the snakebite lower than her heart. When they arrived at the hospital thirty minutes later, Maya was quickly <u>saw</u> by a doctor. *seen*

LO 7 Identify progressive forms.

Progressive Forms
(-*ing* verbs)

Most verbs have progressive tenses. The **progressive tense**, formed with *be* and the -*ing* form of the verb, indicates that an action is, was, or will be in progress. For example, the present progressive indicates that an action is happening right now or for a temporary period of time. The following time line illustrates both the simple and progressive tenses.

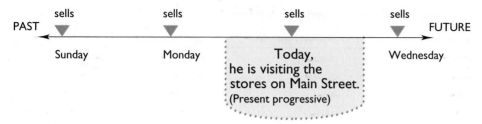

Every day, he sells leather wallets. (Simple present)

	sells	sells	sells	sells	
PAST	▼	▼	▼	▼	FUTURE
	Sunday	Monday	Today, he is visiting the stores on Main Street. (Present progressive)	Wednesday	

To form the progressive, use the appropriate tense of the verb *be* with the *-ing* verb.

Present progressive	Right now, I **am** <u>working</u>.
Past progressive	We **were** <u>sleeping</u> when you phoned us.
Future progressive	Tomorrow, at noon, I **will be** <u>driving</u>.
Present perfect progressive	The receptionist **has been** <u>working</u> since 8:00 A.M.
Past perfect progressive	She **had been** <u>speeding</u> when the officer stopped her.
Future perfect progressive	Next year, when Enrique retires, he **will have been** <u>working</u> for thirty years.

Common Errors in the Progressive Form

* Do not use the progressive form when an action happens regularly.

  complains
  Every day he ~~is complaining~~ about the weather.

* In the progressive form, use the correct form of the verb *be*.

  is
  Right now, Ron ~~be~~ talking with his customer.

* In the progressive form, always include the complete helping verb.

  is   *have*
  Right now, the customer discussing the problem. They been talking for hours.

* Only use the past progressive tense when an action was ongoing at a specific past time or was interrupted.

  agreed
  Yesterday, I ~~was agreeing~~ to meet the new client.

Nonprogressive Verbs

Some verbs do not take the progressive form because they indicate an ongoing state or a perception rather than a temporary action.

Examples of Nonprogressive Verbs

Perception Verbs	Preference Verbs	State Verbs	Possession
admire	desire	believe	have*
care	doubt	know	own
hear	feel	mean	possess
see	hate	realize	
seem	like	recognize	
smell*	look	suppose	
taste*	love	think*	
	prefer	understand	
	want		

*Some verbs have more than one meaning and can be used in the progressive tense. Compare the following pairs of sentences.

Nonprogressive	Progressive
He **has** a franchise. (expresses ownership)	He **is having** a bad day.
I **think** it is unethical. (expresses an opinion)	I **am thinking** about you.

PRACTICE 9

Underline and correct one verb error in each sentence.

EXAMPLE: Daniel ~~been~~ traveling for six months when he injured himself. *had*

1. For years, U.S. companies ~~been~~ marketing their products overseas. *had*

2. These days, translating advertising slogans becoming more of a priority for such companies. *it's*

3. For instance, Withers and Associates are currently work on a slogan for a burger company's franchises in Germany. *ing*

4. Many bad translations are humorous, such as the ones I been reading online. *had*

5. In the 1990s, KFC be planning to introduce its "Finger Lickin' Good" campaign internationally, but the phrase translated to "Eat Your Fingers Off" in Chinese. *was* *was*

6. When the Dairy Association was brainstorm their "Got Milk?" ad

campaign, they didn't expect that it would translate to "Are You Lactating?"

in Spanish.

7. Pepsi's "Come Alive with the Pepsi Generation" is meaning *~~mean~~* "Pepsi Brings

Your Ancestors Back from the Dead" in China.

8. In another case, Coors was making *~~made~~* a mistake when it translated its "Turn It

Loose" campaign to "Suffer from Diarrhea" in Spanish.

9. Right now, Minh Trong works *is working* on an advertising slogan for Vietnam.

FINAL REVIEW

Underline and correct fifteen errors in verb form or tense.

EXAMPLE: Many people were ~~trample~~ *trampled* that night.

1.   Since the early 1900s, nightclubs *have* been popular. Nightclubs pose fire safety

problems because people are pack*ed* together in dark rooms. For example, few

people remember the Station nightclub fire that ~~was~~ *occurred* occurring in Rhode

Island on February 20, 2003. The fire be *was* one of the deadliest nightclub

fires in America; one hundred people ~~losed~~ *lost* their lives in the blaze. Perhaps

everyone should know*ed* some basic strategies to survive a fire in a crowded

venue.

2.   That night, at 11:00 P.M., Great White, a metal band, stepped onto the

stage. While the band be *was* playing "Desert Moon," the curtains behind the

drummer began to burn. A journalist who *had* been filming the show captured

people's reactions. At first, while the flames were flicker*ing*, most audience

members didn't react~~ed~~. Great White's drummer, who had ~~saw~~ *seen* the curtains ignite, looked confused. Then he kept drumming as if nothing has happened. *had*

Only one music fan pointed frantically at the exit, but he was ignore by the

others. Two minutes later, while the room was fill with smoke, everyone *ing*

panicked and ran toward the front door. Soon, the door was block, but the *ed*

crowd still didn't look for alternative exits.

3.   Unfortunately, during fires, people often freeze and lose precious seconds. *froze*

They also forget that buildings have several fire exits. Fire safety information

should be teached to everyone. *taught*

MyWritingLab™

Complete these
writing assignments at
mywritinglab.com

Chapter 28

MyWritingLab™   **THE WRITER'S ROOM**

Write about one of the following topics. Proofread your writing, and
ensure that your verbs are formed correctly.

1. Describe a moment when you thought you were in danger. What
   happened? Use imagery that appeals to the senses.

2. What are the reasons that people travel? How does a trip outside the
   country affect people? Describe the causes and effects of traveling.

Checklist: Verb Tenses

When you edit your writing, ask yourself these questions.

☐ Do I use the correct present and past tense forms? Check for errors in these cases:

–verbs following third-person singular nouns

–irregular present or past tense verbs

–question and negative forms

             lost

Sherry ~~losed~~ her backpack.

☐ Do I use the correct form of past participles? Check for errors in the following:

–spelling of irregular past participles

–present perfect and past perfect verbs

–passive and active forms

                                have

Since the 1970s, some travel companies ^made bad business decisions.

☐ Do I use *-ing* forms correctly? Check for the overuse or misuse of progressive forms. Also ensure that progressive forms are complete.

                 was

In 2010, while I ~~be~~ swimming, I saw a shark fin.

29 Problems with Verbs

SECTION THEME: Travel and Survival

LEARNING OBJECTIVES

LO 1 Maintain verb consistency. **(p. 396)**

LO 2 Avoid double negatives. **(p. 398)**

LO 3 Avoid nonstandard verb forms *gonna*, *gotta*, *wanna*, and *ain't*. **(p. 399)**

LO 4 Recognize problems in conditional forms. **(p. 400)**

LO 5 Avoid nonstandard verb forms *would of*, *could of*, and *should of*. **(p. 402)**

LO 6 Recognize gerunds and infinitives. **(p. 403)**

In this chapter, you will read about travel destinations and tourism controversies.

LO 1 Maintain verb consistency.

Verb Consistency

A verb tense gives your readers an idea about the time that an event occurred. A **faulty tense shift** occurs when you shift from one tense to another for no logical reason. When you write essays, ensure that your tenses are consistent.

Faulty tense shift	Jean Roberts traveled to Santiago, Chile, where she interviews a salon owner.
Correct	Jean Roberts traveled to Santiago, Chile, where she **interviewed** a salon owner.

HINT ◀ *Would* and *Could*

When you tell a story about a past event, use *would* instead of *will* and *could* instead of *can*.

                            couldn't
Last summer, Jill wanted to travel. She ~~can't~~ afford to fly anywhere.
              would
She knew that it ~~will~~ be too expensive.

PRACTICE 1

Underline and correct ten faulty tense shifts in the next paragraphs.

                                      rode
EXAMPLE: He climbed onto his bike and <u>rides</u> down the hill.

1.   In 1995, Rob Penn started a three-year bicycle odyssey throughout Europe and Asia. At that time, he decided that he will ride a bike because he can't afford a car, and he didn't want to take public transit. For three years, Penn traveled to thirty-one different countries. Quickly, Penn realized that others trusted him because he is on a bicycle.

2.   One day, while Penn was riding through rural Kyrgyzstan, he falls off his bicycle while going down a steep hill. Limping badly, Penn decided that he will go to the nearest farm for help. At first, the farmer pointed his gun and speaks in a menacing manner. But when the farmer noticed the bicycle, Penn can see the difference in the old man's attitude. The farmer put away his gun, invited Penn indoors, and offers him food.

3.   During his travels, Penn noticed that people will treat him differently as soon as they saw his bicycle. Perhaps others recognized that he had to work hard to get from one place to another, and they can appreciate his effort.

LO 2 Avoid
double negatives.

Avoiding Double Negatives

A double negative occurs when a negative word such as *no* (*nothing, nobody, nowhere*) is combined with a negative adverb (*not, never, rarely, seldom,* and so on). The result is a sentence that has a double negative. Such sentences can be confusing because the negative words cancel each other.

Double negative   Mr. Lee <u>doesn't</u> want <u>no</u> problems.
(According to this sentence, Mr. Lee wants problems.)

He <u>didn't</u> know <u>nothing</u> about it.
(According to this sentence, he knew something about it.)

How to Correct Double Negatives

There are two ways to correct double negatives.

1. Completely remove *one* of the negative forms. Remember that you may need to adjust the verb to make it agree with the subject.

   Mr. Lee **doesn't** want ~~no~~ problems.

   Mr. Lee ~~doesn't~~ wants **no** problems.

2. Change *no* to *any* (*anybody, anything, anywhere*). Also change *never* to *ever*.

   Mr. Lee doesn't want ~~no~~ ^{any} problems. He doesn't ~~never~~ ^{ever} complain.

> ### HINT ‹ Words with Negative Meanings
>
> Remember that words such as *barely, scarcely,* and *hardly* function as negative words, so don't use "not" with them.
>
> hardly spoke
> I ~~didn't hardly speak~~ during the class.

PRACTICE 2

Underline and correct six errors with double negatives. There are two ways to correct most of the errors.

EXAMPLE: Jacob <u>doesn't want no</u> conflicts.
^{wants no or doesn't want any}

1.   People who travel by bicycle don't have no transportation costs, but they should know how to repair a flat tire or a broken gear. They should also be careful because drivers don't always see cyclists, especially at night.

Chapter 29

2.　At the start of his recent cycling journey, Jacob Steel barely knew nothing

about the problems of traveling by bicycle. Sometimes, after cycling all day,

he wouldn't have no more energy. If there weren't no hostels in the area,

he would ask a local homeowner to let him sleep on a couch. Most people

were very friendly. However, when there wasn't nowhere to stay, he slept

outdoors. On one occasion, he miscalculated the distance between two

towns in Australia. He suffered from heat exhaustion and became severely

ill. At that time, he vowed that he wouldn't never make that mistake again.

In the future, when Steel travels, he will plan his itinerary more carefully.

Nonstandard Forms—*Gonna, Gotta, Wanna, Ain't*

L03 Avoid nonstandard verb forms *gonna, gotta, wanna,* and *ain't*.

Some people commonly say *I'm gonna, I gotta, I wanna,* or *I ain't.* These are nonstandard forms, so avoid using them in written communication.

* Write *going to* instead of *gonna.*
      going to
      My friend is ~~gonna~~ visit Montana.
* Write *have to* instead of *gotta* or *got to.*
      have to
      We ~~gotta~~ bring our tents.
* Write *want to* instead of *wanna.*
      want to
      We ~~wanna~~ camp.
* Write the correct form of *be* or *have* instead of *ain't.*
      hasn't   *isn't*
      Kendra ~~ain't~~ traveled. She ~~ain't~~ going to take a vacation this year.

PRACTICE 3

Underline and correct eight nonstandard verbs.
      have to
EXAMPLE: I <u>gotta</u> work, so I can't travel.

1.　If you wanna travel, there are several steps to take. First, you gotta save some

money for your trip. It ain't as hard as it seems. For instance, Marika wanted to travel after she finished high school. She worked as a waitress, and she didn't spend money on movies or restaurants. She disciplined herself to save her tips each month.

2.   At the end of a year, she had enough money to travel to Asia. "I thought it was gonna cost a lot to travel there, but I was really surprised," she said. She spent a lot on her flight, but the cost of living in Thailand was very low. She could usually get a dorm bed in a travel hostel for about $5 a night. Marika didn't wanna spend a lot on food, so she found inexpensive restaurants and bought food in food stalls.

3.   Thus, if you wanna see the world, make it a priority. You don't gotta spend a fortune. It ain't as difficult as many people believe.

L04 Recognize problems in conditional forms.

Problems in Conditional Forms

In **conditional sentences**, there is a condition and a result. There are three types of conditional sentences, and each type has two parts, or clauses. The main clause depends on the condition set in the *if* clause.

First Form: Possible Present or Future

The condition is true or very possible. Use the present tense in the *if* clause and the present or future tense in the result clause.

condition (*if* clause)   result
If you **ask** her, she **will travel** with you.

Second Form: Unlikely Present

The condition is not likely, and probably will not happen. Use the past tense in the *if* clause and use *would* or *could* in the result clause. In formal writing, when the condition contains the verb *be*, always use "were" in the *if* clause.

condition (*if* clause)   result
If I **had** more money, I **would** (or **could**) **visit** New Zealand.

Third Form: Impossible Past

The condition cannot happen because the event is over. Use the past perfect tense in the *if* clause, and use the past form of *would* (*would have* + past participle) in the result clause.

condition (*if* clause)   result

If Samson **had taken** that flight, he **would have been** in the plane crash.

HINT ◀ **Be Careful with the Past Conditional**

In "impossible past" sentences, the writer expresses regret about a past event or expresses the wish that a past event had worked out differently. In the "if" part of the sentence, remember to use the past perfect tense.

if & past perfect tense   ,   would have (past participle)

had
If the driver ~~would have~~ panicked, the accident would have been worse.

PRACTICE 4

Write the correct conditional forms of the verbs in parentheses.

EXAMPLE: If he (make) _____*had made*_____ a travel blog, others would have enjoyed it.

1.   Some people try risky travel adventures because they want to break

a world record. For instance, in 2010, sixteen-year-old Abby Sunderland

wanted to be the youngest person to sail around the world unaccompanied.

Her parents permitted her to try the adventure. If they (know)

_____ about the outcome, perhaps they

(reconsider) _____ their decision.

2.   On February 6, 2010, the young sailor set out from Marina Del Rey, California.

At that time, if anyone (ask) _____ to accompany

her, she would have said "no." To break the record, she had to sail alone. For

three months, she passed through rough waves and strong storms. Then when

she was about 3,000 miles from Australia, gale-force winds knocked down her mast. If the boat (capsize) _____, she (be)

_____ in extreme danger. Luckily, it didn't capsize.

A beacon was set off, and the Australian government sent out search planes. A

French fishing vessel rescued the girl. Even though she didn't break the record,

she was satisfied. Of course, if she (break) _____

the record, she (be) _____ happier.

3.　　If people get into trouble while doing an adventure sport, should

they pay for their own rescue? Sunderland's rescue was estimated to cost

about $300,000. Perhaps if her family had had the money, they (pay)

_____ for it, but they didn't. Instead, French

and Australian taxpayers picked up the tab.

4.　　If you (have) _____ a sailboat, would you sail around

the world? Even if someone (pay) _____ me, I wouldn't

do it.

LO 5 Avoid nonstandard verb forms *would of*, *could of*, and *should of*.

Nonstandard Forms—*Would of, Could of, Should of*

Some people commonly say *would of, could of,* or *should of*. They may also say *woulda, coulda,* or *shoulda*. These are nonstandard forms, and you should avoid using them in written communication. When you use the past forms of *should, would,* and *could,* always include *have* with the past participle.

Dominique Brown is a nurse, but she really loves real estate. She ~~should of~~ should have become a real-estate agent. She ~~woulda~~ would have been very successful.

PRACTICE 5

Underline and correct nine errors in conditional forms or in the past forms of *could* and *should*.

have
EXAMPLE: Calvin should <u>of</u> stayed home.

1.   If you search the Internet, you would find information about "orphan

tourism." In 2008, Calvin Rice went to Siem Reap, Cambodia. He saw an organized

group of orphans begging in a tourist area. He coulda just visited the temples,

but instead, he chose to work in that orphanage. If he woulda known about the

problems related to orphan tourism, perhaps he would of done something else.

2.   First, he noticed that many visitors just came to look at the orphans, so it

sometimes felt like a zoo. The orphanage even permitted a man to take out

an orphan for a day, with no supervision, so anything coulda happened to

the child. Rice also learned that many of the taxi drivers, tour operators,

and orphanage directors make a lot of money from orphan tourism. In

2012, UNICEF said that of the nearly 12,000 children living in Cambodian

orphanages, 72 percent have at least one living parent.

3.   In the past, some desperate parents coulda sold their children to an

orphanage. If Rice would of known about the greed and corruption in the

orphanage industry, he woulda done another type of volunteer work. He says

that he should of learned about orphan tourism before he did that volunteer

job. These days, issues related to orphan tourism are being debated openly.

Recognizing Gerunds and Infinitives

LO 6 Recognize gerunds and infinitives.

Sometimes a main verb is followed by another verb. The second verb can be a gerund or an infinitive. A **gerund** is a verb with an *-ing* ending. An **infinitive** consists of *to* and the base form of the verb.

verb + gerund
Edward <u>finished</u> **repairing** his bicycle.

verb + infinitive
He <u>wants</u> **to take** weekends off.

Some verbs in English are always followed by a gerund. Do not confuse gerunds with progressive verb forms.

Progressive verb	Julie is working now.
	(Julie is in the process of doing something.)
Gerund	Julie finished **working**.
	(*Working* is a gerund that follows *finish*.)

Some Common Verbs Followed by Gerunds

acknowledge	deny	keep	recall
admit	detest	loathe	recollect
adore	discuss	mention	recommend
appreciate	dislike	mind	regret
avoid	enjoy	miss	resent
can't help	finish	postpone	resist
consider	involve	practice	risk
delay	justify	quit	suggest

Some Common Verbs Followed by Infinitives

afford	decide	manage	refuse
agree	demand	mean	seem
appear	deserve	need	swear
arrange	expect	offer	threaten
ask	fail	plan	volunteer
claim	hesitate	prepare	want
compete	hope	pretend	wish
consent	learn	promise	would like

Some Common Verbs Followed by Gerunds or Infinitives

Some common verbs can be followed by gerunds or infinitives. Both forms have the same meaning.

begin   continue   like   love   start

Elaine likes **to read**. Elaine likes **reading**.

(Both sentences have the same meaning.)

Stop, *Remember*, and *Used to*

Some verbs can be followed by either a gerund or an infinitive, but there is a difference in meaning depending on the form you use.

Term	Form	Example	Meaning
Stop	+ infinitive	He often stops to buy gas every Sunday.	To stop an activity (driving) to do something else.
	+ gerund	I stopped smoking five years ago.	To permanently stop doing something.
Remember	+ infinitive	Please remember to lock the door.	To remember to perform a task.
	+ gerund	I remember meeting him in 2004.	To have a memory about a past event.
Used to	+ infinitive	Jane used to smoke.	To express a past habit.
	+ gerund	Jane is used to living alone.	To be accustomed to something.

Prepositions Plus Gerunds

Many sentences have the structure *verb + preposition + object*. A gerund can be the object of a preposition.

verb + preposition + gerund

I dream **about** traveling to Greece.

Some Common Words Followed by Prepositions plus Gerunds

accuse of	(be) excited about	(be) good at	prohibit from
apologize for	feel like	insist on	succeed in
discourage him from*	fond of	(be) interested in	think about
dream of	forbid him from*	look forward to	(be) tired of
(be) enthusiastic about	forgive me for*	prevent him from*	warn him about*

*Certain verbs can have a noun or pronoun before the preposition.

PRACTICE 6

Complete the sentence with the appropriate verb. Underline either the gerund or the infinitive form.

1. Some travelers can't afford (to stay / staying) in hotels. Today, they have many other options. For instance, they can consider (to couch surf / couch surfing), which means "to sleep on someone's couch or in a spare bedroom." There are many "free hospitality" Web sites, including *Couchsurfing* and *BeWelcome.* Couch surfing has become a relatively safe and inexpensive way to travel.

2.   If you decide (to try / trying) couch surfing, there are a few things you should do. First, read profiles carefully, as couch surfing hosts are rated by users. Also, remember (to give / giving) back in some way. For instance, I recommend (to cook / cooking) and (to clean / cleaning) up after meals. Also, be prepared (to contribute / contributing) to the host's food bill. Don't expect to receive free meals.

3.   Finally, if you like the couch surfing experience, you may become a couch surfing host. Last summer, Mila Gomeshi was excited (to go / going / about going) to Dallas, Texas. She looked forward (to stay / staying / to staying) in the apartment of a translator named Jennifer. Jennifer hosts guests in her home because she enjoys (to meet / meeting) new people. At first, Mila was nervous, but soon she stopped (to worry / worrying / to worrying) about staying with a stranger. Today, Mila remembers (to be / being) surprised by Jennifer's hospitality. She is interested (to become / becoming / in becoming) a couch surfing host one day.

FINAL REVIEW

Underline and correct fifteen errors with verbs and with double negatives.

EXAMPLE: The tourists should not ~~of~~ *have* painted so quickly.

1.   Many people enjoy to travel and wanna do volunteer work overseas. They look online for an organization, but often they don't know nothing about the issues involved in the "voluntourism" industry. If youths really hope to help others, they gotta do some research first.

2.   Some tour operators make money from travel volunteers. They charge their idealistic workers a fee for housing, and then the money ain't distributed to those in need. For instance, Natalia Morova worked in Ghana for an organization that helped AIDS orphans. She didn't know that the money

was only gonna help the organization's founder. She met children who didn't receive nothing from the charity, yet their names were on the charity's list.

3.   In another case, Daniela Papi was an eager volunteer who looked forward to help others. In Thailand, she paid for a bike tour that was done with an aid organization. The young bikers painted a school in a rural area. Papi believed that her team will make a difference. According to Papi, everyone was tired after a long day of riding, so a lot of the paint ends up on the floor. After they left, someone finished to paint the walls properly because the volunteers had done such shoddy work. In retrospect, Papi says that they should of given the money to the school. The school needed teachers and supplies, not paint. The school coulda hired another teacher with the money that the cyclists contributed.

4.   According to Papi, people shouldn't stop to believe in the value of volunteer work. However, they should be realistic and see volunteer work as a learning opportunity. Also, there are good organizations, but people should learn choosing wisely.

MyWritingLab™
Complete these
writing assignments at
mywritinglab.com

MyWritingLab™   **THE WRITER'S ROOM**   Topics for Writing

Write about one of the following topics. Ensure that your verbs are correctly formed.

1. If you had lived one hundred years ago, what job would you have done? Describe the job using details that appeal to the senses.

2. Describe the different types of thrill seekers. You might begin by defining the term and then dividing it into categories. To get ideas, see the photos on the next page.

Chapter 29

READING LINK

To find out more about traveling and survival, see the following essays.

"Botched Tan" by Sarah Stanfield (page 106)

"With an Open Mouth" by Sy Montgomery (page 125)

"The Rules of Survival" by Laurence Gonzales (page 557)

"Into Thin Air" by Jon Krakauer (page 562)

"Slum Tourism" by Eric Weiner (page 565)

"Guy" by Maya Angelou (page 569)

Checklist: Other Verb Forms

When you edit your writing, ask yourself these questions.

☐ Are my verb tenses consistent? Check for errors with the following:

–shifts from past to present or present to past

–*can*/*could* and *will*/*would*

                 would
Whenever she flew, she ~~will~~ ask for a window seat.

☐ Do I use the correct conditional forms? Check for errors in the following:

–possible future forms (*If I meet . . . , I will go . . .*)

–unlikely present forms (*If I met . . . , I would go . . .*)

–impossible past forms (*If I had met . . . , I would have gone . . .*)

      had
If he ~~would have~~ sold shoes, he would have been successful.

☐ Do I use standard verbs? Do not write *gonna, wanna, gotta, shoulda*, etc.

     want to   have to
If you ~~wanna~~ know the truth about orphan tourism, you ~~gotta~~ do some research.

Nouns, Determiners, and Prepositions

30

SECTION THEME: Inventions and Discoveries

In this chapter, you will read about some of the inventions in the first decade of the new century.

LEARNING OBJECTIVES

LO 1 Distinguish count and noncount nouns. **(p. 409)**

LO 2 Use determiners correctly. **(p. 410)**

LO 3 Use prepositions correctly. **(p. 412)**

Count and Noncount Nouns

LO 1 Distinguish count and noncount nouns.

In English, nouns are grouped into two types: count nouns and noncount nouns.

Count nouns refer to people or things that you can count such as *tree*, *house*, or *dog*. Count nouns have both a singular and plural form.

> She wrote three <u>articles</u> about famous inventors.

Noncount nouns refer to people or things that you cannot count because you cannot divide them, such as *sugar* and *imagination*. Noncount nouns have only the singular form.

> <u>Oil</u> has become a very expensive commodity.

Here are some examples of common noncount nouns.

Common Noncount Nouns

Categories of Objects		Food	Nature	Substances	
clothing	machinery	bread	air	chalk	paint
equipment	mail	fish	electricity	charcoal	paper
furniture	money	honey	energy	coal	
homework	music	meat	environment	fur	
jewelry	postage	milk	heat	hair	
luggage	software	rice	ice	ink	
			radiation		
			weather		

Abstract Nouns

advice	education	health	knowledge	proof
attention	effort	help	logic	research
behavior	evidence	history	peace	speculation
creativity	extinction	information	progress	violence

HINT ◄ Latin Nouns

Some nouns that are borrowed from Latin or Greek keep the plural form of the original language.

Singular	Plural	Singular	Plural
millennium	millennia	paparazzo	paparazzi
datum	data	phenomenon	phenomena

LO 2 Use determiners correctly.

Determiners

Determiners are words that will help you determine or figure out whether a noun is specific or general. Examples of determiners are articles (*a*), demonstratives (*this*), indefinite pronouns (*many*), numbers (*three*), possessive nouns (*Maria's*), and possessive adjectives (*my*).

The students are working on <u>four</u> new robotics projects.

Commonly Confused Determiners

Some determiners can be confusing because you can only use them in specific circumstances. Review this list of some commonly confused determiners.

a, an, the

A and *an* are general determiners and *the* is a specific determiner.

A friend bought a new hybrid car. The car can run for 60 miles on a tank of gas.

Use *a* and *an* before singular count nouns but not before plural or noncount nouns. Use *a* before nouns that begin with a consonant (*a storm*), and use *an* before nouns that begin with a vowel (*an institute*).

Use *the* before nouns that refer to a specific person, place, or thing. Do not use *the* before languages (*He speaks Italian*), sports (*They watch tennis*), or most city and country names (*Two of the coldest capital cities in the world are Ottawa and Moscow*). Two examples of exceptions are *the United States* and *the Netherlands*.

many, few, much, little

Use *many* and *few* with count nouns.

Many people invent products, but few inventions are really successful.

Use *much* and *little* with noncount nouns.

Scientists are spending too much time on the project. They are making little progress.

this, that, these, those

This and ***these*** refer to things that are physically close to the speaker or at the present time. Use *this* before singular nouns and *these* before plural nouns. ***That*** and ***those*** refer to things that are physically distant from the speaker or in the past time. Use *that* before singular nouns and *those* before plural nouns.

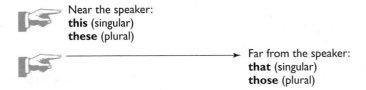

Near the speaker:
this (singular)
these (plural)

Far from the speaker:
that (singular)
those (plural)

This report on my desk is about new satellite technology. The year 1957 was an important time. In that year, the Russians launched the first artificial satellite into space. In those days, Americans worried that the Russians were winning the space race. These days, the United States is making fantastic advances in satellite technology.

PRACTICE 1

Underline the correct noun or determiner in parentheses. If the noun does not require a determiner, underline X.

EXAMPLE: The twenty-first century may be referred to as (the / a / X) Age of Communication.

1.   Although (this / that) century is still young, (many / much) interesting (invention / inventions) are changing how we communicate. (These / Those) days, (few / little) people in (a / the / X) United States have never used (a / an / X) iPod, iPhone, or iPad. There has been (many / much) progress in other methods of mass communication. For example, in 2005, online video sharing was rare, but (this / that) year, three friends from (a / the / X) California created YouTube. (This / That / These) days, over one hundred million YouTube videos are watched daily. In fact, some people believe that there is too (much / many) (information / informations) on that site.

2.   Some other inventions are less well known. Ryan Patterson is interested in electronics. In 2001, when he was seventeen years old, he had (a / an / the) idea. While eating at (a / an / X) restaurant, Ryan saw (a / the / X) group of people who were hearing impaired. They communicated in sign language with their translator, who then repeated their order to their server. Ryan started to think of ways to help people with hearing loss to become more independent. With (little / few) (money / monies), he developed (a / an / X) product called the Braille Glove. It can translate hand signs into words. When (a / the / X) person uses sign language, electronic sensors built into (a / the / X) glove signal (a / an / X) computer. It then displays corresponding letters on (a / an / X) small screen. People who have (a / the / X) problems communicating may find Ryan's glove very convenient. Ryan received the top prize for (a / an / X) invention from Intel's 2002 Science Talent Search contest.

L0 3 Use prepositions correctly.

Prepositions

Prepositions are words that show concepts such as time, place, direction, and manner. They show connections or relationships between ideas.

In 2014, Fred bought an electric car.

In March, his sister borrowed it for a few days.

Prepositions of Time and Place

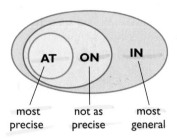

	Prepositions of Time	Prepositions of Place
in	in a year, month, or century (in February)	in a city, country, or continent (in Phoenix)
on	on a day of the week (on Monday) on a specific date (on June 16) on a specific holiday (on Memorial Day)	on a specific street (on Lacombe Ave.) on technological devices (on TV, on the radio, on the phone, on the cell phone, on the computer)
at	at a specific time of day (at 9:15) at night at breakfast, lunch, dinner	at a specific address (at 18 Oriole Crescent) at a specific building (at the hospital, at home)
from . . . to	from one time to another (from 10:00 AM to 1:00 PM)	from one place to another (from Fort Lauderdale to Orlando)
for	for a period of time (for five hours)	for a distance (for two miles)

Commonly Confused Prepositions

to Versus *at*

Use **to** after verbs that indicate movement from one place to another. Use **at** after verbs that indicate being or remaining in one place (and not moving from one place to another). Exception: Do not put *to* directly before *home*.

Every day, the inventor drives <u>to</u> his office and sits <u>at</u> his desk.

for, during, since

Use **during** to explain when something happens, **for** to explain how long it takes to happen, and **since** to indicate the start of an activity.

<u>During</u> the semester, students study robotics <u>for</u> five weeks.

<u>Since</u> 2012, we have been doing surveys <u>during</u> the fall semester.

PRACTICE 2

Write the correct preposition in the blanks.

EXAMPLE: We heard about the Segway _____*on*_____ the radio.

1. _____ all three weeks of the 2008 Summer Olympics

   _____ Beijing, spectators noticed security police zipping around on

   two-wheeled electric vehicles. All over the world, tourists can often be seen

   going _____ one site _____ another using such machines.

   Segway Personal Transporters are a fun way of getting around.

2. _____ 2001, Dean L. Kamen, an inventor, was _____ home

   when he had an inspiration. He worked on his idea _____ several

   days. _____ the following Monday, Kamen discussed his ideas with his

   colleagues. He and his team eventually developed the Segway. It contains a step

   with two wheels, and a person uses body movements to steer the machine. The

   Segway is powered by electricity and can travel _____ about twenty-four

   miles on one battery charge.

3. Dean Kamen first showed his transporter _____ the television

   program *Good Morning America*. He believes that Segways are more

   convenient than cars. _____ Israel and Italy, people may ride the

   Segway _____ city streets. Other countries have specific restrictions

   for Segways. People seem to be content using Segways.

Common Prepositional Expressions

Many common expressions contain prepositions. These types of expressions usually express a particular meaning. The meaning of a verb will change if it is used with a specific preposition. Examine the difference in meaning of the following expressions.

to turn on—to start a machine or switch on the lights

to turn off—to stop a machine or switch off the lights

to turn down—to decline something

to turn over—to rotate

to turn up—to arrive

The next list contains some of the most common prepositional expressions.

accuse (somebody) of	depend on	insulted by	responsible for
acquainted with *not a friend*	dream of / about	interested in	satisfied with
afraid of	escape from	long for	scared of
agree with	excited about	look forward to	search for
apologize for	familiar with	participate in	similar to
apply for	fond of	patient with	specialize in
approve of	forget about	pay attention to	stop (something) from
associate with	forgive (someone) for	pay for	succeed in
aware of	friendly with	prevent (someone) from	take advantage of
believe in	grateful for	protect (someone) from	take care of
capable of	happy about	proud of	thank (someone) for
comply with	hear about	provide (someone) with	think about / of
confronted with	hope for	qualify for	tired of
consist of	hopeful about	realistic about	willing to
count on	innocent of	rely on	wish for
deal with	insist on	rescue from	worry about

PRACTICE 3

Write the correct prepositions in the next paragraphs. Use the preceding list of prepositional expressions to help you.

EXAMPLE: Many people are afraid _____*of*_____ spiders.

1.   Spider web material is stronger and more flexible than steel. Until recently,

   textile makers could only dream ____*about / of*____ making cloth from spider

   webs. But in 2009, two British experts succeeded ____*in*____ creating

   an eleven-foot-long cloth made from spider threads.

2.   The two designers specialize ____*in*____ developing different

   types of textiles. The designers became interested ____*in*____ making

   spider silk cloth after they heard that priests in Madagascar had made

   such a cloth in the 1800s. It took the British designers about four years and

   seventy thousand helpers to make the spider silk. Every day, they searched

   ____*for*____ golden orb spiders and harvested the silk. About fourteen thousand spiders make one ounce of silk, and the textile cloth weighs about two and a half pounds. So the textile experts had to be realistic _about_ the time and effort required to make the silk.

3. Manufacturers became excited _about_ this project because they want to produce material that is as tough and pliable as spider silk. But they will have to forget _about_ such a scheme because it is not cost effective. Scientists have not been able to duplicate spider silk in laboratories.

FINAL REVIEW

Correct fifteen errors in nouns, determiners, and prepositions.

EXAMPLE: ~~Much~~ Many science fiction fans are acquainted ~~in~~ with artificial intelligence.

1. In ~~a~~ the film *Star Wars: A New Hope*, robots exhibit human characteristics. R2-D2 and C-3PO travel from one planet ~~in~~ to another and give their owners useful advices. As technology progresses, the fantastic innovations in the world of science fiction may soon become reality.

2. People have been fascinated with androids since a long time. Scientists are making much advances in the field of artificial intelligence (AI). Currently, researchers are searching ~~with~~ for ways to build machines that have human intellectual abilities such as logics. ~~On~~ In February 2011, a robot named Watson appeared ~~at~~ on television. ~~This~~ That day was unforgettable for fans of *Jeopardy!* because Watson defeated his two opponents, the quiz show's

champions. The audience was astonished that the robot had so

~~many~~ *much* knowledge.

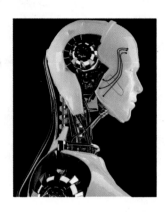

3.　Scientists have also developed a type of robot called a

chatterbot. It can converse with humans through systems such

as instant messaging. ~~At~~ *In* 2008, Elbot, a chatterbot, succeeded ~~on~~ *in*

convincing three of twelve judges of a contest that he was a human

being.

4.　As technology advances, however, society will be confronted ~~about~~ *with*

ethical issues. If robots can develop intelligence, will they also develop

feelings? Will society grant intelligent robots legal rights? Or will robots

become human slaves? Right now, there is very ~~few~~ *little* information about

these topics.

MyWritingLab™ 　**THE WRITER'S ROOM**　 **Topics for Writing**

MyWritingLab™
Complete these writing assignments at mywritinglab.com

Write about one of the following topics. Proofread your text to ensure that there are no errors in singular or plural forms, determiners, and prepositions.

1. Have you ever bought any useless gadgets? Give some examples.
2. Is there a gadget or invention you could not live without? Explain your reasons, or describe how the object affects your life.

Chapter 30

Checklist: Nouns, Determiners, and Prepositions

When you edit your writing, ask yourself these questions:

☐ Do I use the correct singular or plural form of nouns? Check for errors with the spelling of regular and irregular plurals and count and noncount nouns.

> Many people   a music   on
> ~~Much persons~~ have ~~an musics~~ app ~~in~~ their cell phone.

☐ Do I use the correct determiners? Check for errors with *a*, *an*, *the*, *much*, *many*, *few*, *little*, *this*, *that*, *these*, and *those*.

> These   much   the
> ~~This~~ days, there is too ~~many~~ information about ~~a~~ impact of new technology.

☐ Do I use the correct prepositions? Check for errors with *in*, *on*, *at*, and *to*; with *for* and *during*; and with prepositional expressions.

> For   to
> ~~During~~ three months each winter, students look forward ~~in~~
>   in
> competing ~~on~~ the World Gadget Competition.

Chapter 30

In this chapter, you will read about profitable inventions.

Pronoun–Antecedent Agreement

LO 1 Practice pronoun–antecedent agreement.

Pronouns are words that replace nouns (people, places, or things) and phrases. Use pronouns to avoid repeating nouns.

Gary Dahl is an inventor. ~~Gary Dahl~~ *He* invented the Pet Rock.

A pronoun must agree with its **antecedent**, which is the word to which the pronoun refers. Antecedents are words that the pronouns have replaced, and they always come before the pronoun. Pronouns must agree in person and number with their antecedents.

Sarah played games on **her** computer when **she** was young.

Compound Antecedents

Compound antecedents consist of two or more nouns joined by *and* or *or*. When nouns are joined by *and*, use a plural pronoun to refer to them.

James and Reid use **their** satellite phones regularly.

When singular nouns are joined by *or*, use a singular pronoun. When plural nouns are joined by *or*, use a plural pronoun.

> Does <u>the radio station or the TV station</u> have **its** own program on new inventions?

> Do <u>environmentalists or activists</u> update **their** Web sites?

GRAMMAR LINK
For a list of common collective nouns, see page 372 in Chapter 27.

Collective Nouns

Collective nouns refer to a group of people or things. The group usually acts as a unit; therefore, most of the time, the collective noun is singular.

> The <u>company</u> was fined for copyright infringement. **It** had to pay a large sum of money.

PRACTICE 1

Circle each pronoun and underline its antecedent.

EXAMPLE: Although many <u>inventions</u> are useless, (they) are popular.

1. In 1975, Gary Dahl's friends complained about their German Shepherd.

2. Ursula and Mickey Thibo did not want to take care of their dog.

3. So Dahl invented the Pet Rock, and his invention became very popular.

4. The Pet Rock was a great pet because it did not have to be fed or walked.

5. Dahl established a company, and it made a huge profit from the Pet Rock.

6. Does eBay or ThinkGeek sell the Pet Rock on its Web site?

LO 2 Use indefinite pronouns correctly.

Indefinite Pronouns

Use **indefinite pronouns** when you refer to people or things whose identities are not known or are unimportant. This chart shows some common singular and plural indefinite pronouns.

Indefinite Pronouns

Singular				
	another	each	no one	other
	anybody	everybody	nobody	somebody
	anyone	everyone	nothing	someone
	anything	everything	one	something
Plural	both, few, many, others, several			
Either singular or plural	all, any, half (and other fractions), none, more, most, some			

Singular

When you use a singular indefinite antecedent, use a singular pronoun to refer to it.

<u>Nobody</u> remembered to bring **his** or **her** laptop.

Plural

When you use a plural indefinite antecedent, use a plural pronoun to refer to it.

The two men rushed into the street, and <u>both</u> carried **their** own smartphones.

Either Singular or Plural

Some indefinite pronouns can be either singular or plural depending on the noun to which they refer.

Many scientists spoke at the conference. <u>All</u> gave important information about **their** research.

(*All* refers to scientists; therefore, the pronoun is plural.)

I read <u>all</u> of the newspaper and could not find **its** business section.

(*All* refers to the newspaper; therefore, the pronoun is singular.)

HINT ◢ Avoid Sexist Language

Terms like *anybody*, *somebody*, *nobody*, and *each* are singular antecedents, so the pronouns that follow must be singular. At one time, it was acceptable to use *he* as a general term meaning "all people." However, today it is more acceptable to use *he or she*.

Sexist	<u>Everyone</u> should bring **his** laptop to the meeting.
Solution	<u>Everyone</u> should bring **his** or **her** laptop to the meeting.
Better Solution	<u>People</u> should bring **their** laptops to the meeting.
Exception	In the men's prison, <u>everyone</u> has **his** own cell.
	(If you know for certain that the subject is male or female, then use only *he* or only *she*.)

PRACTICE 2

Correct eight errors in pronoun–antecedent agreement by changing either the antecedent or the pronoun. If you change any antecedents, make sure that your subjects and verbs agree.

EXAMPLE: Some customers buy ~~his~~ *their* Chia Pets online.

1.   Everyone feels embarrassed when they buy a useless product. One huge fad was the Chia Pet. Chia Pets are animal-shaped terracotta pots that sprout tiny plants. The plants look like the animal's fur. In 1982, many people bought Chia Pets. Some especially loved his first Chia Pet. Anybody who forgets to water their Chia gets a surprise: The Chia's "fur" dies.

2.   Since the 1980s, some people have become enthusiastic Chia collectors, and he can buy and sell the pets on the Internet. Anyone can add to their collection. Some Chias are cartoon characters such as Bugs Bunny. Others take its image from popular culture. For example, there are Chia Presidents, Chia Statues of Liberty, and so on.

3.   Someone gave me two Chia Pets as a present. Both are on my desk, and its "fur" is green and growing. The Chias are unique, and nobody else I know has one of their own.

Vague Pronouns

LO 3 Avoid using vague pronouns.

Avoid using pronouns that could refer to more than one antecedent.

Vague   My father asked my brother where <u>his</u> instruction manual was.
(Whose instruction manual? My father's or my brother's?)

Clearer   My father asked my brother where **my brother's** instruction manual was.

Avoid using confusing pronouns such as *it* and *they* that have no clear antecedent.

Vague   <u>They</u> say that millions of people have bought the new iPad.
(Who are *they*?)

Clearer   **Reporters** say that millions of people have bought the new iPad.

Vague   It stated in the newspaper that robots are being used to perform dangerous tasks.
(Who or what is *it*?)

Clearer   **The *New York Times*' article** stated that robots are being used to perform dangerous tasks.

This, that, and *which* should refer to a specific antecedent.

Vague   My girlfriend said that the seminar was boring. I was glad she told me this.
(What is *this*?)

Clearer   My girlfriend said that the seminar was boring. I was glad she told me **this information**.

> ## HINT ◄ Avoid Repeating the Subject
>
> When you clearly mention a subject, do not repeat the subject in pronoun form.
>
> Technology ~~it~~ is advancing at a fast pace.

PRACTICE 3

The next paragraphs contain vague pronouns or repeated subjects. Correct the eight errors in this selection. You may need to rewrite some sentences.

EXAMPLE: ~~They~~ Experts say that many items are invented accidently.

1.   When Frank Epperson was eleven years old, he accidentally left a fruit

   drink with a stick in it outside. The temperature plummeted overnight.

   This caused the liquid to freeze, and the Popsicle was

   created. They say that Epperson introduced the "Epsicle

   ice pop" at a fireman's ball in 1922. The firemen, they

   were thrilled with the "stick of frozen juice." Epperson's

   children later convinced their father to name the

   ice pop "Popsicle."

2.   People started talking about the product. This caused reporters to interview Frank Epperson. Frank was told by his friend Jack Steele that he was going to become famous. Jack he advised Frank to take out a patent. Frank took Jack's advice. Three years later, in 1925, it stated that the Joe Lowe Company bought Epperson's patent, and the Popsicle became even more popular. Children, as well as adults, like to eat Popsicles. This has led to the creation of other similar products, such as the Fudgsicle and the Creamsicle.

Pronoun Shifts

LO 4 Avoid unnecessary pronoun shifts.

If your essays contain unnecessary shifts in person or number, you may confuse your readers. They will not know exactly who or how many you are referring to. Carefully edit your writing to ensure that your pronouns are consistent.

Making Pronouns Consistent in Number

If the antecedent is singular, then the pronoun must be singular. If the antecedent is plural, then the pronoun must be plural.

    singular   his or her

The **director** is showing ~~their~~ 3D films to a major distributor.

    plural   their

Many companies market new apps for ~~its~~ cell phones.

Making Pronouns Consistent in Person

Person is the writer's perspective. For some writing assignments, you might use the first person (*I*, *we*). For other assignments, especially most college essays, you will likely use the third person (*he, she, it, they*).

Shifting the point of view for no reason confuses readers. If you begin writing from one point of view, do not shift unnecessarily to another point of view.

When **parents** buy **their** sons or daughters a new video game, **they** should be careful. **They** should read about the video game. ~~You~~ *They* should avoid buying violent video games.

PRACTICE 4

Correct five pronoun shift errors.

they
EXAMPLE: Potato chips are very popular, and it can come in a variety of flavors.

In 1853, George Crum, a chef, was cutting potatoes when you heard customers complaining about the thickness of his fried potatoes. He cut thinner fries, but the women still complained. He knew that you should please the customer. Finally, with a very sharp knife, Crum cut potatoes so thinly that it could not be eaten with a fork. Crum had invented the potato chip. He realized that you could sell the product and make a profit.

I love potato chips, and I often eat them as a snack. My friend Paul does not like potato chips, and one never buys them.

Pronoun Case

Pronouns are formed according to the role they play in a sentence. A pronoun can be the subject of the sentence or the object of the sentence. It can also show possession. This chart shows the three main pronoun cases: subjective, objective, and possessive.

LO 5 Use the three main pronoun cases correctly.

Pronoun

Singular	Subjective	Objective	Possessive	
			Possessive Adjective	**Possessive Pronoun**
1st person	I	me	my	mine
2nd person	you	you	your	yours
3rd person	he, she, it, who, whoever	him, her, it, whom, whomever	his, her, its, whose	his, hers
Plural				
1st person	we	us	our	ours
2nd person	you	you	your	yours
3rd person	they	them	their	theirs

Chapter 31

Subjective Case and Objective Case

When a pronoun is the subject of the sentence, use the subjective form of the pronoun. When a pronoun is the object in the sentence, use the objective form of the pronoun.

subject   subject object

He left the umbrella at work, and **I** asked **him** to bring it home.

Possessive Case

A possessive pronoun shows ownership.

* **Possessive adjectives** come before the noun that they modify.

   She finished **her** research on electric cars, but we did not finish **our** research.

* **Possessive pronouns** replace the possessive adjective and the noun that follows it. In the next sentence, the possessive pronoun *ours* replaces both the possessive adjective *our* and the noun *research*.

   possessive adjective   possessive pronoun

   She finished **her** research on electric cars, but we did not finish **ours**.

Problems with Possessive Pronouns

GRAMMAR LINK
For more information about apostrophes, see Chapter 36.

Some possessive adjectives sound like certain contractions. When using the possessive adjectives *their*, *your*, and *its*, be careful that you do not confuse them with *they're* (they + are), *you're* (you + are), and *it's* (it + is).

          hers   theirs

The book on gadgets is ~~her's~~. The robotics magazine is ~~their's~~.

HINT ◄ Choosing *His* or *Her*

To choose the correct possessive adjective, think about the possessor (not the object that is possessed).

If something belongs to a female, use **her** + noun.

  Malina and **her** husband are inventors.

If something belongs to a male, use **his** + noun.

  Cliff used **his** new camera to make videos.

PRACTICE 5

Underline the correct possessive pronouns or possessive adjectives in parentheses.

EXAMPLE: Hedy Lamarr received praise for (<u>her</u> / hers) invention.

1.   Many people have become famous for (their / there / they're) inventions. For example, Alfred Nobel invented dynamite, and (its / it's / their) usefulness made Nobel rich. Women have also invented products, but (their / there / theirs) are often not as well known.

2.   Hedy Lamarr was famous during (her / hers) lifetime. She was known as an actress, not as an inventor. However, she and (her / his) friend George Antheil developed a secret communications system during World War II. (Their / They're / Theirs) invention altered radio waves and created an unbreakable coding system. The code prevented the enemy from understanding classified messages.

3.   For (our / ours) film studies class, we made a documentary about Hedy Lamarr. All of the students submitted (their / they're / there) films to a contest. (Our / Ours) won first prize. We would like you to see (our / ours) documentary, and we want to watch (your / yours).

Pronouns in Comparisons with *Than* or *As*

Avoid making errors in pronoun case when the pronoun follows *than* or *as*. If the pronoun is a subject, use the subjective case, and if the pronoun is an object, use the objective case.

If you use the incorrect case, your sentence may have a meaning that you do not intend it to have. Review the next examples. Notice that when the sentence ends with the subjective pronoun, it is advisable to add a verb after the pronoun.

objective case

a) I like gizmos as much as **him**.

    (I like gizmos <u>as much as I like him</u>.)

subjective case

b) I like gizmos as much as **he** (does).

    (I like gizmos <u>as much as he likes gizmos</u>.)

HINT ◀ Complete the Thought

To test which pronoun case to use, complete the thought.

Eva understands him more than **I** [understand him].
(Do I want to say that Eva understands him more than I understand him?)

Eva understands him more than [she understands] **me**.
(Or, do I want to say that Eva understands him more than she understands me?)

Pronouns in Prepositional Phrases

In a prepositional phrase, the noun or pronoun that follows the preposition is the object of the preposition. Therefore, always use the objective case of the pronoun after a preposition.

> To **him**, a cutback in funding is not a big deal. Between **you** and **me**, I think he's misinformed.

Pronouns with *and* or *or*

Use the correct case when nouns and pronouns are joined by ***and*** or ***or***. If the pronouns are the subject, use the subjective case. If the pronouns are the object, use the objective case.

> She and I
> ~~Her and me~~ had to read about Alexander Graham Bell, and then the instructor
>   her and me
> asked ~~she and I~~ to summarize the information.

>   I
> Frances or ~~me~~ could give a seminar on a new invention. The students asked
>   me
> Frances or ~~I~~ to show how the invention worked.

HINT ◀ **Finding the Correct Case**

To determine that your case is correct, try saying the sentence with either the subjective case or the objective case.

Sentence	The professor asked her and (**I or me**) to research the topic.
Possible answers	The professor asked **I** to research the topic. (This would not make sense.)
	The professor asked **me** to research the topic. (This would make sense.)
Correct answer	The professor asked **her** and **me** to research the topic.

PRACTICE 6

Correct any errors with pronoun case.

           I
EXAMPLE: Clarence and ~~me~~ laughed at the bizarre gadgets.

1. Last week, my friend Clarence and me went to an exhibition of gadgets.

2. Both him and me like gadgets.

3. However, Clarence is an inventor, and he is more interested in useful devices than me.

4. Some of the items on display were funny. For example, an exhibitor showed we visitors a mood ring.

5. The exhibitor asked Clarence or I to try on the mood rings.

6. Clarence was as willing as me to try on the ring. The ring turned green on his finger and red on mine.

Relative Pronouns

LO 6 Use relative pronouns correctly.

Relative pronouns can join two short sentences. Relative pronouns include *who, whom, whoever, whomever, which, that,* and *whose.*

GRAMMAR LINK
For more information about relative pronouns, see Chapter 22.

Choosing *Who* or *Whom*

To determine whether to use *who* or *whom*, replace *who* or *whom* with another pronoun. If the replacement is a subjective pronoun such as *he* or *she*, use **who**. If the replacement is an objective pronoun such as *her* or *him*, use **whom**.

I know a man **who** studies systems design.
(He studies systems design.)

The man to **whom** you gave your résumé is my boss.
(You gave your résumé to him.)

PRACTICE 7

Underline the correct relative pronoun in the parentheses.

EXAMPLE: My friends (who / whom) play parlor games are going to be interviewed for a magazine.

1. Chris Haney and Scott Abbott, (who / whom) I met at a party, created the very popular game *Trivial Pursuit* in 1979.

2. Josh, (who / whom) is my classmate, plays *Trivial Pursuit* every Friday night with a group of people.

3. Josh's friends, (who / whom) I know somewhat, are all members of the Parlor Games Club.

4. Every year, the club holds a *Trivial Pursuit* contest. Josh and his friends, (who / whom) are serious players, have entered to play again this year.

5. Alison Corbett is a reporter (who /whom) is covering the contest for her magazine.

6. Josh, (who / whom) Alison interviewed, will be featured in next month's issue.

FINAL REVIEW

Correct the fifteen pronoun errors in the next paragraphs.

EXAMPLE: Anne and ~~his~~ *her* friends went to an exhibition on robots.

1.   Inventors and they're inventions make fascinating stories. Matt Richtel, whom is a journalist for the *New York Times*, suggests that some well-known inventions had earlier versions. For instance, in February 1878, Thomas Edison patented a sound device. However, they say that an unknown French inventor had made a sound recording seventeen years earlier.

2.   Nobody knows why their ideas are remembered better than somebody else's ideas. For example, consider the cases of Alexander Graham Bell and Elisha Gray. Both filed his telephone device patents on February 14, 1876. Although Elisha Gray is known, Alexander Graham Bell is more famous than him. Moreover, my friend Louis and me discovered that Antonio Meucci had created a sound machine some years earlier. Most people don't know that.

3.   Sometimes, many innovators contribute to new technologies. The two most famous innovators, Bill Gates and Steve Jobs, made his fortunes in the computer industry. But does either Microsoft or Apple deserve their reputation as one of the first developers of personal computers? People don't

know about Dennis Allison. However, if they had read about the history of computers, you would have recognized his name. Between you and I, Dennis Allison deserves some credit as a computer innovator.

4.   My cousin Sarah, who I admire, likes to invent gadgets. You should show her you're inventions, and she will show you her's.

Topics for Writing

THE WRITER'S ROOM

MyWritingLab™

MyWritingLab™
Complete these writing assignments at mywritinglab.com

Write about one of the following topics. Proofread your text to ensure there are no pronoun errors.

1. Explain how to make a Web site or how to choose a cell phone. What are the steps you would take?

2. What is currently the world's most useful invention? Argue that a particular invention is the most useful.

Checklist: Pronouns

When you edit your writing, ask yourself these questions.

☐ Do I use the correct pronoun case? Check for errors with the following:

  –subjective, objective, and possessive cases

  –comparisons with *than* or *as*

  –prepositional phrases

  –pronouns following *and* or *or*

                  me   I (do)
  Between you and ~~I~~, my sister uses new technology more than ~~me~~.

☐ Do I use the correct relative pronouns? Check for errors with *who* or *whom*.

             whom
  My husband, ~~who~~ you have met, is a video game designer.

☐ Do my pronouns and antecedents agree in number and person? Check for errors with indefinite pronouns and collective nouns.

its
The computer crash and ~~their~~ aftermath were reported on the news.

☐ Are my pronoun references clear? Check for vague pronouns and inconsistent points of view.

Scientists
~~They~~ say that the way we communicate will continually change. I

I
read the report, and ~~you~~ could not believe what it said.

In this chapter, you will read about ancient inventions and discoveries.

LO 1 Practice using adjectives.

Adjectives

Adjectives describe nouns (people, places, or things) and pronouns (words that replace nouns). They add information explaining how many, what kind, or which one. They also describe how things look, smell, feel, taste, and sound.

433

The **enthusiastic** students wanted to make a **short** documentary on **ancient mechanical** devices.

HINT ◂ Placement of Adjectives

You can place adjectives either before a noun or after a linking verb such as *be*, *look*, *appear*, *smell*, or *become*.

Before the noun	The **nervous** inventor gave a **suitable** speech.
After the linking verb	The engineer was **disappointed**, and he was **angry**.

Problems with Adjectives

You can recognize many adjectives by their endings. Be particularly careful when you use the following adjective forms.

Adjectives Ending in *-ful* or *-less*

Some adjectives end in *-ful* or *-less*. Remember that *ful* ends in one *l* and *less* ends in double *s*.

The **cheerful** inventor developed many **useless** products.

Adjectives Ending in *-ed* and *-ing*

Some adjectives look like verbs because they end in *-ing* or *-ed*. When the adjective ends in *-ed*, it describes the person's or animal's expression or feeling. When the adjective ends in *-ing*, it describes the quality of the person or thing.

The **frustrated** but **prepared** historian confronted the politician, and his **challenging** and **convincing** arguments got her attention.

HINT ◂ Keep Adjectives in the Singular Form

Always make an adjective singular, even if the noun following the adjective is plural.

        year
Lucia was a forty-five-~~years~~-old woman when she took out a five-
       dollar
thousand-~~dollars~~ bank loan and opened her own antique store.

Adverbs

Adverbs add information to adjectives, verbs, or other adverbs. They give more specific information about how, when, where, and to what extent an action or event occurred. Some adverbs look exactly like adjectives, such as *early, late, soon, often,* and *hard.* However, most adverbs end in *-ly.*

verb   adverb

Archaeologists <u>studied</u> the ancient documents **carefully**.

adverb   adverb

They released the results **quite** <u>quickly</u>.

adverb adjective

The **very** <u>eloquent</u> speaker was Dr. Ying.

Forms of Adverbs

Adverbs often end in *-ly.* In fact, you can change many adjectives into adverbs by adding *-ly* endings.

* If you add *-ly* to a word that ends in *l,* then your new word will have a double *l.*

professional + ly

The journalist covered the story **professionally**.

* If you add *-ly* to a word that ends in *e,* keep the *e.* Exceptions are *true–truly* and *due–duly.*)

close + ly

The two journalists worked together **closely**.

HINT ◄ **Placement of Frequency Adverbs**

Frequency adverbs are words that indicate how often someone performs an action or when an event occurs. Common frequency adverbs are *always, ever, never, often, sometimes,* and *usually.* They can appear at the beginnings of sentences, or they can appear in the following locations.

• Place frequency adverbs before regular present and past tense verbs.

    Politicians **sometimes** <u>forget</u> the importance of ancient structures.

• Place frequency adverbs after all forms of the verb *be.*

    She <u>is</u> **often** an advisor for the historical society.

• Place frequency adverbs after an initial helping verb.

    They <u>have</u> **never** donated to a museum.

PRACTICE 1

Correct eight errors with adjectives or adverbs.

wonderful
EXAMPLE: The ancient Greeks created many ~~wonderfull~~ artifacts.

Usually think
1.   People think ~~usually~~ that computers are a modern invention. In 1900,

Interesting
some Greek sponge divers discovered an interested shipwreck. Among

the plentifull artifacts, the divers stumbled across a piece of stone with

brass in it. They showed the relic to Valerios Stais, a Greek archaeologist.

excited
The exciting archaeologist identified the piece as the Antikythera mechanism.

2.   Recently, experts successfully X-rayed the treasure; it contains thirty

gears. The two-thousand-years-old instrument is the first mechanical analog

computer. Greek astronomers used frequently the instrument to calculate

the movement of stars and planets. Today the Antikythera mechanism is

housed in the National Archaeological Museum in Athens. Scientists

astounding
continue to examine this astounded discovery.

Problems with Adverbs

Many times, people use an adjective instead of an adverb after a verb. Ensure that you always modify your verbs using an adverb.

really quickly   *slowly*
The students read about the scrolls ~~real quick~~. They examined the script ~~slow~~.

PRACTICE 2

Correct ten errors with adjectives or adverbs.

really
EXAMPLE: I read Heron's book ~~real~~ rapidly.

incredible
1.   Heron of Alexandria (10–70 AD) was an incredibly engineer. He gained

greatly
fame quick for his inventions. He contributed great to the technology of his

time. Heron wrote a book, *Mechanics and Optics*, in which he described his work very carefull*ly* The original manuscript is lost, but Arabic texts mention

some of Heron's inventions quite clear*ly* .

2.   One of his inventions was the vending machine. It worked reall*y* smooth*ly*

When someone put a coin into the machine, it squirted out holy water quite

accurate*ly* into a pan. People used Heron's other inventions, such as the wind

wheel and the water pump, very eager*ly* Every time Heron created a new

device, fellow citizens cheered very loud*ly* .

Good and Well / Bad and Badly

Poorly *badly*

Good is an adjective, and *well* is an adverb. However, as an exception, you can use
well to describe a person's health (for example, *I do not feel well*).

| **Adjective** | The archaeologist gave a **good** account of the events. |
| **Adverb** | Archimedes slept **well** after he talked to his mentor. |

Bad is an adjective, and *badly* is an adverb.

| **Adjective** | The antique clock was in **bad** condition. |
| **Adverb** | The historian described the event **badly**. |

HINT ◄ Linking Verbs + Adjectives or Adverbs

The following verbs change their meaning when used with an adverb.

| look good (appearance) | look well (healthy) |
| feel good (state of mind) | feel well (healthy / not sick) |

Blair wants to **look good** for his interview. He bought a new shirt.

Nina has a high fever. She does not **look well**.

PRACTICE 3

Underline the correct adjectives or adverbs.

EXAMPLE: There are many (<u>good</u> / well) books on Egyptian pyramids.

1.   The Aztecs, Mayans, and Egyptians all built pyramids very (good / well) The

pyramids of Egypt are the most famous. There are about 101 pyramids known

in Egypt, but only some remain in (good / well) condition. The step pyramid

was built more than four thousand years ago. It is in a (bad / badly) state, but archaeologists are repairing it. The Great Pyramid at Giza is the largest pyramid. It contains over two million limestone blocks of (good / well) quality.

2.   Researchers are trying to gain a (good / well) understanding of construction practices in ancient Egypt. The pharaohs prepared for the afterlife really (good / well). They believed that if they planned (bad / badly), then they would not reach heaven. They hired laborers who were in (good / well) shape to build the pyramids. Even if the laborers did not feel (good / well), they still had to work. Most laborers wanted to work on the pyramids. The laborers thought their (bad / badly) actions in their present life would be cancelled if they served the pharaoh. Then, they could also have a (good / well) afterlife. The pharaohs also used slaves for construction work. Generally, Egyptian citizens treated their slaves (bad / badly) and provided their slaves with (bad / badly) working conditions. But when slaves worked on the pyramids, they did not live (bad / badly). All workers had to eat (good / well) because they had to work hard. (Good / Well) workers also received a tax break, as well as housing and clothes.

LO3 Distinguish comparative and superlative forms.

Comparative and Superlative Forms

Use the **comparative form** to compare two items. Use the **superlative form** to compare three or more items. You can write comparative and superlative forms by remembering a few simple guidelines.

Using *-er* and *-est* Endings

Add *-er* and *-est* endings to one-syllable adjectives and adverbs. Double the last letter when the adjective ends in *one vowel + one consonant*.

short	short**er** than	the short**est**
hot	hot**ter** than	the hot**test**

When a two-syllable adjective ends in *-y*, change the *-y* to *-i* and add *-er* or *-est*.

happy	happ**ier** than	the happ**iest**

Using *more* and *the most*

Generally, add *more* and *the most* to adjectives and adverbs of two or more syllables.

beautiful   **more** beautiful than   the **most** beautiful

Using Irregular Comparative and Superlative Forms

Some adjectives and adverbs have unique comparative and superlative forms. Study this list to remember some of the most common ones.

good / well	better than	the best
bad / badly	worse than	the worst
some / much / many	more than	the most
little (a small amount)	less than	the least
few	fewer than	the fewest
far	farther / further	the farthest / the furthest

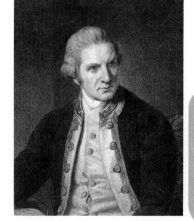

> **GRAMMAR LINK**
> *Farther* indicates a physical distance. *Further* means "additional." For more commonly confused words, see Chapter 34.

PRACTICE 4

Fill in the blanks with the correct comparative and superlative forms of the words in parentheses.

EXAMPLE: Captain Cook was one of the (good) _____*best*_____ navigators of his era.

1.   Captain James Cook is one of the (famous) _*most*_ _*famous*_ explorers of the eighteenth century. He

joined the Royal Navy and acquired many different skills. He

learned to survey, but he liked mathematics the (good)

*the best* of all of his subjects. He

liked rope making the (little) _*least*_ of

his studies.

2.   Cook made three voyages around the world. The first voyage to the eastern

coast of Canada was (short) _*shorter*_ than the next

two. Cook's second expedition was on the ship *Endeavour*. He mapped New

Zealand and parts of Australia. Cook sailed a third time on the ship *Resolution*.

His third voyage was (hazardous) _____*most hazardous*_____ than the

earlier expeditions. After exploring the Easter Islands, he reached the Hawaiian

Islands in 1778. Unfortunately, he fought with the islanders, and in one of the

(bad) _____*worst*_____ skirmishes in the conflict, he was killed.

Problems with Comparative and Superlative Forms

Using *more* and *-er*

In the comparative form, never use *more* and *-er* to modify the same word. In the superlative form, never use *most* and *-est* to modify the same word.

> The photographs of the old radios were ~~more~~ better than the ones of the toasters, but the photos of the gramophones were the ~~most~~ best in the exhibition.

Using *fewer* and *less*

GRAMMAR LINK
For a list of common noncount nouns, refer to page 410 in Chapter 30.

In the comparative form, use *fewer* before count nouns (*fewer people, fewer houses*) and use *less* before noncount nouns (*less information, less evidence*).

> Researchers have **less** <u>time</u> than they used to. They hire **fewer** <u>students</u> than before.

HINT ◀ Using *the* in the Comparative Form

Although you would usually use *the* in superlative forms, you can use it in some two-part comparatives. In these expressions, the second part is the result of the first part.

> action　　　　　　　　　　　　　　　　　result
> <u>The more</u> you read about ancient Egypt, <u>the better</u> you will understand the culture.

PRACTICE 5

Correct the nine adjective and adverb errors in the next paragraphs.

EXAMPLE: The more the public sees the Dead Sea Scrolls, the ~~most~~ *more* interested they become in the origins of the scrolls.

1.　　The Dead Sea Scrolls consist of about one thousand biblical and

nonbiblical texts. They are one of the ~~most~~ largest collections of ancient texts

in Israel. In the late 1950s, the scientific community became real~~l~~ excited
ly

when they heard about the scrolls.

2.   In 1947, a Bédouin boy's goats wandered into a cave near the Dead Sea.
er

The more he tried to coax his goats out of the cave, the farthest they retreated

into the cave. The boy threw rocks into the cave to get the goats out. He

accidently hit some pottery jars, and they broke, exposing the scrolls. The
had

boy never had seen such documents, so he showed them to an archaeologist.
ly

The expert went back to the cave really quick and was relieved to see that
fewer

most of the jars had remained intact. The boy had broken ~~less~~ jars than the

expert had first believed.

3.   At the beginning of their investigation, scientists damaged some of the
dly

scrolls bad. They did not know how fragile the documents were and smoked
worst

while working on the scrolls. The experts discovered that the worse problem

was that the manuscripts faded when exposed to air. Soon, they realized

their mistakes and ever since have been making digital copies of the scrolls.
most

The more the experts analyze the scrolls, the ~~more~~ better they understand

their significance.

FINAL REVIEW

Correct fifteen errors in adjectives and adverbs.

interesting

EXAMPLE: The experts studied the ~~interested~~ artifact.

have

1.   Researchers always ~~have~~ wanted to study the cultural history of North

American tribes. Most native groups have left no written records. Scientists

believe that the more they study human remains, the ~~more~~ better they

READING LINK

The following essays contain more information about inventions and discoveries.

"Journalists Are History's Record Keepers" by Lindsey Davis (page 147)

"Internet Trolls" by Lisa Selin Davis (page 158)

"Marketing New Inventions" by Robert Rodriguez (page 548)

"Brands R Us" by Stephen Garey (page 551)

"Can We Talk?" by Josh Freed (page 554)

understand indigenous history. They want to examine skeletons in burial grounds real carefully. However, distressing native groups feel that the excavation of burial sites is demeaning to their ancestors. The Dickson Mounds Museum in Illinois is one of the most examples of this issue.

2. In 1927, Don Dickson, an Illinois farmer, saw a small hill on his land. The more closely he examined it, the most interested he became. He discovered that the hill was a tribal burial ground. He dug up the area quite quick and saw clear that the site contained beautiful ancient artifacts and human skeletons. The farmer built a museum over the site and opened it for the general public.

3. The museum contained thousand-years-old bones. Scientists came often to analyze the skeletons and to continue hunting for remains. However, archaeologists actually excavated less sites than they wanted. In the 1970s, many native groups protested such excavations. They argued passionate that their ancestors could not rest in peace if their bones were on display. By the 1990s, the government passed a law requiring any federally funded institution to give back its collection to Native American tribes that claimed ownership over burial grounds. The concerning Dickson Mounds Museum officials responded good. In 1992, the museum officials reburied the skeletons because they wanted to respect native groups.

MyWritingLab™

Complete these writing assignments at mywritinglab.com

MyWritingLab™

THE WRITER'S ROOM   Topics for Writing

Write about one of the following topics. Proofread your text to ensure that there are no adjective and adverb mistakes.

1. Compare two inventions from the past.

2. How important is history as a school subject? Should history be a compulsory subject at school?

Checklist: Adjectives and Adverbs

When you edit your writing, ask yourself these questions:

☐ Do I use adjectives and adverbs correctly? Check for errors in these cases:

–the placement, order, and spelling of adjectives

–the placement of frequency adverbs, and the spelling of adverbs ending in -ly

–the adjective and adverb form

–the use of *good/well* and *bad/badly*

>   quietly   interesting
> Magnus Forbes spoke very ~~quiet~~ about the ~~interested~~ shipwreck
>   often
> article at the news conference. He was asked ~~often~~ about historical
>   really well
> findings. The museum director hid his concern ~~real good~~.

☐ Do I use the correct comparative and superlative forms? Check for errors in these cases:

–*more* versus *-er* comparisons

–*the most* versus *-est* comparisons

–*fewer* versus *less* forms

> Samuel Ben Aziz used his ~~most~~ best camera to photograph the mummy.
>   fewer   less
> The organization has ~~less~~ members, but it also has ~~fewer~~ bad publicity.

33 Exact Language

SECTION THEME: Our Natural World

LEARNING OBJECTIVES

LO 1 Use specific and detailed vocabulary. **(p. 444)**

LO 2 Avoid wordiness and redundancy. **(p. 446)**

LO 3 Avoid clichés. **(p. 447)**

LO 4 Use standard English. **(p. 449)**

In this chapter, you will read about plants.

LO 1 Use specific and detailed vocabulary.

Using Specific and Detailed Vocabulary

Effective writing evokes an emotional response from the reader. Great writers not only use correct grammatical structures, but they also infuse their writing with precise and vivid details that make their work come alive.

When you proofread your work, revise words that are too vague. **Vague words** lack precision and detail. For example, the words *nice* and *bad* are vague. Readers cannot get a clear picture from them.

Compare the following sets of sentences.

Vague   The tree was big.

Precise   The 250-foot-tall giant sequoia seemed to touch the cloudless sky.

Vague   The gardener planted some flowers.

Precise   The gardener, Mr. Oliver, planted azaleas, hyacinths, and irises.

HINT ◄ Some Common Vague Words

The following is a list of some frequently used vague words. Try to find substitutes for overly familiar and vague words: *good*, *bad*, *nice*, *pretty*, *big*, *small*, *great*, *happy*, *sad*, *thing*.

Creating Vivid Language

When you choose the precise word, you convey your meaning exactly. Moreover, you can make your writing clearer and more impressive by using specific and detailed vocabulary. To create vivid language, do the following:

- **Modify your nouns.** If your noun is vague, make it more specific by adding one or more adjectives. You could also rename the noun with a more specific term.

Vague	the child	
Vivid	the ecstatic girl	the agile ten-year-old ballerina

- **Modify your verbs.** Use more vivid, precise verbs. You could also use adverbs.

Vague	talk	
More vivid	bicker	debate passionately

- **Include more details.** Add information to make the sentence more detailed and complete.

Vague	Some plants are good for the health.
Precise	Garlic has antibiotic properties that can fight bacteria and viruses.

> **WRITING LINK**
> You can find more information about appealing to the five senses in Chapter 8, "Description."

PRACTICE 1

Underline vague words in the following sentences. Then replace them with more precise and detailed vocabulary.

EXAMPLE: Our town is <u>pretty</u>.

<u>Our town has many Victorian buildings, a Gothic church, and a</u>

<u>small lake surrounded by wildflowers.</u>

Chapter 33

1. The government buildings in our town are surrounded by trees.

   _____

   _____

2. Every spring, people come to admire the tree blossoms.

   _____

   _____

3. Nice flowers bloom beside the lake.

   _____

   _____

4. Town residents can do many activities in the park.

   _____

   _____

5. The park in the town center is pretty.

   _____

   _____

L02 Avoid wordiness and redundancy.

Avoiding Wordiness and Redundancy

Sometimes students fill their writing assignments with extra words to meet the length requirement. However, good ideas can get lost in work that is too wordy. Also, if the explanations are unnecessarily long, readers will become bored.

To improve your writing style, use only as many words or phrases as you need to fully explain your ideas.

The farm was big ~~in size~~.

(*Big* is a measure of size, so you do not need to say "in size.")

Correcting Wordiness

You can cut the number of words needed to express an idea by substituting a wordy phrase with a single word. You could also remove the wordy phrase completely.

                                     because

I don't like gardening ~~due to the fact that~~ I spend most of the time just pulling out weeds.

Some Common Wordy Expressions and Substitutions

Wordy	Substitution	Wordy	Substitution
at this point in time	now, currently	gave the appearance of being	looked like
at that point in time	then, at that time	in close proximity	close or in proximity
big / small in size	big / small	in order to	to
a difficult dilemma	a dilemma	in spite of the fact	in spite of
due to the fact	because	in the final analysis	finally, lastly
equally as good as	as good as	past history	past or history
exactly the same	the same	period of time	period
exceptions to the rule	exceptions	still remain	remain
final completion	end	a true fact	a fact
for the purpose of	for	the fact of the matter is	in fact

PRACTICE 2

Edit the following sentences by crossing out all unnecessary words or phrases. If necessary, find more concise substitutes for wordy expressions.

EXAMPLE: The Bodhi tree has grown to be big ~~in size~~.

1. Some trees around the world have become famous due to the fact that they are associated with myths and legends.

2. A Bodhi tree is located in close proximity to the village of Bodh Gaya, India.

3. Legend states that Siddhartha Gautama, the Buddha, overcame a difficult dilemma and attained spiritual enlightenment near the tree.

4. After he attained enlightenment, the Buddha spent many days in exactly the same spot to illuminate his disciples.

5. Many pilgrims visited the Buddha under the tree in order to hear his teachings.

6. The original Bodhi tree has died, but at this point in time, another tree is sprouting from the ancestor tree.

7. The Bodhi tree still remains an important destination for pilgrims who want to pay homage to the Buddha.

Avoiding Clichés

LO 3 Avoid clichés.

Clichés are overused expressions. Avoid boring your readers with clichés, and use more direct and vivid language instead.

clichés
In this neck of the woods, she is considered
an expert on orchids.

direct words
In this area

Other Common Clichés

a drop in the bucket	calm, cool, and collected
add insult to injury	crystal clear
as luck would have it	easier said than done
at a loss for words	go with the flow
axe to grind	in the nick of time
bend over backwards	keep your eyes peeled
better late than never	time and time again
between a rock and a hard place	tried and true
break the ice	under the weather

HINT ◀ **Modifying Clichés**

To modify a cliché, change it into a direct term. You might also try playing with language to come up with a more interesting description.

Cliché   She was as happy as a lark.

Direct language   She was thrilled.

Interesting description She was as happy as a teenager whose parents had gone away for the weekend.

PRACTICE 3

Cross out the clichéd expression in each sentence. If necessary, replace it with fresh or direct language.

EXAMPLE: I was ~~blown away~~ by the size of the trees.
greatly impressed

1. I kept my eyes peeled for the turn off to Catheral Grove, an old-growth

   forest of majestic Douglas fir trees on Vancouver Island.

2. Many people bend over backwards to visit such beautiful places as old-

   growth forests.

3. The parking lot was full, but as luck would have it, someone was leaving just as we arrived.

4. Near one tree, there was a sign stating that when Christopher Columbus arrived in the New World, the tree was already three hundred years old. When I read the sign, I was at a loss for words.

5. Some of the very ancient trees have time and time again survived windstorms and forest fires.

6. It is crystal clear that we need to protect old-growth forests from logging and other manmade disasters.

Using Standard English

LO 4 Use standard English.

Most of your instructors will want you to write using **standard English**. The word "standard" does not imply better. Standard English is the common language generally used and expected in schools, businesses, and government institutions in the United States. **Slang** is nonstandard language. It is used in informal situations to communicate common cultural knowledge. In any academic or professional context, do not use slang.

Slang	Me an' some bros wanted to make some dough, so we worked on a farm picking apples. We made a bit of coin, and our grub was included. It was real cool. On the weekends, we mostly chilled.
Standard American English	My friends and I wanted to make some money, so we worked on a farm picking apples. We were well paid, and our food was included. We had a memorable time. On the weekends, we mostly relaxed.

HINT ◄ Reasons to Avoid Slang

Slang changes depending on generational, regional, cultural, and historical influences. For example, one group might say "upset" whereas others might say "freaked out" or "having a fit." You should avoid using slang expressions in your writing because they can change very quickly—so quickly, in fact, that you might think that this textbook's examples of slang are "lame."

PRACTICE 4

Substitute the underlined slang expressions with the best possible choice of standard English.

body odor
EXAMPLE: Since ancient times people have eaten garlic even if it causes B.O.

1. Recently, there has been a lot of <u>hype</u> about the medicinal properties of garlic.

2. In the past, when people <u>were under the weather</u>, they believed the magical properties of garlic would help them heal.

3. In Greek mythology, Circe <u>had the hots for</u> Ulysses, who ate garlic to protect himself from her advances.

4. Spanish bullfighters wore garlic necklaces so they would have the <u>guts</u> to fight bulls.

5. Ancient Egyptian <u>chicks</u> would put garlic in their belly buttons to find out if they were <u>knocked up</u>.

6. In Eastern Europe, people wore garlic <u>24/7</u> to ward off evil spirits.

7. Today, scientists believe that garlic is <u>awesome</u> because it may help fight cancer.

FINAL REVIEW

Edit the following paragraphs for twenty errors in wordiness, slang, clichés, and vague language to make the text more effective.

1.   At this point in time, many people are freaking out about genetically modified foods. Genetic modification (GM) is a technology that lets scientists fool around with the genetic composition of plants. Historically, people have always tried to change the characteristics of

plants for the purpose of making them more disease-resistant. That process has traditionally been done through hybridization, a tried and true method. That is, two parent plants from the same genus are bred to create an improved hybrid plant. One true fact is that hybrid wheat is hardier than traditional wheat.

2.   Today, in North America, hundreds of foods are genetically modified. In the final analysis, there is great controversy about genetically modified foods. Proponents of this technology say time and time again that food will contain higher levels of nutrition, be resistant to disease, and produce higher yields. In spite of the fact of such arguments, opponents are all fired up about genetically modified foods because they say that there is not enough knowledge about how such foods will affect human health. They believe such foods might be a death trap. For example, will humans who are allergic to peanuts have a reaction if they eat tomatoes that have been genetically modified with a peanut gene? Furthermore, opponents believe that the loss of diversity in crops and plants really bites. Another worry is that food production will go into the hands of super-sized agricultural companies who will control the growth and distribution of food. Moreover, the bigwigs in this debate stress out about the ethics of mixing genes from species to species.

3.   The genetically modified food industry is growing rapidly in size. But it is important to have a healthy and open debate about this issue. Presently, consumers are faced with a difficult dilemma. Most people are in a fog and unknowingly buy genetically modified foods because such foods

Chapter 33

lack complete labeling. For example, most cooking oil comes from genetically modified grains. The public should be in the know about this technology. Consumers need to be clued in so that they can make the right choices.

MyWritingLab™

Complete these writing assignments at mywritinglab.com

MyWritingLab™   **THE WRITER'S ROOM**   Topics for Writing

Write about one of the following topics. Proofread your text to ensure that you have used detailed vocabulary and avoided wordiness, clichés, and slang.

1. Examine the photo below. What are some terms that come to mind? Some ideas might be *family farm, agribusiness, healthy living, back to basics, farm aid,* or *green thumb.*

2. Why are fast foods and other unhealthy foods so popular? Think of some reasons.

Checklist: Exact Language

When you edit your writing, ask yourself these questions.

☐ Have I used specific and detailed vocabulary? Check for errors with vague words.

Vague	My son likes to garden.
Detailed	My fifteen-year-old son, Kiran, is an enthusiastic gardener.

☐ Have I used exact language? Check for errors with wordiness, clichés, and slang.

now
Julian works in the garden center ~~at this point in time~~.

evident
It is ~~as plain as black and white~~ that many people like organic food.

easy
The biology exam was ~~a no-brainer~~.

34 Spelling and Commonly Confused Words

SECTION THEME: Our Natural World

LEARNING OBJECTIVES

LO 1 Learn and apply spelling rules. **(p. 454)**

LO 2 Review 120 commonly misspelled words. **(p. 457)**

LO 3 Distinguish look-alike and sound-alike words. **(p. 459)**

In this chapter, you will read about insects.

LO 1 Learn and apply spelling rules.

Spelling Rules

It is important to spell correctly because spelling mistakes can detract from important ideas in your work. Here are some strategies for improving your spelling skills.

How to Become a Better Speller

◆ **Look up words** using the most current dictionary because it will contain new or updated words. For tips on dictionary usage, see page 520 in Chapter 40.

◆ **Keep a record of words that you commonly misspell**. For example, write the words and definitions in a spelling log, which could be in a journal or binder. See Appendix 6 for more information about your spelling log.

◆ **Use memory cards or flash cards** to help you memorize the spelling of difficult words. With a friend or a classmate, take turns asking each other to spell difficult words.

◆ **Write out the spelling of difficult words at least ten times** to help you remember how to spell them. After you have written these words, try writing them in a complete sentence.

Six Common Spelling Rules

Memorize the following common rules of spelling. If you follow these rules, your spelling will become more accurate. Also try to remember the exceptions to these rules.

1. **Writing *ie* or *ei***
   Write *i* before *e*, except after *c* or when *ei* is pronounced as *ay*, as in *neighbor* and *weigh*.

i before *e*:	brief	field	priest
ei after *c*:	receipt	deceit	receive
ei pronounced as *ay*:	weigh	beige	vein

   Here are some exceptions:

ancient	either	neither	foreigner	leisure	height
science	species	society	seize	their	weird

2. **Adding *-s* or *-es***
   Add *-s* to form plural nouns and to create present tense verbs that are third-person singular. However, add *-es* to words in the following situations.

   ◆ When words end in *-s*, *-sh*, *-ss*, *-ch*, or *-x*, add *-es*.

noun	box–boxes	**verb**	miss–misses

   ◆ When words end in consonant *-y*, change the *-y* to *-i* and add *-es*.

noun	baby–babies	**verb**	marry–marries

   ◆ When words end in *-o*, add *-es*. Exceptions are *pianos*, *radios*, *logos*, *stereos*, *autos*, *typos*, and *casinos*.

noun	tomato–tomatoes	**verb**	go–goes

◆ When words end in *-f* or *-fe*, change the *-f* to a *-v* and add *-es.* Exceptions are *beliefs* and *roofs.*

> life–lives   wolf–wolves   shelf–shelves

3. **Adding Prefixes and Suffixes**

A **prefix** is added to the beginning of a word, and it changes the word's meaning. For example, *con-, dis-, pre-, un-,* and *il-* are prefixes. When you add a prefix to a word, keep the last letter of the prefix and the first letter of the main word.

> **im** + **m**ature = **imm**ature   mi**s** + **s**pell = mi**ss**pell

A **suffix** is added to the ending of a word, and it changes the word's tense or meaning. For example, *-ly, -ment, -ed,* and *-ing* are suffixes. When you add the suffix *-ly* to words that end in *-l*, keep the *-l* of the root word. The new word will have two *-l*s.

> casua**l** + **l**y = casua**ll**y   factua**l** + **l**y = factua**ll**y

4. **Adding Suffixes to Words Ending in *-e***

If the suffix begins with a vowel, drop the *-e* on the main word. Some common suffixes beginning with vowels are *-ed, -er, -est, -ing, -able, -ent,* and *-ist.*

> bak**e**–baking   creat**e**–created

Some exceptions are words that end in *-ge*, which keep the *-e* and add the suffix.

> outrag**e**–outrageous   manag**e**–manageable

If the suffix begins with a consonant, keep the *-e*. Some common suffixes beginning with consonants are *-ly, -ment, -less,* and *-ful*. Some exceptions are *acknowledgment, argument,* and *truly.*

> sur**e**–surely   awar**e**–awareness

5. **Adding Suffixes to Words Ending in *-y***

If the word has a consonant before the final *-y*, change the *-y* to an *-i* before adding the suffix. Some exceptions are *ladybug, dryness,* and *shyness.*

> pretty–prett**i**est   happy–happ**i**ness

If the word has a vowel before the final *-y*, if it is a proper name, or if the suffix is *-ing*, do not change the *y* to an *i*. Some exceptions are *daily, laid,* and *said.*

> employ–employed   apply–applying   Levinsky–Levinskys

6. **Doubling the Final Consonant**

Double the final consonant of one-syllable words ending in a consonant–vowel–consonant pattern.

> ship–shi**pp**ing   swim–swi**mm**er   hop–ho**pp**ed

Double the final consonant of words ending in a stressed consonant–vowel–consonant pattern. If the final syllable is not stressed, then do not double the last letter.

refer–refe**rr**ed   o<u>ccu</u>r–occu**rr**ed   <u>ha</u>ppen–happened

120 Commonly Misspelled Words

L02 Review 120 commonly misspelled words.

The next list contains some of the most commonly misspelled words in English.

absence	curriculum	loneliness	reference
absorption	definite	maintenance	responsible
accommodate	definitely	mathematics	rhythm
acquaintance	desperate	medicine	schedule
address	developed	millennium	scientific
aggressive	dilemma	minuscule	separate
already	disappoint	mischievous	sincerely
aluminum	embarrass	mortgage	spaghetti
analyze	encouragement	necessary	strength
appointment	environment	ninety	success
approximate	especially	noticeable	surprise
argument	exaggerate	occasion	technique
athlete	exercise	occurrence	thorough
bargain	extraordinarily	opposite	tomato
beginning	familiar	outrageous	tomatoes
behavior	February	parallel	tomorrow
believable	finally	performance	truly
business	foreign	perseverance	Tuesday
calendar	government	personality	until
campaign	grammar	physically	usually
careful	harassment	possess	vacuum
ceiling	height	precious	Wednesday
cemetery	immediately	prejudice	weird
clientele	independent	privilege	woman
committee	jewelry	probably	women
comparison	judgment	professor	wreckage
competent	laboratory	psychology	writer
conscience	ledge	questionnaire	writing
conscientious	leisure	receive	written
convenient	license	recommend	zealous

PRACTICE 1

Edit the next paragraphs for twenty misspelled words.

EXAMPLE: ~~Profesor~~ Wright studies ants.

1.   Most people usualy become anxious when ants invade their homes. They think that ants are aggresive and creepy. But anybody familar with ants knows that they definitly have their positive points.

2.   Ants evolved around 130 million years ago. Scientists have identified over twelve thousand speceis of ants. Ants are social creatures. They are hard working and show a lot of perseverence. Most types of ants use complicated technics to build their colonies.

3.   Ant societies have a queen as their leader. The queen ant is responsable for laying thousands of eggs, which will guarantee the survival of the colony. The female worker ants are very compitant. They search for food, build the nest, take care of the queen and her eggs, and guard the colony from predators. In comparason to her workers, the queen does miniscule amounts of work. Male ants are necesary for only one important duty: They mate with the queen.

4.   Ants are extraordinaryly important insects. Scientists study them in labratories because ant behavor can sometimes parralel human conduct. For example, scientists beleive that unlike most other insects, ants learn from each other. Ants are also important for the enviroment. For instance, ants eat rotting plants and animals, and some animals and fungi eat ants. In addition, ants control pests, aerate soil, and spread the seeds of certain trees. Moreover, in some cultures, people happyly eat ants the way other groups eat tomatos.

Look-Alike and Sound-Alike Words

Sometimes two English words can sound the same but have different spellings and meanings. These words are called **homonyms**. Here are a few commonly confused words and their basic meanings. (For more specific definitions for these and other words, consult a dictionary.)

accept	to receive; to admit	We must <u>accept</u> the vital role that insects play in our culture.
except	excluding; other than	I like all insects <u>except</u> ants.
allowed	permitted	We were not <u>allowed</u> to view the exhibit.
aloud	spoken audibly	We could not speak <u>aloud</u>, so we whispered.
affect	to influence	Pesticides <u>affect</u> the environment.
effect	the result of something	Scientists are examining the <u>effects</u> of pesticides on our health.
been	past participle of the verb *to be*	He has <u>been</u> to the Imax film about caterpillars.
being	present progressive form (the *-ing* form) of the verb *to be*	She was <u>being</u> kind when she donated to the butterfly museum.
by	preposition meaning *next to, on,* or *before*	A bee flew <u>by</u> the flowers. <u>By</u> evening, the crickets were making a lot of noise.
buy	to purchase	Will you <u>buy</u> me that scarab necklace?
complement	an addition; to complete	The film about the monarch butterfly was a nice <u>complement</u> to the exhibit.
compliment	nice comment about someone	The film was informative, and the director received many <u>compliments</u>.
conscience	a personal sense of right or wrong	After spraying pesticides, the gardener had a guilty <u>conscience</u>.
conscious	aware; awake	He made us <u>conscious</u> of the important role insects play in our society.

PRACTICE 2

Underline the correct word in the parentheses.

EXAMPLE: Many people (by / <u>buy</u>) clothes made out of silk.

1.   Silk has (been / being) produced (by / buy) the Chinese for at least four thousand years. The silkworm is actually a caterpillar that eats nothing (accept / except) mulberry leaves, grows quickly, and then encircles itself into a cocoon of raw silk. The cocoon contains a single thread around 300

to 900 yards in length, so it's not surprising that it takes about 2,000 cocoons to make one pound of silk. (Been / Being) very (conscious / conscience) of the long and intense silk-making process, most people (accept / except) the high cost of the material.

2.   The Chinese valued silk and carefully guarded the secret of its making. In ancient China, only the emperor and his family were (allowed / aloud) to wear silk garments. Sometimes, members of royalty wore the fabric as a (complement / compliment) to their regular clothes. Of course, less fortunate people admired the emperor's beautiful clothes and always (complimented / complemented) him.

3.   By the fifth century, the secret of silk-making had been revealed to Korea, Japan, and India. How did the secret get out? Legend says that a princess with no (conscious / conscience) smuggled silkworm larvae to Korea by hiding them in her hair. The emperor was outraged (by / buy) the actions of the princess, and there was great debate about her treachery. The scandal had a negative (affect / effect) on her health.

everyday	ordinary or common	Swatting mosquitoes is an everyday ritual of camping.
every day	each day	Every day, I check my roses for aphids.
imminent	soon to happen	The journalist reported that the arrival of locusts in parts of Africa was imminent.
eminent	distinguished; superior	Professor Maurice Kanyogo is an eminent entomologist.
imply	to suggest	The entomologist implied that he had received a large grant.
infer	to conclude	His students inferred that they would have summer jobs because of the grant.
its	possessive case of the pronoun *it*	The worker bee went into its hive.
it's	contraction for *it is*	It's well known that the queen bee is the largest in the colony.
knew	past tense of *to know*	I knew that I should study for my test on worms.
new	recent or unused	But my new book on honey making was more interesting.
know	to have knowledge of	The beekeepers know that there has been a decline in bees in recent years.
no	a negative	There were no books on beekeeping in the library.

lose	to misplace or forfeit something	Do not <u>lose</u> the mosquito repellent.
loose	too baggy; not fixed	You should wear <u>loose</u> clothes when camping.
loss	a decrease in an amount; a serious blow	Farmers would experience a <u>loss</u> if there were no bees to pollinate crops.
peace	calmness; an end to violence	The <u>peace</u> in the woods was wonderful.
piece	a part of something else; one item in a group of items	The two <u>pieces</u> of amber had insects in them.
principal	director of a school; main	The <u>principal</u> of our school is an expert on beetles. They are his <u>principal</u> hobby.
principle	rule or standard	Julius Corrant wrote a book about environmental <u>principles</u>.
quiet	silent	The crickets remained <u>quiet</u> this evening.
quite	very	They usually make <u>quite</u> a noise.
quit	stop	I would like them to <u>quit</u> making so much noise.

PRACTICE 3

Identify and correct ten word choice errors.

EXAMPLE: I need some ~~piece~~ *peace* and quiet.

1.   Professor Zoe Truger, an imminent entomologist, specializes in butterfly

behavior. I am reading her book. Its very interesting. On it's cover, there is a

beautiful photograph of a butterfly. Everyday, during the summer, thousands

of monarch butterflies are found in southern Canada, their summer home.

As autumn arrives, these butterflies know that migration to warmer climates

is eminent.

2.   The principle of Jake's school took the students on a nature walk to look

for earthworms. The students were very quite when the guide told them

there are 2,700 species of earthworms.

3.   Did you no that beekeeping is one of the world's oldest professions?

Beekeepers wear lose clothing and protective gear. Some beekeepers must

quiet their profession because they are allergic to bee stings.

taught	past tense of *to teach*	I taught a class on pollination.
thought	past tense of *to think*	I thought the students enjoyed it.
than	word used to compare items	There are more mosquitoes at the lake than in the city.
then	at a particular time; after a specific time	He found the termite nest. Then he called the exterminators.
that	word used to introduce a clause	They told him that they would come immediately.
their	possessive form of *they*	They wore scarab amulets to show their respect for the god Khepera.
there	a place or location; an introductory phrase in sentences stating that something does or does not exist	The ant colony is over there. There is a beehive in the tree.
they're	contraction of *they are*	The ants work hard. They're very industrious.
to	part of an infinitive; indicates direction or movement	I want to hunt for bugs. I will go to the hiking path and look under some rocks.
too	very or also	My friend is too scared of bugs. My brother is, too.
two	the number after *one*	There were two types of butterflies in the garden today.
where	question word indicating location	Where did you buy the book on ladybugs?
were	past tense of *be*	There were hundreds of ladybugs on the bush.
we're	contraction of *we are*	We're wondering why we have this infestation.
who's	contraction of *who is*	Isabelle, who's a horticulturist, also keeps a butterfly garden.
whose	pronoun showing ownership	Whose garden is that?
write	to draw symbols that represent words	I will write an essay about the common earthworm.
right	the opposite of the direction left; correct	In the right corner of the garden, there is the compost bin with many worms in it.
		You are right when you say that earthworms are necessary for composting.

PRACTICE 4

Identify and correct fifteen word choice errors.

There
EXAMPLE: ~~Their~~ are many different types of bees.

1. In 2007, their were reports than the honeybee population was mysteriously

   disappearing. According too scientists at Pennsylvania State University,

   a large percentage of honeybee colonies where dying. The demise of the honeybee population was worrisome because bees pollinate crops. People who's livelihoods depended on the agricultural industry worried about losing income. Records showed that, in 2007, honeybee populations declined at a greater rate that at any time in the past. Entomologists traveled to different countries were they observed bee colonies. They taught parasites or a virus might be responsible for the deaths.

2.   Presently, scientists are seeing some confusing statistics. There finding that declines in honeybee populations vary in different countries. Annie May Tricot, whose a specialist in bees, is studying this problem. She has thought to courses on honeybee behavior. Her research shows that honeybee populations in China and Argentina are increasing. Tricot will right an article about this phenomenon. Scientists hope that the situation will write itself in the near future. Were looking forward to hearing what Tricot has to say in her lecture on bees tonight.

FINAL REVIEW

Correct the twenty spelling errors and mistakes with commonly confused words in the essay.

                    carries
EXAMPLE: The bee ~~carrys~~ pollen grains from one plant to another.

1.   Around the world, unatural causes such as climate change, pollution, and human activities are threatening the enviroment. Forests are expecialy vulnerable to these pressures because of loging, increasing pests, and global warming. Conserving biodiversity is important to protect forests.

2.   Biodiversity, a contraction of the words *biological diversity*, means that a variety of plants, animals, and microorganisms coexist in an ecosystem. Today, imminent scientists concerned with species' extinction refer to the necesity of maintaining biodiversity on our planet. Scientists are conscience of the value of each species. Argueing for conserving biodiversity, scientists believe that if species become extinct, than their ecosystem will become unstable.

3.   Insects are crucial to sustaining the biodiversity of an ecosystem and are the most diverse life form on earth. Currently, there are approximately 800,000 identified species of insects, all of which are usefull in balancing the ecosystem. For example, they pollinate plants, and they eat other insects and plants. Their also important to the global economy. For instance, insects are used for honey production, silk making, and agricultural pest control. If an insect species becomes extinct, their will be a variety of consequences for the remaining species in the ecosystem, such as an increase in predatory insects or a lost of another species higher on the food chain. Such a change in the ecosystem would have an eminent effect on all life forms.

4.   Most people think that insects are troublesome and should be eradicated. Of course, insects such as mosquitos carry diseases, including malaria and West Nile virus, which are harmfull to human health. But its important to keep in mind that most insects provide important services for the natural world, to. Were there are insects, there is a thriving ecosystem. Extinction of an insect species will have a serious affect on nature, so the next time you are tempted to swat a fly or step on an ant, you might think twice.

MyWritingLab™

Complete these writing assignments at mywritinglab.com

Topics for Writing

THE WRITER'S ROOM

MyWritingLab™

Write about one of the following topics. Proofread your text to ensure there are no spelling and commonly confused word errors.

1. Discuss types of insects that are particularly annoying, repulsive, or frightening.

2. Are laws banning the use of pesticides on lawns a good idea? Explain your ideas.

Checklist: Spelling Rules

When you edit your writing, ask yourself these questions.

☐ Do I have any spelling errors? Check for errors in words that contain these elements:

–*ie* or *ei* combinations

–prefixes and suffixes

~~Dragonflys~~ are ~~lovly~~. ~~There~~ wings are transparent, but ~~they're~~ bodies
(Dragonflies) (lovely) (Their) (their)

are a variety of colors. They eat other insects such as ~~mosquitos~~.
(mosquitoes)

☐ Do I repeat spelling errors that I have made in previous assignments? I should check my previous assignments for errors or consult my spelling log.

READING LINK

The following readings contain more information on our natural world.

"With an Open Mouth" by Sy Montgomery" (page 125)

"How to Plant a Tree" by Samuel Charland Larivière (page 131)

"Swamps and Pesticides" by Corey Kaminska (page 187)

"My African Childhood" by David Sedaris (page 539)

"Nature Returns to the Cities" by John Roach (page 545)

Chapter 34

35 Commas

SECTION THEME: Human Development

LEARNING OBJECTIVES

LO 1 Practice using commas correctly. **(p. 466)**

LO 2 Use a comma in a series. **(p. 467)**

LO 3 Use commas after introductory words and phrases. **(p. 468)**

LO 4 Use commas around interrupting words and phrases. **(p. 469)**

LO 5 Use commas in compound sentences. **(p. 471)**

LO 6 Use commas in complex sentences. **(p. 472)**

In this chapter, you will read about life stages.

LO 1 Practice using commas correctly.

What Is a Comma?

A **comma (,)** is a punctuation mark that helps identify distinct ideas. There are many ways to use a comma. In this chapter, you will learn some helpful rules about comma usage.

Notice how comma placement changes the meanings of the following sentences.

The baby hits, her mother cries, and then they hug each other.

The baby hits her mother, cries, and then they hug each other.

Commas in a Series

Use a comma to separate items in a series of three or more items. Remember to put a comma before the final "and."

Unit 1	,	unit 2	,	and	unit 3
			,	or	

Canada, the United States, and Mexico have psychology conferences.

The experiment required patience, perseverance, and energy.

Some teens may work part time, volunteer in the community, and maintain high grades at school.

HINT ⟨ Comma Before *and*

There is a trend, especially in the media, to omit the comma before the final *and* in a series. However, in academic writing, it is preferable to include the comma because it clarifies your meaning and makes the items more distinct.

PRACTICE 1

Underline series of items. Then add fifteen missing commas.

EXAMPLE: Some psychological studies are simple, obvious, and extremely important.

1. Child development expert Mary Ainsworth worked in the United States Canada and Uganda. In an experiment called "The Strange Situation," she measured how infants reacted when the primary caretaker left the room a stranger entered and the primary caretaker returned. She determined that children have four attachment styles. They may be secure avoidant ambivalent or disoriented.

2. Secure children may leave their mother's lap explore happily and return to the mother. Avoidant babies are not upset when the mother leaves do

not look at the stranger and show little reaction when the mother returns.

Ambivalent babies are clinging unwilling to explore and upset by strangers.

Disoriented infants react oddly to their mother's return. They look fearful

avoid eye contact and slowly approach the returning mother.

LO 3 Use commas after introductory words and phrases.

Commas After Introductory Words and Phrases

Place a comma after an **introductory word** or **phrase**. Introductory words include interjections (*well*), adverbs (*usually*), or transitional words (*therefore*). Introductory phrases can be transitional expressions (*of course*), prepositional phrases (*in the winter*), or modifiers (*born in Egypt*).

Introductory word(s)	,	sentence.

Introductory word   Yes, the last stage of life is very important.

Introductory phrase   After the experiment, the children returned home.

Feeling bored, he volunteered at a nearby clinic.

PRACTICE 2

Underline each introductory word or phrase. Then add twelve missing commas.

EXAMPLE: Before leaving home, adolescents assert their independence.

1.   In *Childhood and Society*, Erik Erikson explained his views about the stages of life. According to Erikson, there are eight life stages. In his opinion, each stage is characterized by a developmental crisis.

2.   In the infancy stage, babies must learn to trust others. Wanting others to fulfill their needs, babies expect life to be pleasant. Neglected babies may end up mistrusting the world.

3.   During adolescence, a young man or woman may have an identity crisis. Confronted with physical and emotional changes, teenagers must develop

a sense of self. According to Erikson, some adolescents are unable to solve

their identity crisis. Lacking self-awareness, they cannot commit themselves

to certain goals and values.

4.   In Erikson's view, each crisis must be solved before a person develops in

the next life stage. For example, a person may become an adult chronologically.

However, that person may not be an adult emotionally.

Commas Around Interrupting Words and Phrases

LO 4 Use commas around interrupting words and phrases.

Interrupting words or phrases appear in the middle of sentences, and while they interrupt the sentence's flow, they do not affect its overall meaning. Some interrupters are *as a matter of fact*, *as you know*, and *for example*. Prepositional phrases can also interrupt sentences.

Sentence	, interrupter,	sentence.

The doctor, for example, has never studied child psychology.

Adolescence, as you know, is a difficult life stage.

The child, feeling nervous, started to laugh.

HINT ◄ **Using Commas with Appositives**

An appositive gives further information about a noun or pronoun. It can appear at the beginning, in the middle, or at the end of the sentence. Set off an appositive with commas.

> beginning
> A large hospital, the Mayo Clinic has some of the world's best researchers.

> middle
> Gail Sheehy, a journalist, has written about life passages.

> end
> The doctor's office is next to Sims Wholesale, a local grocery store.

PRACTICE 3

The next sentences contain introductory words and phrases, interrupters, and series of items. Add the missing commas. If the sentence is correct, write *C* in the space provided.

EXAMPLE: Last year, I met Malidoma Somé.   _____

1. Malidoma Somé a West African, spent his childhood living at a Jesuit boarding school.   _____

2. He returned to Dano, his parents' village, unable to speak his native language.   _____

3. Feeling confused, twenty-year-old Malidoma wanted to reconnect with his tribe.   _____

4. He convinced the elders to let him undergo a rite of passage, a ceremony usually done during puberty.   _____

5. Without initiation, a person is always considered a child.   _____

6. The process involves living in the wilderness, finding food, and dealing with dangers.   _____

7. Six weeks later, Malidoma emerged from the wilderness with a greater respect for nature.   _____

8. The villagers, including the parents and elders, celebrated the return of the initiates.   _____

9. Each initiate was greeted as an adult, a valuable member of the community.   _____

10. Meaningful rite-of-passage ceremonies, in Malidoma Somé's view, should be created for North American adolescents.   _____

Commas in Compound Sentences

In compound sentences, place a comma before the coordinating conjunction (*for, and, nor, but, or, yet, so*).

Sentence	, coordinating conjunction	sentence.

Adulthood has three stages, **and** each stage has its particular challenge.

Carolina lives with her mother, **but** her sister lives on her own.

She goes to school, **yet** she also works forty hours a week.

HINT ◂ Commas and Coordinators

To ensure that a sentence is compound, cover the conjunction with your finger and read the two parts of the sentence. If one part of the sentence is incomplete, then no comma is necessary. If each part of the sentence contains a complete idea, then you need to add a comma.

No comma   Ben still lives with his parents **but** is very self-sufficient.

Comma   Ben still lives with his parents, **but** he is very self-sufficient.

PRACTICE 4

Edit the next paragraphs, and add twelve missing commas.

EXAMPLE: She is not an adult, yet she is not a child.

1.   Adulthood is another stage in life, but the exact age of adulthood is unclear. Some cultures celebrate adulthood with high school graduation ceremonies, and others celebrate with marriage. Some people define adulthood as the moment a person has full-time work and is self-sufficient, yet many people only become independent in their thirties.

2.   Are you an adult? Researchers asked this question to people in their thirties, and the results were surprising. Most did not feel fully adult until their late twenties or early thirties. Compared with previous generations, people today

move into markers of adulthood slowly. They marry later, and they have

children later.

3.　　Additionally, various cultures treat early adulthood differently. Adela Pelaez

has a culturally mixed background. Her mother's lineage is British, and her

father's lineage is Spanish. At age nineteen, *Introductory* she was encouraged to find an

apartment. Today, twenty-one-year-old Adela pays her own bills, and she

does her own cooking. Alexis Khoury is thirty-one, but she still lives with

her parents. They are Greek immigrants, and they want their daughter to stay

home until she marries. Alexis will respect her parents' wishes, and she will

not leave home until she finds a life partner.

Commas in Complex Sentences

LO 6 Use commas in complex sentences.

A **complex sentence** contains one or more dependent clauses (or incomplete ideas). When you add a **subordinating conjunction**—a word such as *because, although,* or *unless*—to a clause, you make the clause dependent.

dependent clause   independent clause

After <u>Jason graduated from college</u>, he moved out of the family home.

Using Commas After Dependent Clauses

GRAMMAR LINK
For a list of subordinating conjunctions, see Chapter 21, page 319.

If a sentence begins with a dependent clause, place a comma after the clause. Remember that a dependent clause has a subject and a verb, but it cannot stand alone. When the subordinating conjunction comes in the middle of the sentence, it is generally not necessary to use a comma.

Dependent clause	,	main clause.

Comma <u>When I find a better job</u>, I will move into an apartment.

Main clause	dependent clause.

No comma I will move into an apartment <u>when I find a better job</u>.

PRACTICE 5

Edit the following sentences by adding or deleting commas.

EXAMPLE: Although thirty-year-old Samuel Chong lives at home, he is not

ashamed.

1. When he examined the 2001 census, Mark Noble noticed a clear trend.

2. Although most people in their twenties lived on their own, about 40 percent

   of young adults still lived with their parents.

3. In 1981, the results were different because only 25 percent of young adults

   lived at home.

4. After examining the statistics, Noble determined several causes for the shift.

5. Because the marriage rate is declining, fewer people buy their own homes.

6. When the cost of education increases, people cannot afford to study and pay rent.

7. Other young adults stay with their parents because rental rates are so high.

8. Because these conditions are not changing, many young adults will probably

   continue to live with their parents.

Using Commas to Set Off Nonrestrictive Clauses

Clauses beginning with *who, that,* and *which* can be restrictive or nonrestrictive. A **restrictive clause** contains essential information about the subject. Do not place commas around restrictive clauses. In the following example, the underlined clause is necessary to understand the meaning of the sentence.

> **No commas**   The local company <u>that creates computer graphics</u> has
>   no job openings.

A **nonrestrictive clause** gives nonessential or additional information about the noun but does not restrict or define the noun. Place commas around

> **GRAMMAR LINK**
> For more information about choosing *which* or *that,* see Chapter 22, "Sentence Variety."

nonrestrictive clauses. In the following sentence, the underlined clause contains extra information, but if you removed that clause, the sentence would still have a clear meaning.

Commas　Her book, which is in bookstores, is about successful entrepreneurs.

HINT ◄ *Which, That, and Who*

Which　Use commas to set off clauses that begin with *which*.

The brain, **which** is a complex organ, develops rapidly.

That　Do not use commas to set off clauses that begin with *that*.

The house **that** I grew up in was demolished last year.

Who　If the *who* clause contains nonessential information, put commas around it. If the *who* clause is essential to the meaning of the sentence, then it does not require commas.

| **Essential** | Many people **who** have brain injuries undergo subtle personality changes. |
| **Not essential** | Dr. Jay Giedd, **who** lives in Maryland, made an important discovery. |

PRACTICE 6　Homework

Edit the following essay by adding twelve missing commas. Also remove two unnecessary commas.

EXAMPLE: If people want to have longer lives, they can exercise, eat well, and avoid risky behavior.

1.　In 350 BC, Aristotle wrote that humans have a maximum life span and nothing can be done to prolong that span. Until recently, scientists agreed with Aristotle. However a group of researchers believes that human life expectancy will increase significantly in the future.

2.　Dr. James Vaupel a researcher at Duke University, believes that our life spans can be extended. He gives a concrete example. In 1840 the average Swedish woman lived to age forty-five. Today, Japanese women, who live to an average age of eighty-five have the world's longest life expectancy. This huge

increase in life expectancy was partly due to the decrease in infant mortality.

Surgery, vaccines and antibiotics have helped to lower childhood death rates.

Also, because they have access to new medical interventions people over age

sixty-five are living longer. Still, only about 2 percent of the population lives

to one hundred years of age.

3.   According to Dr. Vaupel, today's babies will have much longer life

expectancies than their parents had and half of all newborns could live to

one hundred years of age. Certainly, cures for cancer, and heart disease could

help increase life expectancy. Because so many women delay childbirth the

period of human fertility may lengthen which could have an eventual impact

on life expectancy. Also, some research labs are experimenting with ways of

increasing the life spans of cells. For example scientists have isolated a part of

the chromosome that shrinks with age. If scientists find a way to slow down cell

aging the results could significantly increase life expectancies of all humans.

4.   A very long life expectancy, would force humans to rethink life stages. When

would childhood end? Would you want to live to 150 years of age or more?

GRAMMAR LINK
For information about comma usage in business letters, see Chapter 19, "The Résumé and Letter of Application."

FINAL REVIEW

This essay has twenty punctuation errors. Add eighteen missing commas.
Also, remove two unnecessary commas.

EXAMPLE: The money, which was in the cash box ⌃, disappeared.

1.   Dan Ariely, a professor of psychology at Duke University has

written about honesty in his book *The (Honest) Truth about Dishonesty*.

Although, people like to believe that they are honest they fool

themselves. Furthermore people from all classes and in all societies may be dishonest sometimes.

2. In April 2011 college student Dan Weiss was hired by the Kennedy Center for the Performing Arts in Washington, DC. His job, which was part time was to take the stock inventory at the center's gift shop. Meanwhile about three hundred well-intentioned volunteers worked at the shop. The shop which relied on the volunteers sold about $400,000 of merchandise annually. Each year about $150,000 disappeared. The gift shop which had no cash registers, just had a cash box that volunteers put the money into.

3. Weiss, who worked alone was determined to find the thief. Undoubtedly, the thief was one of the volunteers. He suspected a young man who brought the cash box to the bank each night. Weiss set up a sting operation. He put some marked bills into the box and he and a detective waited in a bush outside the bank. When the young volunteer left the bank they searched him. He had $60 of marked bills in his pocket so he was fired. Nevertheless, the thefts continued.

4. Weiss, who was undeterred discovered that hundreds of the volunteers were pilfering objects or money. He decided to put a cash register and an itemized logbook into the gift shop. Before then, money disappeared every day but no money disappeared after the cash register was installed.

5. We can learn the following lesson from this story: On the one hand all types of people can be dishonest. On the other hand, people's bad behavior can easily be modified when temptation is removed.

Topics for Writing

THE WRITER'S ROOM   My WritingLab™

MyWritingLab™
Complete these
writing assignments at
mywritinglab.com

Write about one of the following topics. After you finish writing, make sure that you have used commas correctly.

1. What problems could occur if the human life expectancy gets a lot longer? Think about the effects of an increased life expectancy.

2. Which life stage is the most interesting? Give supporting examples to back up your views.

Checklist: Commas

When you edit your writing, ask yourself these questions.

☐ Do I use commas correctly? Remember to use commas in the following situations:

–between words in a series of items

–after an introductory word or phrase

–around an interrupting word or phrase

> The conference will be in Santa Fe, San Francisco, or Phoenix.
>
> Beyond a doubt, many psychologists will attend.
>
> The key speaker, in my opinion, is extremely interesting.

☐ Do I use commas correctly in compound and complex sentences? Remember to use commas in the following situations:

–before the coordinator in a compound sentence

–after a dependent clause that starts a complex sentence

–around nonrestrictive clauses

> She will discuss brain development, and she will present case studies.
>
> When her presentation ends, participants can ask questions.
>
> The questions, which must be short, are about the brain.

36 Apostrophes

SECTION THEME: Human Development

LEARNING OBJECTIVES

LO 1 Explain the purpose of an apostrophe. **(p. 478)**

LO 2 Form contractions with apostrophes. **(p. 478)**

LO 3 Use apostrophes to show ownership. **(p. 480)**

LO 4 Use apostrophes in expressions of time. **(p. 482)**

In this chapter, you will read about artistic ability and creativity.

LO 1 Explain the purpose of an apostrophe.

What Is an Apostrophe?

An **apostrophe** is a punctuation mark showing a contraction or ownership.

Emma **Chong's** art gallery is very successful, and **it's** still growing.

LO 2 Form contractions with apostrophes.

Apostrophes in Contractions

To form a **contraction**, join two words into one and add an apostrophe to replace the omitted letter(s). The following are examples of common contractions.

1. **Join a verb with *not*.** The apostrophe replaces the letter "o" in *not*.

   is + not = isn't   has + not = hasn't
   are + not = aren't   have + not = haven't
   could + not = couldn't   should + not = shouldn't
   did + not = didn't   was + not = wasn't
   do + not = don't   were + not = weren't
   does + not = doesn't   would + not = wouldn't

   Exception: will + not = <u>won't</u>, can + not = <u>can't</u>

2. **Join a subject and a verb.** Sometimes you must remove several letters to form the contraction.

I + will = I'll	she + will = she'll
I + would = I'd	Tina + is = Tina's
he + is = he's	they + are = they're
he + will = he'll	we + will = we'll
Joe + is = Joe's	who + is = who's
she + has = she's	who + would = who'd

Note: Do not contract a subject with *was, were,* or *did.*

HINT ◀ **Common Apostrophe Errors**

Do not use apostrophes before the final *-s* of a verb or a plural noun.

            wants   *galleries*
Mr. Garcia ~~want's~~ to open several ~~gallerie's~~.

In contractions with *not*, remember that the apostrophe replaces the missing *o.*

        doesn't
He ~~does'nt~~ understand the problem.

PRACTICE 1

Edit the next sentences for twelve apostrophe errors. You may need to add, move, or remove apostrophes.

                                isn't
EXAMPLE: Making a great work of art ~~isnt~~ a simple process.

1.   Whos a great artist? Why do some people have amazing artistic abilities whereas others do'nt? Neurologists look inside the brain to answer questions about creativity. Theyve said that the left portion of the brains responsible for logical processing and verbal skills. The right sides responsible for artistic, abstract thinking. In the past, neurologists did'nt believe that the left side of the brain had an impact on creative impulses, but recent brain scan's have shown that both sides of the brain are used in creative thinking.

2.   Whats the source of creativity? Maybe its never going to be understood.

What everybody know's for certain is that artistic talent isnt evenly

distributed. Some people are'nt as talented as others.

HINT ◂ Contractions with Two Meanings

Sometimes one contraction can have two different meanings.

   I'd = I had *or* I would   **He's** = he is or he has

When you read, you should be able to figure out the meaning of the contraction by looking at the words in context.

   Joe's working on a painting. **Joe's** been working on it for a month.
   (Joe is)   (Joe has)

PRACTICE 2

Look at each underlined contraction, and then write out the complete words.

EXAMPLE: They <u>weren't</u> ready to start a business.   _____*were not*_____

1. <u>Banksy's</u> a very good graffiti artist.   _____

2. <u>He's</u> been a graffiti artist since 2002.   _____

3. <u>He's</u> an extremely creative man.   _____

4. I wish <u>I'd</u> gone to art school.   _____

5. <u>I'd</u> like to be an artist, too.   _____

LO 3 Use apostrophes to show ownership.

Apostrophes to Show Ownership

You can also use apostrophes to show ownership. Review the following rules.

Possessive Form of Singular Nouns

Add -'s to the end of a singular noun to indicate ownership. If the singular noun ends in *s*, you must still add -'s.

   Lautrec's artwork was very revolutionary.

   Morris's wife is a professional dancer.

Possessive Form of Plural Nouns

When a plural noun ends in -*s*, just add an apostrophe to indicate ownership. Add -'*s* to irregular plural nouns.

Many **galleries'** Web sites contain images from their exhibits.

The **men's** and **women's** paintings are in separate rooms.

Possessive Form of Compound Nouns

When two people have joint ownership, add the apostrophe to the second name. When two people have separate ownership, add apostrophes to both names.

Joint ownership   Marian and **Jake's** gallery is successful.

Separate ownership Marian's and **Jake's** studios are in different buildings.

PRACTICE 3

Write the possessive forms of the following phrases.

EXAMPLE: the sister of the doctor _____ *the doctor's sister* _____

1. the brush of the artist _____

2. the brushes of the artists _____

3. the rooms of the children _____

4. the entrances of the galleries _____

5. the photo of Ross and Anna _____

6. the photo of Ross and the photo of Anna _____

HINT ◀ **Possessive Pronouns Do Not Have Apostrophes**

Some contractions sound like possessive pronouns. For example, *you're* sounds like *your*, and *it's* sounds like *its*. Remember that the possessive pronouns *yours*, *hers*, *its*, and *ours* never have apostrophes.

              its
The conference is on ~~it's~~ last day.

       yours   *hers*
The document is ~~your's~~ and not ~~her's~~.

PRACTICE 4

Underline and correct ten errors. You may need to add or remove apostrophes.

            museum's
EXAMPLE: The <u>museums</u> collection includes the famous George Tooker painting *The Subway.*

1.   Many artist's paintings are unique. Have you ever heard of George Tooker? The American painter's work earned him the National Medal of Honor in 2007. Several of his painting's have appeared in museums, and most art school's programs mention his work. His paintings are part of the movement known as "magic realism." What makes his work unique is it's dark overtones. One of his most famous paintings is of a group of people trapped in a subway. Theyre gathered in a low-ceilinged subway car, incapable of escaping. Its a powerful and disturbing image.

2.   Tooker's work was not appreciated for much of his life. However, in recent years, many peoples' choice of "favorite artist" has been George Tooker. Hes known for making mundane situations seem ominous or threatening, and his despondent view of the modern world has influenced contemporary artists. Both George Tooker and Fernando Botero's paintings appear in many art galleries collections.

LO 4 Use apostrophes in expressions of time.

Apostrophes in Expressions of Time

If an expression of time (*year, week, month, day*) appears to possess something, use the possessive form of that word.

Alice Ray gave two **weeks'** notice before she left the dance company.

When you write out a year in numerals, an apostrophe can replace the missing numbers.

The graduates of the class of **'99** hoped to find good jobs.

However, if you are writing the numeral of a decade or century, do not put an apostrophe before the final *-s*.

In the **1900s**, many innovations in art occurred.

PRACTICE 5

Underline and correct ten errors. You may need to add or remove apostrophes.

wasn't
EXAMPLE: Jackson Pollock <u>wasnt</u> a conventional artist.

1.   In 1992, truck driver Teri Horton shopped for the weeks groceries, and then she passed by a thrift shop. She bought a painting for $5. She had planned to give it to a friend as a gag gift, but the large painting wouldnt fit through the door of her friends mobile home. A few month's after that, Horton put the artwork in her garage sale.

2.   Three hour's later, a local art teacher saw the painting and said, "Maybe its Jackson Pollocks work!" Horton spent the rest of the 1990's trying to prove that shed bought an original Pollock. Today, art expert's opinions are still divided.

FINAL REVIEW

Underline and correct eighteen apostrophe errors. You may need to add, remove, or move apostrophes.

EXAMPLE: What is an <u>artists</u> motivation to create?
                        artist's

1.   The street artist Banksy grew up in Bristol, England. When he was fourteen year's old, he began to paint graffiti on walls. He noticed that many of his friend's favorite graffiti spots were being watched by police officers. Banksy was worried; he didnt want to be arrested. One day, while he was hiding from a policewoman, he noticed the stenciled letters on the officers cruiser. Banksy realized that he could paint more quickly if he used stencils. "I wasnt very good at free-hand drawing," he said in an interview. "I was too slow."

2.   In the early 2000's, many of Banksy's stencils began to have political content. For example, he painted several murals on the wall in Israels' West Bank. In one image, there appear's to be a hole in the wall with a sandy beach on the

other side. Under the hole are two smiling children, and the childrens' buckets are full of sand. Banksy has also snuck his art into some of the worlds most prestigious galleries'. In 2003, he used tape to post a painting on the wall of Londons Tate gallery. Its amazing that the security guards didnt see him do it.

3. The artists reputation has increased because his images have captured the publics' imagination. In fact, in 2013, someone went to the trouble to remove a London stores brick wall, which had a Banksy mural on it. An auction house sold the work for $1.1 million. Although he now has international fame, Banksy doesnt want people to discover his true identity.

MyWritingLab™
Complete these writing assignments at mywritinglab.com

My WritingLab™   **THE WRITER'S ROOM**   Topics for Writing

Write about one of the following topics. After you finish writing, make sure that you have used apostrophes correctly.

1. What are some jobs that require creativity? List examples of such jobs, and describe how they are creative.

2. Define a term or expression that relates to this photo. Some ideas might be *creativity, graffiti, art, vandalism,* or *beauty.*

Checklist: Apostrophes

When you edit your writing, ask yourself these questions.

☐ Do I use apostrophes correctly? Check for errors in these cases:

  –contractions of verbs + *not* or subjects and verbs

  –possessives of singular and plural nouns (*the student's* versus *the students'*)

  –possessives of irregular plural nouns (*the women's*)

  –possessives of compound nouns (*Joe's and Mike's cars*)

  > shouldn't   Wong's
  > You ~~should'nt~~ be surprised that Chris ~~Wongs~~ going to exhibit his paintings.

  > Chris's
  > ~~Chris'~~ artwork will be on display next week.

☐ Do I place apostrophes where they do not belong? Check for errors in possessive pronouns and present tense verbs.

  > looks   its
  > It ~~look's~~ as though the gallery is moving ~~it's~~ collection to Houston.

37 Quotation Marks, Capitalization, and Titles

SECTION THEME: Human Development

LEARNING OBJECTIVES

LO 1 Use quotation marks correctly. **(p. 486)**

LO 2 Use quotations in research essays. **(p. 489)**

LO 3 Learn capitalization rules. **(p. 492)**

LO 4 Style titles correctly. **(p. 494)**

In this chapter, you will read about artists and musicians.

LO 1 Use quotation marks correctly.

Quotation Marks (" ")

Use **quotation marks** to set off the exact words of a speaker or writer. When you include the exact words of more than one person in a text, then you must make a new paragraph each time the speaker changes. If the quotation is a complete sentence, punctuate it in the following ways.

- Capitalize the first word of the quotation.
- Place quotation marks around the complete quotation.
- Place the end punctuation inside the closing quotation marks.
- Generally, attach the name of the speaker or writer to the quotation in some way.

Oscar Wilde declared, "All art is useless."

Review the following rules.

1. **Introductory Phrase** When the quotation is introduced by a phrase, place a comma after the introductory phrase.

    Pablo Picasso said, "Art is a lie that makes us realize the truth."

2. **Interrupting Phrase** When the quotation is interrupted, place a comma before and after the interrupting phrase.

    "In the end," says dancer Martha Graham, "it all comes down to breathing."

3. **End Phrase** When you place a phrase at the end of a quotation, end the quotation with a comma instead of a period.

    "Great art picks up where nature ends," said Marc Chagall.

    If your quotation ends with other punctuation, put it inside the quotation mark.

    "Who is the greatest painter?" the student asked.

    "That question cannot be answered!" the curator replied.

4. **Introductory Sentence** When you introduce a quotation with a complete sentence, place a colon (:) after the introductory sentence.

    George Balanchine explains his philosophy about dance: "Dance is music made visible."

5. **Inside Quotations** If one quotation is inside another quotation, then use single quotation marks (' ') around the inside quotation.

    To her mother, Veronica Corelli explained, "I am not sure if I will succeed, but you've always said, 'Your work should be your passion.' "

HINT ◀ Integrated Quotations

> If the quotation is not a complete sentence, and you simply integrate it into your sentence, do not capitalize the first word of the quotation.
>
> Composer Ludwig van Beethoven called music "the mediator between the spiritual and the sensual life."

PRACTICE 1

In each sentence, the quotation is set off in a color. Add quotation marks and periods, commas, or colons. Also, capitalize the first word of the quotation, if necessary.

EXAMPLE: Producer Rick Rubin asks , "W~~where~~ are the great singers? "

1. Famous music producer Rick Rubin says   right now, if you listen to pop, everything is in perfect pitch, perfect time, and perfect tune

2. Auto-tune was originally created to fix pitch and tone problems in singers' voices   according to Anna Pulley.

3. The auto-tune effect just worked for my voice   proclaimed rapper T-Pain.

4. I know auto-tune better than anyone   said T-Pain   and even I'm just figuring out all the ways I can use it to change the mood of a record

5. *Time* journalist Josh Tyrangiel says that technology   can transform a wavering performance into something technically flawless

6. It makes singers sound too perfect   says music lover Andrea Berezan   and perfect singing is boring

7. Guitarist Pierre Roi shows his contempt for auto-tune   when singers use auto-tune, their voices sound fake

8. Too many pop stars also lip-synch in concert   declares Jay Segal.

9. Neil McCormack mentions an incident at a live show   I saw Madonna drop her microphone, and her singing was still audible

10. Music fan Chelsea Oberman says   When I pay $80 to see a live concert, and the singer lip-synchs, I sometimes shout   use your voice

PRACTICE 2

Correct ten punctuation errors in the next dialogue.

EXAMPLE: She told me, "Your future is in your hands."

Maya confronted her son, "Your drums are too loud"!

Jonell looked at his mother and replied: "I need to practice for my band."

"How will you make a living as a drummer" she asked?

He replied, "I do not need to earn a lot of money to be happy."

"You're being very naive." Maya responded.

Jonell said, "I'm just following your advice. You always say, "Find work that you love." "

"Perhaps you have to take some chances" his mother responded, "and learn from your own mistakes."

Jonell stated firmly, "my decision will not be a mistake!"

Using Quotations in Research Essays

LO2 Use quotations in research essays.

Use quotations to reveal the opinions of an expert or to highlight ideas that are particularly memorable and important. When quoting sources, remember to limit how many you use in a single paper and to vary your quotations by using both direct and indirect quotations.

Direct and Indirect Quotations

A **direct quotation** contains the exact words of the speaker or writer, and it is set off with quotation marks.

> Amy Kurtz Lansing writes, "Connecticut has long been a center for the visual arts in America."

An **indirect quotation** keeps the author's meaning but is not set off by quotation marks. Note that an indirect quotation is also called a paraphrase.

> Amy Kurtz Lansing writes that Connecticut is one of America's artistic centers.

Integrating Quotations

Short Quotations

Introduce short quotations with a phrase or sentence. (Short quotations should not stand alone.) Read the following original selection, and then view how the quotation has been introduced using three common methods. The selection, written by Michael J. Strada, appeared on page 60 of his book *Through the Global Lens*.

Original Selection

Maps turned out to be very helpful to London officials a century ago, when they were used to track the spread of a cholera epidemic to the city's water system. Since maps aim to simulate reality, the drawing of maps may seem simple and straightforward. The process, however, is anything but simple.

Phrase Introduction

In *Through the Global Lens,* Michael J. Strada writes, "Since maps aim to simulate reality, the drawing of maps may seem simple and straightforward" (60).

Sentence Introduction

In his book, *Through the Global Lens,* Michael J. Strada suggests that drawing maps can be complicated: "Since maps aim to simulate reality, the drawing of maps may seem simple and straightforward" (60).

Integrated Quotation

In *Through the Global Lens,* Michael J. Strada reveals that drawing a map "is anything but simple" (60).

HINT ◀ Words That Introduce Quotations

Here are some common words that can introduce quotations.

admits	concludes	mentions	speculates
claims	explains	observes	suggests
comments	maintains	reports	warns

The doctor **states**, "_____."

"_____," **observes** Dr. Hannah.

Dr. Hannah **speculates** that _____.

Long Quotations

If you use a quotation in MLA style that has four or more lines (or in APA style, more than forty words), insert the quotation in your research paper in the following way.

* Introduce the quotation with a sentence ending with a colon.
* Indent the entire quotation about ten spaces (one inch) from the left margin of your document.
* Use double spacing.
* Do not use quotation marks.
* Cite the author and page number in parentheses after the punctuation mark in the last sentence of the quotation.

Review the next example from a student essay about art history that uses MLA style. The quotation is from page 132 of Germaine Greer's *The Obstacle Race.* The explanatory sentence introduces the quotation and is part of an essay.

Much great art has been lost owing to a variety of factors:

> Panels decay as wood decays. Canvas rots, tears, and sags. The stretchers spring and warp. As color dries out, it loses its flexibility and begins to separate from its unstable ground; dry color flakes off shrinking or swelling wood and drooping canvas. (Greer 132)

HINT ◄ Using Long Quotations

If your research paper is short (two or three pages), avoid using many long quotations. Long quotations will only overwhelm your own ideas. Instead, try summarizing a long passage or using shorter quotations.

Using Ellipses (. . .)

If you want to quote key ideas from an author, but do not want to quote the entire paragraph, you can use **ellipses**. Ensure that your new sentence, with the ellipses, is grammatically correct. These three periods show that you have omitted unnecessary information from a quotation. Leave a space before and after each period. If the omitted section goes to the end of the sentence or includes one or more complete sentences, insert a final period before the ellipses (. . . .). The original selection appeared on page 173 of the book *Crossroads* by Elizabeth F. Barkley.

Original Selection
The guitarist slides the steel bar across the strings, which are tuned to a single cord, and the steel bar changes the pitch of the chord by its location on the strings. The sliding of the bar gives the guitar a distinctive wavering timbre.

Quotation with Omissions
In *Crossroads*, Elizabeth F. Barkley writes, "The guitarist slides the steel bar across the strings. . . . The sliding of the bar gives the guitar a distinctive wavering timbre" (173).

PRACTICE 3

Read the quotation, and then answer the questions. The selection, written by Richard Paul Janaro, appeared on page 200 of *The Art of Being Human*.

Original Selection
Blues music is almost always about the empty aftermath of a once burning passion. The songs are written from either a male or a female point of view. Men sing of the faithlessness of women, and women return the compliment about men.

1. Write a direct quotation. Remember to introduce the title and author.

   _____

   _____

   _____

2. Write a direct quotation with an omission. Remember to introduce the title and author.

   _____

   _____

   _____

LO 3 Learn capitalization rules.

Capitalization

Remember to capitalize the following:

* **the pronoun _I_ and the first word of every sentence**

   My brothers and **I** share an apartment.

* **days of the week, months, and holidays**

   | Thursday | June 22 | Labor Day |

   Do not capitalize the seasons: summer, fall, winter, spring.

* **titles of specific institutions, departments, companies, and schools**

   | Microsoft | Department of Finance | Elmwood High School |

   Do not capitalize general references.

   | the company | the department | the school |

* **names of specific places such as buildings, streets, parks, cities, states, and bodies of water**

   | Eiffel Tower | Times Square | Los Angeles, California |
   | Sunset Boulevard | Florida | Lake Erie |

   Do not capitalize general references.

   | the street | the state | the lake |

* **names of specific planets but not the sun or the moon**

   | Earth | Mars | Venus |

◆ **specific languages, nationalities, tribes, races, and religions**

| Greek | Mohawk | Buddhist | a French restaurant |

◆ **titles of specific individuals**

| General Franklin | President Obama | Doctor Blain |
| Professor Sayf | Prime Minister Trudeau | Mrs. Robinson |

If you are referring to the profession in general, or if the title follows the name, do not use capital letters.

| my doctor | the professors | Ted Kennedy, a senator |

◆ **specific course and program titles**

| Physics 201 | Marketing 101 | Advanced Algebra |

If you refer to a course without mentioning the course title, then it is unnecessary to use capitals. Also, do not capitalize the names of programs.

| He is in his math class. | I am in the music program. |

Do not capitalize academic degrees when spelled out. Only capitalize the abbreviated form.

Mike has a master of arts in literature, but his sister did not complete her **MA**.

I have a bachelor of science degree, and Melissa has a **PhD**.

◆ **the major words in titles of newspapers, magazines, and literary or artistic works**

| *Miami Herald* | *Great Expectations* | *The Daily Show* |

◆ **historical events, eras, and movements**

| World War II | Post-Impressionism | Baby Boomers |

HINT ◢ **Capitalizing Computer Terms**

Always capitalize the following computer terms.

| Internet | Google | World Wide Web | Microsoft Office |

PRACTICE 4

Add fifteen missing capital letters to the following paragraphs.

EXAMPLE: The musician was born on m̶arch 21.

1.   The New York academy of Sciences has examined how people respond to music. The study, done in april 2005, examines whether musical training can make people smarter. The researchers found that listening to a song such as "in my life" can enhance brain functions.

2.   Gordon Shaw, who passed away in 2005, earned his bachelor of science degree and later completed a doctorate in physics at cornell university. He was the co-founder of the Music intelligence neuronal development institute. He also wrote the book *Keeping Mozart in mind*. Shaw determined that music can enhance math abilities. I wish I had known that when I took math 401 at Greendale high school. Maybe I will study music in college.

Titles

LO 4 Style titles correctly.

Place the title of a short work in quotation marks. Italicize the titles of longer documents, or underline such titles when the document is handwritten.

Short Works		**Long Works**	
short story	"The Lottery"	**novel**	*Catch-22*
chapter	"Early Accomplishments"	**book**	*The Art of Emily Carr*
newspaper article	"The City's Hottest Ticket"	**newspaper**	*New York Times*
magazine article	"New Artists"	**magazine**	*Rolling Stone*
Web article	"Music Artists Lose Out"	**Web site**	*CNET News*
essay	"Hip-Hop Nation"	**textbook**	*Common Culture*
TV episode	"The Search Party"	**TV series/ film title**	*Lost/Rush*
song	"Mouths to Feed"	**CD**	*Release Therapy*
poem	"Howl"	**anthology**	*Collected Poems of Beat Writers*

Capitalizing Titles

When you write a title, capitalize the first letter of the first word and all the major words.

To Kill a Mockingbird   "Stairway to Heaven"

Do not capitalize the word ".com" in a Web address. Also, do not capitalize the following words, unless they are the first word in the title.

articles	a, an, the
coordinators	for, and, nor, but, or, yet, so
prepositions	of, to, in, off, out, up, by, . . .

HINT   ◀ **Your Own Essay Titles**

In essays that you write for your courses, do not underline your title or put quotation marks around it. Simply capitalize the first word and the main words.

Why Music Is Important

PRACTICE 5

Add ten capital letters to the next selection, and add quotation marks or underlines to ten titles. Add quotation marks to the titles of short works. For long works, underline titles to show that they should be in italics.

EXAMPLE: The magazine <u>business week</u> featured successful singers.
　　　　　　　　　　　　ᴮ　　　ᵂ

1.　　Rolling stone, a music magazine, published an article called The 500 Greatest songs of All Time. The first item on the list is the Bob Dylan song Like a Rolling Stone. According to the magazine, the greatest album is Sergeant Pepper's Lonely Hearts Club band.

2.　　I heard my favorite song in a movie. The song Mad World was first recorded by the british band Tears for Fears. Released in august 1982 on the album The hurting, the song was moderately successful. Then, for the 2001 movie Donnie Darko, the song was redone in a slower tempo with piano music. The version by Gary Jules mesmerized filmgoers and helped give the movie a cult following. In fact, last friday, when the movie played at a theater on arrow street in Cambridge, Massachusetts, the film sold out. The song has appeared as background music in television shows such as Third Watch and

Without a trace. Then, in 2009, Adam Lambert sang it during an episode of American Idol. Once again, the song became a great hit.

FINAL REVIEW

Identify and correct twenty-five errors. First, correct fourteen errors with capitalization. Then correctly set off six titles by adding quotation marks or by underlining titles that should be in italics. Finally, correct five other punctuation errors.

EXAMPLE: The marketing manager said '"Virtual singers are here to stay."

1. Hatsune Miku, with her turquoise pigtails and her sweet voice, has become a star in Asia. The article Virtual Singer Tops the Charts on the online site Web Japan points out, "she is no girl at all". Hatsune Miku is actually an artificial voice accompanied by a virtual avatar. The avatar is clearly meant to represent a pop star from a typical High School.

2. The british fashion magazine Clash featured Miku's virtual character on the cover of its 59th issue. The character also appeared in the manga magazine *Comic rush*. Miku's voice is the result of a voice-synthesizing software program. It uses an audio library of samples from japanese voice actress Fujita Saki to create new, synthesized songs. In the article Pixel perfect, Karley Sciortino

describes the world of Miku, "Her creative output is created by her fans." For under $200, aspiring songwriters buy a software program and then write songs for Miku. "I hope my song becomes a hit" says super fan Aki Kiyuka.

3.   The company called Crypton future Media created the avatar. In 2007, Hatsune Miku was the top-selling computer program in Japan. In april 2010, an updated version was released. In the newspaper Los Angeles Times, journalist Tiffany Hsu said: "The virtual diva's albums have topped the Japanese charts."

4.   The virtual character has a strong media presence. She advertises products and is also one of the hosts of the television program The Net Star. Most surprisingly, thousands of fans show up to Miku concerts. "Miku played her first live gig in Saitama, Japan, on saturday august 22, 2009. Her image was projected to the audience as a giant 3D hologram." says Sciortino. At her concerts, fans show up in Miku costumes "And wave glowsticks," Sciortino continues. Miku also has some fans in the United States. In 2011, she performed at Anime Expo in Los Angeles. The show was at the Los Angeles convention Center, at 1201 South Figueroa street. Could Miku change the way music is produced?

Topics for Writing   **THE WRITER'S ROOM**   MyWritingLab™

MyWritingLab™

Complete these writing assignments at mywritinglab.com

Write about one of the following topics. Include some direct quotations. Proofread to ensure that your punctuation and capitalization are correct.

1. List some characteristics of your generation. What political events, social issues, music, and fashion bind your generation?

2. List three categories of art. Describe some details about each category.

3. Examine the photograph. What do you think the people are talking about? Write a brief dialogue from their conversation.

Checklist: Quotation Marks

When you edit your writing, ask yourself these questions.

☐ Are there any direct quotations in my writing? Check for errors with these elements:

  –punctuation before or after quotations

  –capital letters

  –placement of quotation marks

  "Art is making something out of nothing and selling it," said musician Frank Zappa.

☐ Do my sentences have all the necessary capital letters?

  Munch's greatest works were painted before World ~~w~~ War II.

  W

☐ Are the titles of small and large artistic works properly punctuated?

  Edvard Munch's painting was called *The ~~s~~cream.*

  S

Numbers and Additional Punctuation 38

SECTION THEME: Human Development

In this chapter, you will read about photography and photographers.

LEARNING OBJECTIVES

LO 1 Review the rules for using numbers in academic writing. **(p. 499)**

LO 2 Learn about additional forms of punctuation. **(p. 501)**

LO 1 Review the rules for using numbers in academic writing.

Numbers

There are two basic styles for number usage. Business and technical documents use one style, and academic writing uses another. **In business and technical fields**, use numerals instead of words in charts, statistics, graphs, financial documents, and advertising. The numbers one to ten are written as words only when they appear in sentences.

However, **in academic writing**, numbers are spelled out more often. Review the rules for using numbers in academic writing.

◆ Spell out numbers that can be expressed in one or two words.

We spent **eighteen** days in Mexico City.

There were **forty-seven** people waiting for another flight.

The airline had room for **four hundred**.

That day, **thousands** of people cleared customs.

◆ Use numerals with numbers of more than two words.

The manager booked rooms for **358** guests.

◆ Spell out fractions.

Only **one-third** of the residents have their own homes.

◆ When the sentence begins with a number, spell out the number. If the number has more than two words, do not place it at the beginning of the sentence.

Three hundred people were invited to the gallery.

There were **158** guests.

◆ Use a numeral before million or billion, but spell out *million* or *billion*. (It is easier to read *20 million* than *20,000,000*.)

The company hopes to sell about **14 million** units.

◆ Use numerals when writing addresses, dates, times, degrees, pages, measurements, or divisions of a book. Also use numerals with prices and percentages. Always write out *percent*. For prices, you can write *dollars* or use the $ symbol.

A yearly subscription costs **$29**, which is about **15** percent less than the cover price.

HINT ◀ Several Numbers in a Sentence

When writing two consecutive numbers, write out the shorter number.

We used **two 35-mm** rolls of film.

Be consistent when writing a series of numbers. If some numbers require numerals, then use numerals for all of the numbers.

The gallery guests consumed **300** appetizers, **8** pounds of cheese, and **120** glasses of wine.

PRACTICE 1

Correct any errors with numbers in the next sentences.

nine
EXAMPLE: She was just 9 years old when she picked up a camera.

1. Nature photographer Jillian Wolf has four digital cameras, 3 printers, and

one hundred and sixteen pieces of photography paper.

2. She has worked professionally as a photographer for 5 years.

3. Last year, Wolf published her own photography book, and each book sold

    for ninety-five dollars.

4. She self-published 50 132-page books.

5. She rented a gallery space and exhibited 25 of her nature photos.

6. 65 people came to see her photos.

Additional Punctuation
Semicolon (;)

L0 2 Learn about additional forms of punctuation.

Use a semicolon

* between two complete and related ideas.

    The photograph was stunning; Sherman was very pleased.

* between items in a series of ideas, if the items have internal punctuation or are very long.

    Sherman's works were exhibited in Birmingham, Alabama; Fort Worth, Texas; Toronto, Ontario; and London, England.

Colon (:)

Use a colon

* after a complete sentence that introduces a quotation.

    The photographer Henri Cartier-Bresson stated his view: "Photographers are dealing with things that are continually vanishing."

* to introduce a series or a list after a complete sentence.

    The new museum includes the work of some great photographers: Ansel Adams, Cindy Sherman, Edward Weston, Alfred Stieglitz, Dorothea Lange, and Annie Leibovitz.

* to introduce an explanation or example.

    The tiny sculpture is outrageously expensive: $2.5 million.

* after the expression "the following."

    Please do the following: read, review, and respond.

> **GRAMMAR LINK**
> For practice using semicolons, see Chapters 21 and 24.

♦ to separate the hour and minutes in expressions of time.

> The exhibit will open at 12:30 P.M.

Hyphen (-)

Use a hyphen

♦ with some compound nouns. (Note that *compound* means "more than one part.") The following nouns always require a hyphen.

| sister-in-law | mother-in-law | show-off |

♦ when you write the complete words for compound numbers between twenty-one and ninety-nine.

| twenty-five | ninety-two | seventy-seven |

♦ after some prefixes such as *self-*, *mid-*, or *ex-*.

| self-assured | mid-December | ex-husband |

♦ when you use a compound adjective before a noun. The compound adjective must express a single thought.

| one-way street | well-known actor | thirty-year-old woman |

There is no hyphen if the compound adjective appears after the noun.

| The street is one way. | The actor was well known. | The woman is thirty years old. |

> **HINT** ◀ **Nonhyphenated Compound Adjectives**
>
> Some compound adjectives never take a hyphen, even when they appear before a noun. Here are some common examples.
>
> | World Wide Web | high school senior | real estate agent |

Dash (—)

You can use dashes to indicate long pauses or to dramatically emphasize words. Use dashes sparingly.

> Ansel Adams waited until the sun was setting to capture the image—the perfect moment.

> The gallery owner—hiding his excitement—offered to buy the rare photo.

Parentheses ( )

You can use parentheses to set off incidental information such as a date or abbreviation. Use parentheses sparingly.

> Lange's photo of the migrant mother, which was taken during the height of the Depression era (1936), has become an enduring image.

> The United Press Photographer's Association (UPPA) was founded in 1946.

HINT ◄ Using Abbreviations

An **abbreviation** is the shortened form of a word. Avoid using abbreviations in academic writing except for titles and time references.

> Dr. = Doctor   Mr. = Mister   P.M. = post meridiem (after noon)

An **acronym** is formed with the first letters of a group of words. Many companies and organizations use acronyms. In an academic paper, give the complete name of the organization the first time you mention it and put the acronym in parentheses immediately after the full name. Use the acronym in the rest of the essay.

> The North Atlantic Treaty Organization (NATO) signed the agreement in 1949. Today, NATO's headquarters are in Belgium.

PRACTICE 2

Add any missing colons, hyphens, dashes, or parentheses.

EXAMPLE: The ten year old truck broke down.

1. Florence Thompson and her husband, Cleo, were living in Merced Falls, California, when there was a tragedy the Crash of 1929.

2. In 1936, Florence, a thirty two year old woman, decided to keep her children with her "I made a promise to Cleo to see his six kids raised, and by God I'm going to keep that promise!"

3. In the back of her truck were Florence's possessions a small stove, a few pieces of clothing, some blankets, and a canvas tent.

"Migrant Mother," portrait of Florence Owens Thompson and children, by Dorothea Lange for the Farm Security Administration, Nipomo, California, 1936.

4. Florence and her children did many low wage jobs they struggled and rarely had enough to eat.

5. One day, Florence was in a tent by the highway waiting for her son to return a day that would make her famous.

6. That day, photographer Dorothea Lange was working for the Farm Security Administration FSA and was traveling around Nipomo Valley in California.

7. Lange described what happened "I saw and approached the hungry and desperate mother, as if drawn by a magnet."

8. Sitting in her dust covered canvas tent, Florence Thompson was holding her baby, and her children were crowded around her.

9. During a twenty minute session, Lange took many photos of the migrant mother.

10. The compassionate photographs of Dorothea Lange 1895–1965 have influenced modern documentary photography.

FINAL REVIEW

Identify and correct any errors in numbers, colons, hyphens, dashes, or parentheses.

EXAMPLE: Richard Avedon took large format photos.

1. Richard Avedon 1923–2004 was a great fashion photographer.

2. Before he joined the Merchant Marines, his father in law gave him a camera a gift that changed his life.

3. At the beginning of his career, he took photos with his ten year old Rolleiflex camera.

4. He became a staff photographer for *Vogue* he also worked for *Harper's Bazaar*.

5. Many of his photos featured three items a chair, a white backdrop, and a face.

6. One of his greatest photos a masterpiece of shadow and light showed Audrey Hepburn's face.

7. He took 100s of photos of Hepburn, his favorite model.

8. His photographs have been exhibited at New York's Museum of Modern Art MOMA.

9. He published the best selling book *Portraits*, and he co authored another book, *The Sixties*.

10. His book has twenty-nine fashion shots, 125 portraits, and twelve war images.

11. One of his photos—an iconic image of Marilyn Monroe has been reproduced in 1000s of books and magazines.

12. Avedon compared photography to music "The way I see is comparable to the way musicians hear."

READING LINK
Read more about human development and creativity.

"Priceless Euphoria" by Lisa Monique (page 79)

"We're Watching What We Eat" by Al Kratina (page 89)

"Do You Have What It Takes to Be Happy?" by Stacey Colino (page 141)

"How Cults Become Religions" by John D. Carl (page 572)

"The Untranslatable Word 'Macho' " by Rose del Castillo Guilbault (page 575)

"Chance and Circumstance" by David Leonhardt (page 578)

"The Happiness Factor" by David Brooks (page 582)

"Medicating Ourselves" by Robyn Sarah (page 585)

MyWritingLab™

Complete these writing assignments at mywritinglab.com

Chapter 38

MyWritingLab™

THE WRITER'S ROOM

Topics for Writing

Write about one of the following topics. Proofread for errors in numbers or punctuation.

1. Describe a personal photograph that you cherish. When was the photo taken? What is in the photo? Why is it so compelling?

2. Compare two art forms. For example, you could compare a photograph and a painting or two pieces of music.

Checklist: Numbers and Punctuation

When you edit your writing, ask yourself these questions.

☐ Are there any numbers in my writing? Check that your numbers are consistently written, and verify that you have used words rather than numerals when necessary.

thousands
Lange took ~~1000s~~ of photographs.

☐ Are my semicolons, colons, hyphens, dashes, and parentheses used in a correct and appropriate manner?

She brought the following supplies; a camera, a well used chair, and a camera stand.

Editing Practice 39

LEARNING OBJECTIVE

LO 1 Practice revising and editing essays and different types of writing. **(p. 507)**

To conquer Mount Everest, climbers meet the physical and mental challenges through practice and training. To write good essays, students perfect their skills by revising and editing.

Why Bother Editing?

LO 1 Practice revising and editing essays and different types of writing.

After you finish writing the first draft of an essay, always make time to edit it. Editing for errors in grammar, punctuation, sentence structure, and capitalization can make the difference between a failing paper and a passing one or a good essay and a great one. Editing is not always easy; it takes time and attention to detail. However, it gets easier the more you do it. Also, the more you edit your essays (and your peers' essays, too), the better your writing will be, and the less time you will need to spend editing!

PRACTICE 1

Correct fifteen errors in this essay. An editing symbol appears above each error. To understand the meaning of each symbol, refer to the revising and editing symbols on the inside back cover of this book.

1.   Films such as *Into the ~~Wild~~* ^{cap} and television shows such as *Survivor* is very ^{agr}

popular. But watching shows about survival is not the same as surviving

alone in the outdoors. If you enjoy hiking in the wild, you should definitly [sp] [del]
learn basic outdoor survival techniques.

2.   First, plan your trip in advance. Buy a detailed map of the area, and

find out informations [pl] about the weather. Also, take a survival kit with you.

Packing essential items is more important than to buy buying expensive equipment.

For example, a butane lighter and a tarp are necessary, Especially [frag] if you are

hiking in the outback. Most importantly, tell someone where you are going

and when you are returning before you set off on an outdoor trip. This

information will prove vital if something unexpected happened. [vt]

3.   Second, if you get lost [p] try to remain calm. Panic can cause you to make

the wrong choices. The most best [ad] way to stop the panic is to sit down and

breathe deep [ad] deeply. You should probably stay where you are because [ro] you have informed

someone of your plans.

4.   Next, build a shelter. People Persons [pl] have died from extreme temperatures. For

example, Mike and Janice were hiking in the Grand Tetons when it started

to rain. They were stranded on the side of a mountain wearing [m] wet clothes.

Fortunately, they knew how to build a shelter and had packed extra clothes.

5.   By following these basic rules, you will increase you're chances of survival
[*sp*] *yours*

in an emergency. Outdoor hiking is a lot of fun, but we should always
[*shift*] *You*

remember the Boy Scouts motto: Be prepared.

PRACTICE 2

Correct twenty errors in this essay. An editing symbol appears above each error.
To understand the meaning of each symbol, refer to the revising and editing
symbols on the inside back cover of this book.

1.   Since 1900, many products been defective. In his book *Business ethics*,
[*vt*] *had*   [*cap* E]

Richard T. De George discusses a famous product defect case. In the early

1970s, American automakers was losing market share to smaller Japanese
[*p*]   [*agr*] *were*

imports. Lee Iacocca, the CEO of Ford Motor Company wanted to produce
[*p*]

a car that was inexpensive, lightweight, and had an attractive look. Engineers
[*//*]

developped the Ford Pinto.
[*sp*]

2.   Because Ford wanted the product on the market real quickly, the car
[*ad*] *really*

was not test for rear-end impacts. After the Pintos been produced, they were
[*vt*] *tested*   [*vt*] *has*

put in collision tests, they failed the tests. When the Pinto was hitted from
[*ro*] *but*   [*sp*] *hi*

behind, a bolt on the bumper will sometimes puncture the fuel tank And
[*wc*] *would*   [*frag*] *and*

cause an explosion.

3.   Ford conducted a study and determined that ~~a~~ inexpensive baffle [wc]

could be placed between the bumper and the gas tank. After conducting

a cost–benefit analysis, a decision was made. *by Ford.* It was less expensive to fight

lawsuits than inserting the baffle. [//]

4.   In 1976, Pintos had thirteen explosions from rear-end impacts.

Comparable cars had less problems. *Fewer* [ad] When it ~~be~~ too late, the company *was* [vt]

realized that the lawsuits and the bad publicity were worst for the company [ad]

than the cost of the repairs would have been. After seven years and many

deaths, the Pintos were recalled.

PRACTICE 3 EDIT A FORMAL LETTER

Correct fifteen errors in this formal business letter.

> **GRAMMAR LINK**
> Learn more about business letter formatting in Chapter 19

George Bates

5672 Manet street west

Lazerville, TX 76202

August 15, 2014

Customer Service

The Furniture store

1395 Division avenue

Denton, TX 76205

Subject: Desk

Attention: Sales manager

I bought a desk from your store on august 13 2014, and the store delivers it thursday morning. After the delivery people had left, I discovered a large scratch on the surface of the desk. Its also lopsided. Because I have always found your products to be of excellent quality I would like to have a replacement desk delivered to my home. If you do not have replacement desk, then I would like to have a full reimbursement.

Thank you very much for your cooperation in this matter, I look forward to receive my new desk.

Yours Sincerely,

George Bates

George Bates

PRACTICE 4 EDIT A WORKPLACE MEMO

Correct ten errors in the following excerpt from a memo.

To: Career development faculty members

From: Maddison Healey

Re: Internships

I'm gonna take this opportunity to remind you that their are financial resources to hiring two new interns for the Career development

Program. If anyone wishes to participate in this collaboration, please let Danielle or I know. The current deadline for applying to the internship program is the beginning of april. The internship program, provides valuable mentoring to college students. Treating interns with respect, it is very important. If you hire an intern, you are responsible for training them. For those who are interested, please let me know as quick as possible.

PRACTICE 5 EDIT A SHORT ARTICLE

Correct fifteen errors in the next selection.

1.   The solar system no longer has nine planets; on August 24, 2006, the International Astronomical union, which has a voting membership of about 2,500 scientists, met in Prague. It decided to demote Pluto from a planet to a dwarf planet. The astronomers said that Pluto does not exhibit the same characteristics as the other major planets. According to scientists, a planet must orbit the sun, it must be having a spherical shape, and it must have a clear orbit. Unfortunatly, Pluto's orbit overlaps Neptune's orbit.

2.   At the begiming of the twentieth century, much astronomers suspected the possibility of another planet in the solar system. In 1930, while working for the Lowell Conservatory in Flagstaff, Arizona, astronomer Clyde Tombaugh took photographs of a sphere that was composed mainly of ices and rocks. It also had a satellite, Charon, orbiting it. Evenitaly, this sphere was named the nineth planet in the solar system.

3. Scientists were very exciting ~~ed~~ about the discovery. People from all over

the world suggested names for the new planet. The scientists from the

observatory received so many suggestions that they had difficulty choosing

one. An eleven-years-old girl from Oxford, England, suggested the name

Pluto.

4. The scientific community and the public have had a mixed reaction to the

declassification of Pluto. ~~As~~ as a planet. Some refuse to accept it. But I wonder

why ~~are they~~ they are resistant. Perhaps teachers don't ~~wanna~~ want to change astronomy

textbooks. Maybe people feel particularly wary when the scientific

community revises what it once asked ~~us~~ them to accept as fact.

Part V

Reading Selections and Strategies

In this chapter, the essays are organized according to the same themes used in the grammar chapters. The predominant writing pattern of each essay is shown in parentheses.

40 From Reading to Writing

LEARNING OBJECTIVES

LO 1 Practice reading strategies. **(p. 516)**

LO 2 Analyze reading selections. **(p. 522)**

Aspiring actors study ordinary people, psychological profiles, and the work of other actors to fully develop the characters they play. In the same way, by observing how different writers create their work, you can learn how to use those techniques in your own writing.

LO 1 Practice reading strategies.

Reading Strategies

The reading strategies discussed in this chapter can help you develop your writing skills. They can also help you become a more active reader. You will learn about previewing, finding the main and supporting ideas, understanding difficult words, and recognizing irony. When you read, you expand your vocabulary and learn how other writers develop topics. You also learn to recognize and use different writing patterns. Finally, reading helps you find ideas for your own essays.

Previewing

Previewing is like glancing through a magazine in a bookstore; it gives you a chance to see what the writer is offering. When you **preview**, look quickly for the following visual clues so that you can determine the selection's key ideas:

* titles or subheadings (if any)
* the first and last sentence of the introduction
* the first sentence of each paragraph

- the concluding sentences
- any photos, graphs, or charts

Previewing prepares you for the next step, which is reading the essay.

Finding the Main Idea

After you finish previewing, read the selection carefully. Search for the **main idea**, which is the central point that the writer is trying to make. In an essay, the main idea usually appears somewhere in the first few paragraphs in the form of a thesis statement. However, some professional writers build up to the main idea and state it only in the middle or at the end of the essay. Additionally, some professional writers do not state the main idea directly.

HINT ◄ **Making a Statement of the Main Idea**

If the reading does not contain a clear thesis statement, you can determine the main idea by asking yourself who, *what*, *when*, *where*, *why*, and *how* questions. Then, using the answers to those questions, make a statement that sums up the main point of the reading.

Making Inferences

If a professional writer does not state the main idea directly, you must look for clues that will help you to **infer** or figure out what the writer means to say. For example, the next paragraph does not have a topic sentence. However, you can infer the main idea. Underline key words that can lead you to a better understanding of the passage.

> What is wrong with this picture? Every year, mass shootings occur in public places such as schools, movie theaters, or post offices. Such tragic events dominate headlines and ignite endless and futile debates. And, of course, there are the everyday shootings: children mishandling the family firearm, alcohol-fueled street fighters killing their opponents, or jealous lovers executing their partners. Americans have more guns, on average, than any other citizens in the world. In an article for the *Guardian*, journalist Henry Porter pointed out that more Americans have been killed by privately owned guns since 1968 than have been killed in all U.S. wars. The British writer, baffled by the "lunacy" of gun lovers, calls the constitutional right to bear arms "archaic."
>
> —Adele Berridge

PRACTICE 1

Ask yourself the following questions.

1. What is the subject of this text?

2. What points can you infer that the writer is making?

_____

_____

_____

Finding the Supporting Ideas

Different writers use different types of supporting ideas. They may give steps for a process, use examples to illustrate a point, give reasons for an argument, and so on. Try to identify the author's supporting ideas.

Highlighting and Making Annotations

After you read a long text, you may forget some of the author's ideas. To help you remember and quickly find the important points, you can highlight key ideas and make annotations. An **annotation** is a comment, question, or reaction that you write in the margins of a passage.

Each time you read a passage, follow these steps:

* Look in the introductory and concluding paragraphs. Underline sentences that sum up the main idea. Using your own words, rewrite the main idea in the margin.
* Underline or highlight supporting ideas. You might even want to number the arguments or ideas. This will allow you to understand the essay's development.
* Circle words that are important ideas or that you do not understand.
* Write questions in the margin if you do not understand the author's meaning.
* Write notes beside passages that are interesting or that relate to your own experiences.
* Jot down any ideas that might make interesting writing topics.

Here is an annotated passage from "The Rules of Survival" by Laurence Gonzales on page 557 of this textbook.

main point ➤

Ralston from
movie _127 Hours?_ ➤
I would have ➤
panicked

steps to ➤
control fear
look up word ➤

1   In the initial crisis, survivors are not ruled by fear; instead, they make use of it. Their fear often feels like (and turns into) anger, which motivates them and makes them feel sharper. Aron Ralston, the hiker who had to cut off his hand to free himself from a stone that had trapped him in a slot canyon in Utah, initially panicked and began slamming himself over and over against the boulder that had caught his hand. But very quickly he stopped himself, did some deep breathing, and began thinking about his options. He eventually spent five days progressing through the stages necessary to convince him of what decisive action he had to take to save his own life.

Understanding Difficult Words

When you come across an unfamiliar word in a passage, do not stop reading to look up its definition in the dictionary. First, try using context clues to figure out the term's meaning on your own. If you still do not understand the word, circle it to remind you to look up its meaning in the dictionary when you have finished reading through the passage. You can keep a list of new vocabulary. See Appendix 6 for information about creating a vocabulary log.

Using Context Clues

Context clues are hints in the selection that help to define a word. To find a word's meaning, try the following:

♦ **Look at the word.** Is it a noun, a verb, or an adjective? Knowing how the word functions in the sentence can help you guess its meaning.

♦ **Look at surrounding words.** Look at the entire sentence and try to find a relation between the difficult word and those that surround it. There may be a **synonym** (a word that means the same thing) or an **antonym** (a word that means the opposite), or other terms in the sentence that help define the word.

♦ **Look at surrounding sentences.** Sometimes you can guess the meaning of a difficult word by looking at the sentences, paragraphs, and punctuation marks surrounding it. When you use your logic, the meaning becomes clear.

In most cases, you can guess the meaning of a new word by combining your own knowledge of the topic with the information conveyed in the words and phrases surrounding the difficult word.

PRACTICE 2

Can you define the words *strewn, emanate,* and *haven*? Perhaps you are not quite sure. Looking at the words in context makes it much easier to guess the definitions of the words.

> When I arrived in my hometown, I was baffled by the changes in my old neighborhood. Garbage was **strewn** across front lawns, paint peeled on the graying wooden homes, and roofs sagged. The auto body shop on the corner **emanated** horrible fumes of turpentine and paint, forcing me to cover my nose when I passed it. I wondered what had happened to my former safe **haven**.

Now write your own definition of the words as they are used in the context.

strewn _____ emanated _____ haven _____

HINT ◀ Cognates

Cognates (also known as word twins) are English words that may look and sound like words in another language. For example, the English word *responsible* is similar to the Spanish word *responsable*, although the words are spelled differently.

If English is not your first language, and you read an English word that looks similar to a word in your language, check how the word is being used in context. It may or may not mean the same thing in English as it means in your language. For example, in English, *sensible* means "to show good sense," but in Spanish, *sensible* means "emotional." In German, *bekommen* sounds like "become" but it really means "to get," and the German word *gift* means "poison" in English. If you are not sure of a word's meaning, you can always consult a dictionary.

Using a Dictionary

If you cannot understand the meaning of an unfamiliar word even after using context clues, then look up the word in a dictionary. A dictionary is useful if you use it correctly. Review the following tips for proper dictionary usage:

◆ **Look at the dictionary's front matter.** The preface contains explanations about the various symbols and abbreviations. Find out what your dictionary has to offer.

◆ **Read all of the definitions listed for the word.** Look for the meaning that best fits the context of your sentence.

◆ **Look up root words, if necessary.** For example, if you do not understand the word *unambiguous*, remove the prefix and look up *ambiguous*.

Here is an example of how dictionaries set up their definitions:

Word-Break Divisions
Your dictionary may indicate places for dividing words with heavy black dots.

Stress Symbol (′) and Pronunciation
Some dictionaries provide the phonetic pronunciation of words. The stress symbol lets you know which syllable has the highest or loudest sound.

Parts of Speech
The *n* means that *formation* is a noun. If you do not understand the "parts of speech" symbol, look in the front or the back of your dictionary for a list of symbols and their meanings.

for•ma′•tion / fòr′mā shen/*n* 1, the process of starting a new organization or group. 2, the process by which something develops into a particular thing or shape.

From *The Longman Dictionary of Contemporary English*, http://www.ldoceonline.com/dictionary/formation.

HINT ◀ Online Dictionaries

There are many good online dictionaries, including those that provide a pronunciation link and a thesaurus. Some good Web sites are Longman's Online Dictionary at *ldoceonline.com* and *Dictionary.com*.

Determining Connotation and Denotation

A **denotation** is the literal meaning for a word that may be found in the dictionary. For example, the dictionary definition of *mother* is "a female parent." A **connotation** is the implied or associated meaning. It can be a cultural value judgment. For instance, the word *mother* may trigger feelings of comfort, security, anger, or resentment in a listener, depending on that person's experience with mothers.

Authors can influence readers by carefully choosing words that have specific connotations. For example, review the next two descriptions. Which one has a more negative connotation?

Terry left his family.   Andrew abandoned his family.

PRACTICE 3

Read the next passages and underline any words or phrases that have strong connotations. Discuss how the words support a personal bias.

1. Furthermore, in too many states, welfare keeps flowing while the kids are in jail, or middle-class parents continue to claim children as tax deductions even as the state pays for their upkeep in detention facilities. We must demand that parents reimburse the state for housing their failures.

    —from "Enough Is Enough" by Judy Sheindlin

2. Rohe could have chosen to give a substantive speech detailing why she believes "pre-emptive war is dangerous and wrong"—or as she so categorically put it, how she "knows" that it is. Instead she took the easy way out by insulting the speaker and throwing out some leftist chestnuts about the still missing Osama bin Laden and weapons of mass destruction. But the former would have required her to grapple with ideas; she chose to take potshots.

    —from "The Real Meaning of Courage" by Linda Chavez

From Reading to Writing

After you finish reading a selection, you could try these strategies to make sure that you have understood it.

Summarize the reading. When you summarize, you use your own words to write a condensed version of the reading. You leave out all information except for the main points. You can find a detailed explanation about summaries in Chapter 16.

Outline the reading. An outline is a visual plan of the reading that looks like an essay plan. First, you write the main idea of the essay, and then write down the most important idea from each paragraph. You could make further indentations, and under each idea, include a detail or example.

Analyze the reading. When you read, look critically at the writer's arguments and evaluate them, point by point. Also analyze how the writer builds the argument and ask yourself questions such as *Do I agree? Are the author's arguments convincing?* Then, when you write your analysis, you can break down the author's explanations and either refute or agree with them, using your own experiences and examples to support your view.

Write a response. Your instructor may ask you to write about your reaction to a reading. These are some questions you might ask yourself before you respond in writing.

* What is the writer's main point?
* What is the writer's purpose? Is the writer trying to entertain, persuade, or inform?
* Who is the audience? Is the writer directing his or her message at someone like me?
* Do I agree or disagree with the writer's main point?
* Are there any aspects of the topic to which I can relate? What are they?

After you answer the questions, you will have more ideas to use in your written response.

LO 2 Analyze reading selections.

Reading Selections

Theme: Conflict

READING 1

The *CSI* Effect

Richard Willing

Richard Willing is a journalist for *USA Today*. In the next article, he discusses the impact of crime scene shows on courtrooms across the nation.

1   Television shows such as *CSI* (Crime Scene Investigation) are affecting action in courthouses by, among other things, raising jurors' expectations of what prosecutors should produce at trial. Prosecutors, defense lawyers, and judges call it "the *CSI* effect," after the crime-scene shows that are among the hottest attractions on television. The shows feature high-tech labs and gorgeous techies. By shining a glamorous light on a gory profession, the programs also have helped to draw more students into forensic studies.

2   The programs also foster what analysts say is the mistaken notion that criminal science is fast and infallible and always gets its man. That's affecting the way lawyers prepare their cases, as well as the expectations that police

and the public place on real crime labs. Real crime-scene investigators say that because of the programs, people often have unrealistic ideas of what criminal science can deliver.

3   Many lawyers, judges, and legal consultants state they appreciate how *CSI*-type shows have increased interest in forensic evidence. "Talking about science in the courtroom used to be like talking about geometry—a real jury turnoff," says jury consultant Robert Hirschhorn of Lewisville, Texas. "Now that there's this obsession with the shows, you can talk to jurors about scientific evidence and just see from the looks on their faces that they find it fascinating."

4   But some defense lawyers remark that *CSI* and similar shows make jurors rely too heavily on scientific findings and unwilling to accept that those findings can be compromised by human or technical errors. Prosecutors also have complaints: They say the shows can make it more difficult for them to win convictions in the large majority of cases in which scientific evidence is irrelevant or absent.

5   Lawyers and judges note the *CSI* effect has become a phenomenon in courthouses across the nation. For example, in Phoenix, jurors in a murder trial noticed that a bloody coat introduced as evidence had not been tested for DNA. The jurors alerted the judge. The tests were unnecessary because, early in the trial, the defendant admitted his presence at the murder scene. The judge decided that TV had taught jurors about DNA tests but not enough about when to use them.

6   Juries are sometimes right to expect high-tech evidence. Three years ago in Richmond, Virginia, jurors in a murder trial asked the judge whether a cigarette butt found during the investigation could be tested for links to the defendant. Defense attorneys had ordered DNA tests but had not yet introduced them into evidence. The jury's hunch was correct—the tests exonerated the defendant, and the jury **acquitted** him.

acquitted: pronounced not guilty

7   The *CSI* effect is also being felt beyond the courtroom. At West Virginia University, forensic science is the most popular undergraduate major for the second year in a row, attracting 13 percent of incoming freshmen this fall. In June, supporters of an Ohio library drew an overflow crowd of 200-plus to a luncheon speech on DNA by titling it "CSI: Dayton." The Los Angeles County Sheriff's Department crime lab has seen another version of the *CSI* effect. Four technicians have left the lab for lucrative jobs as technical advisers to crime-scene programs. "They found a way to make science pay," lab director Barry Fisher says.

8   The stars of crime shows often are the equipment—DNA sequencers, mass spectrometers, photometric fingerprint illuminators, scanning electron microscopes. But the technicians run a close second. "It's 'geek chic,' the idea that kids who excel in science and math can grow up to be cool," says Robert Thompson, who teaches the history of TV programming at Syracuse

University. "This is long overdue. . . . Cops and cowboys and doctors and lawyers have been done to death."

9   Some of the science on crime shows is state-of-the-art. Real lab technicians can, for example, lift DNA profiles from cigarette butts, candy wrappers, and gobs of spit, just as their Hollywood counterparts do. But some of what's on TV is far-fetched. Real technicians don't pour caulk into knife wounds to make a cast of the weapon. That wouldn't work in soft tissue. Machines that can identify cologne from scents on clothing are still in the experimental phase. A criminal charge based on "neuro-linguistic programming"—detecting lies by the way a person's eyes shift—likely would be dismissed by a judge.

10   Real scientists feel the main problem with crime shows is this: The science is always above reproach. "You never see a case where the sample is degraded or the lab work is faulty or the test results don't solve the crime," says Dan Krane, president and DNA specialist at Forensic Bioinformatics in Fairborn, Ohio. "These things happen all the time in the real world."

MyWritingLab™

Complete additional reading comprehension questions for this selection at mywritinglab.com

Comprehension and Critical Thinking

1. Find a word in paragraph 2 that means "cultivate or advance." _____

2. What is the meaning of *exonerated* in paragraph 6?
    a. convicted   b. determined   c. cleared

3. Underline the thesis statement; that is, find a sentence that sums up the main idea of the essay.

4. In which paragraphs are there examples of the following?

    Anecdotes: _____

    Statistics: _____

    Expert opinions: _____

5. What can you infer, or guess, after closely reading paragraph 6?
    a. The defendant left a cigarette butt at the crime scene.
    b. The defendant did not leave a cigarette butt at the crime scene.
    c. The DNA proved that the defendant was at the crime scene.

6. What do lawyers and judges appreciate about crime-scene shows?

    _____

    _____

    _____

    _____

7. What problems do crime-scene shows cause for lawyers? Think of at least two answers.

_____

_____

_____

8. Crime-scene shows glamorize forensic science. How might the reality of life as a forensic scientist be different from what is shown on TV?

_____

_____

_____

_____

9. How are crime-scene shows great for science "geeks"?

_____

_____

10. Why do real scientists object to crime-scene shows?

_____

_____

_____

Writing Topics

Write about one of the following topics. Remember to explore, develop, and revise and edit your work.

1. You have just read about crime-scene shows. Think about another type of television series or movie, and describe how it influences viewers. For example, you might choose soap operas, medical dramas, or mobster movies.

2. What are the possible benefits of sitting on a jury? What effects could a criminal trial have on jury members?

READING 2

Types of Rioters

David Locher

David A. Locher is an author and college professor at Missouri Southern State College. The next excerpt about rioters is from his book _Collective Behavior_.

1   In March of 1992, Los Angeles was a city with a long history of conflict between racial groups. That year, a videotape of Rodney King being brutally beaten was shown over and over again on local, regional, and national television news reports. What almost no one realized at the time was that they were seeing an edited tape. KTLA, the Los Angeles television station that first acquired the videotape, edited out the first few seconds of the video because it was blurry. Most reporters, together with the public, saw only the edited, sixty-eight-second version of the video. They were not aware of the missing thirteen seconds, which apparently showed Rodney King charging at the police officers. The vast majority of Americans who saw the televised video believed that the beating had been totally unprovoked and that the officers were therefore guilty. The untelevised thirteen seconds were enough to convince many jurors that the beating was at least partially provoked. Legally, they believed that the beating was excessive but not sufficient grounds for conviction in a court of law.

2   The videotape created a presumption throughout the country that the officers would be found guilty. When the not guilty verdict was announced, it led to the South-Central Los Angeles riot, which was the bloodiest, deadliest, most destructive riot in modern American history. At the time the riots were beginning, no one blamed the prosecutors; most blamed the jury and the system itself. The generalized belief throughout much of the country and shared by the rioters was that guilty verdicts could not have been reached, no matter what. Participants believed that legal justice was beyond their reach, but revenge was right at hand.

3   In all riots, there are categories of participants. Five categories can be labeled ego-involved, concerned, insecure, curious spectators, and ego-detached exploiters. Each category of participant may be operating under a different generalized belief, and possibly even a different set of structural strains.

Ego-Involved

4   Ego-involved participants feel a deep connection to the concerns expressed. In Los Angeles, the ego-involved participants were the ones who felt the most empathy for Rodney King, the most hatred for the **LAPD**, and the most outrage over the verdicts. They fully accepted the generalized beliefs and believed that it was up to them to do something. These individuals placed themselves into the position of responsibility. They threw bricks or started fires because they believed that doing so would produce real change and that their violent actions were the only way to produce that change. Ego-involved participants actually started the riot. Anger, outrage, and disappointment drove their actions. They believed that those actions were necessary, desirable, or unavoidable.

LAPD:
Los Angeles Police
Department

Concerned

5   Concerned riot participants are not so personally involved. They have a more general interest in the event. The concerned participants were those who took part in the rioting, but who focused their attention on following the lead of others. They accepted the generalized belief and engaged in riotous actions, but they did so as much out of empathy with the other rioters as empathy for Rodney King. These individuals helped the ego-involved start fires, break windows, and so on. Under only slightly different circumstances, they could just as easily have followed leaders in a peaceful march. In Los Angeles, the concerned participants were acting out of hatred of the system or of authority in general. They followed the lead of the ego-involved but did not choose the course of action themselves.

Insecure

6   Insecure participants just want to be a part of something or are afraid of missing out. They may not have any understanding of the riot's causes. In this sense, they may get confused. They see others throwing objects and smashing windows, and they engage in the same behavior themselves. However, it could be that the ego-involved and concerned participants are all attacking a particular building because of what it represents, while the insecure simply smash whatever is handy. Insecure riot participants revel in the power that they feel by taking part, and they seek safety in numbers.

7   In the South-Central riot, the insecure participants went along with the actions of the others because it made them feel powerful. They were standing up to authority, spitting in the eye of society, and all from the relative safety of a large and anonymous crowd. Individuals who would never think of talking back to a police officer suddenly felt secure enough to throw rocks at them. The meek became powerful; the tame became dangerous. These participants turned the violence away from symbols of authority and toward anyone or anything that stood in the path of the crowd.

Spectators

8   In any form of collective behavior, there may be those who want to watch the actions of participants but do not wish to get directly involved. Photographs and videotaped segments of the Los Angeles riots frequently reveal more people standing around watching the action than participants. At one point during the riot, Reginald Denny, a truck driver who was passing through the area, was pulled out of his truck and nearly beaten to death by rioters. There were many more people watching the attack on Denny than there were actually hitting him. For spectators, the riot was simply an exciting form of entertainment.

9   Spectators are important for several reasons. In a deadly riot, they can frequently become targets for the hostile participants. They may also get

caught up in the excitement and decide to join the action. They may take the side of participants against police. Sometimes social control agents force them into action. Social control agents usually do not attempt to distinguish between spectators and active participants. Circumstances often make it impossible for them to do so. In Los Angeles, many spectators joined in the looting, and the police, soldiers, and guardsmen made no real attempt to distinguish between active participants and spectators. Everyone on the streets not wearing a uniform was perceived as a riot participant and treated accordingly. This sort of treatment sometimes outrages spectators to the extent that they become active in resisting social control.

Ego-Detached Exploiters

10   The ego-detached participant does not care about the issues that drive a riot. They do not accept the generalized belief shared by many other participants. They might not even know why the riot started in the first place. None of these issues matter to the ego-detached. They only want to exploit the conditions created by the riot for their own personal gain. An individual who throws a brick at a policeman might be driven by outrage over the verdicts (ego-involved), by a general hatred of the police (concerned), or by a sense of power and group identity (insecure). An individual who throws a brick at a store window to steal a television is driven by the desire for a free TV. Looting is an act of exploitation by those who are detached from the strain and generalized belief of the riot. Looters use the circumstances created by the riot to gather as many material goods as possible for themselves. No deep sense of outrage over a legal injustice drives an individual to steal a freezer. The exploiter uses the chaos, confusion, and temporary lack of social control to acquire commercial goods for free. They carry out their own personal agendas under cover of the collective episode.

11   The Los Angeles riot was literally taken over by exploiters. The pattern of destruction reveals that the targets changed within the first few hours. Rioters first attacked buildings that symbolized authority or individuals who, through their race, symbolized those with authority. By nightfall, however, they started attacking liquor stores. Before long, any business was fair game. If it could be moved, it was stolen. If it couldn't be moved, it was destroyed. The actions of the exploiters are not difficult to pick out in Los Angeles: They removed any object with any potential value before setting fire to each building. This is not the action of social revolutionaries; it is the action of greedy individuals looking to score. The passion of the ego-involved and concerned participants may fade out within a brief period of time, but the greed of the exploiters does not go away. Only the return of effective social control or the absence of anything to steal ends looting.

12   By the time a riot as big as the South-Central riot has begun, the ego-involved participants may be dramatically outnumbered by those from other

categories. This may make the entire event seem pointless or illogical to outside observers. "If they are so mad at the LAPD, why are they burning down their own houses?" was a common question asked by many Americans during the 1992 riot. These critics were overlooking the simple fact that many of the riot participants were not deeply concerned with the issues that caused the riot in the first place. Insecure participants blindly following the crowd and exploiters using the breakdown of social order for their own material gain can vastly outnumber those who actually care about the issues that caused the riot to begin in the first place. Spectators might outnumber all participants combined.

Comprehension and Critical Thinking

MyWritingLab™

Complete additional reading comprehension questions for this selection at mywritinglab.com

1. What does Locher mean by *generalized beliefs* in paragraph 4?

   _____

   _____

2. What is the meaning of *revel* as it is used in paragraph 6?
   a. feel drunk   b. enjoy   c. abuse

3. Which type of rioter simply wants to benefit materially from the riot?

   _____

4. Using your own words, briefly sum up the main characteristics of each type of rioter.

   Ego-involved: _____

   _____

   Concerned: _____

   _____

   Insecure: _____

   _____

   Spectators: _____

   _____

   Ego-detached exploiters: _____

   _____

5. Locher used emphatic order to organize his essay. Specifically, how does he organize the types of riot participants?

   _____

   _____

6. Does Locher feel that the riots were justified? You will need to infer, or read between the lines.

   _____

   _____

   _____

7. Although this is mainly a classification essay, it also touches on causes and effects of the Los Angeles riot. Briefly sum up some of the main causes and effects.

   Causes: _____

   _____

   _____

   Effects: _____

   _____

   _____

8. The author starts this essay by telling an anecdote. Why is this anecdote crucial to the main focus of the essay?

   _____

   _____

   _____

9. Who is the audience for this essay? Look closely at the tone and vocabulary.

   _____

   _____

Writing Topics

Write about one of the following topics. Remember to explore, develop, and revise and edit your work.

1. What are some types of media reports? Divide media reporting into at least three categories.

2. When an event such as a celebrity divorce, a terrorist attack, or a sports scandal occurs, how do you react? Does one topic excite your interest more than others? Discuss at least three types of audiences for media reporting.

READING 3

My Bully, My Best Friend

Yannick LeJacq

Yannick LeJacq is a freelance writer and photographer living in New York City. His work has appeared in *Kill Screen*, the *Wall Street Journal*, the *Atlantic*, and other publications. In the following essay, he relates a personal experience about bullying.

1   The first time someone called me a "faggot," I didn't hear it at all. That's because my head was being slammed against a locker, the syllables crashing together like cymbals in my ear. In the locker room after lacrosse, Fred, tall, clear-skinned, and golden, would snap at my ankles with his stick. I lived the next months in fear. Before the start of high school, I asked my brother if he could teach me how to punch somebody. But I didn't have to learn. Fred left our school. I heard his dad was seen screaming in the office about what a screw-up his son was, a detail I relished with a grim smile. Mostly, I was relieved Fred was gone, and I could stop jumping every time I heard a locker slam.

2   Life was good. It got even better when I met John during soccer practice. He was quirky; he wore the same pair of purple sweatpants to school every day, and he joked about how much he masturbated. We became best friends.

3   I was happy to have someone to sit with at lunch, but eventually John started to do something I didn't understand—he would constantly tell me I was gay. He wrote it on my textbook in biology, where we sat together, and he would whisper it while pointing at me. At that point, I was fourteen and barely knew what sex was beyond the definitions I'd gleaned from health class and pornography. But I knew that "gay" meant more than having sex with men. "Gay" was a word that boys tossed around like a hot potato, everyone hurling the insult in the vain hope it wouldn't stick to them. It was a word to be feared, but still buoyant enough not to always be taken seriously. I figured John was using it playfully, among friends, the way he would also call me "Jew."

4   A few weeks later, John invited me to join an online conference using our school's in-house e-mail system for a movie he wanted to make. The film was about one of our heavier friends, Drew, escaping from fat camp. Fat. Gay. Jew. The words were piling up, but I didn't care. I had finally wedged my foot in the door. We went over to John's house to mess around with a camera one Saturday, but all we ended up filming was Drew chasing a line of bagels rolling down the street while chanting "donut, donut, donut!" Instead,

the conference became a place to jab at each other while sitting on school computers. Eventually, John started making more of his gay jokes.

5   At first I was flattered. This was still a form of attention. And, frankly, I craved attention. But things got weird around spring break. John wrote stories about me taking little boys and animals into the woods to have sex with them and other stories about me being molested by priests and loving it.

6   Finally, I asked him to stop. The insults meant nothing, I told him in an e-mail, but I would bow out of the group. Still, I stayed up late at night at the family computer, reading and re-reading more elaborately crafted insults and waiting for the page to refresh. "Since Yannick isn't reading any more," he posted, "I can now say, 'Yannick is GAY GAY GAY GAY GAY GAY GAY GAY.'" It went on like that for a while. The other boys just laughed.

7   One morning, I checked my e-mail in the school library and saw a note from our IT adviser. He had discovered the online conference. The news spread quietly through the administration, which did its best to stop any further damage. A faculty member reminded kids during Monday announcements to be mindful of the correspondence we keep on the school's e-mail. John was identified as the ringleader and quietly whisked away for probation. I was rushed in to meet with the head of the upper school, my old lacrosse coach. He asked me that bland, unanswerable question, "Are you OK?" Tears were in his eyes as he apologized for what the school had let happen to me.

8   There's a weird tension once authorities become involved in teenage arguments. It was a relief that someone finally made it stop. But it was equally bizarre to hear our conversations reinterpreted by adults who were trying to determine the arbitrary moment when a cruel jest slid into unacceptable hatred.

9   The night the news broke at school, John's mother called me. She was livid with him, she said, and didn't understand why someone would do something like this. She couldn't say she was sorry enough. I stammered out the same response I would learn to tell everybody: "It's okay, I'm fine." Then she put John on the phone. It was the first time we'd spoken since an army of adults swarmed around us. It was the last time we would really speak for almost three years.

10   "Yannick?" John's voice was frail, as if he had barely finished crying. I thought about his parents standing above him as he sat on the couch in his living room, face buried in his palms, trying to explain things he couldn't and didn't want to. It was the same position I had been in earlier that day, the same position I would be in many times in the coming weeks. "I'm really sorry."

11   "It's okay," I said. "I'm fine."

12   "I really don't know why I did that. I don't know what I was thinking. Still friends?" he asked me.

13   "Still friends."

14   We both knew the words were hollow. I switched seats in biology, and we avoided each other. My mother called John a monster. My brother fumed about how the school needed to expel him. Everyone wanted me to be angry, but all I wanted was to have my friend back.

15   Hating Fred was much simpler. The violence of getting my head kicked into a locker is so obvious, and I could redirect it. At night, I would stare at the knife rack in my kitchen and wonder what it would be like to make one of us bleed. But John hadn't hurt me in a way I understood. So I did my best to disappear. I spent days down in the photo lab, bringing my lunch there to avoid the cafeteria. I took as many classes as I could. I pretended to search through my locker until the hallway was empty so I could walk to class alone. I tied and retied my shoes. Then the next fall, I dropped out of soccer. The coach didn't ask why.

16   John went to the varsity team and became class president. Every time he did something remotely public, someone would whisk me into an office and ask how I felt. "It's okay," I would say. "I'm fine." For a long time, I didn't hate the people in high school so much as I loathed the school itself.

17   We can gaze aghast at the horror of bullies every time a new tragedy surfaces, but asking where this violence truly comes from is much more difficult. Years later, after my school recorded its first case of cyber-bullying, the same administrator who cried in front of me in his office did his best to stop the school's Gay Straight Alliance from hosting a queer prom. Lower-school parents, he explained, had seen posters in the high school hallways and didn't want their children to be affected.

Comprehension and Critical Thinking

MyWritingLab™

Complete additional reading comprehension questions for this selection at mywritinglab.com

1. In paragraph 3, what does *gleaned* mean?
   a. joyful feeling
   b. discovered
   c. engaged in
   d. forgotten

2. How did Yannick react when he was first called "gay" by John? See paragraph 3.

   _____

3. In paragraph 4, the writer says, "I had finally wedged my foot in the door." What is he referring to in that statement?

   _____

4. How did Yannick's relationship with John evolve? List the main events of what happened from the time they first met.

_____

_____

_____

_____

_____

_____

_____

_____

5. How did Yannick respond when school authorities and then parents got involved in the conflict?

_____

_____

6. In paragraph 14, Yannick says, "We both knew the words were hollow." What words is he referring to? Also, what does he mean by _hollow_?

_____

_____

7. The writer compares his hatred of John with his hatred of Fred. What are the similarities or differences?

_____

_____

_____

8. After adults learn about the name-calling, Yannick repeatedly tells them that he is "okay." But how does his experience with being called "gay" actually affect Yannick?

_____

_____

_____

9. Find examples in paragraph 1 of imagery that appeals to the following senses. (For a detailed explanation of imagery, see pages 113–114 in Chapter 8.)

Sight: _____

_____

Sound: _____

_____

Touch: _____

_____

10. What point is the writer making in the concluding paragraph?

_____

_____

_____

_____

_____

Writing Topics

Write about one of the following topics. Remember to explore, develop, and revise and edit your work.

1. Write about a time when you felt like an outsider. What happened to make you feel that way?

2. Narrate your encounter with someone who is different from others. What did that person show you or teach you? Describe a specific incident and explain what happened.

3. What can school administrators do to reduce bullying in schools? Suggest some clear actions that schools should take.

Theme: Urban Development and Our Natural World

READING 4

....
Living Environments
....
Avi Friedman

Avi Friedman is a professor at the McGill School of Architecture. In the following article, which appeared in the *Montreal Gazette*, Friedman reflects on designing an appropriate house for the individual needs of families.

1   When invited to design a home, I first like to know what kind of dwellers my clients are. In our first meeting, I ask them to take me on a guided tour of their current residence and describe how each room is used—when and by whom. Walking through hallways, scanning the interior of rooms, peeping into closets, looking at kitchen cupboards, and pausing at family photos have helped me devise several common categories of occupants.

2   The "neat" household regards the house as a gallery. The home is spotless. The placement of every item, be it hanging artwork, a memento on a shelf, or furniture, is highly choreographed. The color scheme is coordinated and the lighting superb. It feels as if one has walked into an *Architectural Digest* magazine spread. Recent trends, professional touches, and carefully selected pieces are the marks of the place.

pragmatic:
practical

3   The "utilitarian" family is very **pragmatic**. They are minimalists, believing that they get only what they need. Environmental concerns play an important role in buying goods. The place, often painted in light tones, is sparsely decorated with very few well-selected items. Souvenirs from a recent trip are displayed, and some photos or paintings are on the wall. They will resist excess consumption and will squeeze as much use as they can from each piece.

4   The home of the "collector" family is stuffed to the brim. It is hard to find additional space for furniture or a wall area to hang a painting. Books, magazines, and weekend papers are everywhere. Newspaper cutouts and personal notes are crammed under magnets on the fridge door. The collector family seems to pay less attention to how things appear and more to comfort. Stress reduction is a motto. Being an excessively clean "show house" is not a concern. Placing dirty breakfast dishes in the sink and the morning paper in the rack before leaving home is not a priority as long as things are moving along.

5   Of course, these are only a few household types, but at the end of a house tour, I have a pretty good idea about my clients. More than the notes that I take during a meeting, these real-life images tell me all about my client's home life and desired domestic environment. When I began practicing, I quickly realized house design is about people more than architecture. As hard as I might try, I will never be able to tailor a new personality to someone by placing them in a trendy style, one that does not reflect who they really are. I can attempt to illustrate options other than their current life habits and decorating choices. But in the end, when they move into their new place, they will bring along their old habits.

6   My experience has taught me some homeowners have been trying hard to emulate lifestyles and décors that are really not theirs. The endless decorating shows on television and the many magazines that

crowd supermarket racks provide a tempting opportunity to become someone else. Some homeowners are under constant pressure, it feels, to undergo extreme makeovers and borrow rather than mature into their natural selves. They search for a readymade packaged interior style rather than discovering their own.

7   I am often at a loss when clients ask me what style I subscribe to, or solicit advice on the style they are to adopt. I reply that styles are trendy and comfort is permanent, and that they should see beyond the first day of occupancy into everyday living. Sipping a freshly brewed coffee on the back porch on a summer Sunday and letting the morning paper litter the floor while watching a squirrel on the tree across the yard is a treasured moment. It will never be able to fit into a well-defined architectural style. Home design needs to create the backdrop for such opportunities. It is these types of moments that make us enjoy life.

8   If someone wants to read, why not have a wall of books? Does someone love listening to music? Then a music room or corner should be created, even if it is not trendy. Does someone want to interact with the children? He or she might add a hobby space, even if it is outdated and cannot be found in most magazines.

9   Referring to technological advances, the renowned French architect Le Corbusier once described the home as a "machine for living." It is partially true. Home is the site where mundane and utilitarian activities take place. It is also where special moments, uniquely ours, are created and treasured.

Comprehension and Critical Thinking

MyWritingLab™

Complete additional reading comprehension questions for this selection at mywritinglab.com

1. Find a four-word expression in paragraph 4 that means "completely filled."

   _____

2. Find a word in paragraph 6 that means "to copy."

   _____

3. Underline the thesis statement.

4. Underline the topic sentences in paragraphs 2–7.

5. Paragraph 8 is missing a topic sentence. Which sentence best expresses the main idea of that paragraph?

   a. People can create a music room in their homes.

   b. Everybody should think about his or her likes and dislikes.

   c. People should create spaces in their homes to accommodate their personal interests.

   d. Hobby rooms and bookshelves can help make a home feel unique.

6. How does Friedman assess the needs of families when designing a house?

_____

_____

_____

7. What are the three categories of households that Friedman describes in this article?

_____   _____   _____

8. In your own words, describe the characteristics for each type of household.

_____

_____

_____

_____

9. a. What influences families when they choose a design for their homes?

_____

   b. Does Friedman think that such influences are positive or negative? Explain your answer.

_____

_____

_____

10. According to Friedman, what is the most important factor that home design should take into consideration?

_____

_____

Writing Topics

Write about one of the following topics. Remember to explore, develop, and revise and edit your work.

1. Use a different classification method to describe types of living environments.

2. Friedman writes, "Home is the site where mundane and utilitarian activities take place. It is also where special moments, uniquely ours, are created and treasured." Write about different categories of special or memorable moments.

READING 5

My African Childhood

David Sedaris

David Sedaris is an award-winning essayist and humorist. In the following essay, excerpted from his collection *Me Talk Pretty One Day*, Sedaris contrasts his own childhood with that of his partner, who lived in Africa.

1   When Hugh was in the fifth grade, his class took a field trip to an Ethiopian slaughterhouse. He was living in Addis Ababa at the time, and the slaughterhouse was chosen because, he says, "it was convenient." This was a school system in which the matter of proximity outweighed such petty concerns as what may or may not be appropriate for a busload of eleven-year-olds. "What?" I asked. "Were there no autopsies scheduled at the local morgue? Was the federal prison just a bit too far out of the way?"

2   Hugh defends his former school, saying, "Well, isn't that the whole point of a field trip? To see something new?"

3   "Technically yes, but . . . "

4   "All right then," he says. "So we saw some new things." One of his field trips was literally a trip to a field where the class watched a wrinkled man fill his mouth with rotten goat meat and feed it to a pack of waiting hyenas. On another occasion, they were taken to examine the bloodied bedroom curtains hanging in the palace of the former dictator. There were tamer trips, to textile factories and sugar refineries, but my favorite is always the slaughterhouse. It wasn't a big company, just a small rural enterprise run by a couple of brothers operating out of a low-ceilinged concrete building. Following a brief lecture on the importance of proper sanitation, a small white piglet was herded into the room, its dainty hooves clicking against the concrete floor. The class gathered in a circle to get a better look at the animal that seemed delighted with the attention he was getting. He turned from face to face and was looking up at Hugh when one of the brothers drew a pistol from his back pocket, held it against the animal's temple, and shot the piglet, execution-style. Blood spattered, frightened children wept, and the man with the gun offered the teacher and bus driver some meat from a freshly slaughtered goat.

5   When I'm told such stories, it's all I can do to hold back my feelings of jealousy. An Ethiopian slaughterhouse. Some people have all the luck. When I was in elementary school, the best my class and I ever got was a trip to Old Salem or Colonial Williamsburg, one of those preserved brick villages where time supposedly stands still and someone earns his living as a town crier. There was always a blacksmith, a group of wandering patriots, and a

collection of bonneted women hawking corn bread or gingersnaps made "the old fashioned way." Every now and then we might come across a doer of bad deeds serving time in the stocks, but that was generally as exciting as it got.

6   Certain events are parallel, but compared with Hugh's, my childhood was unspeakably dull. When I was seven years old, my family moved to North Carolina. When he was seven years old, Hugh's family moved to the Congo. We had a collie and a house cat. They had a monkey and two horses named Charlie Brown and Satan. I threw stones at stop signs. Hugh threw stones at crocodiles. The verbs are the same, but he definitely wins the prize when it comes to nouns and objects. An eventful day for my mother might have involved a trip to the dry cleaner or a conversation with the potato chip deliveryman. Asked one ordinary Congo afternoon what she'd done with her day, Hugh's mother answered that she and a fellow member of the Ladies' Club had visited a leper colony on the outskirts of Kinshasa. No reason was given for the expedition, though chances are she was staking it out for a future field trip.

7   Due to his upbringing, Hugh sits through inane movies never realizing that they're often based on inane television shows. There were no pokerfaced sitcom Martians in his part of Africa, no oil rich hillbillies or aproned brides trying to wean themselves from the practice of witchcraft.[1] From time to time a movie would arrive packed in a dented canister, the film scratched and faded from its slow trip around the world. The theater consisted of a few dozen folding chairs arranged before a bed sheet or the blank wall of a vacant hangar out near the airstrip. Occasionally a man would sell warm soft drinks out of a cardboard box, but that was it in terms of concessions.

8   When I was young, I went to the theater at the nearby shopping center and watched a movie about a talking Volkswagen. I believe the little car had a taste for mischief, but I can't be certain, as both the movie and the afternoon proved unremarkable and have faded from my memory. Hugh saw the same movie a few years after it was released. His family had left the Congo by this time, and they were living in Ethiopia. Like me, Hugh saw the movie by himself on a weekend afternoon. Unlike me, he left the theater two hours later to find a dead man hanging from a telephone pole at the far end of the unpaved parking lot. None of the people who'd seen the movie seemed to care about the dead man. They stared at him for a moment or two and then headed home, saying they'd never seen anything as crazy as that talking Volkswagen. His father was late picking him up, so Hugh just stood there for an hour, watching the dead man dangle and turn in the breeze. The death was not reported in the newspaper, and when Hugh related the story to his friends, they said, "You saw the movie about the talking car?"

---

[1]Sedaris is referring to *My Favorite Martian, The Beverly Hillbillies,* and *Bewitched,* popular television shows in the 1960s.

9   I could have done without the flies and the primitive theaters, but I wouldn't have minded growing up with a houseful of servants. In North Carolina, it wasn't unusual to have a once-a-week maid, but Hugh's family had houseboys, a word that never fails to charge my imagination. They had cooks and drivers, and guards who occupied a gatehouse, armed with machetes. Seeing as I had regularly petitioned my parents for an electric fence, the business with the guards strikes me as the last word in quiet sophistication. Having protection suggests that you are important. Having that protection paid for by the government is even better, as it suggests your safety is of interest to someone other than yourself.

10   Hugh's father was a career officer with the U.S. State Department, and every morning a black sedan carried him off to the embassy. I'm told it's not as glamorous as it sounds, but in terms of fun for the entire family, I'm fairly confident that it beats the sack race at the annual IBM picnic. By the age of three, Hugh was already carrying a diplomatic passport. The rules that applied to others did not apply to him. No tickets, no arrests, no luggage search: He was officially licensed to act like a brat. Being an American, it was expected of him, and who was he to deny the world an occasional tantrum?

11   They weren't rich, but what Hugh's family lacked financially they more than made up for with the sort of exoticism that works wonders at cocktail parties, leading always to the remark, "That sounds fascinating." It's a compliment one rarely receives when describing an adolescence spent drinking **Icees** at the North Hills Mall. No fifteen-foot python ever wandered onto my school's basketball court. I begged, I prayed nightly, but it just never happened. Neither did I get to witness a military **coup** in which forces sympathetic to the colonel arrived late at night to assassinate my next-door neighbor. Hugh had been at the Addis Ababa teen club when the electricity was cut off, and soldiers arrived to evacuate the building. He and his friends had to hide in the back of a jeep and cover themselves with blankets during the ride home. It's something that sticks in his mind for one reason or another.

Icees: iced drinks

coup: attempt to overthrow a government (coup d'etat)

12   Among my personal highlights is the memory of having my picture taken with Uncle Paul, the legally blind host of a Raleigh children's television show. Among Hugh's is the memory of having his picture taken with Buzz Aldrin on the last leg of the astronaut's world tour. The man who had walked on the moon placed his hand on Hugh's shoulder and offered to sign his autograph book. The man who led Wake County schoolchildren in afternoon song turned at the sound of my voice and asked, "So what's your name, princess?"

13   When I was fourteen years old, I was sent to spend ten days with my maternal grandmother in western New York State. She was a small and private woman named Billie, and though she never came right out and asked, I had the distinct impression she had no idea who I was. It was the way she looked at me, squinting through her glasses while chewing on her

lower lip. That, coupled with the fact that she never once called me by name. "Oh," she'd say, "are you still here?" She was just beginning her long struggle with Alzheimer's disease, and each time I entered the room, I felt the need to reintroduce myself and set her at ease. "Hi, it's me. Sharon's boy, David. I was just in the kitchen admiring your collection of ceramic toads." Aside from a few trips to summer camp, this was the longest I'd ever been away from home, and I like to think I was toughened by the experience.

14   About the same time I was frightening my grandmother, Hugh and his family were packing their belongings for a move to Somalia. There were no English-speaking schools in Mogadishu, so, after a few months spent lying around the family compound with his pet monkey, Hugh was sent back to Ethiopia to live with a beer enthusiast his father had met at a cocktail party. Mr. Hoyt installed security systems in foreign embassies. He and his family gave Hugh a room. They invited him to join them at the table, but that was as far as they extended themselves. No one ever asked him when his birthday was, so when the day came, he kept it to himself. There was no telephone service between Ethiopia and Somalia, and letters to his parents were sent to Washington and then forwarded on to Mogadishu, meaning that his news was more than a month old by the time they got it. I suppose it wasn't much different than living as a foreign-exchange student. Young people do it all the time, but to me it sounds awful. The Hoyts had two sons about Hugh's age who were always saying things like "Hey, that's *our* sofa you're sitting on" and "Hands off that ornamental stein. It doesn't belong to you."

A pet monkey

15   He'd been living with these people for a year when he overheard Mr. Hoyt tell a friend that he and his family would soon be moving to Munich, Germany, the beer capital of the world. "And that worried me," Hugh said, "because it meant I'd have to find some other place to live."

16   Where I come from, finding shelter is a problem the average teenager might confidently leave to his parents. It was just something that came with having a mom and a dad. Worried that he might be sent to live with his grandparents in Kentucky, Hugh turned to the school's guidance counselor, who knew of a family whose son had recently left for college. And so he spent another year living with strangers and not mentioning his birthday. While I wouldn't have wanted to do it myself, I can't help but envy the sense of **fortitude** he gained from the experience. After graduating from college, he moved to France knowing only the phrase "Do you speak French?"—a question guaranteed to get you nowhere unless you also speak the language.

fortitude: strength

17   While living in Africa, Hugh and his family took frequent vacations, often in the company of their monkey. The Nairobi Hilton, some suite of high-ceilinged rooms in Cairo or Khartoum: These are the places his people recall when gathered at a common table. "Was that the summer we spent in

Beirut or, no, I'm thinking of the time we sailed from Cyprus and took the *Orient Express* to Istanbul."

18   Theirs was the life I dreamt about during my vacations in eastern North Carolina. Hugh's family was hobnobbing with chiefs and sultans while I ate hush puppies at the Sanitary Fish Market in Morehead City, a beach towel wrapped like a hijab around my head. Someone unknown to me was very likely standing in a muddy ditch and dreaming of an evening spent sitting in a clean family restaurant, drinking iced tea and working his way through an extra-large seaman's platter, but that did not concern me, as it meant I should have been happy with what I had.

19   Rather than surrender to my bitterness, I have learned to take satisfaction in the life that Hugh has led. His stories have, over time, become my own. I say this with no trace of a **kumbaya**. There is no spiritual symbiosis; I'm just a petty thief who lifts his memories the same way I'll take a handful of change left on his dresser. When my own experiences fall short of the mark, I just go out and spend some of his. It is with pleasure that I sometimes recall the dead man's purpled face or the report of the handgun ringing in my ears as I studied the blood pooling beneath the dead white piglet. On the way back from the slaughterhouse, we stopped for Cokes in the village of Mojo, where the gas-station owner had arranged a few tables and chairs beneath a dying canopy of vines. It was late afternoon by the time we returned to school, where a second bus carried me to the foot of Coffeeboard Road. Once there, I walked through a grove of eucalyptus trees and alongside a bald pasture of starving cattle, past the guard napping in his gatehouse, and into the warm arms of my monkey.

kumbaya: the title of a spiritual song popular in the 1960s that was thought to have African ties and symbolized peace, harmony, and unity among people

Comprehension and Critical Thinking

MyWritingLab™

Complete additional reading comprehension questions for this selection at mywritinglab.com

1. What is the meaning of *inane* in paragraph 7?
    a. fascinating   b. serious   c. ridiculous

2. Find a word in paragraph 7 that means "to reduce" or "to stop."

    _____

3. Highlight the thesis statement. Remember that it may not be in the first paragraph.

4. Look in paragraph 4, and underline examples of imagery that appeal to hearing and sight.

5. How were the writer's school field trips different from Hugh's?

    _____

    _____

    _____

6. What nationality is Hugh? Look carefully at paragraph 10.

_____

7. Briefly describe the writer's childhood. Give a few details.

_____

_____

_____

8. In paragraph 13, the writer describes the summer he spent with his grandmother, and in paragraph 14, he describes Hugh's year with the Hoyt family. What are some similarities and differences in their experiences?

_____

_____

_____

_____

9. In paragraph 4, the writer describes Hugh's trip to a slaughterhouse. In paragraph 8, he describes Hugh's trip to a theater, and in paragraph 11, he discusses a military coup that Hugh witnessed. What do the anecdotes about Hugh's childhood have in common?

_____

_____

10. The writer uses humor to describe his partner's childhood. How does humor affect the reader's perception of events?

_____

_____

11. On the surface, the writer appears to envy Hugh's childhood. What is he also suggesting?

_____

_____

12. Think about the title. Why does Sedaris call this essay "My African Childhood"?

_____

_____

Writing Topics

Write about one of the following topics. Remember to explore, develop, and revise and edit your work.

1. Describe a particularly happy, exciting, or dangerous moment in your childhood. Where were you? What happened? Include imagery that appeals to the senses.

2. Reflect on how you were parented. How do you parent your own children, or how would you like to parent your future children? Compare and contrast your parenting style with the style of the people who raised you.

READING 6

Nature Returns to the Cities

John Roach

John Roach is a writer for *National Geographic*, and he has written many articles about nature. In the next essay, he describes animal life in our concrete jungles.

An urban raccoon

1   The concrete jungle isn't just for people anymore. Thirty years of good environmental stewardship combined with wildlife's innate ability to adapt has given rise to a resurgence of nature in America's urban centers. In New York City, raccoons have walked through the front door and into the kitchen to raid the refrigerator. In southern California, mountain lions have been seen cooling off under garden sprinklers and breaking into homes near Disneyland. In Chicago, beavers gnaw and fell trees and snarl traffic. In her book *Wild Nights: Nature Returns to the City,* Anne Matthews describes such incidents as she explores the resurgence of wildlife in New York and other cities. "Thirty years of environmental protection and absence of hunting [in cities] have allowed animal populations to soar," she notes.

2   The implications of the wildlife resurgence in cities vary. People may marvel at the presence of a falcon nest on the twenty-seventh floor of New York Hospital. On the other hand, some people were literally sickened to death in the fall of 2000 by the West Nile virus, which had been carried to the city by migrating birds and transmitted to mosquitoes, which passed it on to humans.

3   Overcrowded cities and urban sprawl have put more people and wild animals in proximity than at any other time in American history, says Matthews. Encounters between these two groups are beginning to exceed what scientists call the cultural carrying capacity, defined in *Wild Nights* as

"the moment humans stop saying 'Aww' and start calling 911." This change in the nature of the relationship between people and wildlife, says Matthews, is forcing people to reconsider their ethical and practical role as top predator.

4   Nature's return to U.S. cities has resulted in part from passage of the Clean Air Act in 1970 and the Clean Water Act in 1972. These laws of environmental protection that helped make air safer to breathe and water safer to drink also made cities more hospitable to wildlife, according to Matthews. After being cleaned up, New York Harbor is now home to booming populations of blue crabs and fiddler crabs, which in turn attract thousands of long-legged wading birds such as herons and egrets. With the air now cleaner, owls have flocked in growing numbers to the suburbs in search of easy prey: pets such as schnauzers, chihuahuas, and cats. In parts of the South and Midwest, forests that were logged in the nineteenth century have grown back over the last hundred years, allowing animal populations to recover. Car collisions with moose are now common along Interstate 95, the main East Coast traffic corridor. Crocodiles, who were all but erased by development pressure in Florida, are now breeding at four times their normal rate in the cooling canals of Florida's nuclear power plants.

5   Some creatures, such as rats, never really left the city. Today, an estimated 28 million rats—which are nonnative, like much of the city's human population—inhabit New York. The greater New York area is home to eight million people, which means there are more than three rats to every person. Matthews explains how it happened. "Rats are smart," she writes. "Although a fast-forward version of natural selection has made rats in many big cities immune to nearly all conventional poisons, they still may press one pack member into service as a taster; if the test rat dies, the others resolutely avoid the bait."

6   Matthews says the strong adaptive ability of nonnative species has begun to change the definition of wilderness. Rats were introduced into U.S. cities in the 1700s after arriving as stowaways on merchant ships. Zebra mussels, which have caused major problems in the Great Lakes by clogging intake pipes, were imported in the ballast water of international ships. "The most important thing is to realize that a city is wilder than we tend to imagine, and the land we think of as untouched or wild really isn't," says Matthews. "There has been so much human interference and reshaping that we really don't know what a pristine planet is." Matthews thinks people should not try to undo the effects of this increased interference with wildlife but to improve their understanding of it and continue to make room for nature in their lives.

7   Matthews says it's crucial that people consider what kind of world they want their grandchildren to inherit and act to ensure that such a world will exist. One immediate concern is what the impacts of global warming will be in fifty years. Citing the results of computer models showing future

conditions if no action is taken to mitigate global warming, Matthews says much of New York will be under water, as sea levels rise three feet. New Orleans, Louisiana, already eight feet below sea level, might become the next Atlantis. What can we do? "What you can do is as small as don't use air conditioning as much, don't use your gas-guzzling [sport utility vehicle], walk more," says Matthews. "On the macro level, urge your congressperson to do something about environmental issues."

Comprehension and Critical Thinking

1. In paragraph 1, circle a word that means "reappearance."

2. Define *prey*. Look in paragraph 4 for context clues.

   _____

3. Underline the thesis statement.

4. What are at least two reasons the writer gives for animals returning to urban environments?

   _____

   _____

   _____

   _____

5. What are at least three effects of wildlife in cities?

   _____

   _____

   _____

   _____

6. In paragraph 4, what is the writer implying?
   a. The Clean Air and Clean Water Acts did not help the environment.
   b. The Clean Air and Clean Water Acts were quite effective in helping to improve the quality of the air and water.
   c. Logging practices are much more detrimental to the environment today than they were in the past.
   d. Many dangerous predators such as crocodiles now roam the cities.

7. What is Matthews's opinion about abundant wildlife in the city?

   _____

   _____

MyWritingLab™

Complete additional reading comprehension questions for this selection at mywritinglab.com

8. What is Matthews's definition of wilderness in paragraph 6?

_____

_____

9. Although this is mainly a cause and effect essay, there are also elements of process. Which paragraph gives the readers clear steps to take to help the environment? _____

10. What incorrect assumption or belief do many people today have about the relationship between wildlife and cities?

_____

_____

_____

Writing Topics

Write about one of the following topics. Remember to explore, develop, and revise and edit your work.

1. Describe your own experiences with wildlife in your home, yard, or neighborhood. What causes or caused the bird, animal, or insect to invade your area? How does it or how did it affect you and your neighbors?

2. Do you have a pet in your home? Why or why not? Describe the causes or effects (or both) of your decision about having pets.

Theme: Inventions and Discoveries

READING 7

Marketing New Inventions

Robert Rodriguez

Robert Rodriguez is a journalist for McClatchy Newspapers. In the next essay, he lists some problems that can occur when someone tries to market a new invention.

1   When a Fresno mother-and-daughter duo's idea for a hide-and-seek doll made it onto the shelves of one of the nation's largest toy stores, they felt as if they had won the lottery. Shelly Conte and her mother, Cindy Reichman, were riding high. Their patented Hide-N-Seek Hayley doll was being sold at Toys R Us stores nationwide, becoming a top seller during the 2005 holiday season. "I remember someone telling us that we were going to be millionaires," said Ms. Conte. "And I was thinking about it, no doubt." But

the pair's dreams of fame and fortune began to unravel about a year later when a major player in the industry put a new spin on its popular Care Bear by introducing a hide-and-seek version. It soon edged out Hide-N-Seek Hayley, whose sales began to plummet. Business experts say that in a fiercely competitive market for new products, copycats and timing all play a part in whether a new product stays on a store's shelves or is relegated to the bargain bin. To survive, an entrepreneur must be market savvy, develop brand loyalty, and "sleep with one eye open."

The Hula-Hoop

2   "This can be a very tough business, and knockoff products are commonplace," said Tim Walsh, a Florida-based toy inventor and author of *Timeless Toys*, a book that looks at classic toys and the people who created them. "The problem is that success often prompts others to want in on what you are doing." Mr. Walsh said a classic example is the Hula-Hoop. The name was trademarked in 1958 by Wham-O, but it didn't stop others from cashing in on the plastic hoop's popularity. Mr. Walsh estimated over the years Wham-O has kept only a quarter of the market.

3   Inventors say they never rest easy: The possibility of a much larger competitor taking them out is always a chief concern. "I know I could wake up one day, and it could all be gone," said Kathleen Whitehurst, who is co-inventor of DaysAgo, a digital day-counter that attaches to food containers and measures freshness of refrigerated products. "It is a cruel world out there, and that's why you have to cover all your bases." Part of Ms. Whitehurst's strategy was to get her product distributed in foreign markets, where copycats often spring up. The DaysAgo counter is sold in the United States, Canada, Sweden, Norway, Iceland, Australia, and Japan. "You basically have to get out there first and establish yourself as the recognizable brand," she says. "But you are never safe. You just have to keep pedaling as fast as you can." Jennifer Barney, a Fresno mom who created Barney Butter, an almond spread, credits her survival to maintaining strong relationships with the grocery stores that carry her product. She holds product demonstrations in as many of the stores as she can. It is exhausting because her butter is sold in six states and 106 stores.

4   Rookie inventors Reichman and Conte said their tumble from Toys R Us taught them many hard lessons; the most sobering is that patents don't always protect inventors from copycats. Shocked and frustrated by their abrupt sales slide, the team terminated their contract last year with Hayley's manufacturer, the Kid-riffic toy company in St. Louis, which they fault for a lack of promotion. "We are almost in the exact same position we were eight years ago, when we started this idea," Ms. Reichman said. "We should not be in this position. This was a once-in-a-lifetime chance for us, and look at what's happened." They considered suing Play Along, the Florida-based Care Bear makers, but backed off after a lawyer specializing in such cases advised that they didn't have a strong enough case. Their patent attorney, Richard

Ryan, says Play Along was careful not to copy the name "Hayley" or the specific technology used by the doll to play hide and seek.

5   Mike Summers, director of technology development and commercialization at California State University, said bringing an idea to the marketplace can be daunting for inventors who lack the experience and knowledge. An inventor himself, Summers developed a lifesaving device that inflates when hurled into water. Rather than compete head-to-head with much larger companies that also produce lifesaving devices, he approached the No. 2 player in the market. After some negotiation, that company agreed to buy his idea. "Sometimes the collaborative route is the easier route to take," Summers said. The "enemy" could end up being a best friend.

MyWritingLab™

Complete additional reading comprehension questions for this selection at mywritinglab.com

Comprehension and Critical Thinking

1. In paragraph 4, what does *sobering* mean?
    a. discouraging   c. falling
    b. abstaining from alcohol   d. reliable

2. Find a word in paragraph 5 that means "thrown." _____

3. Underline the thesis statement in the introduction.

4. What is the essay illustrating?
    a. the reasons to invent a new product
    b. great marketing success stories
    c. examples of successes and failures of new products
    d. the value of patenting a product

5. In paragraph 3, what is the meaning of the expression "You just have to keep pedaling as fast as you can"?

    _____

    _____

6. Explain what happened to each of the following products.

    Hide-N-Seek Hayley: _____

    _____

    Hula-Hoop: _____

    _____

    DaysAgo Counter: _____

    _____

Barney Butter: _____

_____

7. According to the essay, which product is most widely distributed?

   a. Hide-N-Seek Hayley   b. DaysAgo counter   c. Barney Butter

8. What are the main problems that can occur when you try to market a new product?

_____

_____

9. What are possible problems with patents, according to paragraph 4?

_____

_____

10. What did Mike Summers do with his inflatable lifesaving device?

_____

Writing Topics

Write about one of the following topics. Remember to explore, develop, and revise and edit your work.

1. List some of your greatest successes or your worst mistakes. Provide specific details about each event.

2. What are some of the most useful or useless inventions that humans have developed? Think about products that you love or hate.

READING 8

Brands R Us

Stephen Garey

Stephen Garey is a writer and a former advertising industry creative executive. He has published many articles about consumption and the environment. In the following essay, he makes a powerful argument about advertising.

1   Most people don't believe, don't remember, and don't think about advertising. Focus groups and other forms of testing have proven time and time again that the majority of ads are inefficient and ineffective. Indeed, it's been estimated that some 80–85 percent of all advertising is neither consciously "seen" nor remembered by the consuming public. Within a

few minutes after being exposed to an advertising message and brand, consumers have a hard time remembering the message *or* the brand that delivered it!

2   And yet, there's a direct connection between an individual's level of exposure to advertising and levels of product consumption. How can this be? If advertising is largely ineffective, if most advertising is neither seen nor remembered by most people, and if—two minutes after being exposed to a particular message or brand—consumers can't remember the brand or the message, then where's the connection? How does something so seemingly **benign** and banal impact consumption patterns and habits?

benign: harmless

3   While we may not be paying much attention to each and every individual message that comes our way, the collective effect of all this advertising is quite powerful. All during our waking hours, some 3,000 to 5,000 messages per day *per individual* are instructing us to Buy, Buy, Buy and Buy Some More. Sometimes these messages are delivered quietly. Many times the advertisers shout them from the rooftops. But no matter how these messages are delivered to us—and as much as we might tend to consider advertising mere background or "wallpaper" in our day-to-day lives—there's little doubt that advertising *as a whole* strongly influences overall consumer behavior. In other words, by itself, the advertising for Hyundai automobiles has little effect upon one's personal life. But Hyundai ads combined with Apple Computer ads, Tide detergent TV commercials, Chivas Regal outdoor boards, GE television program sponsorships, and Johnson's Floor Wax coupons in the Sunday newspaper—not to mention the specials down each and every aisle at the local department store or supermarket—have a very powerful *collective* effect indeed.

4   Because advertising is generally so lighthearted and entertaining, this collective messaging practically gives us permission to ignore the long-term consequences of our daily purchasing decisions. The almost comedic presentation of most advertising carries with it the underlying suggestion that we shouldn't take any of it too seriously.

5   But we should . . . and we must.

6   At one time, advertising's collective message to buy—and to replace what we have rather than repair what we have—served us well. When we were far fewer in numbers, when nations and communities were growing and businesses large and small were trying to build their customer base, consumption of goods in high volume was not only desirable, it was also respectable. But our population has exploded, and we're no longer naïve about the hazards of our consumer culture. It's all too clear that advertising's collective power and our collective responses to it over time

have had a profound, often adverse, impact upon people's lives and the planet we all share.

7   **Wanton** consumption now presents serious dangers to our health and well-being. It's a way of life that has outlived its usefulness, and what needs to change is *us*, not the advertising that influences us. We need to change our view of advertising as a banal and benign medium and fully recognize its powerful, collective effect.

wanton: unrestrained

8   We most certainly need to reduce consumption, and one of the first steps we can take towards consuming fewer unnecessary goods is to consume less advertising. Keep counters in the kitchen free of brand names; use unbranded containers. Take the roads less traveled: Use local streets at the edge of town and the old back highways as a way of avoiding exposure to commercial clutter. Steer clear of T-shirt advertising: Why should you be a walking, unpaid billboard? Watch less commercial television; listen to less commercial radio. Implementing just one or two of these suggestions can help you consume less advertising and, in turn, fewer products. And that's the whole idea.

Comprehension and Critical Thinking

MyWritingLab™

Complete additional reading comprehension questions for this selection at mywritinglab.com

1. What is the meaning of *adverse* in paragraph 6?

    _____

2. Who is the audience for this essay?

    _____

3. There is no clear thesis in the opening paragraphs. Instead, the writer builds his argument. Using your own words, describe the main point, or thesis, of the essay.

    _____

    _____

    _____

4. What is the main point of paragraph 3?

    _____

    _____

5. How does listing so many brand names in paragraph 3 help the writer's argument?

    _____

    _____

6. The writer mentions that advertising in the past had a positive effect. What was it?

    _____

    _____

7. In paragraphs 6 and 7, the writer says that overconsumption presents serious dangers to our health and our planet. Infer or guess what dangers he is referring to.

    _____

    _____

8. List at least three steps that consumers should take to reduce the negative effect of advertising.

    _____

    _____

9. How does the writer conclude the essay?
    a. prediction   b. suggestion   c. quotation

Writing Topics

Write about one of the following topics. Remember to explore, develop, and revise and edit your work.

1. Should advertising aimed at children be banned? Explain your answer.

2. Kalle Lasn, founder of *Adbusters* magazine, says, "Advertisements are the most prevalent and toxic of the mental pollutants." Agree or disagree with this statement. Develop your argument with specific examples.

3. Many brands have cult-like devotees. For example, Apple computers and Harley Davidson motorcycles have fanatic followers. Describe someone who is a "brand fan," and explain which brands that person loves. Another option is to choose some major brands, and describe the types of people who love those brands.

READING 9

· ·

Can We Talk?

· ·

Josh Freed

Josh Freed is an award-winning columnist for the *Montreal Gazette*. Freed has published many books, including *Fear of Frying and Other Fax of Life*. In this essay, Freed ponders technology and privacy.

1   We keep hearing that technology is destroying our privacy by spreading our personal information on the Web—from our credit card passwords to our naked beach photos on Facebook. But technology is also creating more privacy than we've ever had and probably more than we need.

2   Phoning friends has become a more isolating experience. For much of my life, I called my friends at home and never knew who'd pick up the phone. I might end up talking to their spouse or their kids or their cleaning person. I would have interesting, unexpected chats. But during the last couple of years, I barely remember my friends' home numbers. I just call their cell phones, which they answer immediately. As a result, I never have random chats with whoever else answers because no one else does. Even when I do call friends' homes, I get an answering machine because family members see my name flashing and know it's not for them, so they don't answer. It's all more efficient, but it has practically wiped out my chance personal conversations and shrunk my sense of community.

3   In our new technology-tailored world, it's rarer and rarer to have an unexpected conversation with people we don't know well. In recent years, bank machines have ended our chats with tellers, while the phone operator has long vanished, replaced by PRESS 1 machines. It is the same when we phone offices. In the past, I used to speak with personal secretaries whom I would gradually get to know. But now a voice machine answers instead. An hour later, the person returns my call and leaves a message, and later I call and leave one for that person. By the time we're through messaging, we have said what we have needed to say and don't end up speaking with one another.

4   When we travel, it is increasingly difficult to have a good yak with a stranger because technology gets in the way. On airplanes, no one talks to his or her seatmate anymore. We're all too busy watching our little television screens. Everyone is wearing earphones, so our seatmates won't hear us even if we shout, "The plane is on fire!" Cabbies used to be great chatterers; they were armchair experts on everything from traffic jams to politics in their native lands. But now they always yak on their cell phones, using hands-free headsets, while I yak on mine. Ask them a question, and they'll say, "I am very sorry, sir, but I am talking to my mother in Cairo here." Taxis are even more isolating in New York where most now have passenger TVs, so I end up watching my own screen in back while the driver chats privately up front. I don't even talk at the end of the ride. I just slide my credit card along the bottom of the TV screen and then leave—with barely a word spoken between us. We may as well have robot-taxis, which would probably be chattier. "Welcome to Robo-Cab. Please state your destination."

5   The future looks even more private and isolating. Most teens don't even talk to their own friends on

the phone anymore—they text. They don't hang out in streets or parks together—they gather online where they only chat with those they choose. We adults aren't much better. We don't call office colleagues anymore to chat about work decisions. We e-mail them to avoid conversation because less time is lost in random chatter.

6   Something else is lost as we live more insular and isolated lives. We walk in crowds of people, all talking on cell phones, while ignoring those around us; we listen to iPods, isolated in our own soundtracks; we stare at iPhones and iPads, lost in our own world and literally screening out those beside us. The irony is that we are eliminating the idea of "long distance" phone calls, as rates to faraway countries fall drastically. But we are putting long distance into the relationships in our own lives.

7   For now, home landlines and accidental conversations still exist, but cell phone companies are advertising 2,500-minute monthly plans and soon they'll be 50,000 minutes. Eventually the idea of a shared family phone will be history. We will all get our own cell phones at two years old and live in our own private cells.

MyWritingLab™

Complete additional reading comprehension questions for this selection at mywritinglab.com

Comprehension and Critical Thinking

1. In paragraph 3, what does "technology-tailored world" mean?

    make for specific conditions

2. Look in paragraphs 2 and 4, and underline three slang words. Suggest standard alternatives for those words.

    _____

    _____

3. Highlight the thesis statement.

4. List some examples of technology the author gives that prevent us from communicating with strangers.

    _____

5. According to the author, what is the difference between how people used phones in the past and how they use phones in the present?

    Personal conversation, in the past
    we used to talk with everybody in
    the family

6. According to the author, how has travel become an isolating experience? Give two examples.

Everyone is wearing earphones.

Everyone is on their cell phone.

7. In paragraph 6, the author states, "But we are putting long distance into the relationships in our own lives." What does he mean by that statement?

People don't interact between them

No more talks

8. How does the author think our future communication with others will change?

No more share family share, Everyone will get their own

9. What is the author's attitude toward his subject? Cell phone at two years old

10. Irony conveys the opposite meaning of what is stated or intended. What is ironic about the way technology affects our lives?

We are eliminate the idea of long distance phone call, But people are putting long distance into the relationships in own lives.

Writing Topics

1. List some ways in which technology has changed the world.

2. How has technology made your life better or worse? Provide specific examples.

Theme: Travel and Survival

READING 10

The Rules of Survival

Laurence Gonzales

Laurence Gonzales won the National Magazine Award in 2001 and 2002. His work has appeared in such publications as *Harper's*, *National Geographic Adventure*, and *Smithsonian Air and Space*, just to name a few. The next excerpt is from his latest book, *Deep Survival*.

1   As a journalist, I've been writing about accidents for more than thirty years. In the last fifteen or so years, I've concentrated on accidents in outdoor recreation in an effort to understand who lives, who dies, and why. To my surprise, I found an eerie uniformity in the way people survive seemingly impossible circumstances. Decades and sometimes centuries apart, separated by culture, geography, race, language, and tradition, the most successful survivors—those who practice what I call "deep survival"—go through the same patterns of thought and behavior, the same transformation and spiritual discovery, in the course of keeping themselves alive. It doesn't seem to matter whether they are surviving being lost in the wilderness or battling cancer; the strategies remain the same.

2   Survival should be thought of as a journey or vision quest of the sort that Native Americans have had as a rite of passage for thousands of years. Once people pass the precipitating event—for instance, they are cast away at sea or told they have cancer—they are enrolled in one of the oldest schools in history. Here are a few things I've learned about survival.

Stay Calm

3   In the initial crisis, survivors are not ruled by fear; instead, they make use of it. Their fear often feels like (and turns into) anger, which motivates them and makes them feel sharper. Aron Ralston, the hiker who had to cut off his hand to free himself from a stone that had trapped him in a slot canyon in Utah, initially panicked and began slamming himself over and over against the boulder that had caught his hand. But very quickly he stopped himself, did some deep breathing, and began thinking about his options. He eventually spent five days progressing through the stages necessary to convince him of what decisive action he had to take to save his own life.

Think, Analyze, and Plan

4   Survivors quickly organize, set up routines, and institute discipline. When Lance Armstrong was diagnosed with cancer, he organized his fight against it the way he would organize his training for a race. He read everything he could about it, put himself on a training schedule, and put together a team from among friends, family, and doctors to support his efforts. Such conscious, organized effort in the face of grave danger requires a split between reason and emotion in which reason gives direction and emotion provides the power source. Survivors often report experiencing reason as an audible "voice."

5   Steve Callahan, a sailor and boat designer, was rammed by a whale, and his boat sunk while he was on a solo voyage in 1982. Adrift in the Atlantic for seventy-six days on a five-and-a-half-foot raft, he experienced his survival voyage as taking place under the command of a "captain" who

gave him his orders and kept him on his water ration, even as his own mutinous (emotional) spirit complained. His captain routinely lectured "the crew." Thus under strict control, he was able to push away thoughts that his situation was hopeless and take the necessary first steps of the survival journey: to think clearly, analyze his situation, and formulate a plan.

Celebrate Every Victory

6   Survivors take great joy from even their smallest successes. This attitude helps keep motivation high and prevents a lethal plunge into hopelessness. It also provides relief from the unspeakable strain of a life-threatening situation.

7   Lauren Elder was the only survivor of a light plane crash in the High Sierra. Stranded on a 12,000 foot peak, one arm broken, she could see the San Joaquin Valley in California below, but a vast wilderness and sheer and icy cliffs separated her from safety. Wearing a wrap-around skirt and blouse but no underwear, with two-inch heeled boots, she crawled "on all fours, doing a kind of sideways spiderwalk," as she put it later, "balancing myself on the ice crust, punching through it with my hands and feet." She had thirty-six hours of climbing ahead of her—a seemingly impossible task. But Elder allowed herself to think only as far as the next big rock. Once she had completed her descent of the first pitch, Elder said that she looked up at the impossibly steep slope and thought, "Look what I've done! Exhilarated, I gave a whoop that echoed down the silent pass." Even with a broken arm, joy was Elder's constant companion. A good survivor always tells herself, "Count your blessings—you're alive."

Enjoy the Survival Journey

8   It may seem counterintuitive, but even in the worst circumstances, survivors find something to enjoy, some way to play and laugh. Survival can be tedious, and waiting itself is an art. Elder found herself laughing out loud when she started to worry that someone might see up her skirt as she climbed. Even as Callahan's boat was sinking, he stopped to laugh at himself as he clutched a knife in his teeth like a pirate while trying to get into his life raft. And Viktor Frankl ordered some of his companions in **Auschwitz** who were threatening to give up hope to force themselves to think of one funny thing each day. Singing, playing mind games, reciting poetry, and doing mathematical problems can make waiting tolerable, while heightening perception and quieting fear.

Auschwitz: a Nazi concentration camp

Never Give Up

9   Yes, you might die. In fact, you will die—we all do. But perhaps it doesn't have to be today. Don't let it worry you. Forget about rescue. Everything you

need is inside you already. Dougal Robertson, a sailor who was cast away at sea for thirty-eight days after his boat sank, advised thinking of survival this way: "Rescue will come as a welcome interruption of . . . the survival voyage." One survival psychologist calls that "resignation without giving up. It is survival by surrender."

10   Survivors are not easily discouraged by setbacks. They accept that the environment is constantly changing and know that they must adapt. When they fall, they pick themselves up and start the entire process over again, breaking it down into manageable bits. When *Apollo 13*'s oxygen tank exploded, apparently dooming the crew, Commander Jim Lovell chose to keep on transmitting whatever data he could back to mission control, even as they burned up on re-entry. Elder and Callahan were equally determined and knew this final truth: If you're still alive, there is always one more thing that you can do.

MyWritingLab™

Complete
additional reading
comprehension questions
for this selection at
mywritinglab.com

Comprehension and Critical Thinking

1. What is the meaning of *precipitating* in paragraph 2?
   a. ending   b. unexpected   c. initiating or triggering

2. In paragraph 7, what is the meaning of *pitch*?
   a. throw   b. slope   c. tone

3. How does the author introduce the text?
   a. general background   c. anecdote
   b. historical background   d. contrasting position

4. In this process essay, the author describes the experiences of several survivors. Briefly explain what challenge the following people faced.

   Aron Ralston: _____

   _____

   Lance Armstrong: _____

   _____

   Lauren Elder: _____

   _____

   Viktor Frankl: _____

   _____

   Dougal Robertson: _____

   _____

5. a. What do most of the stories of survival have in common? What kinds of threats were they surviving?

    _____

    _____

    b. How is Frankl's journey different from those of the others mentioned in the essay?

    _____

    _____

6. This process essay also uses narration and cause and effect. What are some of the effects of positive thinking while in a dangerous situation?

    _____

    _____

7. What is the author's specific purpose?

    _____

    _____

8. Who was probably the targeted audience for this essay?
    a. an academic or intellectual audience   c. a general audience
    b. children

    Give some reasons for your choice.

    _____

    _____

9. What lessons does this essay have for the reader?

    _____

    _____

    _____

10. Using your own words, explain why it is important to enjoy the survival journey.

    _____

    _____

Writing Topics

Write about one of the following topics. Remember to explore, develop, and revise and edit your work.

1. Describe a difficult physical ordeal that you or someone you know went through. What happened? What steps were taken to get through the ordeal?

2. Explain the steps people should take when they have an emotional crisis. For example, how can they survive a breakup, a public humiliation, or the loss of a friend?

READING 11

Into Thin Air

Jon Krakauer

Jon Krakauer is a mountaineer and writer. In his memoir, *Into Thin Air*, Krakauer recounts the tragic tale of the 1996 Mount Everest climbing expedition in which he participated. During this expedition, many people who were Krakauer's climbing companions died when a sudden ferocious storm engulfed them. The next reading is an excerpt from Krakauer's best-selling book.

1   The literature of Everest is rife with accounts of hallucinatory experiences attributable to hypoxia and fatigue. In 1933, the noted English climber Frank Smythe observed "two curious looking objects floating in the sky" directly above him at 27,000 feet: "[One] possessed what appeared to be squat underdeveloped wings, and the other a protuberance suggestive of a beak. They hovered motionless but seemed slowly to pulsate." In 1980, during his solo ascent, Reinhold Messner imagined that an invisible companion was climbing beside him. Gradually, I became aware that my mind had gone haywire in a similar fashion, and I observed my own slide from reality with a blend of fascination and horror.

2   I was so far beyond ordinary exhaustion that I experienced a queer detachment from my body, as if I were observing my descent from a few feet overhead. I imagined that I was dressed in a green cardigan and wingtips. And although the gale was generating a windchill in excess of seventy below zero Fahrenheit, I felt strangely and disturbingly warm.

Climber on Mount Everest

3   At 6:30, as the last of the daylight seeped from the sky, I'd descended to within 200 vertical feet of Camp Four. Only one obstacle now stood between me and safety: a bulging incline of hard, glassy ice that I would have to descend without a rope. Snow pellets borne by 70-knot gusts stung my face; any exposed flesh was instantly frozen. The tents, no more than 650 horizontal feet away, were only intermittently visible through the whiteout. There was no margin for error. Worried about making a critical blunder, I

marshal: gather

sat down to **marshal** my energy before descending further.

4   Once I was off my feet, inertia took hold. It was so much easier to remain at rest than to summon the initiative to tackle the dangerous ice

slope. I just sat there as the storm roared around me, letting my mind drift, doing nothing for perhaps forty-five minutes.

5   I'd tightened the drawstrings on my hood until only a tiny opening remained around my eyes, and I was removing the useless, frozen oxygen mask from beneath my chin when Andy Harris suddenly appeared out of the gloom beside me. Shining my headlamp in his direction, I reflexively recoiled when I saw the appalling condition of his face. His cheeks were coated with an armor of frost, one eye was frozen shut, and he was slurring his words badly. He looked in serious trouble. "Which way to the tents?" Andy blurted, frantic to reach shelter.

6   I pointed in the direction of Camp Four, and then warned him about the ice just below us. "It is steeper than it looks!" I yelled, straining to make myself heard over the tempest. "Maybe I should go down first and get a rope from camp—." As I was in midsentence, Andy abruptly turned away and moved over the lip of the ice slope, leaving me sitting there dumbfounded.

7   Scooting on his butt, he started down the steepest part of the incline. "Andy," I shouted after him, "it's crazy to try it like that! You're going to blow it for sure!" He yelled something back, but his words were carried off by the screaming wind. A second later he lost his purchase, flipped ass over teakettle, and was suddenly rocketing headfirst down the ice.

8   Two hundred feet below, I could just make out Andy's motionless form slumped at the foot of the incline. I was sure he'd broken at least a leg, or maybe his neck. But then, incredibly, he stood up, waved that he was okay, and started lurching toward Camp Four, which at the moment was in plain sight, 500 feet beyond.

9   My backpack held little more than three empty oxygen canisters and a pint of frozen lemonade; it probably weighed no more than sixteen or eighteen pounds. But I was tired and worried about getting down the incline without breaking a leg, so I tossed the pack over the edge and hoped it would come to rest where I could retrieve it. Then I stood up and started down the ice, which was as smooth and hard as the surface of a bowling ball.

10   Fifteen minutes of dicey, fatiguing **crampon** work brought me safely to the bottom of the incline where I easily located my pack, and another ten minutes after that I was in camp myself. I lunged into my tent with my crampons still on, zipped the door tight, and sprawled across the frost-covered floor too tired to even sit upright. For the first time I had a sense of how wasted I was: I was more exhausted than I'd ever been in my life. But I was safe.

crampon: steel spikes attached to the soles of mountain-climbing boots to create a better grip on ice and prevent slipping

MyWritingLab™

Complete additional reading comprehension questions for this selection at mywritinglab.com

Comprehension and Critical Thinking

1. In paragraph 1, *protuberance* means

    a.   a bulge   b.   a disturbance   c.   a bird

2. In paragraph 3, what is the meaning of *blunder?*

    _____

3. What type of narration is used in this essay?
    a. first-person   b. third-person

4. What can you infer or guess about Krakauer's personality?

    _____

    _____

5. In your own words, sum up the story in a couple of sentences. Answer who, what, when, where, why, and how questions.

    _____

    _____

    _____

6. Describe the author's physical and mental state at the beginning of the essay.

    _____

    _____

7. What were some obstacles that the narrator faced during his descent to Camp Four?

    _____

    _____

    _____

8. This excerpt contains examples of imagery (description using the senses). Give examples of imagery that appeal to touch, sight, and hearing.

    touch: _____

    _____

    sight: _____

    _____

    hearing: _____

    _____

9. Which organizational method does the author use in this essay?
    a. time order   b. space order   c. emphatic order

10. The author uses dialogue in this essay. What is the purpose of the dialogue?

_____

_____

Writing Topics

Write about one of the following topics. Remember to explore, develop, and revise and edit your work.

1. Have you or someone you know participated in a risky activity? What happened? Include descriptive details that appeal to the senses.

2. In Krakauer's story, he describes his reactions during a challenging moment from his past. Think about a time when you felt extremely excited, ashamed, or moved. Where were you and what were you doing? Describe what happened, and include descriptive details.

READING 12

Slum Tourism

Eric Weiner

Eric Weiner is the author of *The Geography of Bliss: One Grump's Search for the Happiest Places in the World.* In his essay, Weiner analyzes slum tourism.

1   Michael Cronin's job as a college admissions officer took him to India two or three times a year, so he had already seen the usual sites— temples, monuments, and markets—when one day he happened across a flier advertising slum tours. "It just resonated with me immediately," said Mr. Cronin, who was staying at the posh Taj Hotel in Mumbai where, he noted, a bottle of champagne cost the equivalent of two years' salary for many Indians. "But I didn't know what to expect," he said.

2   Soon, Mr. Cronin, forty-one years old, found himself skirting open sewers and ducking to avoid exposed electrical wires as he toured the sprawling Dharavi slum, home to more than a million. He joined a cricket game and saw small-scale industry, from embroidery to tannery, which quietly thrives in the slum. "Nothing is considered garbage there," he said. "Everything is used again." Mr. Cronin was briefly shaken when a man, "obviously drunk," rifled through his pockets, but the two-and-a-half-hour tour changed his image of India. "Everybody in the slum wants to work, and everybody wants to make themselves better," he said.

3   Slum tourism, or "poorism," as some call it, is catching on. From the shantytowns of Rio de Janeiro to the townships of Johannesburg to the garbage dumps of Mexico, tourists are forsaking, at least for a while, beaches and museums for crowded, dirty—and in many ways surprising—slums. When a British man named Chris Way founded Reality Tours and Travel in Mumbai two years ago, he could barely **muster** enough customers for one tour a day. Now, he's running two or three a day and recently expanded to rural areas.

muster: gather
together

4   Slum tourism isn't for everyone. Critics charge that ogling the poorest of the poor isn't tourism at all. It's voyeurism. The tours are exploitative, these critics say, and have no place on an ethical traveler's itinerary. "Would you want people stopping outside of your front door every day, or maybe twice a day, snapping a few pictures of you and making some observations about your lifestyle?" asked David Fennell, a professor of tourism and environment at Brock University in Ontario. Slum tourism, he says, is just another example of tourism finding a new niche to exploit. The real purpose, he believes, is to make Westerners feel better about their station in life. "It affirms in my mind how lucky I am—or how unlucky they are," he states.

Slum in São Paulo, Brazil

5   Not so fast, proponents of slum tourism say. Ignoring poverty won't make it go away. "Tourism is one of the few ways that you or I are ever going to understand what poverty means," says Harold Goodwin, director of the International Center for Responsible Tourism in Leeds, England. "To just kind of turn a blind eye and pretend that poverty doesn't exist seems to me a very denial of our humanity." The crucial question, Mr. Goodwin and other experts say, is not whether slum tours should exist but how they are conducted. Do they limit the excursions to small groups, interacting respectfully with residents? Or do they travel in buses, snapping photos from the windows as if on safari?

6   Many tour organizers are sensitive to charges of exploitation. Some encourage—and in at least one case require—participants to play an active role in helping residents. A church group in Mazatlán, Mexico, runs tours of the local garbage dump where scavengers earn a living picking through trash, some of it from nearby luxury resorts. The group doesn't charge anything but asks participants to help make sandwiches and fill bottles with filtered water. The tours have proven so popular that during high season the church group has to turn people away. "We see ourselves as a bridge to connect the tourists to the real world," said Fred Collom, the minister who runs the tours.

7   By most accounts, slum tourism began in Brazil sixteen years ago, when a young man named Marcelo Armstrong took a few tourists into Rocinha, Rio de Janeiro's largest favela, or shantytown. His company, Favela Tour, grew and spawned half a dozen imitators. Today, on any given day in Rio, dozens of tourists hop in minivans, then motorcycles, and venture into

places even Brazil's police dare not tread. Organizers insist the tours are safe, though they routinely check security conditions. Luiz Fantozzi, founder of the Rio-based Be a Local Tours, says that about once a year he cancels a tour for security reasons.

8   The tours may be safe, but they can be tense. Rajika Bhasin, a lawyer from New York, recalls how, at one point during a favela tour, the guide told everyone to stop taking pictures. A young man approached the group, smiling and holding a cocked gun. Ms. Bhasin said she didn't exactly feel threatened, "just very aware of my surroundings, and aware of the fact that I was on this guy's turf." Still, she said, the experience, which included visiting galleries featuring the work of local artists, was positive. "Honestly, I would say it was a life-changing experience," Ms. Bhasin said. Saying she understood the objections, she **parried**, "It has everything to do with who you are and why you're going."

parried: replied

9   Chuck Geyer, of Reston, Virginia, arrived for a tour in Mumbai armed with hand sanitizer and the expectation of human misery incarnate. He left with a changed mind. Instead of being solicited by beggars, Mr. Geyer found himself the recipient of gifts: fruit and dye to smear on his hands and face as people celebrated the Hindu festival of Holi. "I was shocked at how friendly and gracious these people were," Mr. Geyer said.

10   Proponents of slum tourism say that's the point: to change the reputation of the slums one tourist at a time. Tour organizers say they provide employment for local guides and a chance to sell souvenirs. Chris Way has vowed to put 80 percent of his profits back into the Dharavi slum. The catch, though, is that Mr. Way's company has yet to earn a profit on the tours, for which he charges 300 rupees (around $7.50). After receiving flak from the Indian press ("a fair criticism," Mr. Way **concedes**), he used his own money to open a community center in the slum. It offers English classes, and Mr. Way himself mentors a chess club. Many of those running favela tours in Brazil also channel a portion of their profits into the slums. Luiz Fantozzi contributes to a school and day-care center.

concedes: acknowledges

11   But slum tourism isn't just about charity, its proponents say; it also fosters an entrepreneurial spirit. "At first, the tourists were **besieged** by beggars, but not anymore," said Kevin Outterson, a law professor from Boston who has taken several favela tours. Mr. Fantozzi has taught people, Mr. Outterson said, "that you're not going to get anything from my people by begging, but if you make something, people are going to buy it."

besieged: overtaken

12   Even critics of slum tourism concede it allows a few dollars to trickle into the shantytowns but say that's no substitute for development programs. Mr. Fennell, the professor of tourism in Ontario, wonders whether the relatively minuscule tourist revenue can make a difference. "If you're so concerned about helping these people, then write a check," he said.

MyWritingLab™

Complete
additional reading
comprehension questions
for this selection at
mywritinglab.com

Comprehension and Critical Thinking

1. In paragraph 3, what is the meaning of *forsaking*? Read the word in context before making your guess.

   _____

2. In paragraph 4, find a word that means "staring."

   _____

3. In your own words, define slum tourism.

   _____

   _____

4. How did slum tourism develop?

   _____

   _____

5. What are some criticisms of slum tourism?

   _____

   _____

6. What arguments support slum tourism?

   _____

   _____

   _____

7. List two examples of how people's outlook was changed when they toured slums.

   _____

   _____

   _____

8. How should tourists behave when they tour slums?

   _____

   _____

   _____

9. According to the article, what is the best way to help slum dwellers?

   _____

   _____

Writing Topics

1. What is the opposite of a slum? Come up with a new term for a wealthy neighborhood, and define it. Use examples to support your definition.

2. Compare two very different places that you have visited. You can compare two neighborhoods, two towns, or a rural area with an urban area.

3. Is touring a slum *tourism* or *voyeurism*? Argue your point of view by using examples from your own city, state, or country.

READING 13

Guy

Maya Angelou

Maya Angelou is a poet, writer, director, and producer. Her best-known work, *I Know Why the Caged Bird Sings*, is a memoir of her life as a girl in Arkansas. In the next excerpt, taken from her autobiography *All God's Children Need Traveling Shoes*, Angelou recounts a personal tragedy that she experienced while in Ghana.

1   The breezes of the West African night were intimate and shy, licking the hair, sweeping through cotton dresses with unseemly intimacy, and then disappearing into the utter blackness. Daylight was equally insistent, but much more bold and thoughtless. It dazzled, muddling the sight. It forced through my closed eyelids, bringing me up and out of a borrowed bed and into brand new streets.

2   After living nearly two years in Cairo, I had brought my son Guy to enter the University of Ghana in Accra. I had planned to stay for two weeks with a friend of a colleague, settle Guy into his dormitory, and then continue to Liberia to a job with the Department of Information.

3   Guy was seventeen and quick. I was thirty-three and determined. We were Black Americans in West Africa, where for the first time in our lives the color of our skin was accepted as correct and normal.

4   Guy had finished high school in Egypt; his Arabic was good, and his health excellent. He assured me that he would quickly learn a Ghanaian language, and he certainly could look after himself. I had worked successfully as a journalist in Cairo and failed sadly at a marriage, which I ended with false public dignity and copious secret tears. But with all crying in the past, I was on my way to another adventure. The future was plump with promise.

5   For two days, Guy and I laughed. We looked at the Ghanaian streets and laughed. We listened to the melodious languages and laughed. We looked at each other and laughed out loud. On the third day, Guy, on a pleasure outing, was injured in an automobile accident. One arm and one leg were fractured and his neck was broken.

6   July and August of 1962 stretched out like fat men yawning after a sumptuous dinner. They had every right to gloat, for they had eaten me up. Gobbled me down. Consumed my spirit, not in a wild rush, but slowly, with the obscene patience of certain victors. I became a shadow walking in the white-hot streets, and a dark spectre in the hospital.

solace: comfort

7   There was no **solace** in knowing that the doctors and nurses hovering around Guy were African, nor in the company of the Black American expatriates who, hearing of our misfortune, came to share some of the slow hours. Racial loyalties and cultural attachments had become meaningless.

8   Trying utterly, I could not match Guy's stoicism. He lay calm, week after week, in a prison of plaster from which only his face and one leg and arm were visible. His assurances that he would heal and be better than new drove me into a faithless silence. Had I been less timid, I would have cursed God. Had I come from a different background, I would have gone further and denied His very existence. Having neither the courage nor the historical precedent, I raged inside myself like a blinded bull in a metal stall.

9   Admittedly, Guy lived with the knowledge that an unexpected and very hard sneeze could force the fractured vertebrae against his spinal cord, and he would be paralyzed or die immediately, but he had only an infatuation with life. He hadn't lived long enough to fall in love with this brutally delicious experience. He could lightly waft away to another place, if there really was another place, where his youthful innocence would assure him a crown, wings, a harp, ambrosia, free milk, and an absence of nostalgic yearning. (I was raised on the spirituals, which ached to "See my old mother in glory" or "Meet with my dear children in heaven," but even the most fanciful lyricists never dared to suggest that those **cavorting** souls gave one thought to those of us left to **moil** in the world.) My wretchedness reminded me that, on the other hand, I would be rudderless.

cavorting: lively, carefree

moil: work hard

10   I had lived with family until my son was born in my sixteenth year. When he was two months old and perched on my left hip, we left my mother's house and together, save for one year when I was touring, we had been each other's home and center for seventeen years. He could die if he wanted to and go off to wherever dead folks go, but I, I would be left without a home.

Comprehension and Critical Thinking

1. Find a word in paragraph 4 that means "a lot of." _____

2. What type of narrator is telling this story?

    a. first-person   b. third-person

3. Why were the writer and her son in Accra?

    _____

    _____

4. What causes the writer's plans to change?

   _____

   _____

5. What type of relationship does the writer have with her son?

   _____

6. Underline a simile in paragraph 6. (In a simile, two things are compared using
   like or *as*.) Then explain what paragraph 6 is about. What are the writer's
   emotions?

   _____

   _____

   _____

7. While Guy is hospitalized, what is his mood?

   _____

   _____

8. What are the writer's religious feelings while her son is in the hospital?

   _____

   _____

   _____

   _____

9. How does the writer's definition of home change after her son's accident?

   _____

   _____

   _____

   _____

Writing Topics

1. This excerpt is from a memoir by Maya Angelou. Narrate a story about an
   important experience in your life. Explain what happened, and use descriptions
   that appeal to the senses.

2. Define *home*. Give examples to support your definition.

3. Tell a story about a time that you moved from one place to another. What
   were your feelings and experiences? Use descriptive imagery in your essay.

Theme: Human Development

READING 14

....

How Cults Become Religions

....

John D. Carl

John D. Carl is a college professor and textbook author. In the following adapted essay, he discusses how religious institutions evolve.

1   Sociologist Emile Durkheim believed that religion binds the community together through ritual and tradition. Although most societies have some sort of dominant religion, there are many different religions, each of which comes with its own set of beliefs and customs. But how does a set of beliefs become an accepted religion? Religions go through a series of stages as they become an integrated part of society.

2   Sociologically, all religions begin as cults. Cults are new religious movements led by charismatic leaders with few followers. The teachings and practices of cults are often at odds with the dominant culture and religion, so society is likely to reject the cult. For example, since the Chinese revolution, the Chinese government has cracked down on any faith-based group that it considers to be nonconformist, according to Jonathan Kaiman, journalist for the *Guardian*. The Chinese authorities consider a cult such as Falun Gong to be subversive and have tried to obliterate it. In 1999, the Chinese authorities initiated a crackdown on Falun Gong members. According to human rights groups, thousands of practitioners have been imprisoned.

3   A cult demands intense commitment and involvement of its members, and it relies on finding new adherents by using outside recruitment. Most cults fail because they cannot attract enough followers to sustain themselves. However, once a cult has enough members to support itself, it becomes a sect. Sects still go against society's norms, but members have greater social standing and are usually better integrated into society than cult members are. As a result, sect members are less likely to be persecuted by the dominant society. For instance, in the United States, the Church of Scientology and the Unification Church are more or less integrated into society. As time passes and the sect grows, the members tend to become respectable members of society. For example, the Church of Scientology boasts Tom Cruise and John Travolta as followers.

4   Eventually, sects can evolve into a church. The term church does not specifically refer to a building or a denomination of a religion; instead, it is a large, highly organized group of believers. Churches are bureaucratized institutions and may include national and international offices, and leaders

must undergo special training to perform established rituals. A good example is the Catholic Church, where priests go to special colleges to get ordained. The Catholic Church maintains a strict hierarchy in the offices of the Church. According to the Pew Research Center, about 25 percent of the population of the United States is Catholic. There are just under two hundred **dioceses** overseen by bishops, and each diocese has individual parishes, which are run by priests.

diocese: a religious district supervised by a bishop

5   If a church becomes highly integrated into the dominant culture, it may join with the state. A state religion, or theocracy, is formed when government and religion work together to shape society. Citizenship automatically makes one a member, so most citizens belong to the dominant religion. For example, Iran has a theocratic government and goes so far as to place religious leaders at the pinnacle of executive government decision-making. The Grand Ayatollah holds the highest political office and is the moral authority in Iran. Vatican City is another example of a theocracy because the community is ruled by an established religious organization, and the Pope is the head of state.

6   As societies modernize, religions begin going through secularization, which is the overall decline in the importance and power of religion in people's lives. Institutional religion weakens as societies become more scientifically advanced. Sociologists generally argue that as a civilization becomes more complex, people become less tied to the "old ways" and are more inclined to pursue other avenues. This phenomenon seems to indicate that secularization is inevitable. According to the Web site *PollingReport.com*, there has been a decline in the number of people in the United States who say that religion is very important in their lives, while the number of people who say it is fairly important has risen. The number of people who say that religion is not very important in their lives has doubled since 1965.

7   Durkheim argues that religious beliefs and society are intrinsically connected. Cults begin by endorsing practices outside of the dominant religion, but eventually some cults integrate into society. Religions in general function to provide cultural norms and values that bind followers together. Because human beings desire knowledge about the meaning of life and the purpose of death, they have developed complex belief systems, which have developed into various great religions.

Comprehension and Critical Thinking

1. In paragraph 2, what does the word *nonconformist* mean?

_____

_____

MyWritingLab™

Complete additional reading comprehension questions for this selection at mywritinglab.com

2. Find a word in paragraph 2 that means "rebellious." _____

3. Underline the thesis statement of this essay.

4. What type of process does the author use to explain the development of religions?

   a. complete a process   b. understand a process

5. According to paragraph 2, why do societies have a negative attitude toward cults? You may have to infer or guess.

   _____

   _____

6. What are some similarities and differences between a cult and a sect?

   Similarities: _____

   _____

   Differences: _____

   _____

   _____

7. According to paragraph 4, what are three characteristics of a church?

   _____

   _____

   _____

8. In which paragraphs does the author use the following supporting details?

   Informed opinion: _____

   Statistics: _____

   Examples: _____

9. According to the text, what causes the decline of religions?

   _____

   _____

Writing Topics

Write about one of the following topics. Remember to explore, develop, and revise and edit your work.

1. Do you follow a cult, sect, or church, or are you indifferent to religion? Explain the process you went through to develop your current beliefs.

2. Should religious beliefs, such as intelligent design and others, be taught in public schools? Why or why not? Provide examples to back up your argument.

3. According to the author, religion can interfere with politics. Should religious beliefs influence political decisions? Include examples in your own country where religious beliefs may have had an impact on government policy.

READING 15

The Untranslatable Word "Macho"

Rose del Castillo Guilbault

Rose del Castillo Guilbault is a journalist and the editorial director of the ABC affiliate station KGO-TV in San Francisco, California. In this essay, Castillo Guilbault compares how two cultures define the term *macho*.

1   What is *macho*? That depends on which side of the border you come from. Although it's not unusual for words and expressions to lose their subtlety in translation, the negative connotations of *macho* in this country are troublesome to Hispanics.

2   Take the newspaper descriptions of alleged mass murderer Ramon Salcido. That an insensitive, insanely jealous, hard-drinking, violent Latin male is referred to as macho makes Hispanics cringe. *"Es muy macho,"* the women in my family nod approvingly, describing a man they respect. But in the United States, when women say, "He's so macho," it's with disdain.

3   The Hispanic *macho* is manly, responsible, hardworking, a man in charge, and a patriarch. He is a man who expresses strength through silence, or what the Yiddish language would call a *mensch*.

4   The American *macho* is a chauvinist, a brute, uncouth, selfish, loud, abrasive, capable of inflicting pain, and sexually promiscuous. Quintessential *macho* models in this country are Sylvester Stallone, Arnold Schwarzenegger, and Charles Bronson. In their movies, they exude toughness, independence, and masculinity. But a closer look reveals their machismo is really violence masquerading as courage, sullenness disguised as silence, and irresponsibility camouflaged as independence.

5   If the Hispanic ideal of *macho* were translated to American screen roles, they might be Jimmy Stewart, Sean Connery, and Laurence Olivier. In Spanish, macho ennobles Latin males. In English, it devalues them. This pattern seems consistent with the conflicts ethnic minority males experience in this country. Typically, the cultural traits other societies value don't translate as desirable characteristics in America.

6   I watched my own father struggle with these cultural ambiguities. He worked on a farm for twenty years. He laid down miles of irrigation pipe,

recalcitrant:
unmanageable

carefully plowed long, neat rows in fields, hacked away at **recalcitrant** weeds, and drove tractors through whirlpools of dust. He stoically worked twenty-hour days during harvest season, accepting the long hours as part of agricultural work. When the boss complained or upbraided him for minor mistakes, he kept quiet, even when it was obvious the boss had erred.

7   He handled the most menial tasks with pride. At home he was a good provider, helped out my mother's family in Mexico without complaint, and was indulgent with me. Arguments between my mother and him generally had to do with money or with his stubborn reluctance to share his troubles. He tried to work them out in his own silence. He didn't want to trouble my mother—a course that backfired because the imagined is always worse than the reality.

8   Americans regarded my father as decidedly un-macho. His character was interpreted as nonassertive, his loyalty as a lack of ambition, and his quietness as ignorance. I once overheard the boss's son blame him for plowing crooked rows in a field. My father merely smiled at the lie, knowing the boy had done it, but didn't refute it, confident his good work was well known. But the boss instead ridiculed him for being "stupid" and letting a kid get away with a lie. Seeing my embarrassment, my father dismissed the incident, saying, "They're the dumb ones. Imagine, me fighting with a kid." I tried not to look at him with American eyes because sometimes the reflection hurt.

9   Listening to my aunts' clucks of approval, my vision focused on the qualities America overlooked. "He's such a hard worker. So serious, so responsible." My aunts would secretly compliment my mother. The unspoken comparison was that he was not like some of their husbands, who drank and womanized. My uncles represented the darker side of macho.

10   In a patriarchal society, few challenge their roles. If men drink, it's because it's the manly thing to do. If they gamble, it's because it's how men relax. And if they fool around, well, it's because a man simply can't hold back so much man! My aunts didn't exactly meekly sit back, but they put up with these transgressions because Mexican society dictated this was their lot in life.

11   In the United States, I believe it was the feminist movement of the early seventies that changed macho's meaning. Perhaps my generation of Latin women was in part responsible. I recall Chicanas complaining about the chauvinistic nature of Latin men and the notion they wanted their women barefoot, pregnant, and in the kitchen. The generalization that Latin men embodied chauvinistic traits led to this interesting twist of semantics. Suddenly a word that represented something positive in one culture became a negative prototype in another.

12   The problem with the use of macho today is that it's become an accepted stereotype of the Latin male. And like all stereotypes, it distorts truth. The impact of language in our society is undeniable. And the misuse of macho hints at a deeper cultural misunderstanding that extends beyond mere word definitions.

Comprehension and Critical Thinking

MyWritingLab™

Complete additional reading comprehension questions for this selection at mywritinglab.com

1. Find a word in paragraph 2 that means "contempt." _____

2. Underline the thesis statement.

3. What is the writer comparing and contrasting in this essay?

    _____

    _____

4. What connotations does the word *macho* have in Latin culture?

    _____

    _____

5. What connotations does the word *macho* have in American culture?

    _____

    _____

6. According to the writer, why do men like Jimmy Stewart, Sean Connery, and Laurence Olivier better exemplify the word *macho* than men like Sylvester Stallone or Charles Bronson?

    _____

    _____

    _____

7. In paragraph 8, the writer mentions that she tried not to look at her father "with American eyes." In her opinion, how did Americans view her father?

    _____

8. According to the writer, does the word *macho* in Latin cultures only have a positive connotation? Explain your answer.

    _____

    _____

    _____

9. How did the meaning of the word *macho* evolve in Latin communities in North America?

_____

_____

_____

10. Although the predominant pattern in this essay is comparison and contrast, the writer also uses definition and narration. How do they help develop her central argument?

_____

_____

Writing Topics

Write about one of the following topics. Remember to explore, develop, and revise and edit your work.

1. What are some stereotypes of your nationality, religion, or gender? Compare the stereotypes with the reality.

2. Compare and contrast two people in your life who have very different personalities.

READING 16

Chance and Circumstance

David Leonhardt

David Leonhardt is a columnist for the *New York Times*. His columns focus on economics and society. In the following essay, he examines the theories of Malcolm Gladwell and ponders on the definition and the causes of success.

1   In 1984, a young man named Malcolm graduated from the University of Toronto and moved to the United States to try his hand at journalism. Thanks to his uncommonly clear writing style and keen eye for a story, he quickly landed a job at the *Washington Post*. After less than a decade at the *Post*, he moved up to the pinnacle of literary journalism, the *New Yorker*. There, he wrote articles full of big ideas about the hidden patterns of ordinary life, which then became grist for two No. 1 best-selling books. In the vast world of nonfiction writing, he is as close to a singular talent as exists today.

2   Or at least that's one version of the story of Malcolm Gladwell. Here is another: In 1984, a young man named Malcolm graduated from the University of Toronto and moved to the United States to try his hand at

journalism. No one could know it then, but he arrived with nearly the perfect background for his time. His mother was a psychotherapist, and his father a mathematician. Their professions pointed young Malcolm toward the behavioral sciences, whose popularity would explode in the 1990s. His mother also just happened to be a writer on the side. So unlike most children of mathematicians and therapists, he came to learn, as he would later recall, "that there is beauty in saying something clearly and simply." As a journalist, he plumbed the behavioral research for optimistic lessons about the human condition, and he found an eager audience during the heady, proudly geeky '90s. His first book, *The Tipping Point*, was published in March 2000, just days before the **NASDAQ** peaked.

NASDAQ: an electronic stock market started in 1971

3   These two stories about Gladwell are both true, and yet they are also very different. The first personalizes his success. It is the classically American version of his career, in that it gives individual characteristics—talent, hard work, **Horatio Alger**-like pluck—the starring role. The second version does not necessarily deny these characteristics, but it does sublimate them. The protagonist is not a singularly talented person who took advantage of opportunities. He is instead a talented person who took advantage of singular opportunities.

Horatio Alger: American author (1832–1899) who wrote children's adventure novels

4   Gladwell's book *Outliers* is a passionate argument for taking the second version of the story more seriously than we now do. "It is not the brightest who succeed," Gladwell writes, "nor is success simply the sum of the decisions and efforts we make on our own behalf. It is, rather, a gift. Outliers are those who have been given opportunities—and who have had the strength and presence of mind to seize them."

5   He starts with a tale of individual greatness, about the Beatles, the titans of Silicon Valley, or the enormously successful generation of New York Jews born in the early twentieth century. Then he adds details that undercut that tale. So Bill Gates is introduced as a young computer programmer from Seattle whose brilliance and ambition outshine the brilliance and ambition of the thousands of other young programmers. But then Gladwell takes us back to Seattle, and we discover that Gates's high school happened to have a computer club when almost no other high schools did. He then lucked into the opportunity to use the computers at the University of Washington, for hours on end. By the time he turned twenty, he had spent well more than ten thousand hours as a programmer.

6   At the end of this revisionist tale, Gladwell asks Gates himself how many other teenagers in the world had as much experience as he had by the early 1970s. "If there were fifty in the world, I'd be stunned," Gates says. "I had a better exposure to software development at a young age than I think anyone did in that period of time, and all because of an incredibly lucky series of events." Gates's talent and drive were surely unusual. But Gladwell suggests that his opportunities may have been even more so.

anomaly:
peculiarity or
strange quality

Young hockey players

7   Gladwell explores the **anomaly** of hockey players' birthdays. In many of the best leagues in the world, amateur or professional, roughly 40 percent of the players were born in January, February, or March, while only 10 percent were born in October, November, or December. It's a profoundly strange pattern, with a simple explanation. The cutoff birth date for many youth hockey leagues is January 1. So the children born in the first three months of the year are just a little older, bigger, and stronger than their peers. These older children are then funneled into all-star teams that offer the best, most intense training. By the time they become teenagers, their random initial advantage has turned into a real one.

8   At the championship game of the top Canadian junior league, Gladwell interviews the father of one player born on January 4. More than half of the players on his team—the Medicine Hat Tigers—were born in January, February, or March. But when Gladwell asks the father to explain his son's success, the calendar has nothing to do with it. He instead mentions passion, talent, and hard work—before adding, as an aside, that the boy was always big for his age. Just imagine, Gladwell writes, if Canada created another youth hockey league for children born in the second half of the year. It would one day find itself with twice as many great hockey players.

9   *Outliers* is almost a political manifesto. "We look at the young Bill Gates and marvel that our world allowed that thirteen-year-old to become a fabulously successful entrepreneur," he writes at the end. "But that's the wrong lesson. Our world only allowed one thirteen-year-old unlimited access to a time-sharing terminal in 1968. If a million teenagers had been given the same opportunity, how many more Microsofts would we have today?"

10   After a decade—and, really, a generation—in which this country has done fairly little to build up the institutions that can foster success, Gladwell is urging us to rethink. Once again, his timing may prove to be pretty good.

MyWritingLab™

Complete
additional reading
comprehension questions
for this selection at
mywritinglab.com

Comprehension and Critical Thinking

1. Find a word in paragraph 1 that means "height or peak." _____

2. Find a word in paragraph 2 that means "examined deeply." _____

3. What is the introductory style of the essay?
    a. definition   b. contrasting position   c. anecdote

4. Underline a sentence in the essay that defines *outliers*.

5. According to Gladwell, why is Bill Gates an outlier?

   _____

   _____

   _____

   _____

6. According to Gladwell, why is it luckier for hockey players to be born in the first three months of the year?

   _____

   _____

   _____

7. How is Gladwell's perception of successful individuals different from how the general public views successful individuals?

   _____

   _____

   _____

8. In paragraph 9, the writer says that Gladwell's book is "almost a political manifesto." Explain.

   _____

   _____

   _____

9. What is the writer's opinion of Gladwell's thesis?

   _____

   _____

   _____

Writing Topics

Write about one of the following topics. Remember to explore, develop, and revise and edit your work.

1. What is *blind ambition*? Define the term, and use examples to support your ideas.

2. Describe someone you consider "successful." What contributed to that person's success? How has success affected that person? Write about the causes or effects of the person's success.

3. Nowadays, more boys than girls drop out of school. Colleges and universities now have more female than male graduates in many of their programs. Explain what can be done to convince young men to stay in school and pursue higher education.

READING 17

The Happiness Factor

David Brooks

David Brooks writes for the *New York Times*, *The Weekly Standard*, *Newsweek*, and the *Atlantic Monthly*. He is also a commentator on *The NewsHour with Jim Lehrer*. In the following essay, Brooks makes an interesting comparison.

1   Two things happened to Sandra Bullock in 2010. First, she won an Academy Award for best actress. Then came the news reports claiming that her husband was an adulterous jerk. So the philosophic question of the day is: Would you take that as a deal? Would you exchange a tremendous professional triumph for a severe personal blow? On the one hand, an Academy Award is nothing to sneeze at. Bullock has earned the admiration of her peers in a way very few experience. She'll make more money for years to come. She may even live longer. Research by Donald A. Redelmeier and Sheldon M. Singh has found that, on average, Oscar winners live nearly four years longer than nominees that don't win.

2   Nonetheless, if you had to take more than three seconds to think about this question, you are absolutely crazy. Marital happiness is far more important than anything else in determining personal well-being. If you have a successful marriage, it doesn't matter how many professional setbacks you endure, you will be reasonably happy. If you have an unsuccessful marriage, it doesn't matter how many career triumphs you record, you will remain significantly unfulfilled.

3   This isn't just sermonizing. This is the age of research, so there's data to back this up. Over the past few decades, teams of researchers have been studying happiness. Their work, which seemed flimsy at first, has developed an impressive rigor, and one of the key findings is that, just as the old sages predicted, worldly success has shallow roots while interpersonal bonds permeate through and through.

4   For example, the relationship between happiness and income is complicated, and after a point, tenuous. It is true that poor nations become happier as they become middle-class nations. But once the basic necessities have been achieved, future income is lightly connected to well-being. Growing countries are slightly less happy than countries with slower growth

rates, according to Carol Graham of the Brookings Institution and Eduardo Lora. The United States is much richer than it was fifty years ago, but this has produced no measurable increase in overall happiness. On the other hand, it has become a much more unequal country, but this inequality doesn't seem to have reduced national happiness.

Does money buy happiness?

5   On a personal scale, winning the lottery doesn't seem to produce lasting gains in well-being. People aren't happiest during the years when they are winning the most promotions. Instead, people are happy in their twenties, dip in middle age and then, on average, hit peak happiness just after retirement at age sixty-five. People get slightly happier as they climb the income scale, but this depends on how they experience growth. Does wealth inflame unrealistic expectations? Does it destabilize settled relationships? Or does it flow from a virtuous cycle in which an interesting job produces hard work that in turn leads to more interesting opportunities?

6   If the relationship between money and well-being is complicated, the correspondence between personal relationships and happiness is not. The daily activities most associated with happiness are sex, socializing after work, and having dinner with others. The daily activity most injurious to happiness is commuting. According to one study, joining a group that meets even just once a month produces the same happiness gain as doubling your income. According to another, being married produces a psychic gain equivalent to more than $100,000 a year.

7   If you want to find a good place to live, just ask people if they trust their neighbors. Levels of social trust vary enormously, but countries with high social trust have happier people, better health, more efficient government, more economic growth, and less fear of crime (regardless of whether actual crime rates are increasing or decreasing). The overall impression from this research is that economic and professional success exist on the surface of life, and that they emerge out of interpersonal relationships, which are much deeper and more important.

8   The second impression is that most of us pay attention to the wrong things. Most people vastly overestimate the extent to which more money would improve their lives. Most schools and colleges spend too much time preparing students for careers and not enough preparing them to make social decisions. Most governments release a ton of data on economic trends but not enough on trust and other social conditions. In short, modern societies have developed vast institutions oriented around the things that are easy to count, not around the things that matter most. They have an affinity for material concerns and a primordial fear of moral and social ones.

9   This may be changing. There is a rash of compelling books—including *The Hidden Wealth of Nations* by David Halpern and *The Politics of Happiness* by Derek Bok—that argue that public institutions should pay attention to well-being and not just material growth narrowly conceived. Governments keep initiating policies they think will produce prosperity, only to get sacked, time and again, from their spiritual blind side.

MyWritingLab™

Complete additional reading comprehension questions for this selection at mywritinglab.com

Comprehension and Critical Thinking

1. In paragraph 4, what is the meaning of *tenuous*?
   a. unconvincing or questionable   c. complete
   b. strong and convincing

2. In your own words, what is the writer's main point?

   _____

   _____

   _____

3. According to the essay, what factors are associated with increased levels of happiness?

   _____

   _____

4. In which paragraphs does the writer use expert opinion?

   _____

5. In paragraph 5, the writer states that people are happy in their twenties and after retirement, but not in their middle age. Why are people probably less happy in middle age? Make two or three guesses.

   _____

   _____

   _____

   _____

   _____

6. In paragraph 7, the writer mentions social trust but doesn't clearly define it. Infer or guess what social trust is.

   _____

   _____

7. In paragraph 8, the writer criticizes colleges because they don't prepare students to make social decisions. Think of ways that colleges could teach students to make moral and social decisions.

_____

_____

_____

Writing Topics

Write about one of the following topics. Remember to explore, develop, and revise and edit your work.

1. Compare two jobs you've had. What elements in the jobs provided you with the most pleasure?

2. Define personal happiness, and give examples to support your definition.

3. Define social trust. Break the topic down into categories, and list examples for each category. For instance, you could write about trust in the government, trust in the police, and trust in one's neighbors.

READING 18

Medicating Ourselves

Robyn Sarah

Robyn Sarah is a poet and a writer. Her work has appeared in _The Threepenny Review_, _New England Review_, and _The Hudson Review_, and she is a frequent contributor to the _Montreal Gazette_. In the next essay, Sarah reflects on society's overreliance on medication.

1   It is hard to pick up a magazine these days without finding an article attacking or defending some pharmaceutical remedy for syndromes of mood or behavior. These drugs are in vogue because they have shown themselves spectacularly effective for a range of conditions, though their exact workings are not well understood, and their long-term effects are not known. Yet for all the noise we continue to hear about, say, Ritalin, for children with attention deficit disorders and related learning or behavior problems—or Prozac and the new family of anti-depressants prescribed to the stressed and distressed of all ages—the real debate on pharmaceuticals has yet to begin.

2   The enormous strides science has made in understanding brain chemistry have precipitated a revolution no less significant than the "cyber-revolution" now transforming our lives. The biochemical model has brought relief to many suffering individuals and families, removing devastating

anomalous:
unusual

symptoms and lifting blame from parents whose contorted responses to a child's **anomalous** behavior were once mistaken for its cause. But the very effectiveness of corrective pharmacology engenders an insidious imperative: We can, therefore we must. The realization that we can chemically fine-tune personalities—that we may be able to "fix" what were once believed innate flaws of character—has staggering implications for our understanding of morality, our standards for acceptable behavior, our mental pain threshold, and our expectations of self and others.

3   The medication debate should not be a matter of "whether or not," but of where to stop. Mental illness is real and can be life-threatening. But when is

pathologizing:
making a disease of

something truly a disorder, and when are we **pathologizing** human difference, natural human cycles and processes? How do we decide what needs fixing, and who should decide? These are not simple matters.

4   During my own school years, the boy who today would be prescribed Ritalin used to spend a lot of time standing in the hall outside the classroom. His "bad boy" reputation dogged him year to year and became part of his self-image. He learned to wheel-and-deal his way out of trouble by a

subterfuge:
evasion

pariah: outcast

combination of charm and **subterfuge**; he learned to affect a rakish persona to mask what anger he might feel about his **pariah** status. But in spite of his often superior intelligence, anything else he learned in school was hit-and-miss. Such "bad boys" rarely lasted beyond the second year of high school.

5   Defenders of Ritalin point out that in making it possible for such a child to focus and sustain attention, to complete tasks and take satisfaction from them, the stimulant breaks a cycle of disruptive behavior, punishment, anger, and acting out. Begun early, Ritalin can prevent the battering of self-esteem such children undergo in school; introduced later, it allows a child to rebuild self-esteem. These are powerful arguments for a drug that, when it works, can effect what seems a miraculous transformation in a "problem child," giving him a new lease on life in a system that used to chew him up and spit him out.

6   But Ritalin is not a benign drug, and many are alarmed at the frequency and casualness with which it is prescribed (often at the school's prompting) for a disorder that has no conclusive medical diagnosis. Some argue that children who may simply be high-spirited, less compliant, or more physically energetic than the norm are being "drugged" for the convenience of teachers and smooth classroom functioning. Others wonder if the

ADD: attention-deficit disorder

ADHD: attention-deficit hyperactivity disorder

frequency of **ADD** and **ADHD** diagnoses says more about the state of schools than it does about the state of children. Do our schools give children enough physical exercise, enough structure and discipline, or enough real challenge? A proliferation of troublemakers can be an indication of something wrong in the classroom—witness any class with an inexperienced substitute teacher. Pills to modify the behavior of "disturbers" may restore order—at the cost of masking the true problem.

7   Something similar may be going on as diagnoses of depression and other disorders proliferate, especially among groups in the throes of life change (adolescent, mid-life, or geriatric). Just as physical pain is our body's way of alerting us to a problem, psychic pain can be a response to our changed position in the world. Psychic pain might indicate that we should reorient ourselves by reassessing and rebuilding our primary relationships. If I swallow a pill to conceal my existential problems—an "equanimity" pill—I may be easier to live with, but I may also be masking the need for some fundamental work to be done, some exercise of the spirit. Giving a boost to my brain chemistry might help me do this work, but it is just as likely to take away the urgency to do it.

8   I am myself no stranger to depression, but in **eschewing** the chemical solution, I have begun to sense I am swimming against the tide. For a while, I felt all the worse because so many of my peers, with lives no less complicated than mine, seemed to be handling mid-life pressures better than I was. Slowly it emerged that several had taken antidepressants at some point "to get over a rough spot." Some are still taking them.

eschewing: avoiding

9   The arguments are seductive. Why make things harder for ourselves, and why inflict our angst on others, when there is an alternative? One father I know, the stay-at-home parent of small children, told me he put himself back on Prozac (originally prescribed for migraines) because under stress he tended to be irritable, and things were more stressful with a new baby in the house. His irritability was not something he wanted to inflict on his children. Who could fault him for such a decision?

10   If we can really smooth our rough edges by popping a pill, why not make life pleasanter for our loved ones and associates by popping a pill? If a pill can make saints of us all, where is the virtue in resisting this pill? But the effect may be to mask how many people would otherwise be doing "badly," which not only induces the unmedicated to bash themselves for their human frailties, but blinds us all to societal ills that may explain why so many of us get depressed.

11   The new pharmaceutical culture could stigmatize the unmedicated. It could make us all less tolerant of our frailties and those of others. It could keep us reconciled to the values that have put us in the pressure cooker to begin with: the worship of youth and success, the pursuit of comfort and expediency, and a model of wellness based on uninterrupted productivity.

12   Shall we lose the sense of what it is to be unique, struggling, evolving souls in the world, and instead use designer drugs to make ourselves smooth-functioning cogs of an unexamined societal machine? Aldous Huxley predicted it in 1932, in his Utopian novel *Brave New World*. Remember the drug *soma*? It has "the advantages

of Christianity and alcohol; none of their defects [. . .]. Anyone can be virtuous now. You can carry half your morality around in a bottle." Huxley's book, on the high school reading list a generation ago, enjoys that same place today. But I am beginning to think the satire may have been lost on us. Perhaps it was too late for the message even when he wrote it. With our complicity, his vision gets closer every day.

MyWritingLab™

Complete
additional reading
comprehension questions
for this selection at
mywritinglab.com

Comprehension and Critical Thinking

1. In paragraph 7, what does *proliferate* mean? _____

2. Define the word *stigmatize* in paragraph 11. _____

3. In your own words, explain the essay's main point.

   _____

   _____

   _____

4. In which paragraph(s) does the writer acknowledge an opposing viewpoint?

   _____

5. Which strategies does the writer use to support her argument? There is more than one answer.

   a. fact   d. statistics

   b. anecdote   e. logical consequences

   c. quotations from informed sources

   For each type of support that you have identified, underline a sentence from the text.

6. Using your own words, list at least four of the writer's main arguments.

   _____

   _____

   _____

   _____

   _____

   _____

   _____

   _____

7. The writer suggests some causes of overmedicating in our culture. What are they?

    _____

    _____

    _____

8. What are some of the effects of using medication to modify behavior problems?

    _____

    _____

9. How does the writer conclude her essay?

    a. suggestion   b. prediction   c. call to action

10. Why does the writer quote Aldous Huxley in her concluding paragraph?

    _____

    _____

    _____

Writing Topics

Write about one of the following topics. Remember to explore, develop, and revise and edit your work.

1. Argue for the use of mood-altering drugs.

2. Argue that vaccinations should or should not be mandatory. You will have to do some research and support your points with the opinions of experts. See Chapter 17 for information about writing a research essay.

3. What are some of the mental and physical processes people go through to keep looking or feeling good?

READING 19

The Veldt

Ray Bradbury

Ray Bradbury (1920–2012) was a prolific writer of mystery, fantasy, and science fiction. His best-known novels are *The Martian Chronicles* and *Fahrenheit 451*. "The Veldt" was published in 1951 and appeared in his collection of short stories in *The Illustrated Man*.

1   "George," I wish you'd look at the nursery."

2   "What's wrong with it?"

3   "I don't know."

4   "Well, then."

5   "I just want you to look at it, is all, or call a psychologist in to look at it."

6   "What would a psychologist want with a nursery?"

7   "You know very well what he'd want." His wife paused in the middle of the kitchen and watched the stove busy humming to itself, making supper for four.

8   "It's just that the nursery is different now than it was."

9   "All right, let's have a look."

10   They walked down the hall of their soundproofed, Happylife Home, which had cost them thirty thousand dollars installed, this house which clothed and fed and rocked them to sleep and played and sang and was good to them. Their approach sensitized a switch somewhere, and the nursery light flicked on when they came within ten feet of it. Similarly, behind them, in the halls, lights went on and off as they left them behind, with a soft automaticity.

11   "Well," said George Hadley.

12   They stood on the thatched floor of the nursery. It was forty feet across by forty feet long and thirty feet high—it had cost half again as much as the rest of the house. "But nothing's too good for our children," George had said.

13   The nursery was silent. It was empty as a jungle glade at hot high noon. The walls were blank and two dimensional. Now, as George and Lydia Hadley stood in the center of the room, the walls began to purr and recede into crystalline distance, it seemed, and presently an African veldt appeared, in three dimensions; on all sides, in colors reproduced to the final pebble and bit of straw. The ceiling above them became a deep sky with a hot yellow sun.

14   George Hadley felt the perspiration start on his brow.

15   "Let's get out of the sun," he said. "This is a little too real. But I don't see anything wrong."

16   "Wait a moment, you'll see," said his wife.

17   Now the hidden odorophonics were beginning to blow a wind of odor at the two people in the middle of the baked veldtland. The hot straw smell of lion grass, the cool green smell of the hidden water hole, the great rusty smell of animals, the smell of dust like a red paprika in the hot air. And now the sounds: the thump of distant antelope feet on grassy sod, the papery rustling of vultures. A shadow passed through the sky. The shadow flickered on George Hadley's upturned, sweating face.

18   "Filthy creatures," he heard his wife say.

19   "The vultures."

20   "You see, there are the lions, far over, that way. Now they're on their way to the water hole. They've just been eating," said Lydia. "I don't know what."

21   "Some animal." George Hadley put his hand up to shield off the burning light from his squinted eyes. "A zebra or a baby giraffe, maybe."

22   "Are you sure?" His wife sounded peculiarly tense.

23   "No, it's a little late to be sure," he said, amused. "Nothing over there I can see but cleaned bone, and the vultures dropping for what's left."

24   "Did you hear that scream?" she asked.

25   "No."

26   "About a minute ago?"

27   "Sorry, no."

28   The lions were coming. And again George Hadley was filled with admiration for the mechanical genius who had conceived this room. A miracle of efficiency selling for an absurdly low price. Every home should have one. Oh, occasionally they frightened you with their clinical accuracy, they startled you, gave you a twinge, but most of the time what fun for everyone, not only your own son and daughter, but for yourself when you felt like a quick jaunt to a foreign land, a quick change of scenery. Well, here it was!

29   And here were the lions now, fifteen feet away, so real, so feverishly and startlingly real that you could feel the prickling fur on your hand, and your mouth was stuffed with the dusty upholstery smell of their heated pelts, and the yellow of them was in your eyes like the yellow of an exquisite French tapestry, the yellows of lions and summer grass, and the sound of the matted lion lungs exhaling on the silent noontide, and the smell of meat from the panting, dripping mouths.

30   The lions stood looking at George and Lydia Hadley with terrible green-yellow eyes.

31   "Watch out!" screamed Lydia.

32   The lions came running at them.

33   Lydia bolted and ran. Instinctively, George sprang after her. Outside, in the hall, with the door slammed, he was laughing and she was crying, and they both stood appalled at the other's reaction.

34   "George!"

35   "Lydia! Oh, my dear poor sweet Lydia!"

36   "They almost got us!"

37   "Walls, Lydia, remember; crystal walls, that's all they are. Oh, they look real, I must admit—Africa in your parlor—but it's all dimensional superreactionary, supersensitive color film and mental tape film behind glass screens. It's all odorophonics and sonics, Lydia. Here's my handkerchief."

38   "I'm afraid." She came to him and put her body against him and cried steadily. "Did you see? Did you feel? It's too real."

39   "Now, Lydia . . ."

40   "You've got to tell Wendy and Peter not to read any more on Africa."

41   "Of course—of course." He patted her.

42   "Promise?"

43   "Sure."

44   "And lock the nursery for a few days until I get my nerves settled."

45   "You know how difficult Peter is about that. When I punished him a month ago by locking the nursery for even a few hours—the tantrum he threw! And Wendy too. They live for the nursery."

46   "It's got to be locked; that's all there is to it."

47   "All right." Reluctantly he locked the huge door. "You've been working too hard. You need a rest."

48   "I don't know—I don't know," she said, blowing her nose, sitting down in a chair that immediately began to rock and comfort her. "Maybe I don't have enough to do. Maybe I have time to think too much. Why don't we shut the whole house off for a few days and take a vacation?"

49   "You mean you want to fry my eggs for me?"

50   "Yes." She nodded.

51   "And darn my socks?"

52   "Yes." A frantic, watery-eyed nodding.

53   "And sweep the house?"

54   "Yes, yes—oh, yes!"

55   "But I thought that's why we bought this house, so we wouldn't have to do anything?"

56   "That's just it. I feel like I don't belong here. The house is wife and mother now and nursemaid. Can I compete with an African veldt? Can I give a bath and scrub the children as efficiently or quickly as the automatic scrub bath can? I cannot. And it isn't just me. It's you. You've been awfully nervous lately."

57   "I suppose I have been smoking too much."

58   "You look as if you didn't know what to do with yourself in this house, either. You smoke a little more every morning and drink a little more every afternoon and need a little more sedative every night. You're beginning to feel unnecessary too."

59   "Am I?" He paused and tried to feel into himself to see what was really there.

60   "Oh, George!" She looked beyond him, at the nursery door. "Those lions can't get out of there, can they?"

61   He looked at the door and saw it tremble as if something had jumped against it from the other side.

62   "Of course not," he said.

63   At dinner they ate alone, for Wendy and Peter were at a special plastic carnival across town and had televised home to say they'd be late, to go ahead eating. So George Hadley, bemused, sat watching the dining-room table produce warm dishes of food from its mechanical interior.

64   "We forgot the ketchup," he said.

65   "Sorry," said a small voice within the table, and ketchup appeared.

66   As for the nursery, thought George Hadley, it won't hurt for the children to be locked out of it awhile. Too much of anything isn't good for anyone. And it was clearly indicated that the children had been spending a little too much time on Africa. That sun. He could feel it on his neck, still, like a hot paw. And the lions. And the smell of blood. Remarkable how the nursery caught the telepathic emanations of the children's minds and created life to fill their every desire. The children thought lions, and there were lions. The children thought zebras, and there were zebras. Sun—sun. Giraffes— giraffes. Death and death.

67   That last. He chewed tastelessly on the meat that the table had cut for him. Death thoughts. They were awfully young, Wendy and Peter, for death thoughts. Or, no, you were never too young, really. Long before you knew what death was you were wishing it on someone else. When you were two years old you were shooting people with cap pistols.

68   But this—the long, hot African veldt—the awful death in the jaws of a lion. And repeated again and again.

69   "Where are you going?"

70   He didn't answer Lydia. Preoccupied, he let the lights glow softly on ahead of him, extinguished behind him as he padded to the nursery door. He listened against it. Far away, a lion roared.

71   He unlocked the door and opened it. Just before he stepped inside, he heard a faraway scream. And then another roar from the lions, which subsided quickly.

72   He stepped into Africa. How many times in the last year had he opened this door and found Wonderland, Alice, the Mock Turtle, or Aladdin and his Magical Lamp, or Jack Pumpkinhead of Oz, or Dr. Doolittle, or the cow jumping over a very real-appearing moon—all the delightful contraptions of a make-believe world. How often had he seen Pegasus flying in the sky ceiling, or seen fountains of red fireworks, or heard angel voices singing. But now, this yellow hot Africa, this bake oven with murder in the heat. Perhaps Lydia was right. Perhaps they needed a little vacation from the fantasy, which was growing a bit too real for ten-year-old children. It was all right to exercise one's mind with gymnastic fantasies, but when the lively child mind settled on one pattern . . . ? It seemed that, at a distance, for the past month,

he had heard lions roaring, and smelled their strong odor seeping as far away as his study door. But, being busy, he had paid it no attention.

73   George Hadley stood on the African grassland alone. The lions looked up from their feeding, watching him. The only flaw to the illusion was the open door through which he could see his wife, far down the dark hall, like a framed picture, eating her dinner abstractedly.

74   "Go away," he said to the lions.

75   They did not go.

76   He knew the principle of the room exactly. You sent out your thoughts. Whatever you thought would appear.

77   "Let's have Aladdin and his lamp," he snapped.

78   The veldtland remained; the lions remained.

79   "Come on, room! I demand Aladdin!" he said.

80   Nothing happened. The lions mumbled in their baked pelts.

81   "Aladdin!"

82   He went back to dinner. "The fool room's out of order," he said. "It won't respond."

83   "Or"

84   "Or what?"

85   "Or it can't respond," said Lydia, "because the children have thought about Africa and lions and killing so many days that the room's in a rut."

86   "Could be."

87   "Or Peter's set it to remain that way."

88   "Set it?"

89   "He may have got into the machinery and fixed something."

90   "Peter doesn't know machinery."

91   "He's a wise one for ten. That I.Q. of his—"

92   "Nevertheless."

93   "Hello, Mom. Hello, Dad."

94   The Hadleys turned. Wendy and Peter were coming in the front door, cheeks like peppermint candy, eyes like bright blue agate marbles, a smell of ozone on their jumpers from their trip in the helicopter.

95   "You're just in time for supper," said both parents.

96   "We're full of strawberry ice cream and hot dogs," said the children, holding hands. "But we'll sit and watch."

97   "Yes, come tell us about the nursery," said George Hadley.

98   The brother and sister blinked at him and then at each other. "Nursery?"

99   "All about Africa and everything," said the father with false joviality.

100   "I don't understand," said Peter.

101   "Your mother and I were just traveling through Africa with rod and reel; Tom Swift and his Electric Lion," said George Hadley.

102   "There's no Africa in the nursery," said Peter simply.

103   "Oh, come now, Peter. We know better."

104   "I don't remember any Africa," said Peter to Wendy. "Do you?"

105   "No."

106   "Run see and come tell."

107   She obeyed.

108   "Wendy, come back here!" said George Hadley, but she was gone. The house lights followed her like a flock of fireflies. Too late, he realized he had forgotten to lock the nursery door after his last inspection.

109   "Wendy'll look and come tell us," said Peter.

110   "She doesn't have to tell me. I've seen it."

111   "I'm sure you're mistaken, Father."

112   "I'm not, Peter. Come along now."

113   But Wendy was back. "It's not Africa," she said breathlessly.

114   "We'll see about this," said George Hadley, and they all walked down the hall together and opened the nursery door.

115   There was a green, lovely forest, a lovely river, a purple mountain, high voices singing, and Rima, lovely and mysterious, lurking in the trees with colorful flights of butterflies, like animated bouquets, lingering on her long hair. The African veldtland was gone. The lions were gone. Only Rima was here now, singing a song so beautiful that it brought tears to your eyes.

116   George Hadley looked in at the changed scene. "Go to bed," he said to the children.

117   They opened their mouths.

118   "You heard me," he said.

119   They went off to the air closet, where a wind sucked them like brown leaves up the flue to their slumber rooms.

120   George Hadley walked through the singing glade and picked up something that lay in the corner near where the lions had been. He walked slowly back to his wife.

121   "What is that?" she asked.

122   He showed it to her. The smell of hot grass was on it and the smell of a lion. There were drops of saliva on it, it had been chewed, and there were blood smears on both sides.

123   He closed the nursery door and locked it, tight.

124   In the middle of the night he was still awake, and he knew his wife was awake. "Do you think Wendy changed it?" she said at last, in the dark room.

125   "Of course."

126   "Made it from a veldt into a forest and put Rima there instead of lions?"

127   "Yes."

128   "Why?"

129   "I don't know. But it's staying locked until I find out."

130   "How did your wallet get there?"

131   "I don't know anything," he said, "except that I'm beginning to be sorry we bought that room for the children. If children are neurotic at all, a room like that—"

132   "It's supposed to help them work off their neuroses in a healthful way."

133   "I'm starting to wonder." He stared at the ceiling.

134   "We've given the children everything they ever wanted. Is this our reward—secrecy, disobedience?"

135   "Who was it said, 'Children are carpets, they should be stepped on occasionally'? We've never lifted a hand. They're insufferable—let's admit it. They come and go when they like; they treat us as if we were offspring. They're spoiled, and we're spoiled."

136   "They've been acting funny ever since you forbade them to take the rocket to New York a few months ago."

137   "They're not old enough to do that alone, I explained."

138   "Nevertheless, I've noticed they've been decidedly cool toward us since."

139   "I think I'll have David McClean come tomorrow morning to have a look at Africa."

140   "But it's not Africa now, it's Green Mansions country and Rima."

141   "I have a feeling it'll be Africa again before then."

142   A moment later they heard the screams.

143   Two screams. Two people screaming from downstairs. And then a roar of lions.

144   "Wendy and Peter aren't in their rooms," said his wife.

145   He lay in his bed with his beating heart. "No," he said. "They've broken into the nursery."

146   "Those screams—they sound familiar."

147   "Do they?"

148   "Yes, awfully."

149   And although their beds tried very hard, the two adults couldn't be rocked to sleep for another hour. A smell of cats was in the night air.

150   "Father?" said Peter.

151   "Yes."

152   Peter looked at his shoes. He never looked at his father any more, nor at his mother. "You aren't going to lock up the nursery for good, are you?"

153   "That all depends."

154   "On what?" snapped Peter.

155   "On you and your sister. If you intersperse this Africa with a little variety—oh, Sweden perhaps, or Denmark or China—"

156   "I thought we were free to play as we wished."

157   "You are, within reasonable bounds."

158   "What's wrong with Africa, Father?"

159   "Oh, so now you admit you have been conjuring up Africa, do you?"

160   "I wouldn't want the nursery locked up," said Peter coldly. "Ever."

161   "Matter of fact, we're thinking of turning the whole house off for about a month. Live sort of a carefree one-for-all existence."

162   "That sounds dreadful! Would I have to tie my own shoes instead of letting the shoe tier do it? And brush my own teeth and comb my hair and give myself a bath?"

163   "It would be fun for a change, don't you think?"

164   "No, it would be horrid. I didn't like it when you took out the picture painter last month."

165   "That's because I wanted you to learn to paint all by yourself, son."

166   "I don't want to do anything but look and listen and smell; what else is there to do?"

167   "All right, go play in Africa."

168   "Will you shut off the house sometime soon?"

169   "We're considering it."

170   "I don't think you'd better consider it any more, Father."

171   "I won't have any threats from my son!"

172   "Very well." And Peter strolled off to the nursery.

173   "Am I on time?" said David McClean.

174   "Breakfast?" asked George Hadley.

175   "Thanks, had some. What's the trouble?"

176   "David, you're a psychologist."

177   "I should hope so."

178   "Well, then, have a look at our nursery. You saw it a year ago when you dropped by; did you notice anything peculiar about it then?"

179   "Can't say I did; the usual violences, a tendency toward a slight paranoia here or there, usual in children because they feel persecuted by parents constantly, but, oh, really nothing."

180   They walked down the hall. "I locked the nursery up," explained the father, "and the children broke back into it during the night. I let them stay so they could form the patterns for you to see."

181   There was a terrible screaming from the nursery.

182   "There it is," said George Hadley. "See what you make of it."

183   They walked in on the children without rapping.

184   The screams had faded. The lions were feeding.

185   "Run outside a moment, children," said George Hadley. "No, don't change the mental combination. Leave the walls as they are. Get!"

186   With the children gone, the two men stood studying the lions clustered at a distance, eating with great relish whatever it was they had caught.

187   "I wish I knew what it was," said George Hadley. "Sometimes I can almost see. Do you think if I brought high-powered binoculars here and—"

188   David McClean laughed dryly. "Hardly." He turned to study all four walls. "How long has this been going on?"

189   "A little over a month."

190   "It certainly doesn't feel good."

191   "I want facts, not feelings."

192   "My dear George, a psychologist never saw a fact in his life. He only hears about feelings, vague things. This doesn't feel good, I tell you. Trust my hunches and my instincts. I have a nose for something bad. This is very bad. My advice to you is to have the whole damn room torn down, and your children brought to me every day during the next year for treatment."

193   "Is it that bad?"

194   "I'm afraid so. One of the original uses of these nurseries was so that we could study the patterns left on the walls by the child's mind, study at our leisure, and help the child. In this case, however, the room has become a channel toward—destructive thoughts, instead of a release away from them."

195   "Didn't you sense this before?"

196   "I sensed only that you had spoiled your children more than most. And now you're letting them down in some way. What way?"

197   "I wouldn't let them go to New York."

198   "What else?"

199   "I've taken a few machines from the house and threatened them, a
month ago, with closing up the nursery unless they did their homework. I
did close it for a few days to show I meant business."

200   "Ah, ha!"

201   "Does that mean anything?"

202   "Everything. Where before they had a Santa Claus, now they have a
Scrooge. Children prefer Santas. You've let this room and this house replace
you and your wife in your children's affections. This room is their mother
and father, far more important in their lives than their real parents. And now
you come along and want to shut it off. No wonder there's hatred here. You
can feel it coming out of the sky. Feel that sun. George, you'll have to change
your life. Like too many others, you've built it around creature comforts.
Why, you'd starve tomorrow if something went wrong in your kitchen. You
wouldn't know how to tap an egg. Nevertheless, turn everything off. Start
anew. It'll take time. But we'll make good children out of bad in a year, wait
and see."

203   "But won't the shock be too much for the children, shutting the room up
abruptly, for good?"

204   "I don't want them going any deeper into this, that's all."

205   The lions were finished with their red feast.

206   The lions were standing on the edge of the clearing watching the two men.

207   "Now I'm feeling persecuted," said McClean. "Let's get out of here. I
never have cared for these damned rooms. Make me nervous."

208   "The lions look real, don't they?" said George Hadley. "I don't suppose
there's any way—"

209   "What?"

210   "—that they could become real?"

211   "Not that I know."

212   "Some flaw in the machinery, a tampering or something?"

213   "No."

214   They went to the door.

215   "I don't imagine the room will like being turned off," said the father.

216   "Nothing ever likes to die—even a room."

217   "I wonder if it hates me for wanting to switch it off?"

218   "Paranoia is thick around here today," said David McClean. "You can follow
it like a spoor. Hello." He bent and picked up a bloody scarf. "This yours?"

219   "No." George Hadley's face was rigid. "It belongs to Lydia."

220   They went to the fuse box together and threw the switch that killed the
nursery.

221   The two children were in hysterics. They screamed and pranced and threw things. They yelled and sobbed and swore and jumped at the furniture.

222   "You can't do that to the nursery, you can't!"

223   "Now, children."

224   The children flung themselves onto a couch, weeping.

225   "George," said Lydia Hadley, "turn on the nursery, just for a few moments. You can't be so abrupt."

226   "No."

227   "You can't be so cruel."

228   "Lydia, it's off, and it stays off. And the whole damn house dies as of here and now. The more I see of the mess we've put ourselves in, the more it sickens me. We've been contemplating our mechanical, electronic navels for too long. My God, how we need a breath of honest air!"

229   And he marched about the house turning off the voice clocks, the stoves, the heaters, the shoe shiners, the shoe lacers, the body scrubbers and swabbers and massagers, and every other machine he could put his hand to.

230   The house was full of dead bodies, it seemed. It felt like a mechanical cemetery. So silent. None of the humming hidden energy of machines waiting to function at the tap of a button.

231   "Don't let them do it!" wailed Peter at the ceiling as if he was talking to the house, the nursery. "Don't let Father kill everything." He turned to his father. "Oh, I hate you!"

232   "Insults won't get you anywhere."

233   "I wish you were dead!"

234   "We were, for a long while. Now we're going to really start living. Instead of being handled and massaged, we're going to live."

235   Wendy was still crying and Peter joined her again. "Just a moment, just one moment, just another moment of nursery," they wailed.

236   "Oh, George," said the wife, "it can't hurt."

237   "All right—all right, if they'll only just shut up. One minute, mind you, and then off forever."

238   "Daddy, Daddy, Daddy!" sang the children, smiling with wet faces.

239   "And then we're going on a vacation. David McClean is coming back in half an hour to help us move out and get to the airport. I'm going to dress. You turn the nursery on for a minute, Lydia, just a minute, mind you."

240   And the three of them went babbling off while he let himself be vacuumed upstairs through the air flue and set about dressing himself. A minute later Lydia appeared.

241   "I'll be glad when we get away," she sighed.

242   "Did you leave them in the nursery?"

243   "I wanted to dress too. Oh, that horrid Africa. What can they see in it?"

244   "Well, in five minutes we'll be on our way to Iowa. Lord, how did we ever get in this house? What prompted us to buy a nightmare?"

245   "Pride, money, foolishness."

246   "I think we'd better get downstairs before those kids get engrossed with those damned beasts again."

247   Just then they heard the children calling, "Daddy, Mommy, come quick—quick!"

248   They went downstairs in the air flue and ran down the hall. The children were nowhere in sight. "Wendy? Peter!"

249   They ran into the nursery. The veldtland was empty save for the lions waiting, looking at them. "Peter, Wendy?"

250   The door slammed.

251   "Wendy, Peter!"

252   George Hadley and his wife whirled and ran back to the door.

253   "Open the door!" cried George Hadley, trying the knob. "Why, they've locked it from the outside! Peter!" He beat at the door.

254   "Open up!"

255   He heard Peter's voice outside, against the door.

256   "Don't let them switch off the nursery and the house," he was saying.

257   Mr. and Mrs. George Hadley beat at the door. "Now, don't be ridiculous, children. It's time to go. Mr. McClean'll be here in a minute and . . . "

258   And then they heard the sounds.

259   The lions on three sides of them, in the yellow veldt grass, padding through the dry straw, rumbling and roaring in their throats.

260   The lions.

261   Mr. Hadley looked at his wife and they turned and looked back at the beasts edging slowly forward, crouching, tails stiff.

262   Mr. and Mrs. Hadley screamed.

263   And suddenly they realized why those other screams had sounded familiar.

264   "Well, here I am," said David McClean in the nursery doorway.

265   "Oh, hello." He stared at the two children seated in the center of the open glade eating a little picnic lunch. Beyond them was the water hole and the yellow veldtland; above was the hot sun. He began to perspire. "Where are your father and mother?"

266   The children looked up and smiled. "Oh, they'll be here directly."

267   "Good, we must get going." At a distance Mr. McClean saw the lions fighting and clawing and then quieting down to feed in silence under the shady trees.

268   He squinted at the lions with his hand up to his eyes.

269   Now the lions were done feeding. They moved to the water hole to drink.

270   A shadow flickered over Mr. McClean's hot face. Many shadows flickered. The vultures were dropping down the blazing sky.

271   "A cup of tea?" asked Wendy in the silence.

MyWritingLab™

Complete additional reading comprehension questions for this selection at mywritinglab.com

Comprehension and Critical Thinking

1. What are some functions that the Happylife Home can perform? List at least four.

   _____

   _____

   _____

2. What kind of a relationship do the Hadley parents have with their children?

   _____

   _____

3. What is the original purpose of the nursery?

   _____

   _____

4. Why are George and Lydia worried about the nursery?

   _____

   _____

5. What have the children turned the nursery into?

   _____

   _____

6. Provide some examples from the story of imagery that appeal to the following senses. (See pages 113–114 in Chapter 8 for more information about imagery.)

   Sight: _____

   _____

   Sound: _____

   _____

   Smell: _____

   _____

Touch: _____

_____

7. Why do the children become extremely upset with their parents?

_____

_____

8. What does the Happylife Home and nursery represent to the children?

_____

_____

9. What happens to the parents at the end of the story?

_____

_____

10. Although the story is fictional, it presents some universal truths. What is one of the story's messages?

_____

_____

_____

Writing Topics

Write about one of the following topics. Remember to explore, develop, and revise and edit your work.

1. Ray Bradbury wrote this story long before there were personal computers or 3D television screens. Argue that our current world has some similarities to Bradbury's predictions. Support your argument with specific examples from the story.

2. Respond to the story. For information about writing a response essay, see Chapter 18.

3. Narrative writing can be fictional or nonfictional. A work of fiction is created in the writer's imagination. A work of nonfiction presents factual events. Which type of narration do you prefer: fiction or nonfiction? Provide supporting evidence from "The Veldt" and from a narrative essay in this book such as "My Bully, My Best Friend" (page 531), "My African Childhood" (page 539), "Into Thin Air" (page 562), or "Guy" (page 569).

The Basic Parts of a Sentence

Parts of Speech	Definition	Some Examples
Adjective	Adds information about the noun.	small, pretty, red, soft
Adverb	Adds information about the verb, adjective, or other adverb; expresses time, place, and frequency.	quickly, sweetly, sometimes, far, usually, never
Conjunctive Adverb	Shows a relationship between two ideas. It may appear at the beginning of a sentence, or it may join two sentences.	also, consequently, finally, however, furthermore, moreover, therefore, thus
Coordinating Conjunction	Connects two ideas of equal importance.	but, or, yet, so, for, and, nor
Determiner	Identifies or determines if a noun is specific or general.	a, an, the, this, that, these, those, any, all, each, every, many, some
Interjection	Is added to a sentence to convey emotion.	hey, yikes, ouch, wow
Noun	Names a person, place, or thing.	singular: woman, horse, person plural: women, horses, people
Preposition	Shows a relationship between words (source, direction, location, etc.).	at, to, for, from, behind, above
Pronoun	Replaces one or more nouns.	he, she, it, us, ours, themselves
Subordinating Conjunction	Connects two ideas when one idea is subordinate (or inferior) to the other idea.	although, because, even though, unless, until, when
Verb	Expresses an action or state of being.	action verb: look, make, touch, smile linking verb: is, was, are, become

Irregular Verb List

Base Form	Simple Past	Past Participle	Base Form	Simple Past	Past Participle
arise	arose	arisen	fall	fell	fallen
be	was, were	been	feed	fed	fed
bear	bore	borne / born	feel	felt	felt
beat	beat	beat / beaten	fight	fought	fought
become	became	become	find	found	found
begin	began	begun	flee	fled	fled
bend	bent	bent	fly	flew	flown
bet	bet	bet	forbid	forbade	forbidden
bind	bound	bound	forget	forgot	forgotten
bite	bit	bitten	forgive	forgave	forgiven
bleed	bled	bled	forsake	forsook	forsaken
blow	blew	blown	freeze	froze	frozen
break	broke	broken	get	got	got, gotten
breed	bred	bred	give	gave	given
bring	brought	brought	go	went	gone
build	built	built	grind	ground	ground
burst	burst	burst	grow	grew	grown
buy	bought	bought	hang	hung	hung
catch	caught	caught	have	had	had
choose	chose	chosen	hear	heard	heard
cling	clung	clung	hide	hid	hidden
come	came	come	hit	hit	hit
cost	cost	cost	hold	held	held
creep	crept	crept	hurt	hurt	hurt
cut	cut	cut	keep	kept	kept
deal	dealt	dealt	kneel	knelt	knelt
dig	dug	dug	know	knew	known
do	did	done	lay	laid	laid
draw	drew	drawn	lead	led	led
drink	drank	drunk	leave	left	left
drive	drove	driven	lend	lent	lent
eat	ate	eaten	let	let	let

Base Form	Simple Past	Past Participle	Base Form	Simple Past	Past Participle
lie[1]	lay	lain	speak	spoke	spoken
light	lit	lit	speed	sped	sped
lose	lost	lost	spend	spent	spent
make	made	made	spin	spun	spun
mean	meant	meant	split	split	split
meet	met	met	spread	spread	spread
mistake	mistook	mistaken	spring	sprang	sprung
pay	paid	paid	stand	stood	stood
put	put	put	steal	stole	stolen
prove	proved	proved / proven	stick	stuck	stuck
quit	quit	quit	sting	stung	stung
read	read	read	stink	stank	stunk
rid	rid	rid	strike	struck	struck
ride	rode	ridden	swear	swore	sworn
ring	rang	rung	sweep	swept	swept
rise	rose	risen	swell	swelled	swollen
run	ran	run	swim	swam	swum
say	said	said	swing	swung	swung
see	saw	seen	take	took	taken
sell	sold	sold	teach	taught	taught
send	sent	sent	tear	tore	torn
set	set	set	tell	told	told
shake	shook	shaken	think	thought	thought
shine	shone	shone	throw	threw	thrown
shoot	shot	shot	thrust	thrust	thrust
show	showed	shown	understand	understood	understood
shrink	shrank	shrunk	upset	upset	upset
shut	shut	shut	wake	woke	woken
sing	sang	sung	wear	wore	worn
sink	sank	sunk	weep	wept	wept
sit	sat	sat	win	won	won
sleep	slept	slept	wind	wound	wound
slide	slid	slid	withdraw	withdrew	withdrawn
slit	slit	slit	write	wrote	written

[1]*Lie* can mean "to rest in a flat position." When *lie* means "tell a false statement," then it is a regular verb: *lie, lied, lied*.

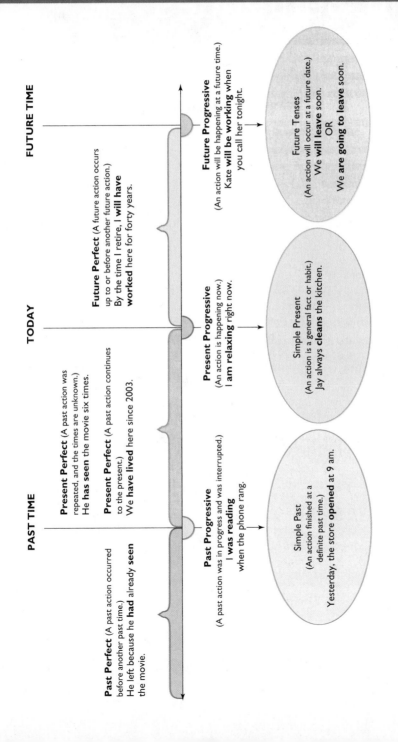

PAST TIME

TODAY

FUTURE TIME

Past Perfect (A past action occurred before another past time.)
He left because he **had** already **seen** the movie.

Present Perfect (A past action was repeated, and the times are unknown.)
He **has seen** the movie six times.

Present Perfect (A past action continues to the present.)
We **have lived** here since 2003.

Future Perfect (A future action occurs up to or before another future action.)
By the time I retire, I **will have worked** here for forty years.

Past Progressive (A past action was in progress and was interrupted.)
I **was reading** when the phone rang.

Present Progressive (An action is happening now.)
I **am relaxing** right now.

Future Progressive (An action will be happening at a future time.)
Kate **will be working** when you call her tonight.

Simple Past
(An action finished at a definite past time.)
Yesterday, the store **opened** at 9 am.

Simple Present
(An action is a general fact or habit.)
Jay always **cleans** the kitchen.

Future Tenses
(An action will occur at a future date.)
We **will leave** soon.
OR
We **are going to leave** soon.

Appendix 4 Combining Ideas in Sentences

Making Compound Sentences

A.

Complete idea

, coordinator
, for
, and
, nor
, but
, or
, yet
, so

complete idea.

B.

Complete idea

;

complete idea.

C.

Complete idea

; transitional expression,
; furthermore,
; however,
; in fact,
; moreover,
; therefore,

complete idea.

Making Complex Sentences

D.

Complete idea

subordinator
although
because
before
even though
unless
when

incomplete idea.

E.

Subordinator
Although
Because
Before
Even though
Unless
When

incomplete idea

,

complete idea.

The American Psychological Association (APA) documentation style is commonly used in scientific or technical fields such as social sciences, economics, and nursing. Before you write a research essay for any course, ask your instructor which style he or she prefers.

HINT ◄ APA Web Site

To get general information about some basic style questions, you can view the APA's Web site. Use the menu on the left side of the page to direct you to specific style questions and answers.

On the same Web site, there is a link to information about online or "electronic" sources. Because the information about online sources is continually being updated, the site has comprehensive information about the latest citation methods.

APA: Including In-Text Citations

Here are two basic options for inserting parenthetical citations in an APA-style research essay.

1. **Enclose the author(s), the publication year, and the page number(s) in parentheses.** Include the last name(s) of the source's author(s). For more than one author, separate the authors' names using *&* (the ampersand sign). Follow with the publication year and then the page number or the page range where the material appears, using *p.* or *pp.* Separate the names, date, and page references with commas, and place the final period after the closing parenthesis.

   Sometimes rioters lose control and "take out their anger and frustration on any individual" (Locher, 2002, p. 92).

   A dozen men are responsible for the development of the movie camera (Giannetti & Eyman, 2006, p. 4).

2. **Introduce the source directly in the text.** When you include a short quotation within a sentence, place the publication year in parentheses immediately after you mention the author's name. Present the quotation, and then write the page number in parentheses immediately after it.

   Sociologist David A. Locher (2002) explains, "Violent mobs often take out their anger and frustration on any individual" (p. 92).

   As Giannetti and Eyman (2006) explained, a dozen men are responsible for the development of the movie camera (p. 4).

APA: Making a References List

Similar to the MLA Works Cited list, the APA References list gives details about each source you have used, and it appears at the end of your paper. Follow these basic guidelines to prepare References using the APA format.

1. Write "References" at the top of the page and center it. Do not italicize it, bold it, underline it, or put quotation marks around it.
2. List each source alphabetically, using the last names of the authors.
3. Indent the second line and all subsequent lines of each reference one-half inch from the left margin.
4. Double-space the list.

HINT ◀ **Writing the Author, Date, Title, and Place Using APA Style**

Author
On the References page, write the complete last name and use the first and middle initials (if provided). Do not write complete first names.

Date of Publication
Put the date of publication in parentheses immediately after the name. If you do not have the author's name, then put the date immediately after the title. If no date is available, write (n.d.).

Title
Capitalize the first word of the title, the first word of the subtitle, and any proper nouns or adjectives in Reference lists. Do not add quotation marks or any other special marks around the titles of short works. Italicize titles of longer works such as books, newspapers, or magazines.

Place of Publication
Mention the name of the city and the postal abbreviation of the state or province.

Here is an example of a complete entry for a References list in APA style.

Brainard, S. (2006). *A design manual*. Upper Saddle River, NJ: Prentice Hall.

Books

Carefully review the punctuation of the following example.

Last name, Initial(s). (date). *Title of the book*. City, State of Publication: Publisher.

One author

Reverse the name of the author. Put the complete last name and the first initial.

Krakauer, J. (1999). *Into thin air*. New York, NY: Random House.

Two or more authors

Reverse the name of each author.

> Ciccarelli, S. K., & Meyer, G. E. (2006). *Psychology*. Upper Saddle River, NJ: Prentice Hall.

Book with an editor instead of an author

Put the editor's name followed by (Ed.).

> Koppleman, S. (Ed.). (1984). *Old maids: Short stories by nineteenth-century US women writers*. Boston, MA: Pandora Press.

Two or more books by the same author

Include the author's name in all references. Arrange the works by year of publication, putting the earliest work first.

> Angelou, M. (1969). *I know why the caged bird sings*. New York, NY: Random House.

> Angelou, M. (2006). *Mother: A cradle to hold me*. New York, NY: Random House.

A work in an anthology

> Munroe, A. (2003). Boys and girls. In R. S. Gwynn & W. Campbell (Eds.), *Literature* (pp. 313–326). Toronto, ON: Pearson Longman.

Encyclopedia and dictionary

> Democracy. (2005). In *Columbia encyclopedia* (6th ed.). New York, NY: Columbia University Press.

> Legitimate. (2003). In *The new American Webster handy college dictionary* (3rd ed.). New York, NY: Signet.

Periodicals

When citing newspapers or magazines, write as much of the following information as is available.

> Last name, Initials. (Year, Month and day). Title of article. *Title of the Magazine or Newspaper, Volume number*, Pages.

Article in a magazine

> Shreeve, J. (2005, March). Beyond the brain. *National Geographic, 207*, 2–31.

Article in a newspaper

> Dugger, C. W. (2006, December 1). Clinton helps broker deal for medicine to treat AIDS. *New York Times*, p. A9.

Article in a journal

Last name, Initials. (Year, Month). Title of article. *Title of Journal.
Volume*(Issue), Pages.

Seligman, M. (1998). The American way of blame. *APA Monitor, 29*(7), 97.

Electronic Sources

If the source was published on the Internet, include as much of the following information as you can find. Keep in mind that some sites do not contain complete source information.

Last name, Initials. (date of most recent update). Title of article. *Title of
Site* or *Online Publication*. Retrieved from http://site_address.html

E-Book

For references, mention the book's DOI or the URL of the site where you downloaded the e-book.

Barnes, J. (2011). *The sense of an ending*. Retrieved from http://
www.amazon.com

Article on a personal web site

Krystek, L. (2006). Crop circles from outer space? *Museum of unnatural
mystery*. Retrieved from http://www.unmuseum.org

Article in an online journal

If the article includes a DOI (digital object identifier), include it instead of the URL. A DOI is a special identification number that will lead you directly to the document on the Internet. If you cannot find the DOI, then go to *crossref.org* and do a DOI search.

Naremore, J. (2008). Films of the year, 2007. *Film Quarterly, 61*(4), 48–61.
doi:10.1525/fq.2008.61.4.48

Government site (or other sites without author information)

If the author is not mentioned on the site, begin with the title followed by the date, and include as much information as you can find. Generally, you do not need to include date of retrieval unless your source is highly changeable such as Wikipedia.

Dangerous jobs. (1997). *US Department of Labor*. Retrieved May 28,
2006, from http://stats.bls.gov/iif/oshwc/cfar0020.pdf

Other Types of Sources

Interview that you conducted

In APA style, do not include a personal interview in your References list. In the actual text, just include the parenthetical notation along with the exact date of the communication. For example: (personal communication, June 15, 2008).

Film or video

> Curtiz, M. (Director). (2003). *Casablanca* [DVD]. United States: Warner Bros. (Original movie released 1942).

Sound recording

> Nirvana. (1994). About a girl. On *Unplugged in New York* [CD]. New York, NY: Geffen.

PRACTICE 1

Imagine that you are using the following sources in a research paper. Arrange the sources for a References page using APA style.

* An article by David Mamet in *Harper's* called "Bambi v. Godzilla." The article, published in the June 2005 issue, appeared on pages 33 to 37.
* A book by David Mamet called *Boston Marriage* that was published by Vintage Books in New York, in 2002.
* A book called *Flashback: A Brief History of Film* written by Louis Giannetti and Scott Eyman. The book was published by Prentice Hall in Upper Saddle River, New Jersey, in 2006.
* A book called *Cultural Anthropology* by Serena Nanda. The book was published by Wadsworth in Belmont, California, in 1991.
* An article called "Biography" on the Web site *Marilyn Monroe*. The site was created in 2006. The Web address is http://www.marilymonroe...bio.com. You cannot find the author's name on the site.

References

_____

_____

_____

_____

_____

_____

_____

_____

_____

_____

Appendix 6 Spelling, Grammar, and Vocabulary Logs

In the first few pages of your writing portfolio or copybook, try keeping three "logs" to help you avoid repeating errors and improve your writing.

Spelling Log

The goal of keeping a spelling log is to stop repeating errors. Every time you misspell a word, record both the mistake and the correction in your spelling log. Then, before you hand in a writing assignment, consult your list of misspelled words.

EXAMPLE:

Incorrect	Correct
finaly	finally
responsable	responsible

Grammar Log

The goal of keeping a grammar log is to stop repeating errors in sentence structure, mechanics, and punctuation. Each time a writing assignment is returned to you, identify one or two repeated errors and add them to your grammar log. Next, consult the grammar log before you hand in new writing assignments in order to avoid making the same errors. For each type of grammar error, you could do the following:

1. Identify the assignment, and write down the type of error.
2. In your own words, write a rule about the error.
3. Include an example from your writing assignment.

EXAMPLE: Cause and Effect Essay (Mar. 10)   Fragment

Sentences must have a subject and a verb and express a complete thought.

Also, an overbearing parent. That can cause a child to become controlling.

Vocabulary Log

The vocabulary log can provide you with interesting new terms to incorporate in your writing. As you use this book, you will learn new vocabulary. Keep a record of the most interesting and useful words and expressions. Write a synonym or definition next to each new word.

EXAMPLE: ubiquitous means widespread

Credits

TEXT

Page 42: From *Flashback: A Brief History of Film*, 3rd Ed. by Louis Giannetti, Scott Eyman, Published by Pearson Education, © 1996; **p. 43:** From *Concise Guide to Jazz*, 6th Ed. by Mark C. Gridley. Published by Pearson Education, © 2009; **p. 50:** From "Bhutan Refugees Find a Toehold in the Bronx" by Kirk Semple from *The New York Times*, September 25, 2009. Copyright © 2009 *The New York Times*. All rights reserved. Used by permission and protected by the Copyright Laws of the United States. The printing, copying, redistribution, or retransmission of this Content without express written permission is prohibited; **p. 51:** From "Let's Stop Being Stupid About IQ" by Dorothy Nixon. Copyright © Dorothy Nixon. Used by the permission of the author; **p. 65:** From *Sociology* by John J. Macionis. Published by Pearson Education © 2012; **pp. 79–80:** Monique, Lisa. "Priceless Euphoria"; **pp. 89–90:** "You are what you eat except on TV" by Al Kratina from Montreal Gazette, April 09, 2011. Copyright © 2011. Material reprinted with the express permission of: Montreal Gazette, a division of Postmedia Network Inc; **pp. 95–97:** McKelvey, Jack. "Rehabilitation"; **pp. 104–105:** "My Journey Down the Grand Canyon" by Andrew Wells; **pp. 106–108:** "I wanted a tan, but I wound up in a hospital" by Sarah Stanfield from Salon.com. March 20, 2011. Copyright © 2011. This article first appeared in Salon.com at http://www.Salon.com An online version remains in the Salon archives. Reprinted with permission; **pp. 114–115:** LaFrance, Judith. "The House with the Brown Door"; **pp. 123–124:** MacDonald, Natalia. "African Adventure"; **pp. 125–126:** "With an Open Mouth" by Sy Montgomery. Reprinted from *The Spell of the Tiger*. Copyright © 2008 by Sy Montgomery with permission of Chelsea Green Publishing (www.chelseagreen.com); **pp. 131–132:** Lariviere, Samuel Charland. "How to Plant a Tree"; **pp. 138–139:** Sanders, Justin. "Steps to Help Out Your First Day of Classes"; **pp. 141–142:** "Do You Have What It Takes to Be Happy?" by Stacey Colino from Shape Magazine, May 2005. Copyright © 2005 by Weider Publications. Used by the permission of Weider Publications; **p. 147:** Quotation by Anthony Mullen, National Teacher of the Year. Copyright © Anthony Mullen. Used by permission of the author; **pp. 147–148:** "Journalists Are History's Record Keepers" by Lindsey Davis; **pp. 156–157:** "Welcome to My World" by Marie-Pier Joly; **pp. 158–159:** From "Internet Trolls" by Lisa Selin Davis from Salon.com, August 01, 2012. Copyright © 2012. This article first appeared in Salon.com at http://www.Salon.com An online version remains in the Salon archives. Reprinted with permission; **pp. 165–166:** "Discrimination in the 21st Century" by Victoria Johnson; **pp. 175–176:** "Flash Mobs, Flash Robs, and Riots" by Diego Pelaez. Reprinted by permission of the author; **pp. 178–181:** "Types of Correctional Officers" by Frank Schmalleger. Copyright © Frank Schmalleger, Ph.D. Used by permission of the author; **pp. 187–188:** "Swamps and Pesticides" by Corey Kaminska; **pp. 197–199:** Adapted from Viral Vigilantes: The Unblinking Panopticon and the Wheelie-Bin Cat Lady by Matthew Fraser. Copyright © 2011. Used by permission of Matthew Fraser; **pp. 204–205:** "College Students and the Challenge of Credit Card Debt" by Katie Earnest; **pp. 212–213:** "Workplace Hostility" by Emilie Dubois. Copyright © by Emilie Dubois. Used by permission; **pp. 215–216:** "Friendless in North America" by Ellen Goodman from The Boston Globe, June 30, 2006. Copyright © 2006 Boston Globe. All rights reserved. Used by permission and protected by the Copyright Laws of the United States. The printing, copying, redistribution, or retransmission of this Content without express written permission is prohibited; **p. 222:** "Graffiti as Art" by Jordan Foster. Used by permission; **pp. 231–232:** "Age Matters" by Chloe Vallieres; **pp. 234–235:** "Keep Your Roses I Hate Admin Day" by Melonyce McAfee from Slate.com. April 26, 2006. Copyright © 2006 The Slate Group. All rights reserved. Used by permission and protected by the Copyright Laws of the United States. The printing, copying, redistribution, or retransmission of this Content without express written permission is prohibited; **p. 250:** From "Top Ten Ways to Beat Stress at Work" by Stephanie Goddard from Work-Stress-Solutions.com. 14 May, 2010 Copyright © 2010. Used by permission of Work-Stress-Solutions.com. (http://www.work-stress-solutions.com); **p. 251:** From "The Case for Debt" by Virginia Postrel from The Atlantic. Copyright © 2008; **p. 251:** From *Consumer Behavior* by Michael R. Solomon. Copyright © 2013 Pearson Education; **p. 266:** Screenshot from "Science Daily". Copyright © 1995–2010. Used by permission of Science Daily; **p. 266:** "The price of popularity: Drug and alcohol consumption" from (University of Montreal) via the AAAS news release service EurekAlert, September 28, 2010. Used by permission of University of Montreal; **pp. 270–271:** From *Consumer Behavior* by Michael R. Solomon. Copyright © 2013 by Pearson Education; **p. 273:** From "Psychology" by Saundra K Ciccarelli. Copyright © 2006 by Pearson Education; **p. 274:** From Think: Social Problems 2 Ed. by John D. Carl. Copyright © 2012 by Pearson Education, Inc., Upper Saddle River, New Jersey; **pp. 283–285:** "The Dangers of Energy Drinks" by Karyne Maheu Corriveau. Used by permission of the author; **pp. 291–293:** "The World of Avatar" by Matthew Fiorentino. Used by permission of the author; **pp. 293–294:** "Lessons from 'For Whom the Bell Tolls'" by Diego Pelaez. Used by permission of the author; **pp. 310–311:** "Factors Contributing to Aggressive Behavior" from *Psychology* by Saundra Ciccarelli. Copyright © 2006 by Prentice Hall; **p. 509:** From Business Ethics by Richard T. DeGeorge. Copyright © 2009 by Prentice Hall; **p. 521:** From "Enough Is Enough" from *Don't Pee On My Leg and Tell Me It's Raining* by Judy Sheindlin. Published by HarperCollins © 1996; **p. 521:** From "The Real Meaning of Courage" by Linda Chavez in The Jewish World Review, May 24, 2006. Copyright © 2006. Used by permission of Linda Chavez and Creators Syndicate, Inc; **pp. 522–524:** *CSI Effect Has Juries Wanting More Evidence"* by Richard Willing from USAToday, August 5, 2004. Copyright © 2004 USAToday. All rights reserved. Used by permission and protected by the Copyright Laws of the United States. The printing, copying, redistribution, or retransmission of this Content without express written permission is prohibited; **pp. 525–529:** *Locher, David; Collective Behavior*, 1st Ed. © 2002. Printed and Electronically reproduced by permission of Pearson Education, Inc., Upper Saddle River, New Jersey; **pp. 531–533:** From "My Bully, My Best Friend" by Yannick LeJacq from Salon.com., May 25, 2012. Copyright © 2012. This article first appeared in Salon.com, at http://www.Salon.com An online version remains in the Salon archives. Reprinted by permission of Salon Media Group; **pp. 535–537:** "Living Environments" by Dr. Avi Friedman from Montreal Gazette. Copyright © by Dr. Avi Friedman. Used by permission; **pp. 539–543:** From: *Me Talk Pretty One Day* by David Sedaris. Copyright © 2000 by David Sedaris. By permission of Little, Brown and Company and by Don Congdon Associates, Inc. All rights reserved; **pp. 545–547:** "Nature Returns to the Cities" by John Roach from *National Geographic News*, July 23, 2001. Copyright © 2001. Used by permission of NGS Images Sales; **pp. 548–550:** From "Toying with Ideas Marketing a New Invention Can Often be a Tough Sell" by Robert Rodriguez from The Fresno Bee, February 10, 2008. Copyright © 2008 McClatchy. All rights reserved. Used by permission and protected by the Copyright Laws of the United States. The printing, copying, redistribution, or retransmission of this Content without express written permission is prohibited; **pp. 551–553:** "Brands R Us: How Advertising Works" by Stephen Garey from Center for Media Literacy. Copyright © 2002–2011. Used by permission of Stephen Garey; **pp. 554–556:** "Can We

615

PHOTOS

Index

Revising Checklist for an Essay

Does the introduction

☐ contain a clearly identifiable thesis statement?

☐ build up to the thesis statement?

Does the thesis statement

☐ convey the essay's controlling idea?

☐ make a valid and supportable point?

☐ appear as the last sentence in the introduction?

☐ make a direct point and not contain expressions such as *I think that* or *I will explain*?

Do the body paragraphs

☐ have **adequate support**? Does each body paragraph have a topic sentence that clearly supports the thesis statement? Are there enough details to support each paragraph's topic sentence?

☐ have **coherence**? Are ideas presented in an effective and logical manner? Do transitional words and phrases help the ideas flow smoothly?

☐ have **unity**? Is the essay unified around one central topic? Does each body paragraph focus on one topic?

☐ have **style**? Are sentences varied in length? Is the language creative and precise?

Does the conclusion

☐ bring the essay to a satisfactory end?

☐ briefly summarize the ideas that the writer discusses in the essay?

☐ avoid introducing new or contradictory ideas?

☐ possibly end with a quotation, suggestion, or prediction?